POWERED VEHICLES

POWERED VEHICLES

By
Reginald Carpenter
Peter Kalla-Bishop
Kenneth Munson
Robert Wyatt

Crown Publishers, Inc • New York

POWERED VEHICLES

has been designed and produced by Tre Tryckare AB, Gothenburg, Sweden, and is the result of cooperation between a number of authors and experts who have collaborated with the Tre Tryckare editorial and art departments under the supervision of Einar Engelbrektson and Turlough Johnston. Index work has been done by Ian D. Huntley and Kerstin M. Stålbrand.

LAYOUT AND ARTWORK

has been made by the Tre Tryckare Studios and the following artists:
John W. Wood Associates
Herlew Studios
Ian D. Huntley

THE AUTHORS

Reginald Carpenter
has written the Introductory Chapter and the Ships section
Robert Wyatt
has written the Cars section
P.M. Kalla-Bishop
has written the Trains section
Kenneth Munson
has written the Flight section

The publishers and authors would like to express their gratitude to the following organizations who have assisted them with advice, information, and material:
Aeroflot, USSR
Aerospatiale, France
Alfa Romeo, Italy
Alsthom, France
ASEA, Sweden
Avions Marcel Dassault, France
Belgian State Railways
British Aircraft Corporation
British Airways
British Motor Corporation
British Railways
Brush Electrical Machines Ltd., England
Canadair, Canada
Cessna Aircraft Company, USA
Chalmers Technical High School, Sweden
Cunard Line, England
Danish State Railways
Dornier, Germany
Fiat Motors, Italy
Finnish State Railways
Fokker-VFW, Netherlands
Ford Motors, USA
French National Railways (SNCF)
General Electric Company, USA
German State Railways
Götaverken, Sweden
Hawker Siddeley Aviation, England
Jaguar Motors, England
Lockheed Aircraft Corporation, USA
Maritime Museum, Gothenburg, Sweden
McDonnel Douglas Corporation, USA
Mercedes Benz Corporation, Germany
Messerschmidt-Bölkow-Blohm, Germany
NASA, USA
National Maritime Museum, England
Opel Motor Corporation, Germany
P. and O. Line, England
Piper Aircraft Corporation, USA
Renault Motors, France
Rolls-Royce, England
Royal Aeronautical Society, England
Saab-Scania, Sweden
Science Museum, England
Smithsonian Institute, USA
Texaco, USA
Tor Line, Sweden
Toyota Motors, Japan
United Aircraft Corporation, USA
Volkswagen, Germany
Volvo, Sweden
Yachting Publishing Corporation, USA

INTRODUCTION 9

The historical development of the four main methods of transportation. Social, political, and economic reasons why transportation became a necessity. Expanding populations, the need for raw materials and overseas markets and the spread of colonial power all help to encourage the development of powered vehicles.

Today we are on the threshold of the supersonic jet airliner era and we face its accompanying problems – pollution and fuel shortages.

THE AGE OF SAIL   18

The sailing ship and its development over thousands of years. Primitive craft. The difference between Northern and Southern European ships. Sails, rigging, and superstructures: how and why they were introduced. The great ships of the heyday of sail – the Baltimore and China clippers, and the large deepwater ships. The ultimate development of the square-rigged steel ship – the *Potosi*.

Competition from the steamship after the First World War is too great and the age of sail comes to an end.

THE DAWN OF STEAM TRACTION   66

Early horse-drawn mining trains. The first steam locomotives. The Stockton & Darlington Railway is opened in England in 1825, its first locomotive being Robert Stephenson's *Locomotion*. Stevens promotes the idea of steam locomotives in the United States. Locomotives are imported from England at first; later an American type is developed. In Europe, the Patentee and Crampton types are the most popular of the early types.

FROM STEAM TO NUCLEAR POWER   36

The theory of steam propulsion and the first steam-driven ships. Steamship companies are formed and regular passenger services are inaugurated. Advances in engine designs are made quickly: the triple expansion reciprocating engine, the steam turbine, the diesel, the turbo-electric.

After the Second World War, airline competition causes the end of regular Atlantic liner services. Cargo transportation is revolutionized: roll-on roll-off ferries, LASH vessels, bulk carriers, and container ships. Hovercraft and hydrofoils become slowly accepted. The search for new means of ship propulsion continues.

LATER LOCOMOTIVE DEVELOPMENT   86

Steam railways are built all over the world. Improved designs increase speeds. The compound locomotive is developed. Von Siemen's electric locomotive, 1879. The Volks Electric Railway opens in Britain. Electric railways spread slowly. Other alternatives to steam traction are introduced: the internal-combustion engine, the diesel, the diesel hydraulic, gas turbine-electric locomotives, and hydro-kinetic transmissions. Today several alternatives to conventional railways are being investigated: monorails, hovertrains, magnetic levitation trains, etc. The latest, linear electric motors, may well increase maximum train speed to the limit.

THE HORSELESS CARRIAGE 110

Steam-powered road vehicles are introduced in the nineteenth century with little success. The main problem, the weight of the engine, is solved by Etienne Lenoir's gas-powered engine in 1860. Siegfried Markus designs a four-stroke gasoline engine and uses it to power his 1875 automobile. The Daimler and Maybach engine of 1885 leads to the first practical automobiles. Automobilism spreads slowly and by 1904 the automobile is regarded as a reliable alternative to the horse-drawn carriage. But only the wealthy can afford an automobile until Henry Ford introduces mass-production techniques.

THE POPULARIZATION OF THE CAR 124

The automobile becomes accessible to the general public. After the Second World War automobile industries come to dominate the economy of many countries. New concepts in design appear. Wankel's rotary piston engine is patented in 1959 and is considered to be the motor of the future. Safety cars are now being experimented upon and safety requirements may very well dominate the future of the automobile.

THE CONQUEST OF THE AIR 154

Early attempts at flight. The first balloon ascent. The discovery of the basic principles of aeronautics. The powered airplanes of the late 1800s fail as the engines are too heavy. Lilienthal's glider experiments demonstrate the importance of control in flight. The Wright brothers' experiments succeed when Orville becomes the first man to make a proper airplane flight in 1903.
The coming of the air age and the popularization of flying. The float-plane. The flying-boat. The great pioneering transatlantic flights. Airline services are opened up, with the Douglas DC-3 being the standard airliner.

FROM JET TO SPACE ROCKET 172

The first jet-plane to fly, the Heinkel He178. Aircraft speeds increase. The first jet passenger aircraft. The breaking of the "sound barrier". The helicopter. VTOL and V/STOL aircraft. Airliners become bigger. The "Jumbo" jets. The supersonic jet transports and their future. The conquest of space. The space shuttle and Skylab.

This section, comprising more than 2,500 entries, is a highly valuable complement to the main part of the book. It provides not only a comprehensive reference index to the book but also much other information in additional entries which together with a glossary are illustrated with more than 100 photographs and line-drawings.

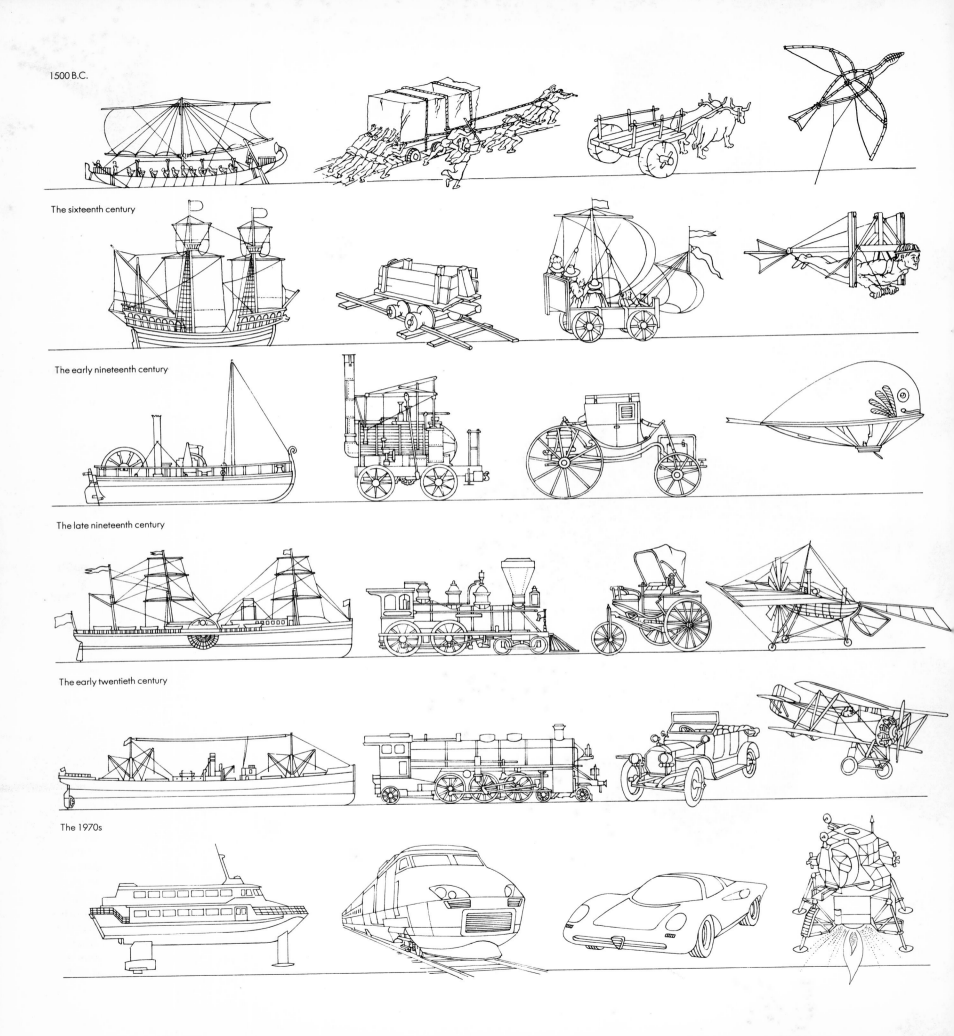

1500 B.C.

The sixteenth century

The early nineteenth century

The late nineteenth century

The early twentieth century

The 1970s

INTRODUCTION

The foundations of the world's present transportation system were laid down thousands of years ago, before recorded history, in a place or places the location of which can only be guessed. Nobody knows who first used the wheel or what form it took, and nobody really knows when and how primitive man learned to train widely differing breeds of animals to carry people and drag loads. Nevertheless, these achievements, together with the equally important discovery that man could float upon water by using suitable materials for support, set him upon a tediously slow road of progress, that only burst into a headlong race once natural forces had been harnessed to propel his vehicles across the land, his ships across the sea, his planes through the air, and, quite recently, his missiles into space. Thus, the history of transportation can be divided into three overlapping sections: the period during which man was dependent upon animals and the wind, the period during which the steam engine and, some time later, the internal-combustion engine changed the old system out of all recognition, and, finally, the era of space travel, which is still in its infancy, yet promises the possibility of greater and more spectacular developments than have ever occurred in the past. Erich von Däniken in his book *Chariots of the Gods* suggests that because of physical evidence upon the surface of the earth, because of tales that have been handed down through generations, through written evidence, notably the Bible, and because of the nature of stone carvings and paintings of some ancient civilizations, it is possible that there was a time when human beings landed upon the earth from spacecraft; this book assumes that we are the first to have witnessed travel in space.

In the earliest days of man's history he had to manage without transportation. Hunting tribes wandered the face of the earth in search of game. Each tribe, or group, was self-contained and relied entirely upon its own efforts for survival. Thousands of years later, when man had learned to cultivate simple crops and to practice animal husbandry, tribal self-sufficiency continued. It is not really known when man began to need transportation in the way in which we now understand it, but it is possible that as he settled, he acquired possessions that needed to be moved from time to time. Crops needed to be harvested, water might also have had to be carried for a considerable distance, and rollers and primitive carts would certainly have produced increased mobility and would have granted some relief to women, who, alongside the horse and the camel, have ranked as "man's" most efficient pack animals.

As man spread across the earth, and tribes started to take advantage of the resources of the particular areas they eventually chose to settle, so they developed individual characteristics. With increasing population and growing pressure on their local resources, tribal territories expanded. Intertribal competition for land and other goods led eventually to the evolution of barter, a simple form of trading transaction. Curiosity must also have been responsible for travel, and in due time more sophisticated peoples became aware of the existence of gold, silver, and precious stones, which came to the Middle East and Europe across the land trade routes from the East. As tribes evolved into embryonic nation states, the possession of these rare and beautiful metals and stones enabled the leaders and other influential men to demonstrate and reinforce their right to power by the extent of their possessions rather than by personal physical superiority or the proof of their prowess in battle or the hunt. Thus, in time, silver and gold, and a number of other metals, came to be used as currency, and the ponderous and often frustrating system of barter tended to fall into disuse. The ever-increasing demand for supplies of precious metals and stones led the kings and princes of Western Europe to seek sea routes to their sources rather than to receive them via the great land routes to the East, the history of which goes back probably beyond recorded history.

In the early fourteenth century the ships that set forth virtually into the unknown were small and of limited seaworthiness. Voyages were confined to the search for the Indies, although valuable commodities such as endless supplies of timber and teeming shoals of fish were discovered on voyages that we now know could never have led around the top of the world to India and the Far East. Voyages for the purpose of colonization did not generally take place until the late sixteenth century. Many of them failed, and where European countries annexed territories, the labor force was often later composed of imported slaves. As a result, the transporting of slaves from Africa to the West Indies and America proved to be an extremely lucrative business.

As is described in later chapters, the sailing ship developed slowly, and the practice of overseas trade being placed almost exclusively in the hands of the monopolistic "companies" did little to induce experimentation to discover how to build faster or more efficient ships. Most developments were brought about by the navies of the European powers, and merchant shipowners were generally content to utilize them once they were satisfied that their adoption would further the interests of their trade. The "Indiamen" were the equivalent in their time of the transatlantic liners. They were large, often in the eighteenth and early nineteenth centuries carrying over 1,000 tons of cargo. Generally, however, merchant ships were much smaller, and a vessel carrying as little as 50 tons was a perfectly economic proposition. East India-

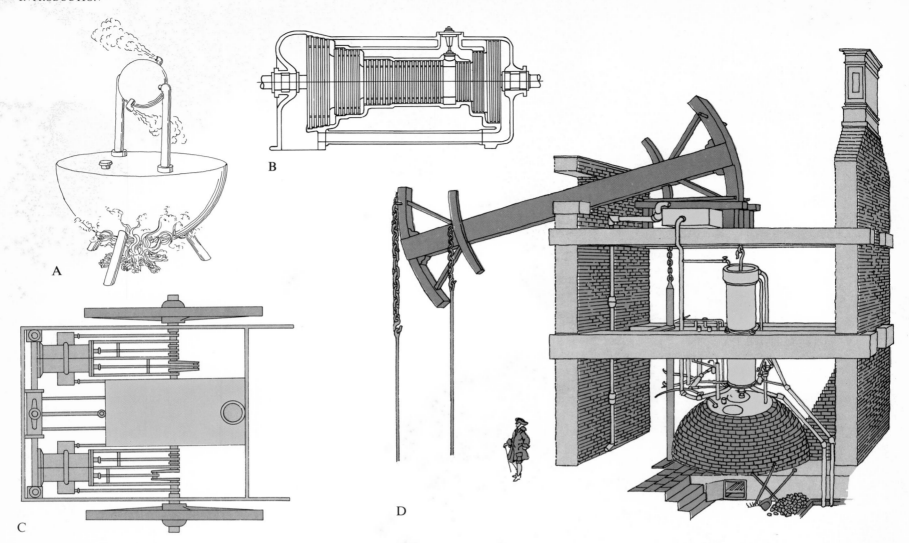

A

B

C

D

men would usually make one round-trip voyage each year, using trade winds and monsoons to ensure fair sailing as far as possible. Progress was leisurely, and it was customary to shorten sail and heave to at night, particularly in dangerous or uncharted waters. Quite often, a ship of this class would only make six voyages before being broken up. It is a surprising fact that for a hundred years from the beginning of the eighteenth century the improvements in size and sailing capacity of ships were very limited.

The newly learned art of making sizable iron plates and the development of more sophisticated tools are expressions of the awakening of scientific and technological interest at the end of the eighteenth century. Throughout Europe, inventors and enthusiastic amateurs sought to solve the problem of turning the theory of steam propulsion, which had been known for hundreds of years, into practice. Many failed, a few succeeded, but for years the inherent difficulties of fabricating a reliable transmission system, and a boiler that could sustain high steam pressure, hampered progress. Early gear

wheels were often made of wood, since no means were available of cutting teeth into iron rims; furthermore, for many years every hole had to be bored by hand. The thermal efficiency of early steam engines (many of which were of the atmospheric type) was astonishingly low, yet with experimentation the time came when the true piston engine drove colliery pumping engines and almost overnight this led to enormously increased productivity. Further outstanding landmarks in technological progress included the development of the Bessemer process of making steel in 1856, and the open-hearth method of steel manufacture eleven years later. These advances were rapidly adopted by the transportation industry.

The first steam locomotives were employed on colliery railways, and it was there that the many difficulties of devising an efficient track and ballast system were overcome. The first public railway was opened in Great Britain in 1825, and although sceptics predicted that speeds above 30 mph (48 km/h) would prove fatal to passengers, the public at large acclaimed the new form of trans-

A AELOPILE
Hero of Alexandria is said to have devised this primitive form of the steam reaction turbine which was a steam-filled ball that was rotated by the expulsion of the steam through opposed escape-nozzles.

B PARSONS'S GAS TURBINE
Sir Charles A. Parsons developed the steam turbine in 1884. The advantage of this engine was that it had only rotating parts. In 1894 Parsons's company built the Turbinia *to test a marine application of this engine.*

C JAMES'S FOUR-CYLINDER MACHINERY
Built by W. H. James for his 1829 steam coach, this comprised, in effect, two separate two-cylinder engines each driving one back wheel to allow for differential action when cornering.

D NEWCOMEN'S ATMOSPHERIC ENGINE
Thomas Newcomen, an Englishman, developed this low-pressure reciprocating steam engine for pumping water out of

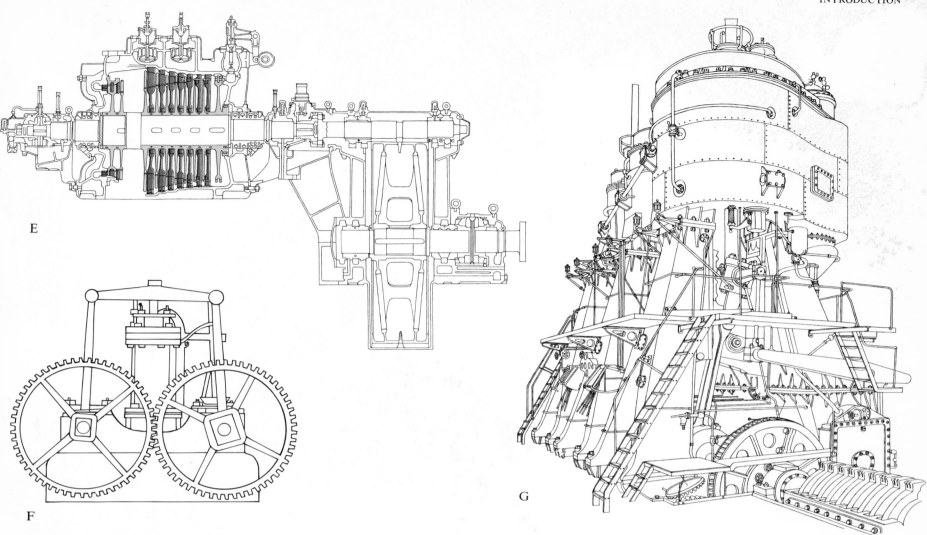

E

F

G

mines in the early eighteenth century. The real power was that of the atmosphere, steam being admitted only to create a vacuum in the bottom of the cylinder by condensation.

E MINESWEEPER TURBINE
Cutaway view of a turbine engine.

F STEVENS'S TWIN-SCREW STEAM ENGINE
In 1802, Colonel John Stevens produced this single vertical cylinder engine with an overhead crosshead from which two connecting rods drove gearing attached to twin propeller shafts for the launch Little Juliana, *which could make a speed of about 4 mph (5.4 km/h).*

G TRIPLE EXPANSION ENGINE
First fitted in Boat No. 30 of the Cie. des Bateaux-Omnibus de la Seine in 1871, the triple expansion engine became the standard machinery installation for ordinary merchant ships even as late as 1930.

portation. The earliest railways were intended to carry goods, but once it was realized that passengers too could be carried in large numbers, Europe, and particularly Great Britain, saw the creation of scores of public companies, which in the fever of the moment built railways that could not possibly produce profits. Routes were uncoordinated, and by the end of the nineteenth century when the fever had subsided, the task of bringing order out of chaos was slowly tackled. Much was achieved by amalgamations and the elimination of costly and unnecessary competition, yet many of the problems remain. The majority of railways are now either nationally controlled or in receipt of government subsidies.

Railways met the demands of the Industrial Revolution in the transportation of both raw materials and finished products. They facilitated the movement of population from the countryside to the growing industrial cities. In Great Britain, 170,000 tons of pig iron were produced in 1802. In 1913 the figure was over 10 million tons. During this time the population rose from about 20 million

to over 45 million. The railways also provided communications between previously isolated communities and brought about sweeping changes in the formerly parochial lives of ordinary people. The early realization of the railways' potential as a large-scale passenger-carrying system produced a situation in which people of moderate means could, for the first time, travel for pleasure. One of the earliest recorded train disasters concerned an excursion train carrying vacationers home from Brighton to London. Just as railways helped in the development of industrial areas—filth and squalor often resulted and became overnight a social problem on a scale that had never been previously encountered—so many seaside resorts and inland vacation centers owe their existence to the railways. Railways thus reaped a double benefit. They eliminated or provided keen competition for the canal and river navigations. Horse transportation, particularly in its role as a carrier of passengers over long distances, was virtually put out of business. The railways remained unchallenged for a long period of time, in fact until the

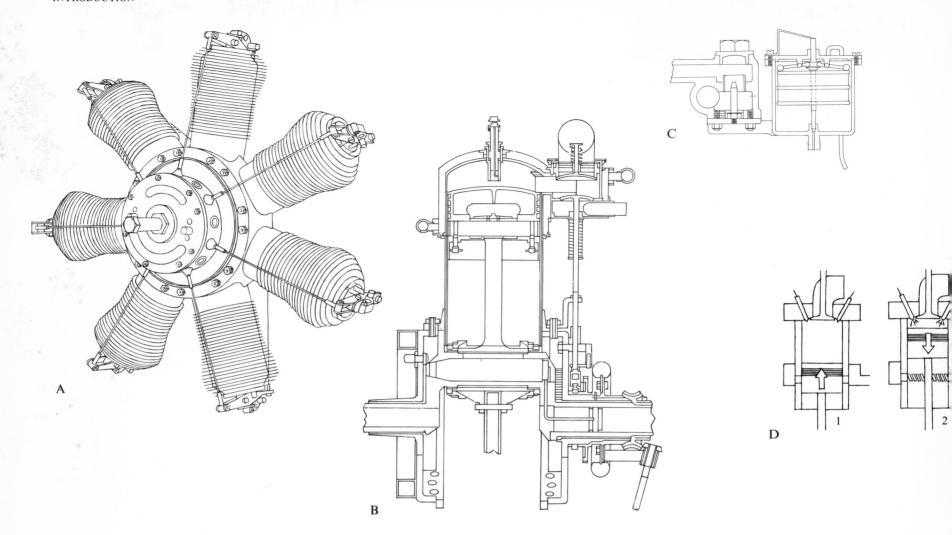

A

B

C

D   1   2

advent of the mass-produced automobile and reliable long distance buses and trucks.

The future of railways, in spite of the introduction of diesel and electric forms of traction, remains problematic. Domestic airlines have made serious inroads into their business. In Great Britain, however, the efforts that have been made to rationalize routes and improve standards of both speed and comfort have resulted in the almost complete discomfiture of airlines within certain specific distances. Railways may still have a role to play if roads fail to keep pace with the pressure of vehicles, if gas shortages continue, if no new means of propelling automobiles are found, and people again discover the many virtues of existing and projected high-speed trains.

The steam engine took longer to make its mark at sea. Early experimental engines were placed in vessels that were little longer than launches, and they were often unable to stem the tides of rivers. Low steam pressures, rudimentary transmissions, and inefficient paddles all contributed to the failure to make marked progress. Coal consumption of early

boilers was so great that even the steamships that eventually made passages across oceans could carry little more than mail and a few passengers. They paid handsomely for "staterooms" and food that hardly matched the glowing promises of the publicity accompanying the introduction of each new steamship service. The enforced practice of using salt water in boilers led to a steady loss of efficiency as the voyage proceeded. The unreliability of the machinery, the vulnerability of the paddles to damage in heavy seas, and the risk of shaft fracture when screws were introduced meant that steamships had to carry auxiliary sail well into the second half of the nineteenth century.

Progress was steady rather than spectacular, and with the invention of the triple-expansion steam engine, the condenser, and the ability to use higher and higher steam pressures, a steam cargo ship, entirely unsubsidized and dependent entirely upon freight charges, eventually became cheaper to run in the long term than a sailing ship. The development of the steamship to the point at which it could carry passengers in large

A GNOME ROTARY ENGINE
Designed by the Seguin brothers in 1907 —08, this marked a complete break from the traditional automobile engine design, the cylinders rotating with the propeller around a fixed crankshaft.

B MANLY'S RADIAL ENGINE
Charles Manly designed this five-cylinder engine in 1903 for S. P. Langley's "Aerodrome." It had a power/weight ratio which was not bettered for twenty years.

C MAYBACH CARBURETOR
Maybach's 1893 float-feed spray carburetor was the ancestor of the modern spray carburetor. It had one jet and the inventor intended that the float and needle-valve should maintain a constant air-petrol mixture.

D TWO-STROKE DIESEL
1 Compression stroke
2 Power stroke
3 Scavenging

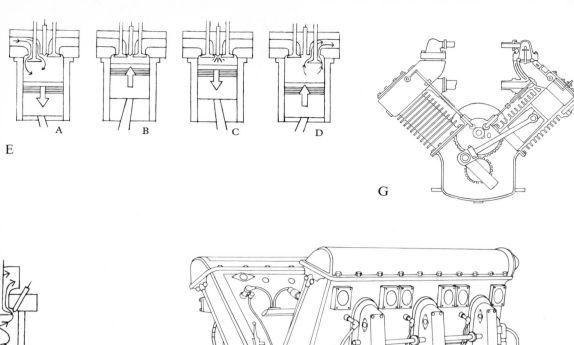

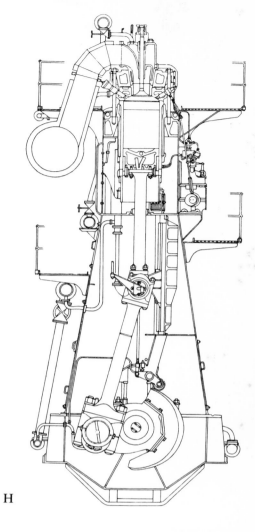

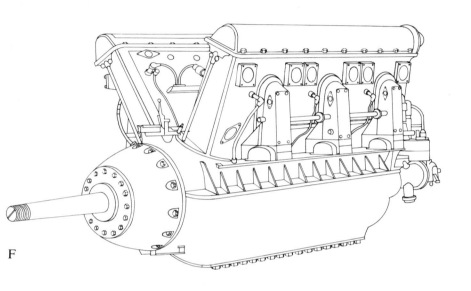

E **FOUR-STROKE DIESEL**
  A Intake stroke
  B Compression stroke
  C Power stroke
  D Exhaust stroke

F HISPANO SUIZA TYPE 12 NBR
After World War I the Spanish firm of Hispano Suiza set up factories in France and produced some very successful aero-engines. The 650 horsepower 12 Nbr was introduced in 1929 and had a reduction gear.

G MORS FOUR-CYLINDER ENGINE
The 1898 Mors automobile had a four-cylinder engine of V-formation with air-cooled cylinder barrels and detachable water-cooled heads.

H DIRECT DRIVE PROPULSION DIESEL
Cross section of a two-stroke, crosshead, direct drive, propulsion diesel engine.

numbers coincided with the main flow of the greatest mass movement in history—the departure overseas from Europe of hundreds of thousands of poverty-stricken, hungry, and oppressed people. By the early 1800s the colonial territories of European powers were attracting people who saw there a new and freer way of life. This movement gathered momentum throughout the century, often as the outcome of the discovery of gold, but it was to the United States that most eyes were directed. The earliest emigrants suffered privation on long journeys in sailing ships, but the steamships, and the government regulations which covered their operation, made conditions more tolerable. Fleets of steamships were built to profit from the flood of emigrants and many of these ships were built in such a way that they could carry a human cargo westward and cattle eastward.

At the other end of the scale, provision for the well-to-do was provided on an increasingly lavish scale, particularly in the Atlantic liners, which were extremely large ships by the beginning of the twentieth century. Ship-owners vied with each other in their efforts

to provide more attractive staterooms and public rooms. They instituted a tradition (which really only ended with the demise of the steamship in its role as a regular passenger liner) of creating mock baronial halls, Palladian lounges, Turkish baths, and dining saloons which in size and opulence often outdid those found in contemporary hotels ashore. In fact, they copied and adapted—some would say distorted—practically all the main styles of European architecture. By present-day standards the ratio of staff to passengers in the heyday of the Atlantic liner was quite outrageous, especially when it is remembered that emigrants were often carried in these huge ships in conditions that we now find difficult to contemplate.

The first marked setback to almost a century of commercial progress occurred in 1914. By that time turbine ships with steel hulls and upperworks were common, and voyages across the Atlantic took less than a week. Many passenger and cargo liners were lost during the 1914—1918 war, but by the middle twenties things were again more or less normal. In 1923 the restrictions placed

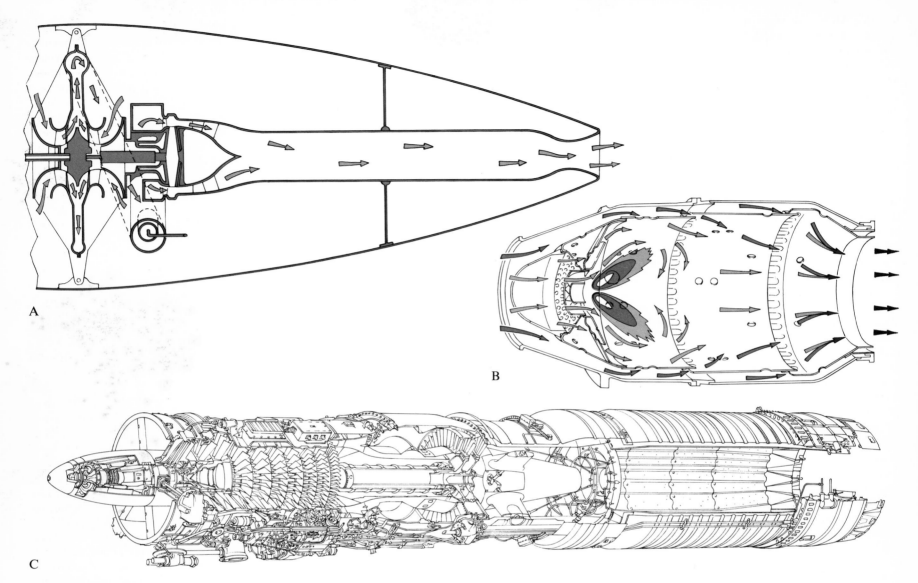

A

B

C

by the United States on immigration and the quota system that was devised had the most profound effect on Atlantic shipping. The International Mercantile Marine Corporation, which had gone well on the way to securing a monopoly of steamship services across this ocean, was particularly hard hit and the measures taken to fill the empty berths were only partially successful. The Wall Street crash in the late 1920s affected the trade of the whole world and its consequences continued to be felt until 1939 when once again the world's fleets were mobilized for war—and sunk as effectively as they had been in 1914—1918 until the convoy escorts finally mastered the U-boat.

For some years before 1939 shipowners had attracted passengers by providing modest yet wholesome accommodations—tourist class is self-explanatory. Cruising as a means of attracting passengers became popular in the late twenties and thirties, and when by the mid-fifties the airlines had sounded the

death knell of passenger ships engaged on scheduled worldwide services, shipowners again turned to this form of activity. Now there are few regular passenger ships left in service, but many new and adapted cruise ships are enticing people to clearly defined areas of the world.

In the last fifteen years the cargo ship has changed almost out of recognition. Short-distance cargo liners have been virtually eliminated and their place taken by container ships or roll-on roll-off ferries. There are now also container ship services based in Europe, Japan, and the United States that serve the majority of the world's established routes. Tankers (very large crude carriers) are in service carrying over 400,000 tons of oil and larger ones are planned. Bulk carriers, too, are now enormous ships and cargoes weighing over 150,000 tons are now not unusual.

Road transportation has been a story of limited endeavor until the advent of the auto-

A WHITTLE ENGINE CHAMBER
The aircraft gas-turbine had to achieve very great heat release in chambers only a few inches across. This is the chamber used in the original Whittle engine of 1937.

B MODERN GAS-TURBINE CHAMBER
This chamber yields a steady stream of hot gas which can be used as the medium to drive the turbine, and, in a jet engine, to provide the propulsive thrust.

C ATAR 9 JET ENGINE
This is one of the four existing versions of the ATAR 9 jet engine, built by the French firm SNECMA. The ATAR 9 is used on, among others, the Dassault Mirage F-1 and the Super-Mystère B2.

mobile. All civilizations had roads, but although we use the word "road", early man had no more than tracks along which he walked or rode. Often he had no shelter and he was the prey of both brigands and natural conditions. Even the great trade routes to the East could have been no more than tracks at best; at worst, the pack animals were led from point to point by reference to landmarks, many of which were often known only to local guides.

The Romans set the pace in road building and the highways that they constructed across the length and breadth of Europe and even into the Middle East and Africa owed their existence primarily to military requirements. As was so often the case, in later years trade followed the army.

During the Dark Ages the art of road building was lost and progress was slow right up until the late nineteenth century. In the Middle Ages few people traveled. Armies, itinerant friars, monks traveling between monasteries, papal dignitaries from Rome, pilgrims, ambassadors, and wealthy traders formed the majority; the village and its immediate surroundings constituted the world for peasants and craftsmen alike. As late as the nineteenth century the majority of people lived and died in the town or village in which they were born. Many of them had perhaps only ventured out of their parish to the nearest market town or cathedral city. Technology was unable to provide comfortable coaches. Tires and springs were, of course, unknown and roads were so excruciatingly bad in winter and summer alike that only those who had business ventured abroad. The horse was the one relatively comfortable means of transportation, but even this noble animal was limited in endurance and speed. Goods were carried in heavy carts with wide-tread wheels, and for thousands of years development was of necessity limited by horse power.

In the eighteenth and nineteenth centuries horse-drawn coaches became equipped with reasonably efficient springs, and comfort of a sort was provided inside. Even then, however, the authorities responsible for the laying and maintenance of roads were under little pressure to exercise diligence in the performance of their duties, and travel continued to be an experience often remembered with distaste. In Great Britain few new roads were built, apart from those diversions caused by the enclosure of land. The practice of turning over road maintenance to private enterprise—the fee being a toll charged to all travelers by the contractor—did much to improve the situation; by the time experiments were being carried out with steam engines

the main towns were linked with regular and relatively fast stagecoaches, 10 mph (16 km/h) being considered an excellent rate of progress. During the toll, or turnpike, era many refinements became possible in the design of private coaches and they also increased quite dramatically in number. Stone sets and the Macadam process were generally used to effect better road conditions. At the height of the stagecoach era some staging inns were known to have maintained over 2,000 horses. The effect of the progress made in road transportation engineering was partly nullified by the advent of railways, but what had been accomplished facilitated the subsequent arrival of the automobile.

One fact that is often forgotten about the steam age is that steam-propelled road vehicles were in operation well before the inauguration of public railways. By 1832 steam coaches and steam buses enjoyed a brief popularity, but they were forced off the turnpike roads by discriminatory tolls; the town buses were put out of business mainly by legislation engineered by interests with heavy involvement in horse transportation.

Experiments with gas and gasoline engines were being carried out as early as 1870, and by 1889 the car was making its first explosive and erratic journeys upon European roads. As with the early forms of all transportation, the automobile was within reach of only the wealthiest, who soon saw its potential. To the man in the street it was little more than a joke; an object to be pursued by jeering small boys and barking dogs. To those who owned horses it was a menace, but its introduction into cities was, ironically, hailed as a great measure to clean up the stinking, filthy, horse-dominated streets.

The internal-combustion engine was used in a number of distinct ways, some successful, others unsuccessful. In general, however, the basic layout and transmission systems had been established by 1914. So fast had been development that the French army could mobilize all the Paris taxis to take reserve infantry to the Battle of the Marne and thus stabilize the line that was to remain virtually static until broken during the German offensive of 1918. London buses were transported to France, where they performed yeoman service as infantry transports. Staff officers soon used cars in preference to horses, tanks and armored cars were in regular use by 1918, and by degrees the world's armies became completely motorized.

In 1908 the Ford Model T astonished the world as the first mass-produced automobile. From 1920 onward more and more people found that they were able to afford

a car. Its pressure upon the roads was enormous, and governments and local authorities have been building and developing roads ever since to contain the increasing number of vehicles that are coming into private and public ownership. In 1939 it was possible to buy a thoroughly reliable automobile for about $350 (£140) and, in spite of heavy taxation, the car remains one of the most economical forms of transportation yet devised. Its social effects have been incalculable. The freedom of movement that railways brought to people traveling in groups has been expanded into freedom of movement on an individual basis, and the purchaser can now select a vehicle that will meet the simplest or most sophisticated needs. Cities are built and adapted to suit the convenience of motor vehicles and the railways have for many years been unable to compete with heavy road transportation except in the conveyance of bulk commodities of low value.

Technical development has now slowed, but within the limits imposed by the manufacturers, one of these apparently being that the product should not last for more than three years. Car enthusiasts—and there are many millions of them—have always discussed the merits of an unending succession of new models and yearned for vehicles which are probably just a little larger and certainly faster than those in their possession. The latest developments, however, have turned eyes toward compact, fuel-economy cars.

The era of air transportation has been even shorter than that of the car, although man's desire to fly has been expressed through mythology and folk tales for countless centuries. As with other forms of transportation, serious efforts to build a heavier-than-air flying machine had to await the invention of the internal-combustion engine and materials for building the light but strong frameworks to contain the engine and wings that, with their delicate contours, could withstand the pressures imposed upon them without collapsing.

The earliest efforts into flight were centered upon balloons. Hot-air balloons had made ascents in the late eighteenth century. They were uncontrollable and inherently dangerous machines. Hydrogen balloons, although similarly subject to winds, were more successful, and one of the first occasions in which balloons were used to practical purpose occurred during the siege of Paris in 1874 when messages were sent out by air from the beleaguered city to the outside world.

Along with the development of balloons, many pioneers were concerned with gliding. Many peculiar ideas were proved to be false and the first halting steps led to the box-kitelike contraptions that were in due course to become the basis of the powered aircraft. The idea of the man-powered flying machine never came to fruition, and even now this intriguing problem-filled idea, which has been the preoccupation of many men for so many years, shows no signs of becoming a practical means of transportation.

Balloons developed into airships (more correctly called dirigibles but often also confusingly called zeppelins). Early versions were actually powered by steam but the gasoline engine soon became the standard form of propulsion. The great enthusiasm for this form of transportation was dashed by the burning of the *Hindenburg* in New Jersey, May 1937, and the almost simultaneous disaster which befell the British R.101 at Beauvais in France. The United States kept the idea alive through the employment of small dirigibles as scouts and antisubmarine spotters for the navy. Now interest has reawakened and investigations are under way to determine the practicability of container-carrying dirigibles, but with one great difference from earlier craft—the use of noncombustible helium in place of hydrogen.

It is generally accepted that the first flight of a heavier-than-air machine took place on December 17, 1903. In 1909 the first crossing of the English Channel was accomplished. By 1914 the opposing powers managed to assemble small forces of ill-assorted planes to augment their experimental military aircraft. In so doing they eliminated almost overnight the use of cavalry as the eyes of the armies. Once tradition-bound commanders understood the role that they could play, aircraft were demanded in ever-increasing numbers. By 1918 they were relatively sophisticated machines, and many of them remained in service as operational units for years afterward.

In 1919 the first direct transatlantic crossing from West to East was made in an adapted twin-engine bomber. The first direct flight in the opposite direction was made by a German single-engine plane in 1928.

Worldwide pioneer flights were carried out by intrepid solo pilots, and newspapers organized races that did much to develop the range and reliability of aircraft. Civil airlines were set up and by 1930 the foundations of the existing worldwide pattern of services had been established. Although faster and faster schedules were the order of the day, pre-1939 flying was a relatively leisurely affair. Few airlines flew during the hours of darkness and it was thought by many experienced people that long-distance

flights would eventually be carried out by flying boats. Much time and effort went into their development, many fine craft were built, and they were actually introduced with great success on several routes. Nevertheless, the clamor for speed was to win the day and the era of the commercial flying boat virtually ended with the end of hostilities in 1945.

As the sea had its Blue Riband for well over a century, so between the wars the air had its Schneider Trophy. This annual race, which was flown over the Solent between the Isle of Wight and the mainland of England, consistently produced new world airspeed records, and the experience gained with the aircraft entered—all by government air forces—was incorporated into the powerful and deadly fighter planes that made their dramatic debut in 1939. Similarly, using the experience gained with heavier machines, the warring factions were able to mount air strikes that hit soldier and civilian indiscriminately. In 1942, just twenty-three years after the first nonstop Atlantic flight, a steady stream of bombers were undertaking the same journey almost without a casualty. In the Pacific arena, American bombers flew vast distances to deliver their deadly loads.

In 1945 civil airlines set about restoring their fortunes and made considerable use of converted bombers and transport planes. Transatlantic commercial flights were soon introduced and the rate of flight development can be illustrated by the fact that when the first successful European airline service was inaugurated between London and Paris in 1919, it flew when the weather was suitable and its sole navigational equipment consisted of a compass and maps, which the pilot used as we now use maps in automobiles. In 1949 the first jet commercial airliner (the first jet fighter plane having made its appearance in the closing months of the 1939–1945 war) was introduced into service. It could fly almost anywhere and carried sophisticated navigational aids, including radar; it could maintain radio contact with airports throughout its journey, where it received continuously updated weather reports and routing instructions.

Today, with Concorde, we stand on the threshold of faster-than-sound commercial flying. Aircraft operation is so complex that the major operators are corporations, very often government-owned or subsidized. The design and development of new engines and aircraft are beyond the resources of all but the largest organizations. Private flying develops swiftly and prices of light aircraft are becoming competitive with those of cars. The need for airports and first-class maintenance

may limit future development, and as yet no vertical takeoff private aircraft has been produced. Helicopters remain primarily within the sphere of military flying and in Europe at least they have not yet been slotted to any extent into the pattern of airliner operations.

A Regency "buck" of 1823 would have laughed at the idea that in 1974 a man could, within twenty-four hours of leaving Europe, be aboard a ship in the Caribbean. It is a fact that even today gives food for thought. Within the field of group transportation, the aircraft has freed man from the remaining shackles which prevented his free movement across and above the earth's surface. The world is now his oyster, and while he has taken an even more significant step forward by probing beyond the earth's atmosphere into space, his existing terrestrial transportation systems remain far from perfect. In reaching the present stage he has created problems, particularly those of pollution and an increasing disequilibrium in the world's ecological balance. People generally are disquieted and a popular and increasingly vocal demand for appropriate measures to be taken is heard across the world. Much of this clamor is uninformed and it is not fully understood that, in order to solve these problems, restrictions will almost certainly have to be brought in that will involve personal sacrifice, particularly as regards freedom of movement in the use of personal transportation. Regrettably, most changes now occur for economic and not social reasons and little will be done until it becomes economically sound. This is well illustrated by the current debate on the validity of transferring many of the goods at present transported by road back to the railways, which not so many years ago had such a large share in this field of transportation.

To predict the future of transportation is indeed difficult for there are so many issues involved. At the time of writing there is an energy crisis throughout the world. It is highly probable that in the decades ahead the consumption of oil will exceed the rate of discovery and exploitation of new resources. Nuclear fission as a means of powering transportation, either directly or through the production of electricity, has not yet produced the results that were once predicted. There is, therefore, a general fear that transportation will eventually be crippled by a failing supply of appropriate fuels. It, nevertheless, is hoped that the level of human ingenuity and development of technology are such that quite new, possibly unknown fuels or sources of motive power will be developed before the earth's resources are finally exhausted.

Brig

The brig is a graceful craft having two masts, both of which carry square sails. On the mainmast there is a small, schooner-type gaff-rigged sail. There are three types of brigs — the full-rigged brig (above), the brigantine, and the hermaphrodite brig (both pictured elsewhere). In all three types, the foremast is made of three separate spars and rigged with square sails, but the main (or after) mast has a different sail rig in each case.

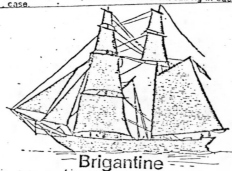

Brigantine

As a class of brig, the brigantine has two masts. The foremast, made of three separate spars, is square-rigged. The mainmast, however, is made up in two spars and carries a fore-and-aft mainsail, over which are two or three yards from which are rigged a square main-topsail and (when there are three yards) a topgallant-sail. No sail is carried on the lower, or main yard.

Hermaphrodite Brig

This type vessel has the foremast of a brig and the mainmast of a schooner. The mainmast is made up of two spars and carries no yards or square sails (as does the foremast). It has a fore-and-aft mainsail and a gaff topsail. With the complicated squaresail rig only on the foremast, this rig offered the advantage of a small crew.

Topsail Schooner

The topsail schooner is a schooner with a little of the squaresail on the foremast. The foremast and its sail plan are nearly identical to the mainmast of the brigantine: a square fore-topsail and fore-topgallant sail over a fore-and-aft foresail. Both masts are composed of two spars, but the lower foremast is a little

Ship

The designation "ship" is properly restricted to the full-rigged vessel — large, square-rigged, with three masts each carrying a full complement of square sails. Each mast is composed of three separate spars — a lower mast, a top-mast, and a topgallant mast. In addition to the square sails on the mizzenmast (closest to the stern), this example also carries a schooner-type gaff-sail called the spanker.

Bark (Barque)

A bark is traditionally a three-masted vessel having her foremast (closest to the bow) and mainmast (in the middle) square-rigged — that is, with rectangular sails hung from yards. The mizzenmast (third from the bow, the last one in this example) is rigged with fore-and-aft sails. In recent times, huge four-and five-masted iron barks were built.

Barkentine (Barquentine)

The barkentine is a three-masted vessel having only the foremast square-rigged and the main and mizzenmasts carrying fore-and-aft mainsails and gaff topsails — rigged and designed to be handled by a small crew. Sometimes one or two additional schooner-rigged masts were added to make a four- or five-masted barkentine.

Schooner

The schooner has two or more masts, all of which are fore-and-aft rigged. The sails can be either full triangle or gaff-rigged (as above). Schooners were popular in coastal trade work and as off-shore fishing boats — widely used off North America. Most popular of the rigs were the three-masted schooners (above) which could be handled by a captain, mate, cook, and four crewmen. Many four-, five-, and six-masted schooners were built. One seven-masted schooner was constructed.

SHIPS

THE AGE OF SAIL

The history of sea transportation falls into two distinct phases: sail and power, except that for a period of about fifty years in the nineteenth and twentieth centuries both sailing ships and powered vessels competed for the world's trade. In the era of power-driven ships, reciprocating engines gave way to turbines, the paddle gave way to the screw and now the diesel engine has become a leading type of marine propulsion.

Sailing ships developed slowly over thousands of years, and until iron and then steel became practical shipbuilding materials their size was limited, among other things, by the inherent weaknesses in wood.

Trade over short distances was an activity that was carried on without significant development for a very long time, but by the Middle Ages the northern European countries traded extensively in products such as wheat, timber, dried fish, hides, wool, and furs. Interocean trade followed the early voyages of discovery, but it was often one-way since the colonies, which eventually became some of the most important markets in the world, were founded by people who had emigrated for reasons little connected with trade. For many years these areas had little to offer the home countries. From China, India, and Southeast Asia the "Companies" brought home such luxuries as spices, tea, exotic woods, fabrics, silk, gold, silver, and precious stones, while from the West Indian plantations Europe received sugar and rum. Until the advent of steam a round-trip voyage to the Far East could take a year or more.

This fact, combined with the policy of the companies to keep the price of their imports high, did little to foster trade or improve ship design.

The increase in the world's population, which became particularly marked in Europe at the end of the eighteenth century produced the need for additional sources of food supply. At the same time the Industrial Revolution led manufacturers to seek markets for the many goods that could not be sold in Europe. The development of the steamship during the first fifty years of the nineteenth century eventually permitted both of these requirements to be met. From this time on, the fleets of merchant ships maintained by Europe and America expanded at a phenomenal rate, and the developing colonies were readily able to export their own surpluses. Many luxuries became commonplace and increasing numbers of people were able to buy tea, sugar, meat, and many other products from the far ends of the earth. As the demand for raw materials increased, so more and more ships were built. Today, ores of various descriptions, crude oil, and grains are becoming increasingly important, and specialized ships have been built to carry them. New types of ships are also being developed to carry a single product in order to reduce the cost of transportation and to ensure safe delivery of the cargo.

The two following chapters describe the evolution of sailing ships and powered ships and the inventions and innovations that assist them to make safe voyages. The sailing ship has gone and the majority of passenger liners have disappeared in the face of air competition. However, ships are still vitally necessary to carry the world's cargoes and the container ships, tankers and vehicle ferries of today are as fascinating as the many types of sailing ships that once sailed the seas long ago crewed by men who faced perils and hardships that very few men now living have experienced.

Throughout history hull shapes have been dictated by the type of construction, mode of construction, mode of propulsion, use, fashion, and whim. Primitive craft ranged from round shapes—woven baskets, skin-covered framework, and even pottery—to the long and narrow, such as bundles of reeds and shaped logs. The most widespread form of hull was the log canoe, which was quickly improved by the addition of one or more planks to each side. For centuries, built-up hulls followed the general shape of such canoes.

The continued existence of the canoe form points to the fact that the main development of ships occurred in the Mediterranean region and in northern Europe. Shipbuilding history is in the main concerned with wooden sailing ships, since metal ships and mechanical propulsion occur only in the later years of the recorded history of shipbuilding. Through most of this time there was a parallel development of the two forms noted above, the "round" ship, or bulky cargo carrier, and the "long" ship which was built for speed.

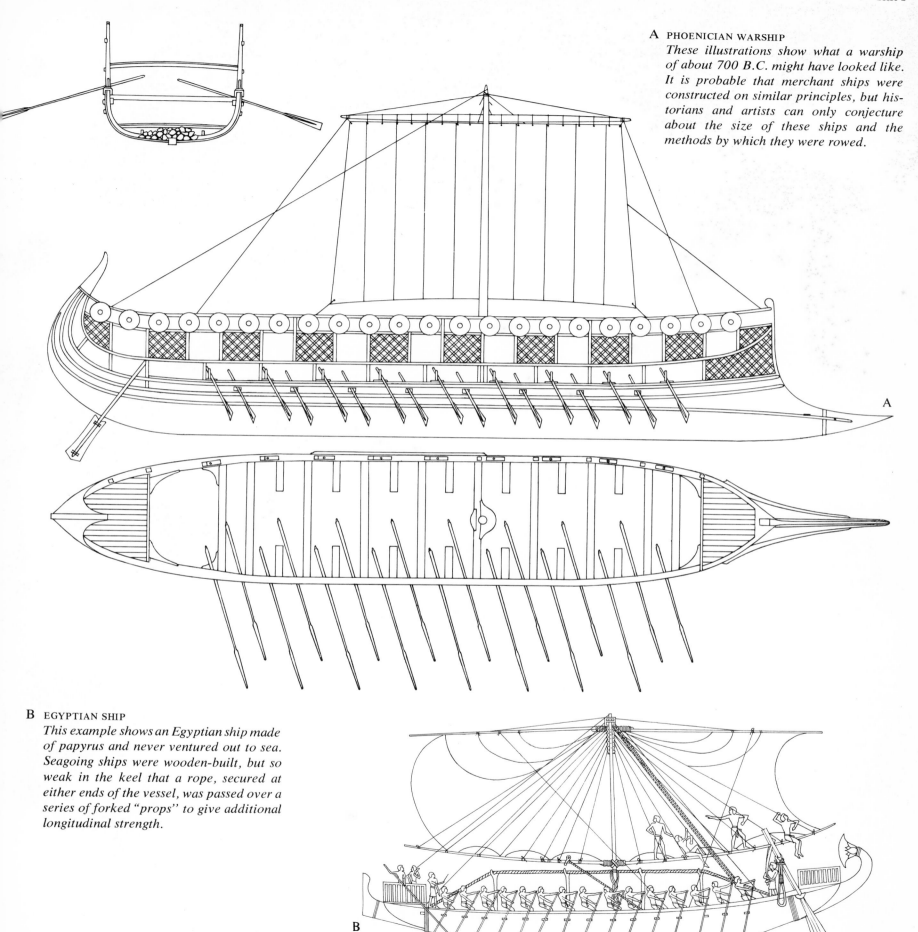

A PHOENICIAN WARSHIP

These illustrations show what a warship of about 700 B.C. might have looked like. It is probable that merchant ships were constructed on similar principles, but historians and artists can only conjecture about the size of these ships and the methods by which they were rowed.

B EGYPTIAN SHIP

This example shows an Egyptian ship made of papyrus and never ventured out to sea. Seagoing ships were wooden-built, but so weak in the keel that a rope, secured at either ends of the vessel, was passed over a series of forked "props" to give additional longitudinal strength.

A SANTA MARIA
An impression of Columbus's Santa Maria. *An impression because nobody knows exactly what this ship looked like. Fifty-two men comprised the crew and conditions on board must have been cramped and unhygienic. Columbus's first voyage lasted about seven and a half months. It is noticeable that by this time the stern castle had become an integral part of the hull.*

B EARLY WORLD MAP
Columbus thought he had discovered India since the map of the world on which he planned his voyage showed a single ocean between Europe and Asia. No European at that time knew of the existence of the continent of America.

C NINA
The Caravel was a common type of ship in the Mediterranean and clearly shows the influence of the lateen sail, which had been used for many years in the Red Sea and the Persian Gulf. This illustration is an impression of the Nina, *a ship of Columbus's expedition, which carried 19 men. She was the fastest sailer in the fleet.*

D PINTA
The third ship of Columbus's expedition was the Pinta, *which carried a crew of 18 men. She was square-rigged and was typical of another type of ship much used by Spain and Portugal.*

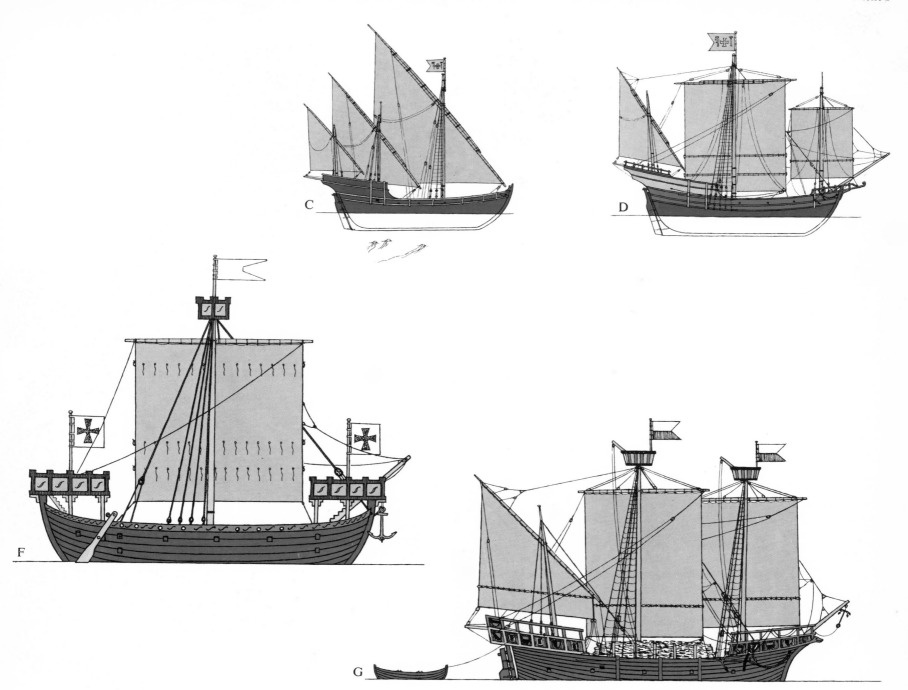

E ROMAN MERCHANT SHIP

This drawing was copied from a marble relief from about 200 A.D. discovered in Ostia. The vessel is carvel-built and has two heavy steering rudders. Apart from the topsails, the Romans also used a spritsail called an "Artemon". Knowledge of the use of this sail appears to have been lost during the Dark Ages, for hundreds of years elapsed before sailing ships in northern Europe used it. Roman ships anchored by the stern to protect the low bow from the force of the sea.

F NORDIC SHIP

This picture shows a Nordic ship from the middle of the thirteenth century. She had a deck under which cargo could be protected from rain and sea, fore-and-after castles, and a "top". In those days sea battles were fought at close quarters by impressed merchant ships or fleets and crews supplied by merchants in return for certain trading rights. The top and the castles were occupied by soldiers whose main weapon was the bow and arrow, and, later on, muzzle-loading guns.

G HULK

The ship illustrated is from the later Middle Ages. While still clinker built, the castles are firmly secured to the hull instead of on strong supports at a higher level. The rig shows considerable development over the earlier roundships, and the rudder, which was controlled by a tiller, was hung from the stern post.

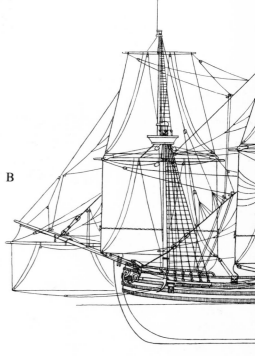

A CARRACK

In the early years of the seventeenth century, many trading voyages were carried out in Carracks, a type of vessel believed to have originated in Italy. By this time the topsail was in common use in larger ships and this, together with the bonnets on the lower sails, allowed a degree of flexibility in suiting the rig to the weather. During his second voyage to America the fleet of Columbus included three vessels which probably looked very much like the vessel illustrated.

B DUTCH FLUTE

By the seventeenth century many different types of sailing ships had been developed. The Dutch Flute was a typical example and would have been employed carrying a wide variety of cargoes between small ports with limited depths of water. The rig was used for all small sailing ships of the period. It is interesting to study the Dutch marine paintings of both the seventeenth and eighteenth centuries to discover the many types of ships which could be seen in a single harbor.

C SWEDISH KRAVEL

The ship illustrated is from the middle of the sixteenth century. By this time two masts each had two sails, but the lateen mizzen was still in common use. The beakhead had been developed to protect the forecastle in head seas. The forecastle had also been moved slightly aft to provide space for the shipping of the heavy bowsprit. During this period ships were highly decorated, especially warships, and the larger merchant ships carried guns as a protection against pirates and warships of enemy nations.

ELIZABETHAN GALLEON
*This seventeenth-century four-masted war-
ship of about 700 tons had a main arma-
ment of culverins and demi-culverins.*

The design of early ships was influenced by the type of tools then available. Northern shipbuilders, for instance, used an adze to shape one plank from each half of a felled tree. These planks were lapped at the edges and fastened by lacings (later by metal rivets) —the present-day clinker planking. Once the planking was secured, the framing was inserted and lashed into place to lugs that had been left on the planks during the original shaping. The main strength of such vessels came from the long, edge-lapped planking.

Southern builders, on the other hand, had the saw with which to produce several planks from each log. These were fastened edge to edge—smooth planking now called carvel-building. Ancient Egyptian shipbuilders were plagued by a shortage of wood suitable for shipbuilding, and so they had to develop ingenious dowels and key-pieces to hold their short planks of acacia wood together. The Egyptian ships were basically riverboats, built without a structural keel, but with a thick plank in its place. These boats were frameless double-enders and had arcform midsections. Heavy rope trusses, fitted from bow to stern, assisted in keeping these weak ships from sagging at the ends. Eventually, heavy framing was added to seagoing vessels to supplement and strengthen the plank edge fastenings, thus eliminating the rope truss. The strength of Southern vessels came from the framing, that of Northern ships from the planking, and it was this essential difference that determined the basic features of Northern and Southern ships up to the time of the Crusades.

Available information indicates that Mediterranean vessels of the Greek and Roman eras were basically double-enders and that their builders had a sound knowledge of structure. Naturally curved timbers formed the framing, and nail-fastened scarf joints were used as needed. The Romans used three kinds of vessels: chubby sailing merchantmen, stout warships used for ramming and propelled with oars, and light speedy galleys for carrying dispatches and transporting important people.

From Roman times to about the twelfth century there was little change in Southern ships. With the slight alteration of lower ends, merchant hulls remained the same as the Roman double-ender with a rather full stern and steering oars. Deck beams, secured to a heavy wale, protruded through the carvel planking, and "castles", which were not part of the hull, were fixed prominently on bow and stern—the square work of house carpenters contrasting with the curved work of the shipwrights. An important change took place when the Roman square rig was replaced by the two- or three-masted lateen rig. From the Greek and Roman multibanked triremes, "long" ships now returned to the single bank of oars. These galleys were fitted with sails that were used occasionally when the winds were favorable.

From 1095, the time of the first Crusade, the features of Northern and Southern "round" ships began to be mingled. Superstructures were added in the North, along with other details, while Southern shipbuilders adopted the stern rudder and returned to the square rig. The standard type that resulted, commonly called the cog, was used from the Mediterranean to the Baltic until the early fifteenth century.

Seagoing ships grew larger during the fifteenth century. In general, the European ship combined a number of features; smooth planking on heavy framing, plus inside supported decks. It is almost impossible today to describe accurately the types of ship that followed the cog, such ships as the galleass, galliot, and galleon, that were derived from oar-propelled craft, and the caravel, carrack, and hulk, the pure sailing vessels.

During the fifteenth and sixteenth centuries the appearance of the ship's hull above water changed considerably. Castles remained large, but lost their angular look and were merged into the main hull. Around 1550 large ships adopted a square stern that gave better support to the superstructure. About the same time, the forecastle lost its triangular form, and its projection was dropped to form a beakhead below the bowsprit in imitation of the galley ram. The major ship type for the next 75 to 100 years was the galleon, which had less sheer and a lower superstructure than earlier types and was longer in relation to the width of its beam.

Around 1600 elaborate stern and quarter galleries, side carvings, and large figureheads were introduced to decorate large merchant ships. By 1800 these were reduced to some stern windows, small quarter galleries, and relatively simple head structures. During these two centuries, superstructures were reduced until even the forecastle and the poop were hidden by a continuous sheer line. In the last days of sail, ships were decorated with only simple figureheads and perhaps a scroll or two on the stern.

The earliest shipbuilding treatises and ship plans preserved date from the early 1400s. About 1670 the results of what were perhaps the first systematic experiments on underwater hull design were recorded in England. Other scientific studies followed, yet during the period there was little real progress in improving the form of ships. Even up to the beginning of the nineteenth century it was difficult to distinguish between merchant ships and warships, except of course the multidecked ships of the line.

In the nineteenth century, many legal and extralegal businesses required the use of small, fast sailing vessels, like those built in Bermuda and the Chesapeake Bay area. Later on this type was known as the Baltimore clipper, and the Western Ocean packet ships were developments of this type. The Baltimore clipper was also adapted for the East India and China trades, where sailing ability in light winds was more necessary than capacity for bulky cargoes. The large extreme clippers lasted as a type from about 1845 until 1860, but economic necessity finally forced a return to the best of the packet forms, ships nearly as fast but capable of carrying more cargo.

Exactly when and where primitive man first rigged a mast and sail remains a mystery, but quite early he must have noticed that if he stood up in his craft, he would drift in the direction in which the wind was blowing. If he wanted to go in this direction, he might well have speeded up his journey by holding up a cloak or animal hide to catch the wind. The length of time that elapsed between this first step and the introduction of the first real mast was considerable.

For many thousands of years a single mast and a single sail were the limit of the ancient sailor's ability to rig a boat, but one break in the monotony came in the Roman era, when sailing ships had a bowsprit that was sometimes seen as a greatly inclined foremast.

In Mediterranean lands the mast and sail evolved somewhat differently than in northern Europe, where the single mast and square sail were prevalent until the beginning of the fifteenth century. The standing rigging was very simple and smaller ships often had none.

The running gear was also very simple. The halyard hoisting the sail was led aft and acted as a backstay, thus also serving to strengthen the mast when sailing. In the early Middle Ages bowlines were added to the sail and led forward to a spar, called the bowsprit, which was rigged out over the bow.

The shrouds were set up with deadeyes and lanyards, and the rigging was rattled down, forming rope ladders to facilitate going aloft. The Northern ship was also given a fighting top at the masthead. This top is actually very old. In fact, our oldest reproduction of the fighting top is to be found on an ancient Egyptian relief dated from about 1200 B.C.

A SWEDISH HUKARE

This unusual type of ship was developed during the 18th century. The mainmast was stepped amidships and there is no foremast. In order to provide a balanced rig large headsails and staysails were carried and the bowsprit and jib boom are extremely long. The topmast was stepped behind the mainmast, and the fore-and-aft sail abaft the mainmast was known as a spencer.

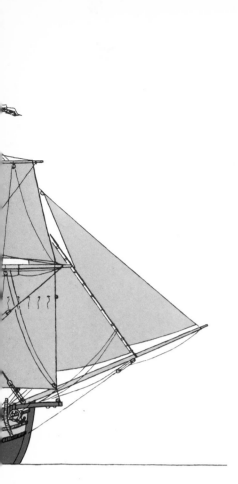

B SWEDISH KREJARE

The eighteenth century Swedish Krejare was in many ways the forerunner of the barkentine which was employed in great numbers right up to the end of the sailing ship era. The Krejare was unusual in that the masts were single poles which permitted the yards to be lowered to the deck. The hull is typical of small merchant ships of the period and little change in design took place until the early years of the nineteenth century.

C GÖTHEBORG

A Swedish East Indiaman of 1787. The ships of the East Indian trading companies were the aristocrats of the sea. They more closely resembled frigates than ships of the line, but were slower and beamier because of the basic requirement to carry cargo. Staysails were carried between the fore and the main masts, and three triangular headsails had replaced the spritsail and the spritsail topsail. Studding sails were set in light weather. Reef points were introduced in the late 1600s, and were now used on all the main sails.

D GUSTAPH ADOLPH

This figure shows a Swedish brig, the type that was called a "snow" during the eighteenth century. This vessel was built in 1783 at Kalmar. She was of a burden of 85 lasts, nearly equal to 210 tons deadweight. It was a plain merchant vessel with a straight stem, full lines, and no figurehead. The cabin is sunk belowdecks, with windows in the broad stern, and around the raised quarterdeck is an open rail extending only as far as the mainmast. In the waist is a detachable rail that could be removed in port to facilitate loading. On deck there are two boats, the longboat and the jolly boat, the small boat being stowed in the large one. The jolly boat was used as the captain's gig.

E SWEDISH TRADING FRIGATE

The illustration shows a ship from about 1770. The bow had assumed the shape it was to retain until the early nineteenth century. Rigging had become quite complicated and square sails were carried on three masts. The lateen mizzen had been superseded by the gaff-rigged sail. Such a ship undertook long voyages and was typical of those of many nations that were developing a flourishing trade with Mediterranean countries. Guns were still carried for piracy was rife. In the Mediterranean it was not finally eradicated until the French occupation of Algiers in 1830 and the destruction of pirate bases in Tripoli by U.S. Marines.

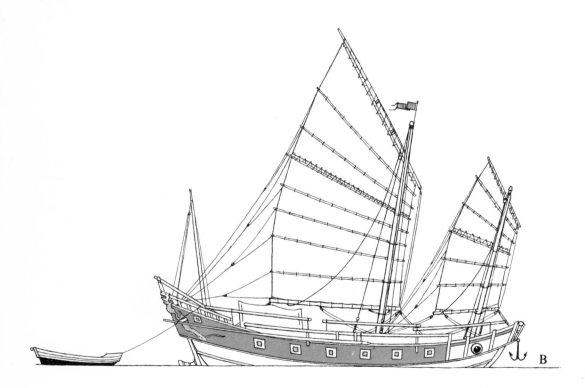

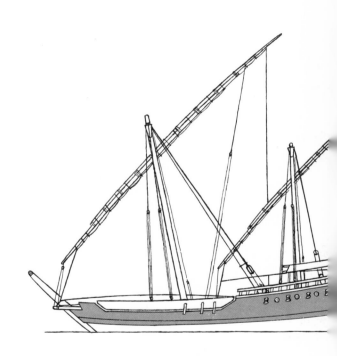

A ALGERIAN XEBECS

These were basically sailing ships, but oars were used during periods of calm and, in the case of the Algerine pirates, when attacking an enemy. Although fast and equipped with a number of small guns these vessels were no match for a warship or a well-armed merchant ship. The rowers, who were almost always prisoners, lived lives of extreme squalor and hardship.

B CHINESE JUNK

There are many different types of Chinese junks, but the matting sails, stiffened with bamboo battens, were commonly used. Nowadays many junks are motorized, yet still retain the characteristics of their predecessors. The eyes which were painted on the bows of Chinese junks—so that the ship could see its way across the seas—is not now so common, but it is a practice which has been carried on in many parts of the world and can still be seen in the Mediterranean.

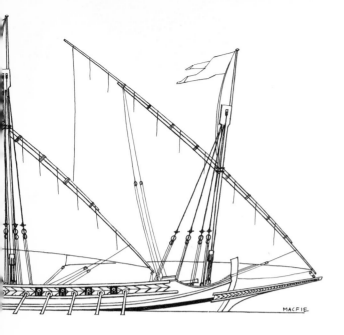

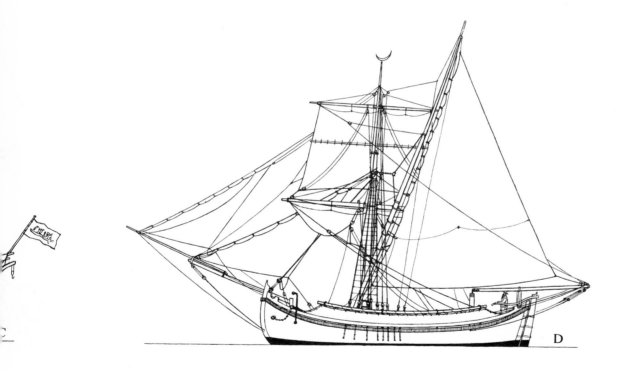

Sometime during the first half of the fifteenth century larger ships were built with two or three masts. In northwestern Europe evolution quickly culminated in three masts. The mainmast kept its location in the middle of the ship and from the beginning the new masts were stepped in the fore- and after-castles. As improvements were made, it was most likely that flags or banners were first flown there, a common practice during the Crusades, and that it was just as easy to hoist a small sail on this same flagpole. One could even go so far as to say that every square sail, except the first, of course, was preceded by a flag on a pole. Thus, big ships unfurled a banner aloft on a staff from the fighting top, and toward the end of the fifteenth century they appeared with a small sail on the same staff. From the beginning this small sail was handled by the men in the top, and it was from this that the name top-sail was derived. The main topsail was soon followed by a second sail on the foremast. Both were small at first, but they continually increased in size as they came to be used more and more.

The triangular lateen sail in general use in galleys and fishing boats in the Mediterranean was eventually used as the mizzen in big ships all along the European coast. Its use had spread all the way to the Baltic Sea by the end of the Middle Ages. There, it gradually supplanted the older square sail as the mizzen. In the 250 years that followed, the lateen mizzen continued to be used in all large ships.

The bowsprit had originally served only to lead the bowlines. By the end of the Middle Ages, however, a square sail had been rigged under the bowsprit. This sail was called a blind in medieval English as it wholly blocked the view ahead. Later it became known as the spritsail.

By the last quarter of the fifteenth century larger ships began to have as many as four masts. The two aftermost masts generally had lateen sails only, but the main mizzen-mast could carry a triangular topsail on a topmast as well. The smaller mizzen, known as the bonaventure mizzen, usually reached abaft the ship where it was sheeted to a spar rigged out over the stern.

The topsail continued to grow in size, and around the middle of the sixteenth century larger ships began to carry a third square sail, the topgallant sail, on the fore and main masts. Until this time, however, the topmasts had been fixed extensions of the masts themselves and could not be rigged down. But around the 1570s, topmasts began to be stepped, to be "fidded", was the term used

C ARABIAN DHOW

There are many types of dhows. This illustration shows a Zambuk, typical of the vessels which for hundreds of years made an annual voyage to East Africa. They sailed southwards before the North East monsoon and returned during the South West monsoon. To East Africa these ships carried salt and dates. Homeward they carried timber, spices, ivory, and slaves. Modernized versions of the Zambuk still make this annual journey although the cargoes carried are vastly different.

D TURKISH CAIQUE

Many different types of local ships were evolved in the Mediterranean and even to-day the characteristics of each can be seen in small beach boats and fishing craft. For hundreds of years the Caique, with its unusual mainsail and double-ended hull was almost the standard type of vessel used in Turkey for the transport of cargo and passengers.

then, so they could be rigged up or taken down depending on circumstances. This innovation, credited to the Dutch, was found to be very practical and was soon adopted for general use. Consequently, the fidded topmasts grew larger in relation to the lower masts; the topsail grew deeper, and the lower sail shallower.

Around 1620 it was common to equip the third mast with a square topsail. At the same time the bonaventure mizzenmast was discarded. This marked the creation of the three-masted ship, with square sails on each mast. These early ships always had one yard less on the mizzenmast than on the fore and main masts.

It was not until the latter half of the eighteenth century that rigging had evolved to the point where each mast had the same number of yards. This was the time when the term "full-rigged ship" became universal. The full-rigged ship usually referred to a merchant vessel, while sailing warships with such a rig were referred to by their rating: ship of the line, frigate, or sloop. The ships of the early seventeenth century were built with low heads and high sterns. This design made them very hard to steer when the wind was abaft the beam, and the need for more headsail was keenly felt. To remedy the problem all larger ships were rigged with a spritsail topsail on a small mast at the end of the bowsprit. This sail was very impracticable, though it was found to be very necessary, and it remained in use for over a hundred years before it was completely replaced with more practical and effective staysails.

During the sixteenth century, the Dutch had developed navigation with small ships in canals and rivers and in the shallow coastal waters between the islands. The inability to beat and especially to tack when using the square sail created the need for new types of sail. Two fore-and-aft sails were evolved: the spritsail and staysail. The former was a simple rectangular sail with one side laced to the mast and extended by a diagonally placed sprit. It became the most commonly used sail in small boats of northern Europe. This sail can still be seen in use in the few surviving Thames barges.

With the spritsail set abaft the mast, there was an empty space under the stay on the forward side of the mast, and it was only natural to set a triangular sail on that stay before the mast. By the middle of the first half of the sixteenth century, boats with a spritsail and fore staysail were in use in Holland. This development was followed by a new staysail called the jib, which was set on a jib boom outside the stem.

A

A AMERICAN WHALER
Many are the tales which have been told about whaling, and this is the type of vessel that was employed in large numbers by the Americans during the nineteenth century. The rig was standard for the period, but noticeable are the whaleboats slung from spar davits. It was from these small boats that the harpooners carried out their deadly work amongst the spermaceti whales. At the very top of the mainmast is the lookout position from which spouting whales were spotted at great distances.

C

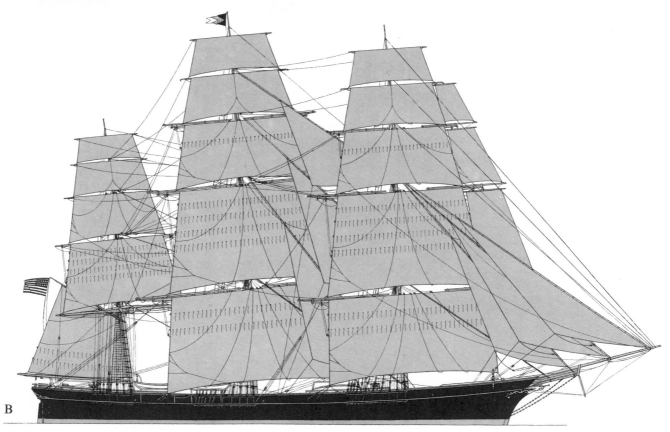

B FLYING CLOUD

American clippers such as the one illustrated, the Flying Cloud, *sailed from the East Coast of America to California with gold prospectors and high-value cargo, then to China in ballast where they loaded tea for England. No British ships of the time could compete with them. The American China clippers and the later British types were undoubtedly the most beautiful square-rigged ships ever built.*

C BALTIMORE CLIPPER

This ship of the early nineteenth century is rigged as a two topsail schooner. Hull design developed rapidly in America during this period and the hull of this vessel bears little resemblance to those in earlier illustrations. The "clipper" bow, which later became concave or hollow was already evident, and the waterline at the bow was much more wedgelike than the bluff bows of earlier ships. The rig was high and the fore-and-aft sails were enormous. Practically all decoration had gone, although later ships sometimes carried figureheads and a little scrollwork at the bow and stern. Fast deep-sea square-rigged ships were developed from these small schooners, and when the British Navigation Acts were repealed in 1849 and gold was discovered in California in the same year, American shipowners were well placed to capture the cream of world trade.

A HANSINA

A small topgallant-rigged schooner, usually called a "topsail schooner". These vessels had no raised forecastle or poop and the ship's boat was slung from wooden davits across the counterstern. The ring of the anchor can be seen secured to the cathead— a balk of timber projecting from the ship's side. The anchor was lowered to the vertical position and then "slipped", the cable running out from the hawse-pipe.

B NORMAN COURT

This is an example of the British clippers that competed with, and later dominated, the American clippers. The opening of the Suez Canal in 1869 cleared the way for steamships and the clippers were forced to seek employment in the Australian wool and other trades.

C FRENCH BARK

The bark Persistent, *built of wood in 1865 shows the final development of the bark rig. Ships of this type undertook the long ocean voyages and three-masted ships were often reduced to this rig when trading conditions made it essential for smaller crews to be carried.*

A

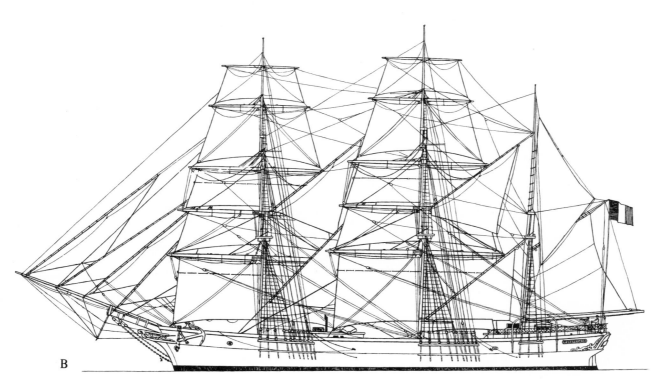

B

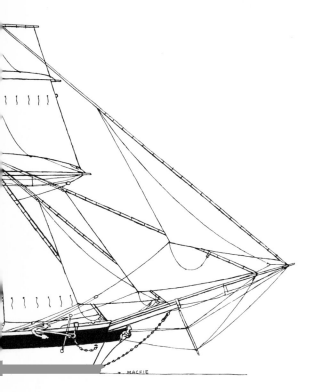

By the 1670s the larger ships began carrying staysails, first between the masts and later over the bowsprit. This fore topmast staysail was difficult to set because of the complicated rigging of the spritsail and sprit topsail. This was also the case with the staysails between the masts, because of the braces and bowlines leading to the stays. The staysails won out over the others, and in the beginning of the eighteenth century the spritsail topmast was discarded and the running gear was gradually changed to make more room for the staysails of the mainmast. This development continued throughout the entire eighteenth century, and by the end of the century larger ships carried a staysail on every possible stay.

When the spritsail topmast was discarded, a new spar, the jib boom, was rigged out on the bowsprit. A new staysail called the jib was placed over it ahead of the fore topmast staysail. After the middle of the eighteenth century the lateen mizzen's long yard was exchanged for a gaff. This change occurred earlier in the smaller vessels than in the large ones.

During the Napoleonic wars, other changes began to take place in the rigging. The mizzen was enlarged and sheeted to a boom extending over the stern. Under the bowsprit a new spar, called the martingale or dolphin striker, was inserted to improve the staying of the jib boom. This all developed into a new spar and staysail, the flying jib boom and flying jib, which were rigged outside the jib. A fourth yard above the topgallant yard, called the royal yard, now became more and more common on larger ships.

The nineteenth century's mechanical revolution gradually began to influence the rigging of sailing ships. At first, it was merely a replacement on masts and yards of rope fittings,

C

A KAJ HVILSOM

One of the last sailing schooners to be commissioned, this wooden-hulled vessel was built at Svendborg in Denmark for a local firm, the Rederi A/S Panis.

B FIVE-MASTED BARK POTOSI

The ultimate development of the square-rigged ship was typified by the German five-masted bark Potosi of 1895. Built of steel, with steel masts and yards, she was one of the largest sailing ships ever constructed and was employed carrying coal to the west coast of South America and saltpeter on the homeward run. The Potosi was 360 feet long with a beam of 49 feet and a depth of hold of 28 feet. The main-mast was 206 feet high above the deck. The five masts carried 24 square sails and 18 fore-and-aft sails. The Potosi could carry 6,000 tons of cargo, but even ships of this size found it progressively more difficult to compete with steamships.

C ARCHIBALD RUSSELL

The British Archibald Russell of 1905 mainly sailed to Australia via the Cape of Good Hope, and returned with grain around Cape Horn. The painted ports were a survival of an earlier tradition in which prominent squares were painted on the side in naval fashion to create the impression of an armed ship. In 1924 the Archibald Russell was purchased by Captain Erikson. She arrived in Hull in 1939 and never sailed again.

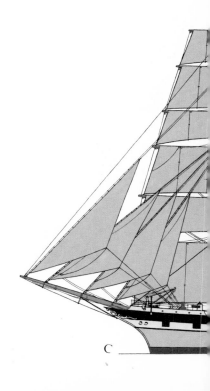

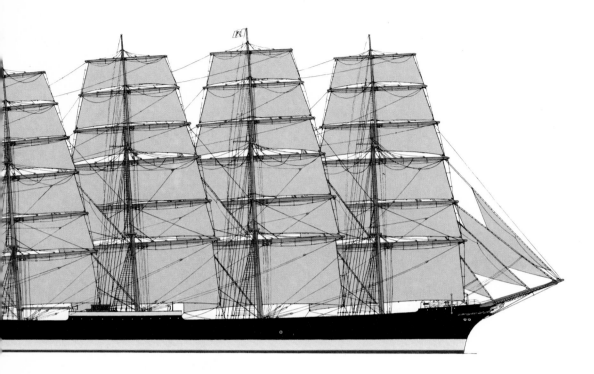

strops, and so on, with forged iron bands. Then the rope trusses of the lower yards were replaced with iron trusses. Wherever possible, the heavier running rigging was replaced with chain. By the middle of the century British ships began to have the standing rigging replaced with wire. The rigging had previously been made of tarred hemp rope, but wire was cheaper and stronger and more durable. It had less surface exposed to the wind, and as the early attempts to build iron vessels were crowned with success, wire rigging was used more and more, especially on steamships, which always had rigging and sails until well on into the century.

The huge topsails on large sailing ships were extremely hard to handle during storms. American developments in the middle of the nineteenth century led to double topsails. Later on the largest ships were fitted with double topgallant sails.

By this time the use of wire for standing rigging and of chain for sheets and halyards was entirely accepted. Standing rigging now featured turnbuckles instead of deadeyes and lanyards, the system used ever since the early Middle Ages. Strong but stiff tarred hemp was replaced by Manila rope for running gear. Manila was softer and easier to work and just as strong, though not as durable as the hemp used formerly. Block sheaves were furnished with roller bearings, which also served to lighten the work on board. In fact, so much was done to ease the work on deck and aloft that the vessels could now be sailed with the same crew as had been required for a smaller ship twenty years earlier. Sail handling became more mechanized in larger ships. In the 1890s a geared mechanical winch was devised that allowed two men to brace the yards in rough weather. In the last of the big ships the topsail and topgallant halyards of chain were replaced with wire regulated by a hand-operated drum winch.

The final chapter of the sailing ship is short. The vessels sunk in the 1914—1918 war were not replaced. In spite of the weak condition of the world economy, many steam tramps were built and were soon competing vigorously for the falling quantities of freight. In spite of the economy measures described above and the rerigging of full-rigged ships to barks and barkentines to secure still further savings in crew numbers, sailing ships became completely uneconomic. By 1933 only twenty sailing ships sailed from Australia to Europe with grain and of these, fourteen were owned by Captain Gustaf Erikson of Mariehamn on the Åland Islands in the Baltic.

FROM STEAM TO NUCLEAR POWER

The theory of steam propulsion has been known for a very long time, and as early as the seventeenth century scientists were debating the type of machinery that would be needed to put the theory into practice. They limited their activities to debating and the production of learned papers, since materials were not available to them in sufficient quantity or quality to permit large-scale experiments. It was not until the eighteenth century that rudimentary boilers and engines were constructed.

Thomas Newcomen (1663—1729) is credited with the construction of the first practical steam engine. Few men of the period, however, seriously considered applying steam power to the propulsion of ships because it was still impossible to generate sufficient power to overcome wind and tide or to carry the enormous amount of coal that the earliest boilers consumed.

It is generally accepted that Claude de Jouffroy d'Abbans was the successful pioneer in the application of steam power to boats. In 1783 his second boat, with French-built engines, moved against the River Seine's current for fifteen minutes; this tiny craft was called the *Pyroscaphe*. In America the engineer John Fitch successfully operated a small steamboat on the River Delaware during the year 1789.

In 1801 Lord Dundas had constructed the canal towboat *Charlotte Dundas*. In 1802 this vessel towed two 70-ton barges on the Forth and Clyde Canal against a strong headwind for a distance of 19$^1/_2$ miles (*c.* 31 km) in six hours. The trials were not repeated because the directors of the canal company felt that the damage done to the banks of the canal by the wash of the *Charlotte Dundas* would more than offset the economies gained by steam towage.

Further development occurred in America in 1807, when Robert Fulton put a steam-boat—the *North River* (sometimes known as the *Clermont*)—into service on the Hudson River. The engines for this craft were manufactured by Messrs. Boulton, Watt and Company, and were the third set allowed to be exported from England.

From this time on development proceeded apace, and Henry Bell's *Comet* of 1812 achieved the distinction of being the first commercial paddle steamer to operate in European waters.

These events had little effect on deep-sea ships. In fact the Americans, in particular, generally ignored them and started to build faster sailing ships, which were later known as Baltimore clippers. These vessels gained the cream of the passenger and cargo trades in many parts of the world. Fixed sailing dates became a reality when, for instance, in January, 1818, the *James Monroe* of the American Black Ball Line sailed from New York for England at the time advertised. It, nevertheless, remained to the steamship in later years to establish the regularity of service which had become such a feature of railway operations.

The voyage of the little *Savannah*, which crossed the Atlantic in 1819, was of little consequence. The *Savannah* was a sailing ship with auxiliary engines which were used for only eighty hours during a voyage of twenty-nine days. On approaching the coast of Ireland a coastguard, seeing smoke belching from her funnel, thought she was on fire. A fast naval vessel was sent to assist but the *Savannah* drew ahead and only halted when warning shots were fired! A far more significant event occurred in 1833 when the Canadian steamship *Royal William* steamed all the way across the Atlantic. This voyage was followed by those of the *Great Western*, designed by Brunel, and the *Sirius*. Both ships arrived in New York harbor on the same day in 1838.

In 1840 the *Britannia* of the Cunard Line inaugurated a regular transatlantic service, while the American Collins Line, owned by the far-seeing Edward Knight Collins, entered the lists in 1850. At first successful and a threat to the Cunard Line, operations ceased within ten years following the loss of two of their finest ships—the *Arctic* and the *Pacific*. This was the first of the many disasters that befell steamship companies during the next thirty or forty years, but by the early sixties passages of ten days were common. Safety records gradually improved and eventually the sailing ship on the North Atlantic was doomed.

In other parts of the world progress was less spectacular. The P. and O. Line pressed steadily ahead with steam services, eventually reaching Alexandria in Egypt where passengers, mail, and cargo were transported overland to join one of the ships that were permanently stationed "East of Suez". It is ironic that in establishing these and later services to Australia, fleets of sailing colliers were employed to stockpile coal at strategic points along the route.

Through the years the development of marine engines and boilers went on at a remarkable pace and the day arrived when boilers were sufficiently advanced to produce the high pressure steam needed for the efficient operation of the compound engine. The condenser permitted the continuous use of distilled water in the boiler. Once these three elements had been brought together, fuel consumption dropped dramatically while the performance of the engine excelled over any of the earlier types. Within a short period new deep-sea ships were built with compound engines and many already in service were reengined. For the first time cargo liners were placed in service carrying general cargo over very long distances with surprising regularity.

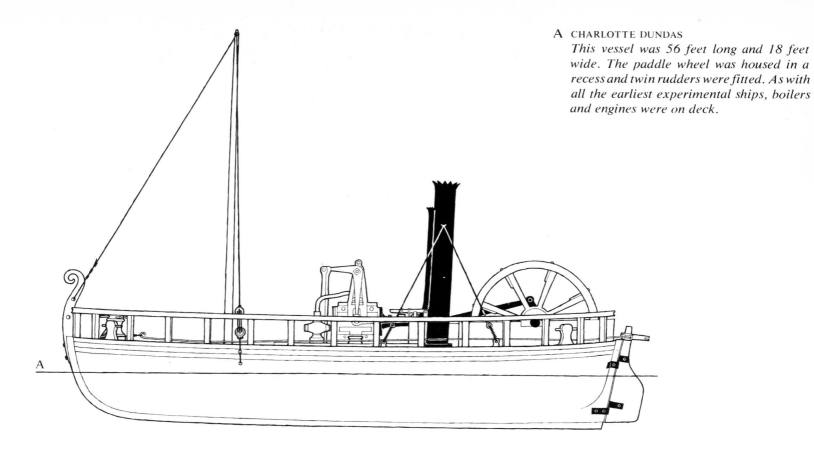

A CHARLOTTE DUNDAS
This vessel was 56 feet long and 18 feet wide. The paddle wheel was housed in a recess and twin rudders were fitted. As with all the earliest experimental ships, boilers and engines were on deck.

B COMET
Henry Bell's Comet. *The hull was typical of small sailing ships of the period. A small saloon was provided for passengers and she was employed commercially on the River Clyde until she was wrecked in 1820.*

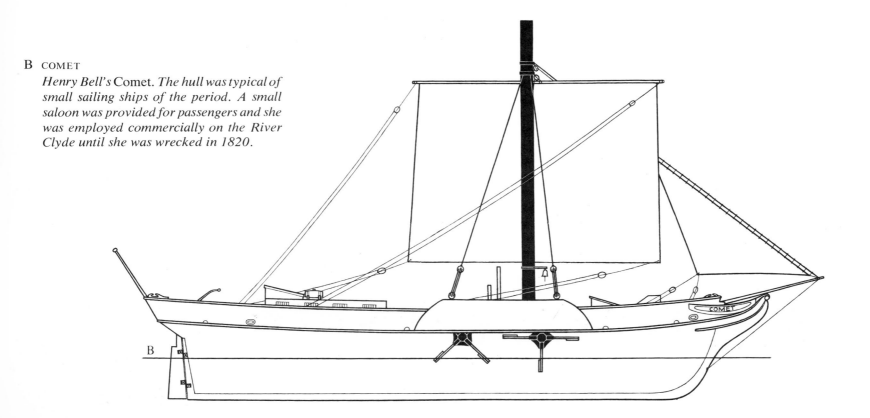

A SAVANNAH

She was rigged as a "ship", and, in fact, was a sailing ship with auxiliary engines. The funnel had a swivel elbow so that smoke and sparks could be directed away from the sails and rigging. The paddle wheels could be unshipped and stowed on deck when not required. Several early screw ships had propellers that could be lifted out of the water to prevent drag when under full sail.

B GREAT BRITAIN

Brunel's famous screw steamship which was built in Bristol in 1843 for the great Western Steamship Company. In 1882 the Great Britain *was converted to a full sailing ship and eventually became a coal hulk in the Falkland Islands. She remained there in a derelict state until recently when she was secured to a steel pontoon and towed to her home port of Bristol. Here she is being restored to her original state.*

C ADRIATIC

The Adriatic *of the Collins Line (New York and Liverpool United States Mail Steamship Company) was built in 1856. She was the last ship built for this ill-fated company and, like many other pioneer steamships, was later converted to a full sailing ship. The* Adriatic *ended her life as a store ship on the west coast of Africa.*

A

B

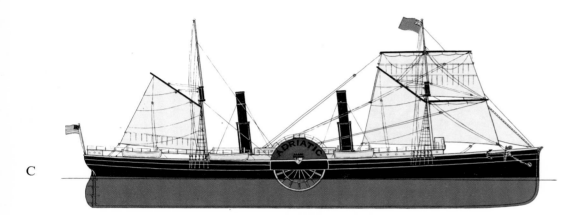

C

D BRITANNIA

The Britannia *of 1840 was an outstanding ship in the history of sea transportation. This vessel and her three sister ships instituted the first regular mail and passenger service on the North Atlantic between Liverpool, Halifax (Nova Scotia), and Boston (Massachusetts). The* Britannia *was 207 feet long and 34 feet wide and made 40 round-trip voyages before being sold out of service. The contemporary press described the accommodations for 115 cabin passengers as luxurious. Charles Dickens crossed in the* Britannia *in 1842 and was far from impressed. He described in more accurate terms what it meant to sail in such a small ship on such a mighty ocean.*

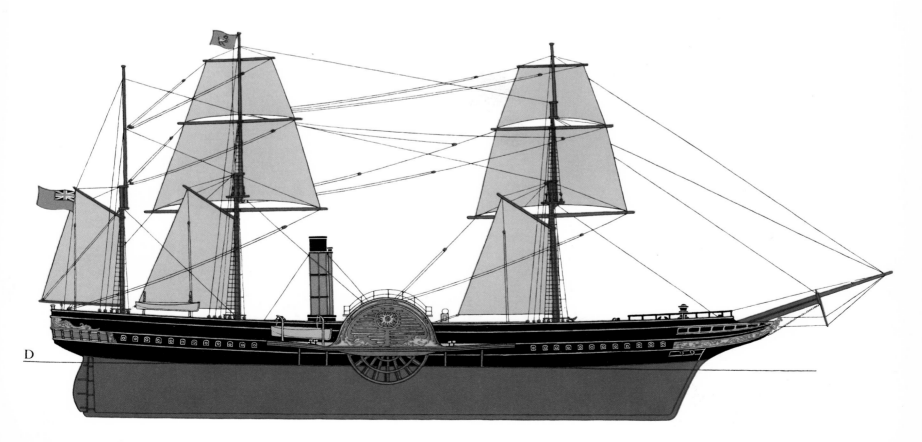

D

A POONAH

The Poonah of 1862 was typical of P. and O. mail liners in service during the late fifties and early sixties. The activities of the fleet were divided into two distinct, but closely linked operations on either side of the Isthmus of Suez. Company ships voyaged by the Cape of Good Hope only to take up station in the East. When the Suez Canal was opened, the P. and O. was forced to rebuild

a major part of its fleet in order to meet the competition of ships that had been built especially to undertake the through voyage to India and the Far East.

B DUNOTTAR CASTLE

Until the amalgamation in 1900 of the Union Line and the Castle Line the competition between these two companies was intense. The Dunottar Castle which was built

in 1890 was typical of the Castle ships of the time and could carry 360 passengers. As a troopship during the Boer War she carried 1,200 troops. The Dunottar Castle was the last ship of this company to carry first class passengers in the after part of the ship. This was a practice inherited from the days of sail, and the first steamship to accomodate first class passengers amidships was the White Star liner Oceanic of 1870.

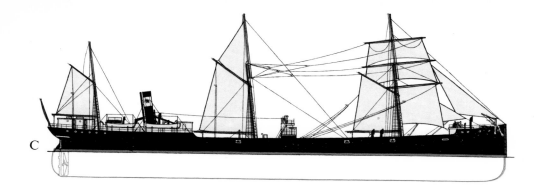

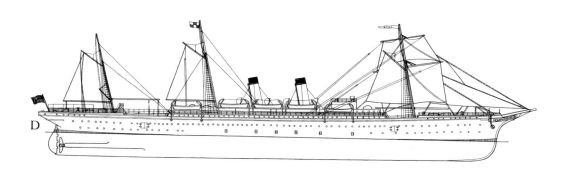

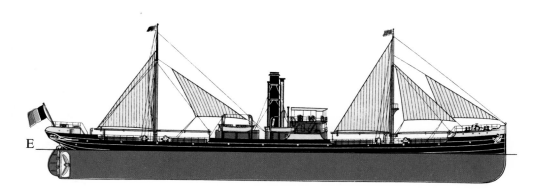

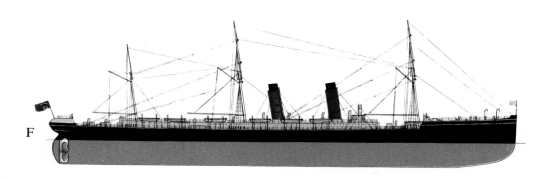

C GLÜCKAUF

The Glückauf *is considered to have been the prototype of the modern oil tanker. She was built specifically for this purpose and the sides of the ship also formed the sides of the tanks. There were nine main tanks, and smaller tanks above them were able to take the oil that expanded out of the tanks in hot weather. The main tanks were also separated from the boiler room by a cofferdam that housed the cargo pumps.*

D EMPRESS OF INDIA

She was built in 1890 and was the first of three sister ships trading between Vancouver and the Far East. With a speed of $17^1/_2$ knots she was a fast ship. The Canadian Pacific Railway held a mail contract and it sometimes proved to be faster to send European mail across the Atlantic and then via Vancouver across the Pacific rather than by the direct route via Suez. Ships trading between America and Japan were often fitted with special rooms to accommodate silk, a highly valuable and delicate cargo.

E COCKERILL

A three-island type small steamer (so called because of the three short superstructures on the weather deck—forecastle, bridge, and poop), the Cockerill *was constructed for the Belgian firm of the same name at Hoboken, New Jersey. Her single screw was driven by a set of triple expansion engines and in good weather she could probably make 10 knots. Sold in 1910 to Armement Adolf Deppe of Antwerp and in 1916 to Baird & Company of West Hartlepools, and renamed* Mabel Baird, *she was torpedoed and sunk in 1917.*

F SERVIA

The Servia *was built in 1861 and was one of many Atlantic record breakers. She was built to meet the competition of the Guion, Inman, and White Star Lines. She was the first steel ship owned by the Cunard Line and carried 450 first- and 600 third-class passengers. By this time few steamships were built with clipper bows and the outfit of sails was less in area than had been provided before. The* Servia *completed 171 round-trip voyages to the United States and also saw service as a troop transport during the Boer War.*

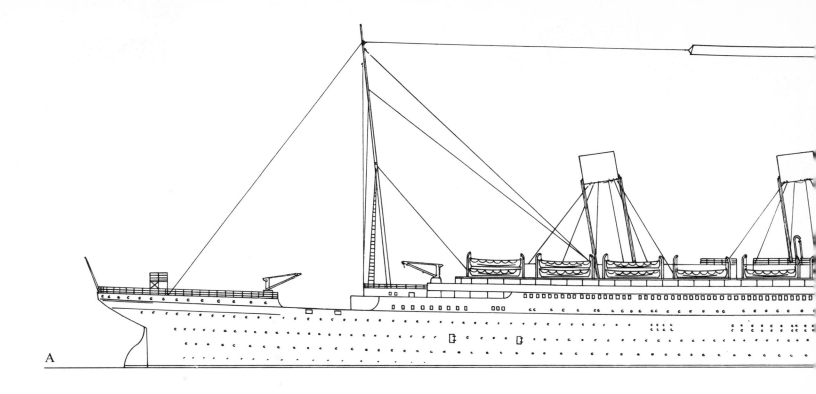

A

A OLYMPIC

The years between 1900 and 1914 saw some of the most interesting developments on the North Atlantic. Many owners had retreated from the expensive business of running record breakers and had opted for greater comfort and less speed. The Olympic *exemplified the period. She was an enormous ship, but was soon eclipsed* *in size by the giant German ships* Bismarck, Vaterland, *and* Imperator. *The* Olympic *had two sister ships, the ill-fated* Titanic *and the* Britannic *which was sunk by a mine in 1916 and never saw service as a passenger ship.*

B VICTORIAN

At the end of the nineteenth century, the Allen Line, which had been engaged in the Canadian trade since 1819, needed new ships to compete with rival lines. It had been intended that the Virginian *and* Victorian *should have reciprocating engines. As such, they would have created little interest. However, plans were*

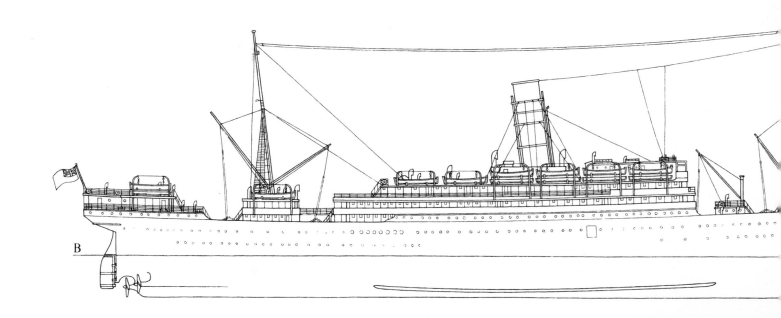

B

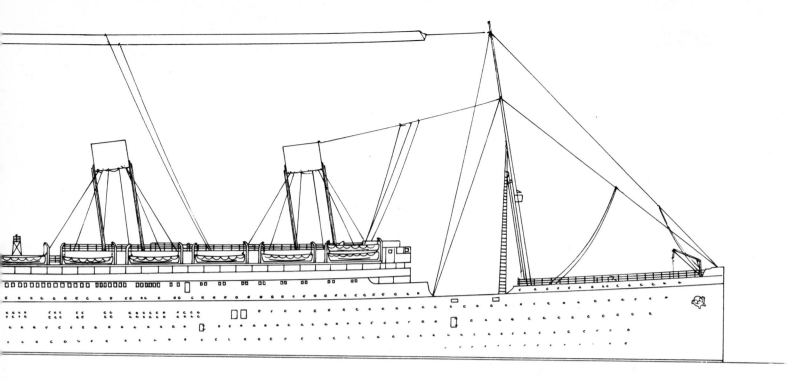

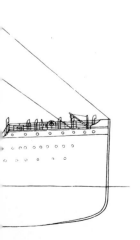

changed while the ships were under construction and both were given turbines. The Victorian *was the first liner to have these engines and her performance was followed with great interest by shipowners, marine engineers, and the public alike. With the advent of the* Mauretania *in 1907, these two ships became of far less interest, but they gave excellent service until recently.*

By the mid-sixties paddles were no longer used for deep-sea ships and iron hulls had become standard. On the Atlantic the Cunard liner *Russia* made an eastward passage at an average speed of 14.22 knots against the *Britannia's* 8.5 knots. The operation of high-speed ships on the Atlantic became the "preserve" of German and British lines, and competition was intense. By the end of the nineteenth century it became apparent to many that the profit gained from these ships was not sufficient and in 1899 the White Star Line built the *Oceanic* of 17,000 gross tons. The *Oceanic* was slower than previous mail ships, but was much larger and introduced standards of luxury that could not be provided in them. The *Oceanic* was followed by bigger and bigger ships, culminating in the German *Bismarck* of 56,551 tons. In addition, shipping companies of many nationalities also ran smaller and still slower ships, which carried considerable quantities of cargo and large numbers of emigrants.

Reverting to the 1880s, the use of steel permitted the construction of lighter and stronger hulls, and the triple expansion reciprocating engine—a logical development of the two-cylinder compound engine—led to the appearance of the steam tramp, the second new type of ship of the nineteenth century. Tramps were built in large numbers and by 1914 the sailing ship, commercially

at any rate, had almost reached the end. The reciprocating engine was also adopted by the largest liners such as the *Olympic*.

The reciprocating engine raised speed to over 20 knots, and several Atlantic record breakers were equipped with them in the late nineteenth and early twentieth centuries. Nevertheless, it was thought that there were limits to the speeds that could be attained with this type of engine. It was considered possible that a rotary engine might provide the required higher speeds and Sir Charles Parsons had for some time been conducting experiments with the steam turbine. This invention, although not new, had so far not been used for marine purposes and the product of Sir Charles's endeavors was the *Turbinia*, 100 ft. long (53.64 m) and with a beam of 9 ft. (4.8 m). The turbine burst upon an astonished world when the *Turbinia* raced through the Fleet Review at Spithead in 1897 at a speed of 34.5 knots.

The first commercial turbine ship was the *King Edward* of 1901. This vessel regularly operated on the River Clyde in Scotland at a speed of 18 1/2 knots until 1951. The first oceangoing ships to be propelled by turbines were the Allen liners *Victorian* and *Virginian*. Both ships were entirely successful. The sixth turbine engined ship was the famous *Mauretania*, placed in service in 1907. From this time on most of the big transatlantic

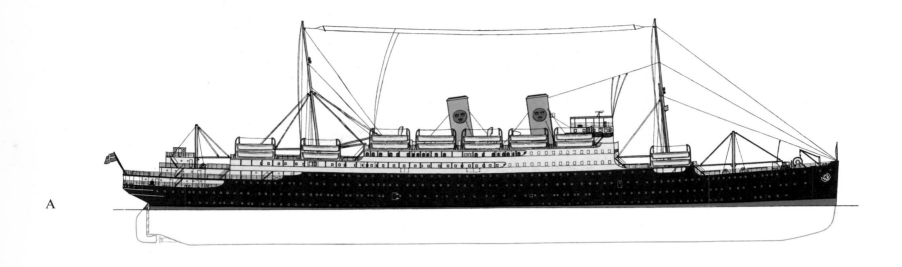

A

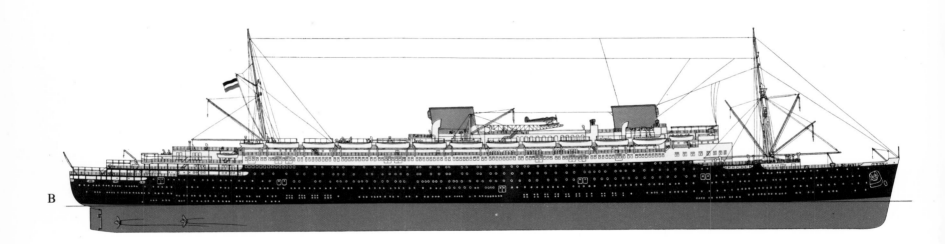

B

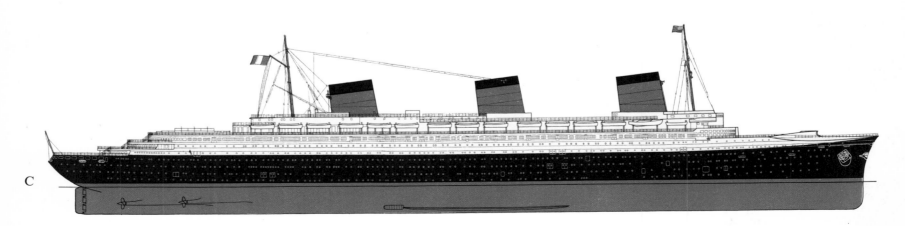

C

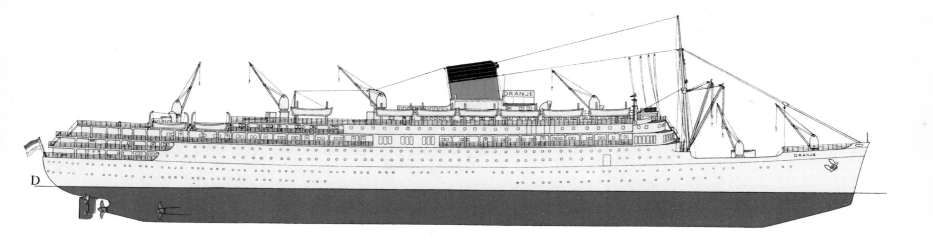

A GRIPSHOLM

The Gripsholm, *which was built in 1925 by Sir W. G. Armstrong, Whitworth and Co., Ltd., for the Swedish America Line, ran between Gothenburg and New York. She was the first motor ship in regular North Atlantic service and was typical of the intermediate liners in service at the time. She carried 91 first-, 355 second- and 1,006 third-class passengers.*

B BREMEN

The Bremen *of the Norddeutscher Lloyd was the first "Atlantic Greyhound" to be built since the* Mauretania. *She captured the Blue Riband in 1929. For a time the* Bremen *had a catapult fitted between the funnels. As she neared her terminal port an aircraft was catapulted off carrying a limited amount of high class mail. Some saving of time resulted, but the experiment was not a success and the catapult was removed. She was damaged beyond repair during an air raid on Bremerhaven in 1941. Her sister ship* Europa *became the French Line's* Liberté.

C NORMANDIE

The pride of France and one of the most beautiful ships ever built, the Normandie *was the first French ship to hold the Blue Riband. It is said by many people that the accommodation of this ship surpassed anything provided before or since. The* Normandie *met an untimely end when she caught fire and capsized in New York in 1942.*

D ORANJE

For many years the Rotterdam Lloyd and the Netherlands Steamship Company operated services to Indonesia. The Oranje *was the last passenger liner built for the latter company. She survived the war, but with the granting of independence to Indonesia, her services were no longer required on the run. After a spell on a round-the-world service, she was sold in 1965 to Achille Lauro. This company completely refitted her and as the* Angelina Lauro *she is now in regular service to Australia and New Zealand. The* Angelina Lauro *is hardly recognizable as the* Oranje, *but the engines that drive her today are those that were originally installed in 1939.*

liners such as the *Bismarck* (later the *Majestic*) had turbine engines. Where speed was not the primary aim liners continued to be built with reciprocating engines.

In the later years of the nineteenth century, Doctor Rudolph Diesel built the first practical engine in which oil fuel provided the motive force. The first seagoing ships with diesel engines were the small Dutch tanker *Vulcanus* and the Danish cargo ship *Selandia*; both of these ships were completed in 1910. In 1920 the first diesel engined liner—the *Aorangi*, owned by the Union Steam Ship Company of New Zealand—entered service on the highly competitive Pacific run.

In 1919 the combatant nations were forced to embark upon large replacement programs. The new ships were generally larger than their predecessors, but no significant increases in speed were recorded. Many propulsive systems were by then available and it is impossible to describe a pattern of development without a detailed analysis of the ships of the major shipowners. The complexity of the position is shown by the following examples. While some lines, such as the Swedish America Line, built motor ships (the term that came to be applied to ships with internal-combustion engines) exclusively, other lines engaged on similar services built turbine ships. Some lines built both turbine and motor ships. The French Line's *Lafayette* was a motor ship, her running partner built three years later—the *Champlain*—was a turbine ship. The P. and O. Line stayed with reciprocating engines until 1929 when they built the *Viceroy of India*. This ship was one of the first turboelectric ships.

In 1929 the race for speed supremacy on the North Atlantic broke out again and the *Bremen* and the *Europa* of the Norddeutscher Lloyd, the *Rex* of the Italia Lines, the French Line's *Normandie* and the Cunard liner *Queen Mary* each held for a short time the Blue Riband. The *Queen Mary* crossed the Atlantic at an average speed of 30.99 knots. The *Queen Elizabeth*, which was employed as a troopship after her secret maiden voyage to New York in 1940, entered service on the North American run soon after World War II broke out. With the Queen Mary she maintained a weekly service between Southampton and New York. As far as the Cunard Line was concerned, the days of the record-breaking runs were over and the *Queen Elizabeth* was never given the opportunity of demonstrating her superior speed.

In 1946 shipyards the world over were busy building ships in large numbers to replace the badly diminished fleets. Passenger liners reflected the process observed in the 1920s although some of the new ships were much faster than those that had been in service before 1939. Just one Atlantic record breaker was built after the war—the United States Lines's *United States*. On her maiden voyage in 1952 this vessel crossed in just under three and a half days at an average speed of 35.59 knots.

Just as many sailing shipowners failed to see the writing on the wall in the 1860s and 1870s, so the world's principal shipowners in the 1950s failed to assess the devastating effect that the steady development of air travel would have within a decade. Many large liners were still being built up to 1961. All the efforts made to counteract the inexorable progress of the airlines failed and the granting of independence to colonial territories accelerated the decline in demand for passenger services. Eventually nearly every passenger line was forced to sell or scrap ships. It is now impossible to cross the Atlantic in winter by regular passenger line services from North European ports, and services are only laid on in the summer to bring American tourists to Europe.

The answer for many companies was to turn to cruising. There are now many liners engaged in cruising, but the pattern is changing. Many conventional passenger liners are not entirely suited to the special needs of cruising and the most recent development is the emergence of ships designed exclusively for this purpose. They carry no cargo, and fewer passengers are carried. They are small enough to enter minor ports and interiors are given over wholly to the needs of passengers whose sole purpose is the pursuit of pleasure.

Since 1946, larger and faster cargo liners have been built, the largest of which can carry more than 16,000 tons of cargo at a speed of over twenty knots. Economic circumstances, however, have made it increasingly difficult for even these ships to earn satisfactory profits, and so the container ship appeared for the first time.

The primary objective of container ships was to cut down the time that cargo liners spent in port and this was achieved by prepacking cargo into large boxes—called containers—which were sent to the docks to be loaded swiftly by gantry cranes into the "cells" of the waiting container ship. Once in place the containers were secure for the voyage and those on the upper deck were firmly lashed.

The earliest container services were established between 1954 and 1956. Almost all the principal cargo liner routes are now served by container ships. As a result, conventional cargo liners are already being sold out of service and the future of those that remain is a doubtful one.

Alongside the container ship there has developed a third new form of sea transportation: roll-on roll-off ferries. The idea was germinated by the LSTs (landing ship tank) which embarked tanks and military vehicles over a ramp in the bow and discharged them in the same way onto the invasion beaches during World War II. The first roll-on roll-off service was probably that inaugurated in 1948 between Preston in England and Larne in Northern Ireland. A trickle of new ships became a flood and many conventional services such as those run by the French, Belgian, and British railways were converted almost completely to roll-on roll-off operations. Deep-sea ships followed and there are now several roll-on roll-off cargo liners competing with container ships.

An American firm of naval architects also designed another new type of ship. This was the *Lash* (lighter aboard ship) vessel. There are now several of these in service. They are equipped with a 500-ton gantry crane which travels on rails for nearly the whole length of the upper deck. The gantry loads and stows loaded lighters (small barges), which have been towed to the ship's stern. At the

A KONINGIN WILHELMINA
This ship which entered service in 1959 was noted for her very untraditional appearance. Although novel at the time later ships have continued to break away from tradition and this trend has been accelerated by the practice of placing the engines at the after end of the ship. The Koningin Wilhelmina *was employed on the Harwich — Hook of Holland day service and was the last purely passenger ship to be built for this route which is now operated by car ferries.*

B CHAMPLAIN
Built in 1931, the Champlain *was one of several intermediate ships built for the North Atlantic at this time. She had accommodations for 643 cabin, 248 tourist, and 122 third-class passengers. Some cabins were interchangeable between tourist and third. The* Champlain *marks the end of a very long period in which emigrants had been carried in large numbers. By 1924 American restrictions on immigration had reduced the numbers carried from Europe from a flood to a trickle and immigration to other countries had shown a sharp decline. The principal shipowners were concerned at the nearly empty steerage accommodations. One man's idea of providing cheap transportation for students was seized upon and steerage accomodations were adapted to a standard that would be more acceptable to tourists. New ships were built with tourist or tourist-third-class spaces and this did much to generate traffic from a class of people who had previously been unable to contemplate extended travel by sea.*

C TAURUS
The Taurus *of 1935 was a cargo liner owned by Wilh. Wilhelmsen of Oslo. She was typical of the advanced types of ship being built by the Scandinavian countries, and in 1938 Wilh. Wilhelmsen's fleet of just over 40 vessels contained no less than 39 motor ships. This company operates worldwide services and is now closely concerned with the operation of container ships to the Far East.*

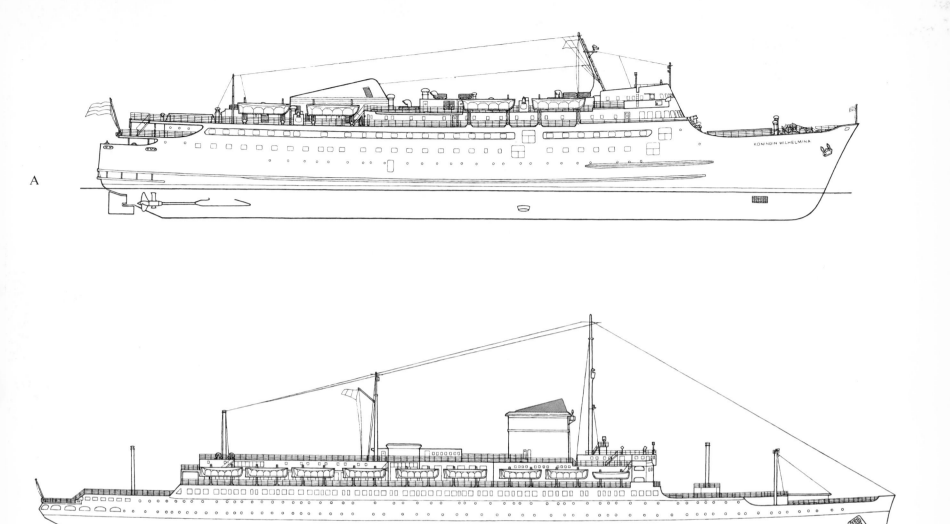

A

B

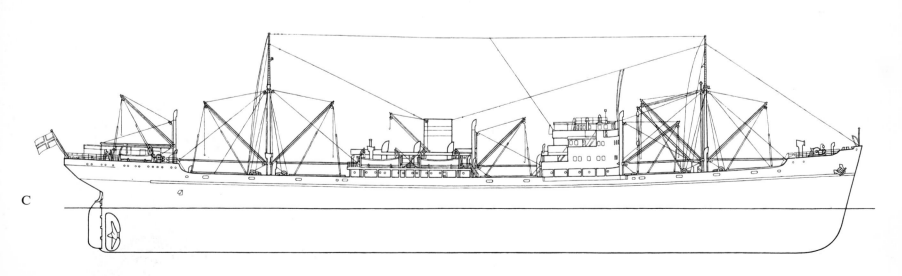

C

A LENIN

The nuclear-powered Soviet icebreaker Lenin *is an outstanding ship of her class and has been in service since her construction in 1957. It is estimated that her three pressurized water reactors contain enough fissionable material to permit her to operate at full power for one year before having to refuel. In outline the* Lenin *is typical of many icebreakers used in northern waters, especially by the Soviet Union and Finland. Finland has probably more experience in building this type of vessel than any other country.*

B TOR GOTHIA

A medium-sized roll-on roll-off ferry of the Swedish Tor Line. These vessels have revolutionized the handling of cargo on short sea routes and they can carry trucks, containers and cargo loaded on flats— strong bases which are towed on board on trailers. Trucks are now able to carry their loads from places as far afield as Teheran and southern Spain to any country in northern Europe without the need to transfer them at any port en route. Ferries have also made it possible for holiday makers, particularly in Britain, to take their cars abroad.

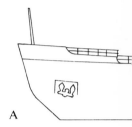

A

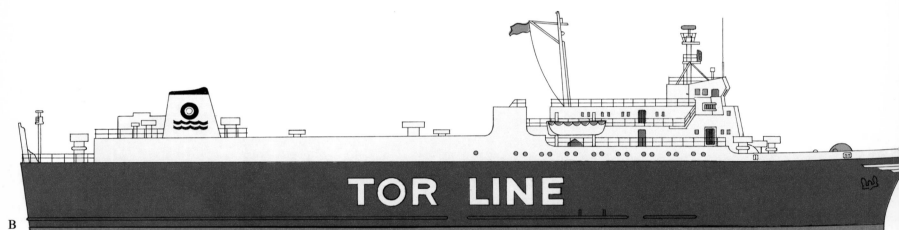

B

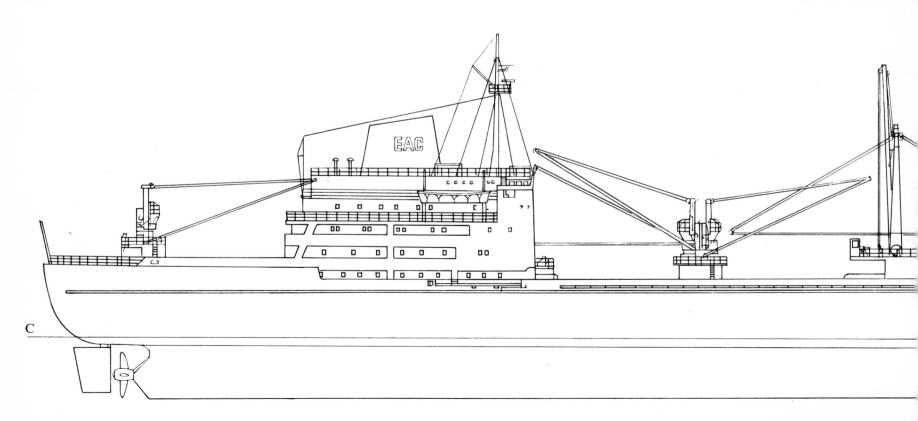

C

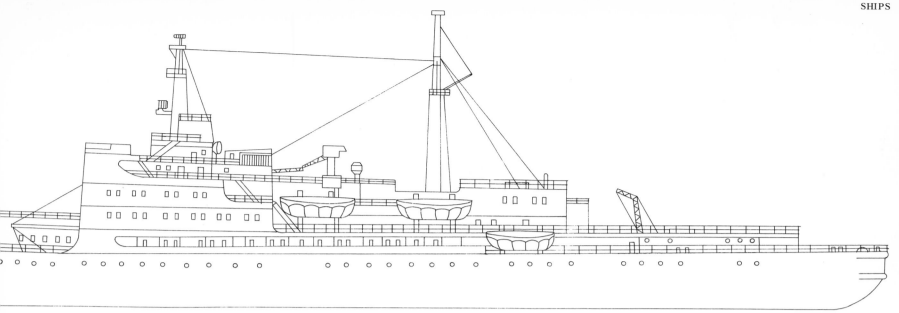

C AROSIA

This is a cargo liner of the Danish East Asiatic Company. Modern cargo liners are a far cry from those operating as recently as the middle 1950s. They now have speeds of up to 26 knots and carry larger cargoes. Twin and triple hatches are served by cranes and modern forms of derricks. Some ships in specialized trades such as that to the Persian Gulf, where heavy equipment is imported for the oil industry, have heavy-lift derricks which can, when used in tandem, lift up to 500 tons.

completion of the voyage the lighters are lowered into the water and towed away to various destinations for unloading.

An important commodity that is also transported by sea is oil. The current energy crisis has greatly increased this importance and will, no doubt, influence the building of new oil tankers. Since 1945 the transportation of crude oil by sea has been revolutionized. The major oil companies have been constantly searching for means by which transportation costs could be reduced. The answer lay in size. In the first years after the war new tankers, with carrying capacities of about 15,000 tons, were only slightly bigger than those that had been in service in the late 1930s. By 1968 a flood of 200,000-ton tankers was entering service. In 1969 there were six tankers that could each carry 312,000 tons of oil. Still larger tankers will soon be in service and it is technically possible to construct ships with capacities in excess of half a million tons. Special dry docks have had to be built to accommodate the giant tankers and there are now fleets of powerful new tugs to handle them at the oil ports.

The need for speed and economy has also been felt in the tramp trades. Twenty-five years ago a tramp ship of 12,000 tons was considered to be a big ship of its type. Now these ships have largely been displaced by much bigger and faster "bulk carriers", many of which can carry 150,000 tons of cargo. Products carried include iron ore, bauxite grain, phosphates, and coal. Smaller bulk carriers will carry as much as 20,000 tons of timber at one time. Now ships have been built that can carry ore or oil according to demand. A more recent type can carry ore, oil, or bulk cargoes.

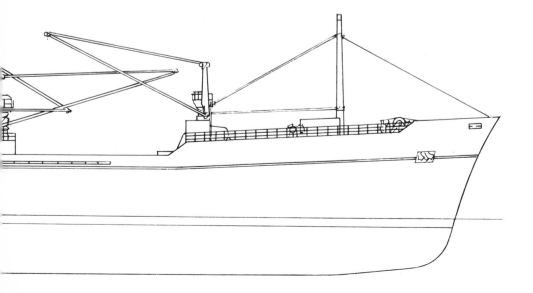

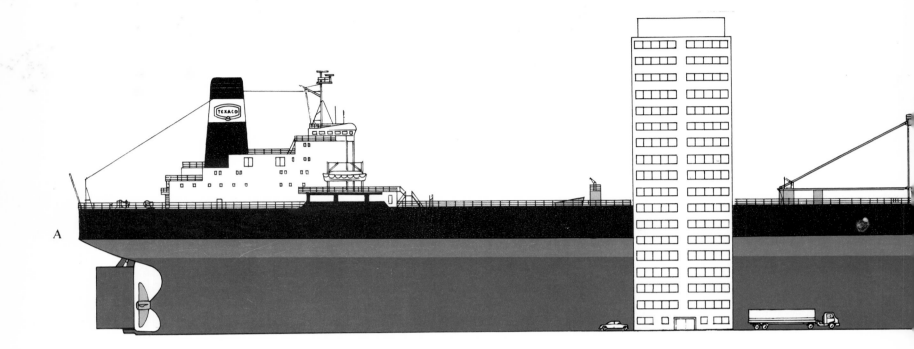

Throughout postwar years internal-combustion engines and turbines have been the most favored means of propulsion. A significant improvement to the internal-combustion engine occurred when it became possible to use boiler fuel in place of the more expensive diesel oil. For the largest ships, slow-revolving large bore engines have been evolved. These engines can produce over 30,000 horsepower. Turbines, too, have continued to increase in efficiency. When used in groups they can produce far higher powers than internal-combustion engines. For instance, the turbines of the *France* produce 160,000 horsepower.

The story of nuclear power in its application to merchant ships has hardly been spectacular. The Russian icebreaker *Lenin* has been in service for some years, but little is known about her performance. The American cargo liner *Savannah*, which in 1960 became the first nuclear-powered ship to cross the Atlantic, is now laid up. Germany and Japan each have a nuclear-powered ship in operation, but there appears to be little interest generally in pursuing this line of development.

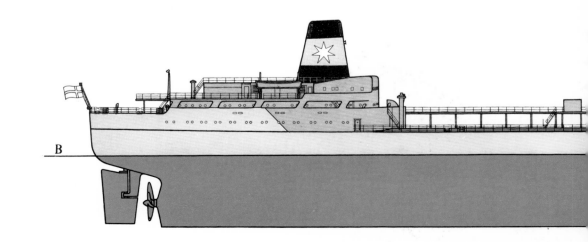

A TEXACO HAMBURG

We have compared this tanker with a high rise apartment block. Tankers of this size are enormous. They are longer than the Queen Elizabeth *and considerably wider. The* Texaco Hamburg *carries over 200,000 tons of oil. There are now many larger ships in service but the additional capacity is taken up by extra beam and draft. The* Globtik Tokyo *will only be marginally longer than the* Texaco Hamburg.*

B EMMA MAERSK

The Emma Maersk, *the largest Danish ship at the time of her construction, was one of the last large tankers to be built with the bridge structure amidships. This vessel carries crude oil and is chartered from the owners—Messrs. A. P. Möller —by oil companies. The* Emma Maersk *is 775 feet long, 109 feet in beam and has a draft of 40 feet. The cargo capacity is 60,750 tons and the De Laval turbines develop 20,000 s.h.p. The service speed is about 17 knots.*

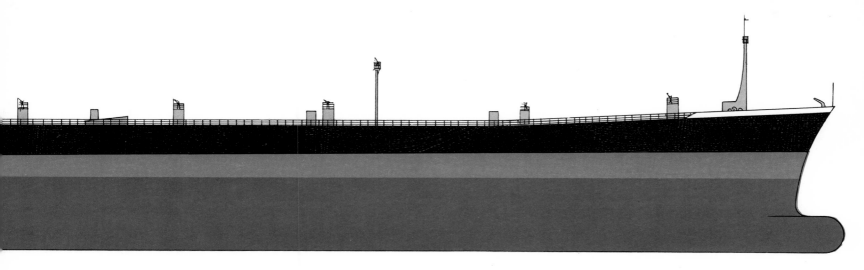

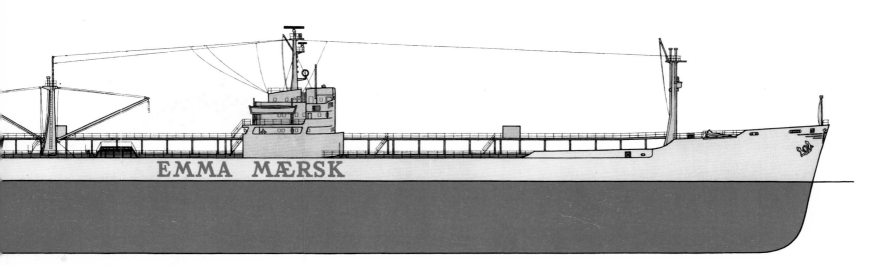

A LASH

The Lash *ship. This illustration shows how the lighters are loaded and stowed. The engine exhausts are taken up close to the ship's side and do not impede the movement of the crane or take up stowage space. A later development is the* Seabee *ship. This type of ship is equipped with a submersible lift and can load and discharge at the remarkable rate of 2,500 tons per hour. The* Doctor Lykes *of this class is the largest general cargo ship ever*

built in the United States and is 875 feet long. Each lighter loaded can carry 850 tons and is as large as a medium-sized coastal ship.

B SYDNEY EXPRESS

This illustration shows how containers are loaded and stowed. The "cells" are bounded by vertical rails which guide containers into position one above the other. The rails are strong enough to hold the containers in place in a seaway although

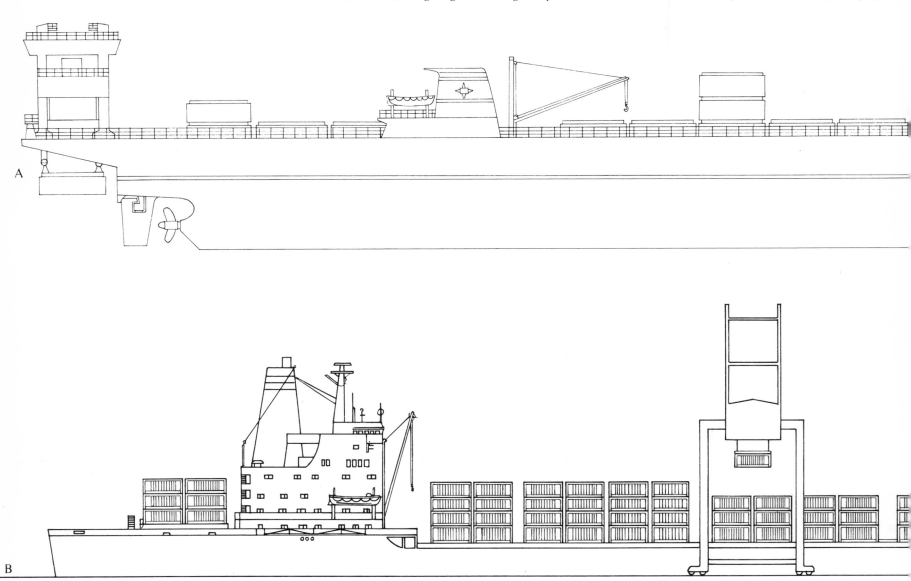

A

B

most big container ships have anti-roll tanks or fins to reduce rolling. Containers have been designed to carry a variety of products including meat, fruit, liquids, and valuable ores. Containers can be seen in any big city on the way to and from the new dock areas which have been built to ensure speedy handling.

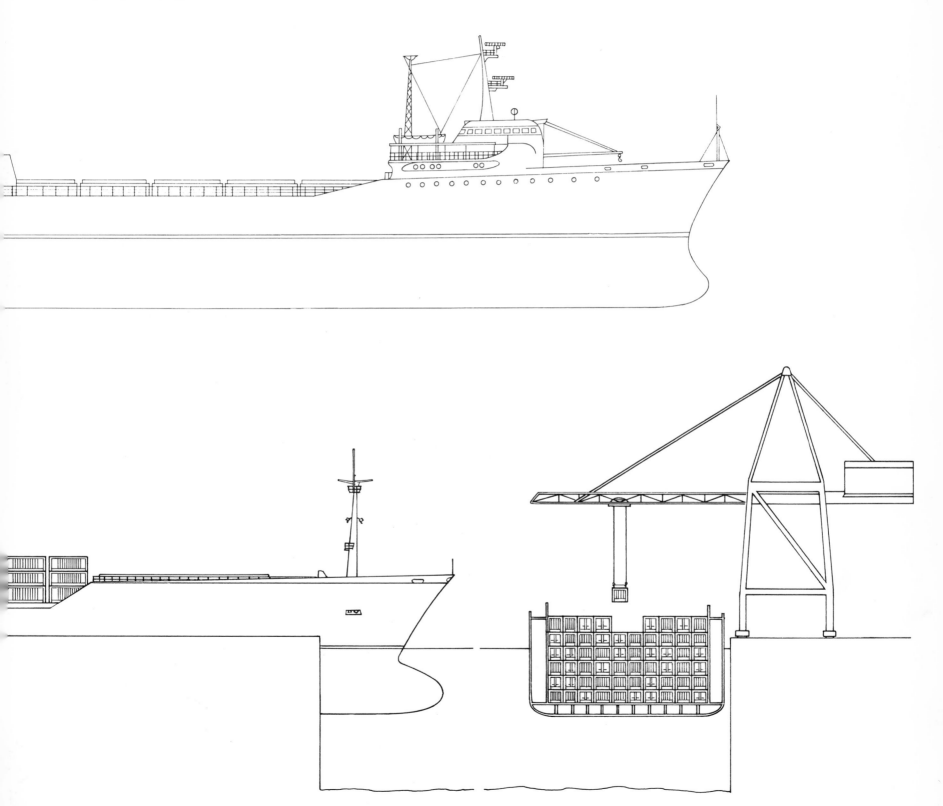

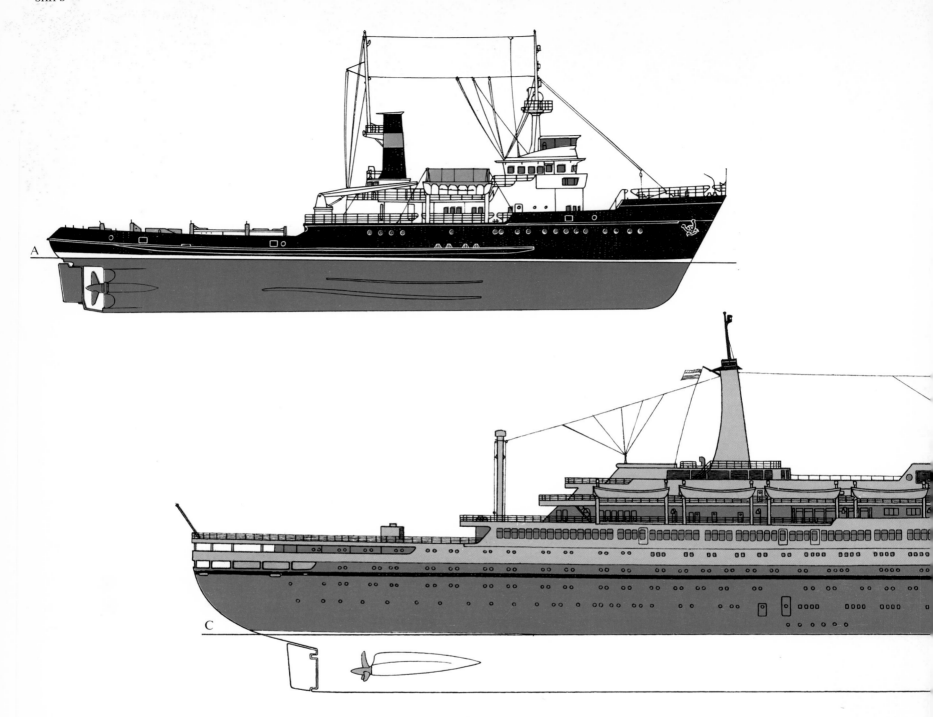

A ZWARTE ZEE

The Zwarte Zee, built in 1962, is a powerful salvage tug in the fleet of L. Smit and Company's International Tug Service of Rotterdam. With a total engine power of 9,000 and a speed of 22 knots the Zwarte Zee can, with another similar tug, tow the largest ships afloat. Later ships can, however, tow the largest tankers and bulk carriers unaided. Tugs such as the Zwarte Zee spend most of their time towing such things as large barges, oil rigs and dredgers on a commercial basis, but some of them are always on salvage station in various parts of the world and ready to go to sea at a moment's notice to aid ships in distress.

B HENGIST

The seas around the shores of northern Europe and the British Isles are crisscrossed with a complicated system of roll-on roll-off services. The ships employed vary considerably in appearance and the Hengist is typical of the modern ferries in the service of British Railways and the French National Railways. Equipped with bow and stern doors to facilitate loading and discharging, the Hengist can carry up to 130 cars on the main vehicle deck and a further 80 on portable car decks. Besides travelers accompanying their own cars this vessel can carry additional passengers, 1,400 in all. Commercial vehicles are carried in large numbers, and one of the British Railways's ships is also equipped to carry passenger carriages and freight wagons. In this way the ship can be switched from one service to another

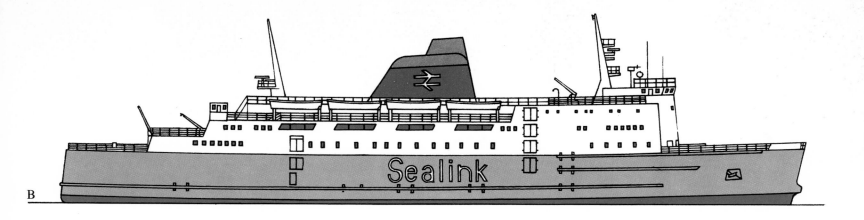

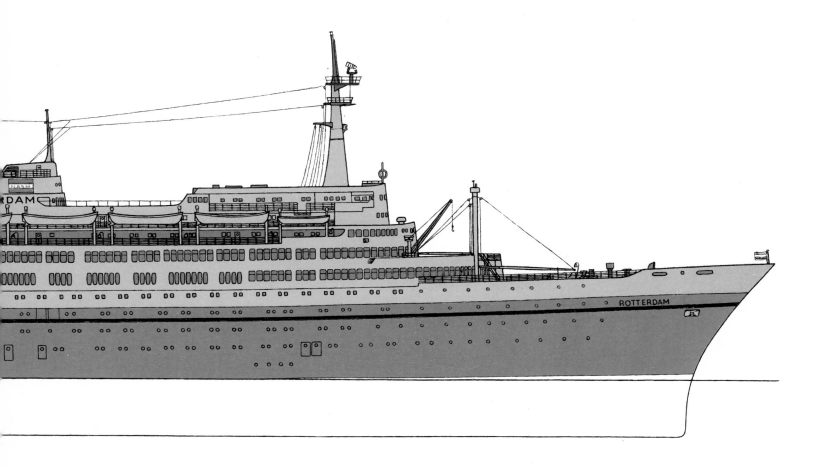

to meet seasonal or occasional peaks in traffic. The Hengist is 385 feet long and has a service speed of 19$\frac{1}{2}$ knots.

C ROTTERDAM

The Holland America Line inaugurated their passenger services to America in 1873. Like other companies they have ceased to operate these services on a regular basis and the Rotterdam is now used for cruising. When she entered service in 1959 she established new standards of accommodation for tourist class pass-

engers. In the past the classes had been divided vertically, but in the Rotterdam, first class and tourist class occupied alternate decks for the full length of the ship. The dining saloons were, however, on the same deck and access to these was by means of a double screw staircase similar in principle to the famous staircase in the Chateau of Chambord. By this means two classes of passengers could use the same "well" without meeting each other. The two-tiered theatre and cinema was entered at two levels; the first class from

their deck into the circle, the tourist class from their deck into the stalls.

The gas turbine, which at one time gave promise of providing a cheap and powerful means of propulsion, has failed to develop, and at the present time there is only one large vessel powered by this means—the American roll-on roll-off cargo liner *Admiral William M. Callaghan*—in service.

The needs of the nations for shipping remains as important as ever. The future is likely to see the development of more specialized ships. Already there are vessels carrying liquid sulfur, liquid methane, and liquid phosphorus. It is possible that many more products still remain that may warrant the construction of special ships for their delivery. The use of airships is being considered for transportation of containers. Who knows whether an inventor may not yet come up with an idea that will make the sailing ship once again a commercial and profitable undertaking?

Hovercraft, which were developed to commercial standards in Great Britain, have not developed as fast as was once thought possible. As yet the ocean-going hovercraft is still not with us and only recently have the problems of short sea passages been generally overcome.

The interior design of these craft permits flexibility between the numbers of passengers and vehicles carried; the standard layout provides for 174 passengers and 34 vehicles. Whilst there are now hovercraft on operation all over the world the two major services are those operated between England and France by Hoverlloyd and Seaspeed (British Railways). After initial difficulties the craft employed maintain a remarkable regularity of service and to cross the Channel by hovercraft is now an accepted and popular form of transport.

As with hovercraft, the development of hydrofoils has been slow and disappointing. The Russians have developed quite large craft for river services and the Italians have also been prominent in this field. Unfortunately the foils on which the craft ride at high speed are delicate and damage is easily caused by striking driftwood and other flotsam. Similarly damage can easily be caused by striking a jetty when coming alongside. Future development is problematical since many pioneering services have been unsuccessful and confidence in these craft is not high. Perhaps the greatest problem to be overcome is the weight/power ratio for as the weight of the craft increases so the power required to drive it at a given speed increases out of all proportion.

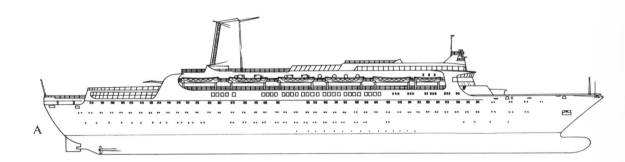

A

A CUNARD ADVENTURER
This purpose-built cruise liner carries approximately 700 passengers in 320 cabins. There are extensive public rooms and cabins on four decks. The Cunard Adventurer *cruises in the Caribbean where several similar ships are operating.*

THE GOKSTAD SHIP (opposite)

A *The shields were fastened by ropes through the shield grips and a batten on the inside of the rail.*

B *The oar holes, sixteen to a side, were cut in the fourteenth plank. They could be closed from the inside by small, neatly-made, hinged wooden discs.*

C *The midship section.*

D *Animals were much smaller than they are today, so that ships, small by present-day standards, could accommodate them as well as the settlers with all their gear. The settlers probably brought their horses ashore in the manner shown here.*

THE GOKSTAD SHIP

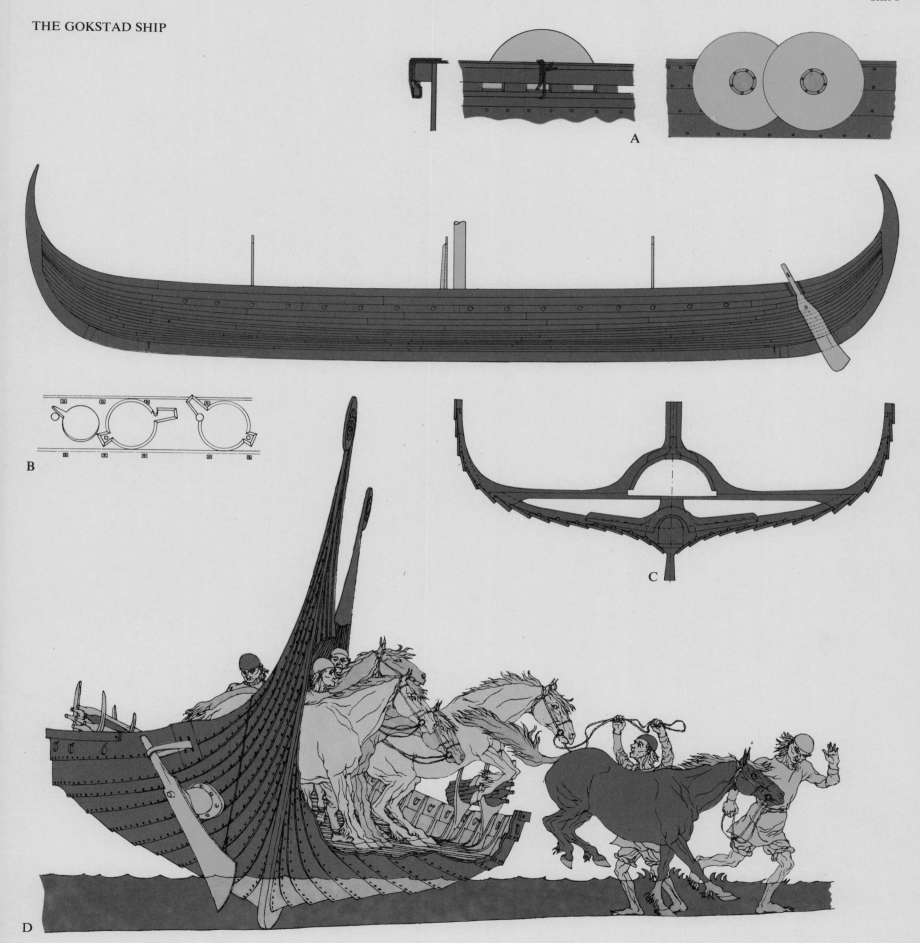

A

B

C

D

WYOMING

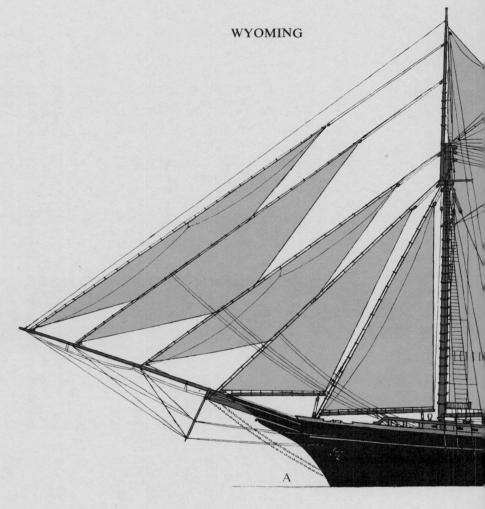

A

DUTCH STATENJACHT

B

SWEDISH MAIL PACKET

C

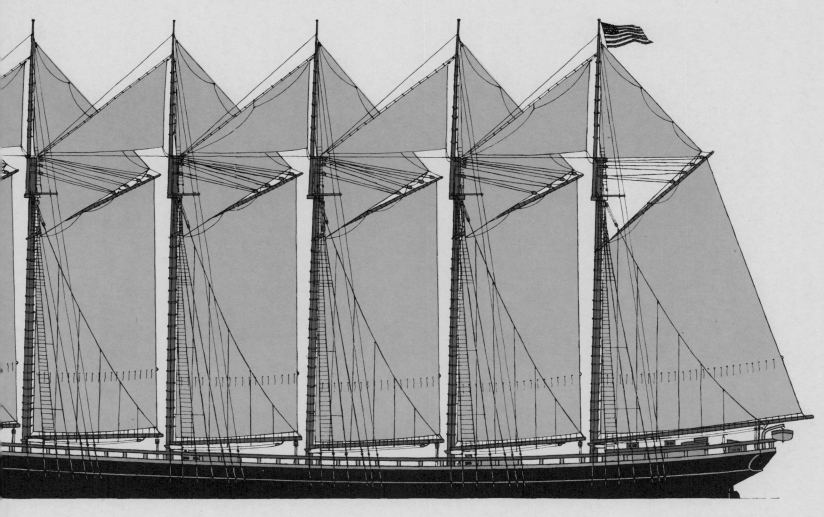

MACFIE

A The American six-masted schooner Wyoming *was the largest wooden sailing ship ever built, being no less than 330 feet long. The* Wyoming *was built in 1909 and sailed exclusively in the American coastal trade, which was and still is reserved for American ships. Sail was assisted by a small auxiliary engine and practically all the sails were hoisted and worked by steam winches. These ships were said to be dangerous when running with the wind and to jibe (to allow the booms to swing across from one side to the other) was almost fatal. Square-rigged ships generally ran safely before the wind, although some were lost through broaching-to (being driven out of control in heavy seas and high winds onto a course at right angles to the wind and sea. The wind laid the ship over and the waves then capsized her).*

B *The Dutch Statenjacht was the forerunner of all yachts and fast dispatch vessels. The egg-shaped board is a leeboard and another was fitted to the port side of the vessel. When sailing, one board was lowered to prevent the ship drifting to lee-ward. It also enabled the ship to sail in shallow water. In modern dinghies and small sailing cruisers the centerboard performs exactly the same function.*

C *Mail packets were often among the fastest ships afloat and well into the nineteenth century they were either owned by governments or chartered and placed under the overall charge of a naval officer. Sizes and rigs of mail packets varied considerably; the illustration is of a small fast ship, classed as a sloop, which carried mail between Ystad and Stralsund in the late seventeenth century.*

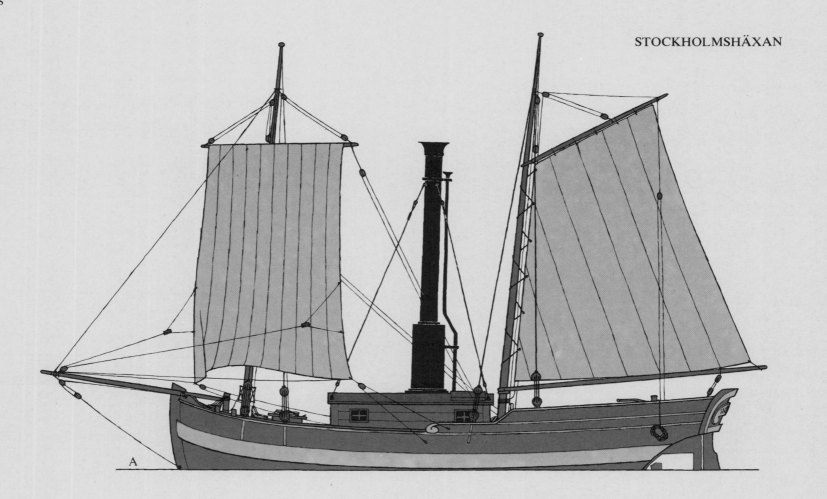

A Taking a typical sloop from Lake Mäla-
ren, Samuel Owen extended her keel aft
and fitted a new sternpost thus providing
an aperture for the propeller. Nearly 5
feet (1.5 m) in diameter, the propeller
had a cast iron frame and four wooden
blades of birch fitted at an angle of 36°
with the shaft line. The after end of the
shaft was supported by the sternpost and
it extended forward under the floor of a
small cabin to the engine room.

B This was a typical single-ended steam
schooner as developed from the first
steam conversions. The first of the so-
called "double-enders" with machinery

amidships was constructed in 1905 but
they were not commonly built until 1916.
Designed to carry a large deck load of
lumber, Willapa had a forecastle and
poop to protect the ends of the load; the
poop was particularly important when
running heavily laden before the wind and
sea down to San Francisco. Many of the
lumber schooners had accommodations
for passengers as for a long period
there was no other means of transportation along the coast.

C This paddle-wheeler had an overall
breadth of 83 feet (25.3 m) and could
carry 5,500 bales of cotton. Supported on

pillars from 15 to 20 feet (4.6—6.1 m)
above the main deck was the work of the
joiners, the hurricane or saloon deck, the
promenade deck, and the "Texas" deck
with the pilot house. Down the middle of
the hurricane deck from the smoke pipes
or chimneys—there was little seagoing lan-
guage on the river—nearly to the stern
was the saloon with its clerestory. It
might be in length from 150—250 feet
(35.7—66.2 m) and was decorated in
white and gilt with numerous glittering
chandeliers. Scenes were painted on the
doors of the staterooms which surrounded
the saloon. There were more staterooms
on the promenade deck above.

WILLAPA

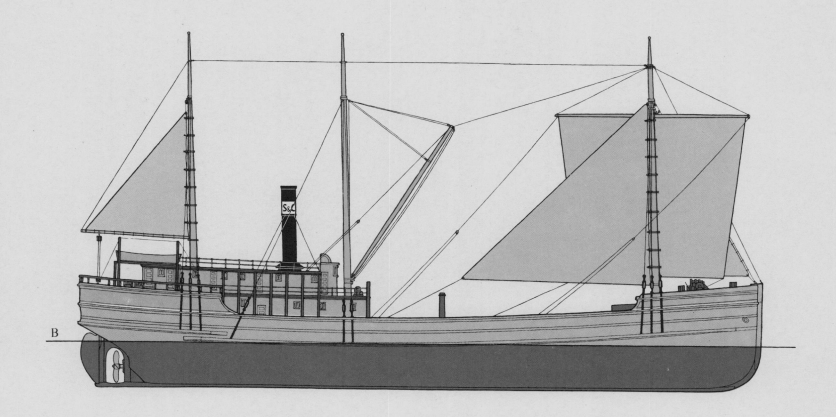

B

NATCHEZ

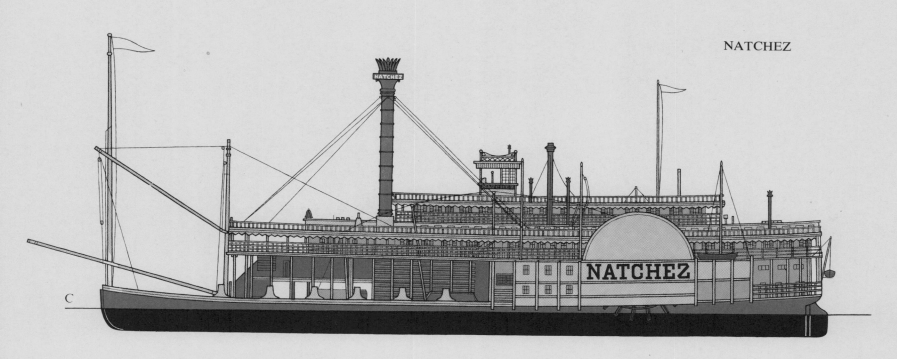

C

KAISER WILHELM DER GROSSE

A *The* Kaiser Wilhelm der Grosse *was a magnificent ship built by the Norddeutscher Lloyd in 1897. On her third homeward voyage she gained the Blue Riband. The* Kaiser Wilhelm der Grosse *carried passengers in three classes. In the first class standards were extremely high and public rooms were two decks high. Promenade spaces were also provided on two decks. Steerage, or third-class, passengers were not so lucky, but their accommodations, too, showed a marked improvement over that of earlier ships. By the 1890s few passenger liners were rigged to carry sails as engines had become capable of reliable performance for months on end without more than routine maintenance.*

B *The* United States *of 1952 is the last of a long line of Atlantic record breakers. She is the largest liner ever to have been built in the United States and the first large ship to be completely air-conditioned. All materials used in her construction are fireproof, or fire retardant, and it is said that the only wood on board is in the pianos and the butcher's block. In spite of*

her attractions, she came upon the scene
too late, and after some years of service
began to lose money. For some time her
future was in doubt and she is now laid up
and unlikely to be used again.

UNITED STATES

THE MOUNTBATTEN HOVERCRAFT CLASS

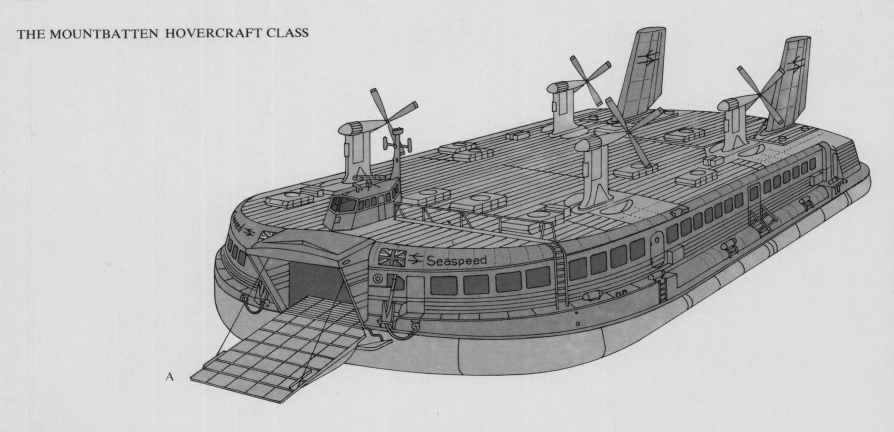

A

A *One of the largest types of hovercraft in service is the Mountbatten Class, built by the British Hovercraft Corporation of East Cowes, England. This craft is supported above the land or sea by air pumped under pressure into spaces below the hull and contained by the skirt. The fans and the propellers which give forward motion are driven by four Rolls-Royce Marine Proteus gas turbines, each of which develops 3,400 shp. Service speeds of between 40 and 50 knots are attained depending upon the state of the water.*

B *The Supramar PT 20 Mk II was the first successful passenger hydrofoil to operate on the open seas. More than seventy PT 20's of various types have been built in Sicily, Japan, Holland, and Norway.*

SUPRAMAR PT 20 MK II

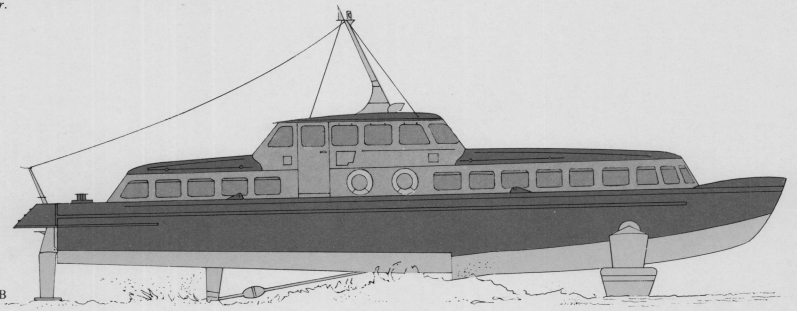

B

TRAINS

THE DAWN OF STEAM TRACTION

Long ago man's wheeled carts made ruts along the way and it was found that the going was easier for all carts if the ruts were followed. By the time of the Roman Empire streets were paved with stone and here and there artificial ruts were built into the paving for traffic to follow. Roman chariots and wagons together made up the first guided transport mode, to use the modern name.

As far as is known, the railway as we know it now first appeared in the fifteenth century in Slovakia in the eastern part of Czechoslovakia. There were iron mines in the mountains and the miners made a track of sorts in the mines with slender straight tree trunks and ran wagons with broad grooved timber wheels over it. The cathedral at Rošňava commissioned an altar painting in 1513 that would depict local industries, and in this painting miners pushing a wagon on rails are to be seen.

There are to be found in books earlier references to railways than the Rošňava painting, and from other references it is known that as early as the sixteenth century iron wheels had appeared running on trimmed timber track. With the advent of the iron wheel if not earlier, the wheel flange was adopted to hold a pair of wheels on a track. Railways to give access to mines spread across Europe in the sixteenth century and what was probably the first British line ran in the late 1590s near Nottingham.

As time passed these railways spread away from the mines and were used to take coal and ore to the nearest waterway, as did the Nottingham line mentioned. Horses were used to haul the wagons for the railways, which could be several miles long. During the eighteenth century iron was used for the track for the first time, cast in L-shaped plates for flangeless wheels. The wheels ran on the foot of the L and were held on the track by the upright.

An important development in 1820 was the patenting of a method for rolling long malleable iron rails by John Birkinshaw of the Bedlington Ironworks near Newcastle in the north of England. The short iron plates and rails soon became a thing of the past and with them vanished the plateway, hence a flanged wheel running on the top of a rail was standard. The first public railway to use steam locomotives was authorized in 1821. It was called the Stockton & Darlington Railway and it was opened to traffic in 1825. The line connected Stockton on the River Tees with collieries inland beyond Darlington. Nevertheless, after the opening day on which a passenger train was hauled by George Stephenson's *Locomotion* (preceded by a horseman carrying a red flag) steam power was confined to coal trains. Passenger services were run by privately owned horse-drawn road coaches adapted to run on rails. Tolls were paid to the railway company.

France followed England with steam-worked railways, obtaining four locomotives from the latter country for the St. Etienne to Lyons Railway in 1828—1829. These were built by Robert Stephenson & Company, founded by Robert Stephenson at the instigation of his father, George Stephenson, who was the builder of *Locomotion* and her sisters. Marc Séguin was the engineer of the St. Etienne to Lyons Railway and he noted that the boilers of the Stephenson locomotives were very poor producers of steam. To remedy this situation he designed and patented a multitubular boiler in 1828, which was fitted to a French-built locomotive that otherwise followed the Stephenson pattern in 1829. James Neville had previously patented a multitubular boiler in England in 1826 and Marc Séguin conceded in later years that Robert Stephenson's *Rocket* was the first actual locomotive to carry a multitubular boiler.

The steam traction happenings in Europe had not gone unnoticed in the United States, where the idea of steam-powered locomotives was promoted by Colonel John Stevens. The colonel built himself a model steam locomotive in 1825, which was demonstrated on a circular track, and later he was president of an early line, the Camden & Amboy. The success of the Stockton & Darlington led to a number of American schemes and the first horse-traction sections of the Baltimore & Ohio Railroad were opened in 1827. This was followed by a railroad auxiliary to the Delaware & Hudson Canal Company in 1829, the Mohawk & Hudson in 1830, and the Charleston & Hamburg (later the South Carolina Railroad), and the Camden & Amboy, both in 1831.

Horatio Allen, the Delaware & Hudson's engineer, ordered four locomotives from England, one from Robert Stephenson & Company named *America*, which was the first to arrive, and three from Foster, Rastrick & Company. Only one Foster, Rastrick locomotive was steamed on the line, the *Stourbridge Lion*. She was considered to be too heavy and the first locomotives in the United States disappeared into history without going into service. Horatio Allen moved south to the Charleston & Hamburg Railroad and convinced the owners that they should use steam traction. This time the locomotives were built in the United States at the West Point Foundry, New York, the first, *Best Friend of Charleston*, inaugurating the line in 1831. Also in 1831 the Camden & Amboy introduced the *De Witt Clinton* on its tracks, another product of the West Point Foundry. Before that in 1830 Peter Cooper had built a small locomotive called *Tom Thumb*, which was demonstrated on the Baltimore & Ohio. This had a vertical boiler and she was the first locomotive to haul passengers in the United States.

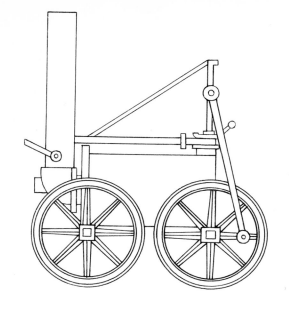

A

B

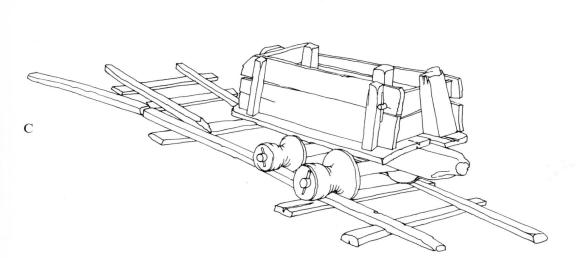

C

D

A CATCH-ME-WHO-CAN
In Richard Trevithick's locomotive built in 1808 he abandoned the great flywheel taken over from stationary engine practice and made a connection direct from the piston rod to the wheels. This little locomotive, with flanged wheels, was shown on a circular track in London and the public could ride behind it at the cost of one shilling per head, the world's first steam railway fare-paying passengers.

B COLLIERY TRAM-WAGON
In the eighteenth century what nowadays would be called technical books were being

published with increasing frequency. This illustration is based on a drawing that appeared in Gabriel Jars's Voyages Metallurgiques *printed in 1765. It shows a British flanged wheel wagon on a colliery tramway in County Durham. Coal was thus transported from the mine to ship loading points called staithes on the Rivers Tyne and Wear.*

C WOODEN MINING TRAMWAY
One of the more remarkable relics of man's transportation experiments is the little truck shown here, now preserved in a German museum. It dates from early

in the sixteenth century and both it and the track it is standing upon are made from timber. Little vehicles like this were used inside mine workings and in the immediate neighborhood of the mine.

D MURDOCK'S STEAM CARRIAGE
The first steam locomotives ran on the roads. Nicholas Cugnot, a Frenchman, devised a machine about 1769 with which he hoped to haul artillery. In England William Murdock built the model steam locomotive shown here in 1784 and Richard Trevithick built a steam road carriage in 1802.

A COLONEL STEVENS'S MODEL
Colonel Stevens's little model steam loco-motive of 1825, the first steam locomotive in the United States. The cylinders drove a pinion that engaged with the gear wheel seen in the center of the locomotive. The gear wheel in turn pulled the locomotive along a rack in the center of the track, the wheels of the locomotive being for carrying purposes only.

B SANS PAREIL
The Sans Pareil *built by Timothy Hack-worth for the Rainhill trials in 1829. Al-though the locomotive took part in the trials (until a boiler feed pump broke down), she was in any case disqualified because she was too heavy. Nevertheless, the locomotive subsequently worked on the Liverpool & Manchester, possibly be-cause many details were well designed*

for the period and the general workman-ship was excellent.

C LIVERPOOL
This design was built for the Liverpool & Manchester Railway by Edward Bury in 1830. For the first time inside horizontal cylinders were combined with a crank axle and, of course, a multitubular boiler. The 6 foot diameter driving wheels were the

C

E

F LOCOMOTION

The Stephenson Locomotion *of 1825 for the Stockton & Darlington Railway. The cast-iron wheel centers shown were a later addition by Timothy Hackworth, the engineer of the line. The Stockton & Darlington locomotive shop at Shildon lacked a wheel-turning lathe of sufficient diameter to handle the wheels, so the centers were made in two halves and fastened together.* Locomotion *had three sister locomotives on the Stockton & Darlington,* Hope, Black Diamond, *and* Diligence.

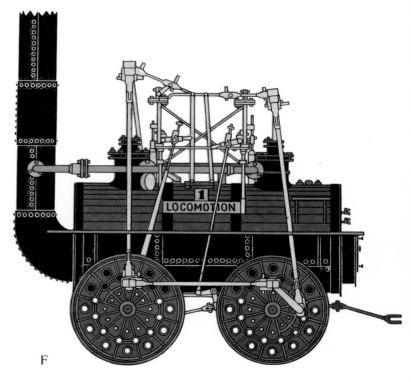

F

largest used up to that time and the locomotive was fully sprung. Other Bury features were bar frames and the D-shaped firebox (in plan) with a hemispherical top, usually known as a haystack firebox.

D SÉGUIN'S ENGINE

Marc Séguin's locomotive with a multitubular boiler for the St. Etienne to Lyons Railway, built in 1829. No exhaust-steam

blast pipe up the chimney was provided and the tender carried a fan whose output was led to the chimney by flexible ducts to make a draft for the fire.

E NOVELTY

The popular favorite of the 1829 Rainhill trials because of its dashing appearance and apparent speed was the little locomotive Novelty *built by John Braithwaite*

and Captain John Ericsson (late of the Swedish army). The blast to blow up the fire was provided by a mechanical bellows. This bellows broke down and lost the locomotive the contest.

A

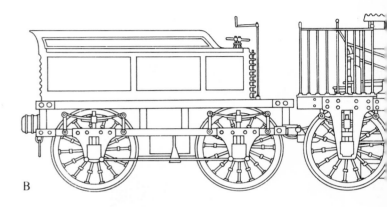

B

A PLANET

Robert Stephenson's Planet, *dated 1830.
Horizontal inside cylinders were combined
with a crank axle, but the frames were
quite different. Both outside and inside
frames were fitted, all with bearings on
the driving axle. Crank axles were difficult
to forge in those days and liable to break
in service. In case of a break the various
frames supported the wheels on the track
and the locomotive did not derail, even
when at speed.*

B DER ADLER

A Patentee *locomotive that has gained
considerable fame was* Der Adler *(The
Eagle) built in England in 1835. She was
the first steam locomotive to run in Germany on the Nuremberg-Fürth Railway
and she was a standard product of the
Robert Stephenson & Co. works at Newcastle.*

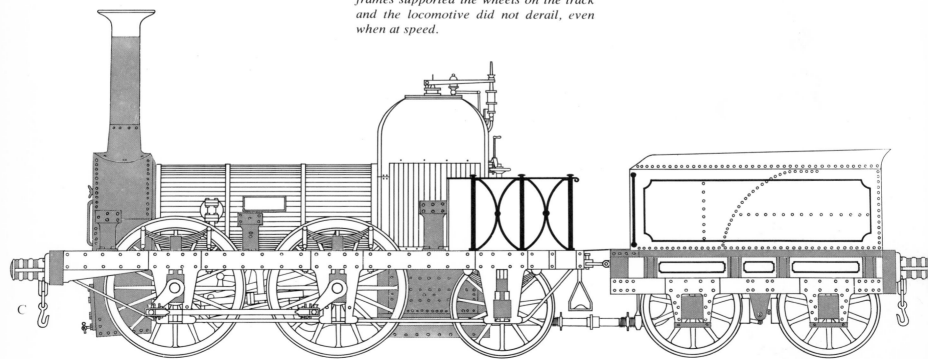

C

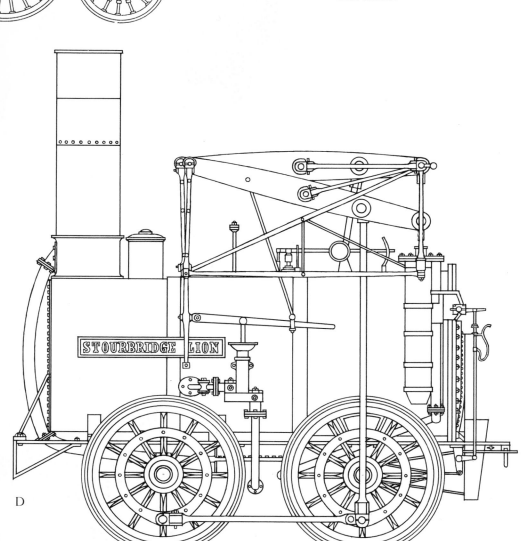

C LION

A typical freight version of the Patentee *type was the* Lion *built for the Liverpool & Manchester in 1838. After a railway life of twenty years she was sold to Liverpool docks for duty as a stationary pumping engine. Seventy years later in 1929 she was still pumping occasionally and was then rescued and put on the rails again. After overhaul she took part in the Liverpool & Manchester centenary celebrations in 1930 and even today is ready to work a train when required.*

D STOURBRIDGE LION

The first locomotive to run on a railroad in the United States was the Stourbridge Lion *supplied to the Delaware & Hudson Canal Co. by Foster, Rastrick & Co. of England in 1829. The locomotive was in fact named* Lion, *but as there were a number of* Lions *the name of the town in which she was built is usually tacked onto that name.*

Hamburg lay just across the river from Charleston, South Carolina and it was from here in 1831 that the Charleston & Hamburg Railroad became the first line to operate a steam-hauled passenger service. The railway used the *Best Friend of Charleston* and various other products of the West Point Foundry. Later in the 1830s passenger trains came to be hauled by single-driver locomotives with a leading bogie, or truck—principal among them being the Norris type. The Norris locomotive, the *Washington Farmer*, built in 1836, succeeded in hauling a train up a gradient of 1 in 14 and thus the type also came to have a reputation as a hill climber. William Norris took some of the features of his locomotives from some Bury single-drivers imported from England. Two driving axles in place of one was the next Norris development, as in the *Hercules* for the Beaver Meadow Railroad built in 1836. At another works in Philadelphia, Eastwick & Harrison's, a similar locomotive to the coupled Norris type was built with the two coupled axle boxes ahead of the firebox. This was the *Gowan and Marx* of 1839.

In the same year, William Norris also built a four-coupled locomotive with bar frames, haystack firebox, leading bogie and with the grate between the driving axles. This was the prototype of the American type of locomotive that was to be the standard locomotive for all types of work in the United States for fifty years or more—except that the haystack firebox gave way to other types after fifteen years or so. Just as with his single-drivers, Norris exported his four-coupled locomotives to Germany, Austria, and Italy, and the design of native-built American locomotives was influenced by them. The chimney spark arrester of the Norris locomotives was copied too in the wood-burning areas of Central Europe.

The Liverpool & Manchester Railway was the world's first all steam public railway, conveying all types of traffic, passengers, livestock, and freight indiscriminately. The route possessed two tracks for trains in either direction, it was equipped with specialized passenger and freight stations, and it worked on a timetable. About the only modern feature that it lacked was a signaling system, and this was developed in the following decade. First class passengers at least enjoyed fully closed carriages and the second class had a roof above their heads, although the coach sides were open. Third-class passengers traveled on benches set in open wagons and such accommodations for the third class lasted in Britain until the Railway Act of 1844.

A

A LAFAYETTE

This machine marks the point where American locomotive design began to follow a separate course. The Lafayette, built in 1837 in Philadelphia, was the Baltimore & Ohio's first engine with a horizontal boiler and more than four wheels. It is still preserved in working order by the company.

B BEST FRIEND OF CHARLESTON

The Best Friend of Charleston *built by the West Point Foundry, N.Y., in 1830. Horatio Allen had persuaded the owners of the Charleston & Hamburg Railroad to use steam traction and this locomotive and her sisters started the train service on the line early in 1831. Vertical boilers like this had quite a vogue in the United States in the 1830s. Unhappily the boiler of the* Best Friend *exploded later, due to maltreatment, and when the locomotive was rebuilt with a different but still upright boiler she was named* Phoenix.

C EXPERIMENT

The West Point Foundry built this little locomotive, the Experiment, *in 1832. An interesting locomotive because for the first time a leading bogie, or truck, was fitted, in this case to help running over the roughly laid American track. The bogie was suggested to a party of American engineers visiting England in 1828 by no less a person than Robert Stephenson.*

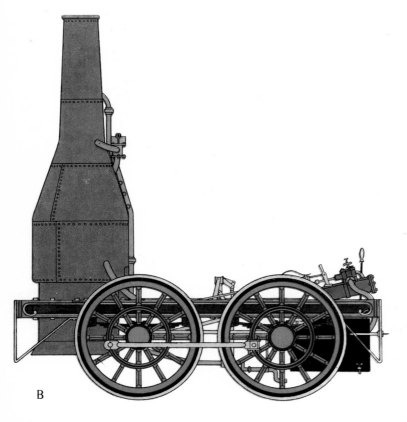

B

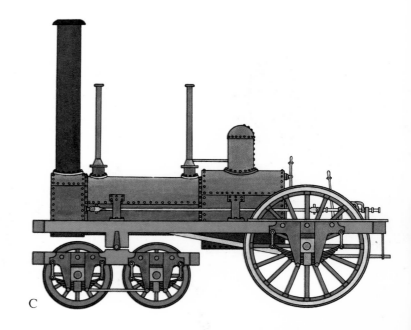

C

D

D ROYAL GEORGE

The Royal George *of 1827, the world's first six-coupled locomotive designed by Timothy Hackworth to work coal trains on the Stockton & Darlington Railway. Like many early locomotives, the design was such that the boiler was fed with fuel at the chimney end. The locomotive normally ran with a coal tender in front and a water tank at the rear.*

E MONSTER

The Monster *built by Isaac Dripps for heavy freight on the Camden & Amboy Railroad in 1836. The connecting rod drives the third axle, which is coupled to the fourth axle. Gearing between the third and second axles drives the coupled first and second axles. The placing of the cylinders and the drive through a rocking lever increase the odd appearance of the locomotive.*

E

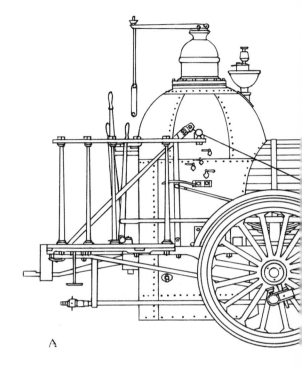

A WASHINGTON FARMER

William Norris of Philadelphia borrowed both Edward Bury's haystack firebox and his bar frames in his locomotive designs, to which he added a leading bogie. The Washington Farmer *shown here was built in 1836 and was of a well-liked type that gained fame for Norris locomotives. So much so that Norris locomotives were exported to England, Germany, and Austria, where in their turn they influenced European locomotive practice.*

B SOUTH CAROLINA

Early American eight-coupled locomotives have already been referred to, and properly South Carolina *built for the South Carolina Railroad in 1832 belongs among them. More particularly she is the world's first purpose-built articulated locomotive, jointed in the middle in order to run through curves more easily. The West Point Foundry built the locomotive and the design is credited to Horatio Allen.*

A

B

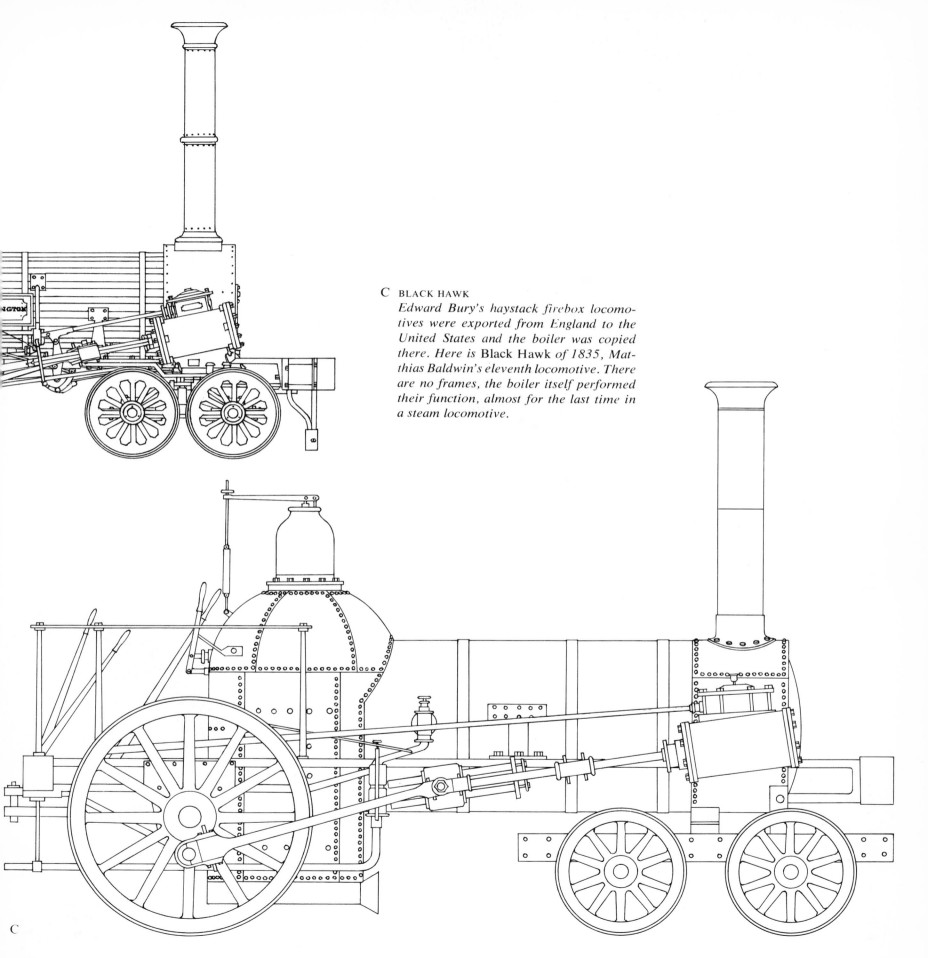

C BLACK HAWK

Edward Bury's haystack firebox locomotives were exported from England to the United States and the boiler was copied there. Here is Black Hawk *of 1835, Matthias Baldwin's eleventh locomotive. There are no frames, the boiler itself performed their function, almost for the last time in a steam locomotive.*

A

B

A FRENCH CRAMPTON

The classic French Crampton locomotive type. This locomotive was built by Cail & Co. for the Northern Railway of France in 1859. She is shown later in life when fitted with a vacuum brake. Vacuum was created by steam ejectors and the twin trumpets for the ejector exhaust are prominent above the boiler. The ineffective cab shown is also a later addition; when she was built there was no protection for the enginemen.

B FINLAND STATE NO. 11

The American locomotive type was also used in Great Britain and built there for other countries, developed as a native design without reference to the United States. Here is a locomotive designed by Dübs & Co. in Glasgow for the Finnish State Railways. As a former part of the Russian Empire, the railways of Finland have the 5 foot gauge instead of the standrad 4 feet 8¹/₂ inches. Wood is the fuel in Finland, hence the spark-arresting chimney fitted to this locomotive.

C CRAMPTON'S LOCOMOTIVE

The pioneer Crampton locomotive was built for the Namur & Liège Railway in Belgium by Tulk & Levy of the Lowca Works, Whitehaven, in 1846. A feature of the Crampton boiler after the early locomotives was a firebox top flush with the top of the boiler. In France in later years such boilers were always known as Crampton boilers. Valve gear outside the frames and driving wheels was another innovation at the time, making for simpler maintenance.

D

D JENNY LIND

Single-driver locomotives long remained popular for express train work in nine-teenth-century Great Britain. The well-known Jenny Lind type featured outside frames to support the carrying wheel axle boxes, while the driving wheels had in-side frame axle boxes. The first of the type shown here was designed by David Joy while working at E. B. Wilson & Co.'s Railway Foundry, Leeds, in 1847. Later on the Railway Foundry was to build one of these locomotives each week, such was the demand in England and in the United States.

E GREAT NORTHERN NO. 1

Patrick Stirling built No. 1 for the Great Northern Railway at Doncaster in 1870 and many more of the class were built there up to 1895. Some British express trains were worked by the locomotives (and by comparable locomotives on other railways) until the first few years of the twentieth century. The leading bogie for fast running was a feature of most British locomotives for express work after 1880 or so.

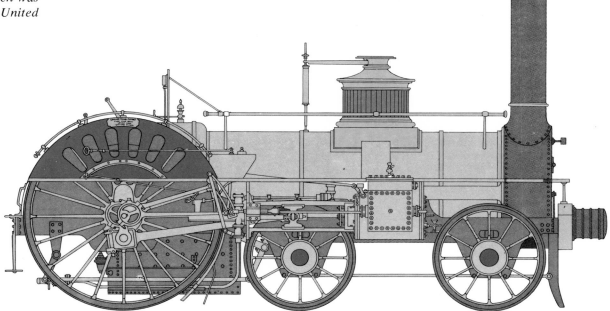

C

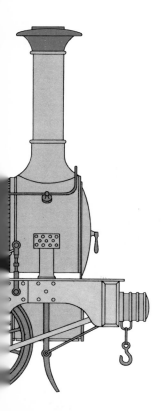

E

A DUTCH STATE PASSENGER LOCOMOTIVE

The Dutch State Railways had fifty passenger locomotives built by Beyer, Peacock & Co. of Manchester, England, during the 1870s. This one was built in 1873 and displays many British characteristics. The design can be contrasted with that of the Hungarian locomotive shown on this page, for both locomotives were built for very much the same sort of duty.

B ERZSEBÈT

This locomotive for the Royal Hungarian State Railways is typical of mid-nineteenth-century locomotive practice in Central Europe. The long boiler and the short wheelbase made the locomotives unsteady at any speed and for this reason some were later rebuilt with a greater distance between the driving axles and with the firebox in between them. The decorations celebrate the building of the 1,000th locomotive at the G. Sigl Works, Wiener Neustadt, the manufacturers of the locomotive in 1870.

A

B

C

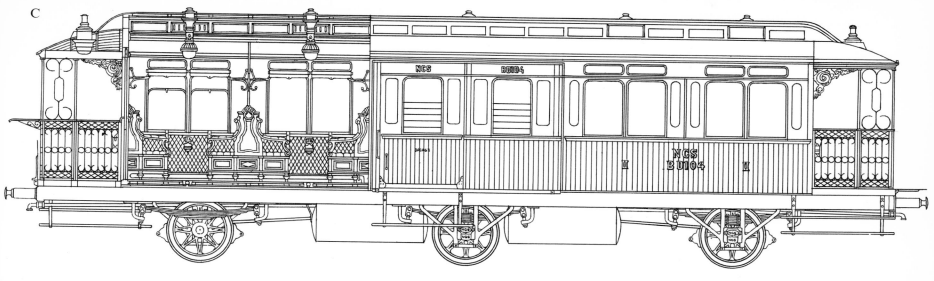

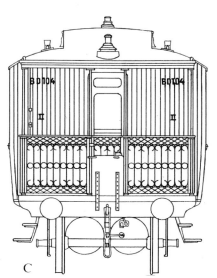

C

C DUTCH SECOND CLASS CARRIAGE
This unusually elegant six-wheel design was built for second-class usage on the internal services of the Netherlands Central Railway during the early 1900s.

D HERNALSER SLEEPER
This sleeping car was built by Hernalser & Co. in Vienna in 1873. The cushioning of the facing seats on either side of the gangway could be pulled out toward each other to make up a lower berth at night, while a second berth was let down from the roof. A stove was located under the floor to heat the coach.

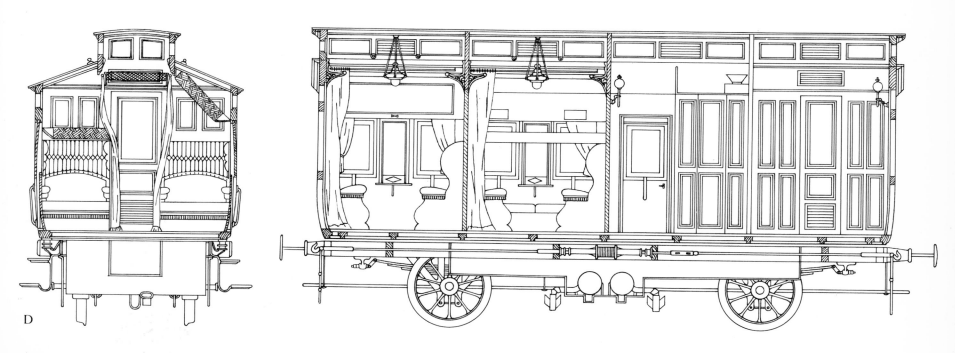

D

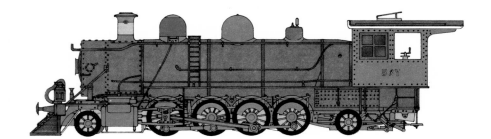

A

A THE 2-8-2 MIKADO TYPE
When the Baldwin Locomotive Works built some locomotives for the Nippon Railway, Japan, in 1897, they supplied a class with a new wheel arrangement, an eight-coupled locomotive with carrying trucks fore and aft. At the time it was the fashion in the United States to give each wheel arrangement an identifying name and in view of the destination of the first locomotives this type became known as the "Mikado". It was widely built for many railways in later years.

B MALLET COMPOUND
In the opening years of the twentieth century United States's freight locomotives grew even more massive. Here is a Mallet compound articulated locomotive, arranged so that the front set of driving

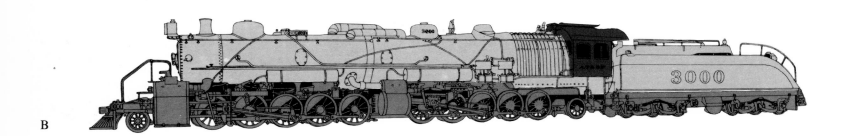

B

C

wheels could swing to take curves in relation to the rear set. She was produced for the Atchison, Topeka & Santa Fe Railway in 1911. The boiler was jointed as well and the steam pipes connecting the front and rear parts can be seen. The locomotives were rebuilt from two ten-coupled locomotives and they were not a success; by 1915 they had all disappeared.

C CHAMPION

The eight-coupled freight locomotive developed rapidly in the United States. Here is one with a leading bogie designed by Philip Hofecker, master mechanic of the Lehigh Valley Railroad. She was built in 1882 for Appalachian mountain coal trains.

What may be called the prototype locomotives for the Liverpool & Manchester have been illustrated already, but in 1833 Robert Stephenson designed the *Patentee* type, which was the first locomotive type to be built in quantity for many other lines as well as the Liverpool & Manchester. It was in effect an enlargement of the *Planet* type with carrying wheels both fore and aft of the single driving wheel, to give much steadier running and the possibility of a larger firebox. *Patentees* with two pairs of driving wheels for freight work were built also, with carrying wheels either behind or in front of the drivers. Many *Patentees* were exported and the first locomotives in Germany (1835), Belgium (1835), Russia (1837), Holland (1839), and Italy (1839) belonged to the type. Such was the demand that other manufacturers were licensed to build the locomotives and thus it came about that the first locomotive to be built in Belgium was a *Patentee*, named *Le Belge* and dated 1835.

On the Stockton & Darlington, the *Locomotion* of 1825 and her sister locomotives quickly proved inadequate for the long coal trains required. Timothy Hackworth at the railway's works at Shildon produced the world's first six-coupled locomotive in 1827, the *Royal George*. The Stockton & Darlington had a number of this type in later years, with modified cylinder arrangements and with multitubular boilers. The *Patentee* locomotives, with a single pair of driving wheels for passenger work and four-coupled for freight, were the Liverpool & Manchester standards, and indeed varying designs of these two types sufficed many European railways until about 1870 or so. Nevertheless, Robert Stephenson & Company designed a six-coupled, inside cylinder locomotive for freight as early as 1834, the first one going to the Leicester & Swannington Railway. Six-coupled locomotives, with inside cylinders in Great Britain and outside cylinders elsewhere in Europe, were the commonest freight locomotives until the end of the century.

In the United States the big locomotive for the heavy freight train was early on the scene. Isaac Dripps built an eight-coupled locomotive for the Camden & Amboy as early as 1836. It was before its time and was later converted into a six-coupled locomotive with a leading bogie. From 1844 the Baltimore & Ohio Railroad had eight-coupled freight locomotives, the first with an upright boiler although the rest were of a more orthodox construction except that the cylinders drove an intermediate jackshaft coupled to the wheels. They were nicknamed "Mud-Diggers", a reference to their tendency to jump

from the track at the slightest opportunity. From 1846 the Baltimore & Ohio and the Philadelphia & Reading Railroad had orthodox eight-coupled locomotives with outside cylinders, a type that was later built in Europe until well into the twentieth century.

The Stephenson *Patentee* type single-driver passenger locomotive and its freight four-coupled derivatives were displaced from 1841 by Robert Stephenson's long boiler locomotives. The boiler was long because all three of the locomotive axles were brought ahead of the firebox—for both single-driver and four-coupled locomotives as well as for six-coupled locomotives. The cylinders could be both inside and outside the frames, and both inside and outside frame *Patentee* locomotives were built. The outside frame, outside cylinder, six-coupled locomotive type was particularly popular in Europe, and when eight-coupled locomotives for mountain work came to be built from the 1860s on, these were long boiler locomotives as well. According to a theory of the time the boiler had to be carried as low down as possible and this created a difficulty in passenger locomotives, for the height of the driving wheel crank or other axle from the ground prevented the desired low height for a boiler of any great diameter. Thomas Crampton had the idea of placing the driving wheels behind the firebox so that carrying wheels only were beneath the boiler.

Crampton's first locomotives were built in 1846, two going to the Namur & Liège Railway in Belgium and the other arriving on the Dundee & Perth Railway in Scotland in 1848. About twenty-five Cramptons were built for British railways at the end of the 1840s, but the type was not popular for it was alleged that the locomotives damaged the track. In France and Germany on the other hand Cramptons were esteemed as high speed machines and nearly 300 were put into service between 1848 and 1864. A few were built in the United States, but it was quickly found that they were quite unsuitable for the American railways.

It has been seen that during the 1830s the three-axle locomotive with four-coupled wheels was evolved to handle freight traffic. In the United States the leading bogie was soon added to aid working over rough track, but in Europe where the track was better laid a leading pair of wheels sufficed, particularly when this axle was carried in a flexible truck as occurred later. This type of four-coupled locomotive joined the six-coupled freight locomotive as the two commonest sorts of locomotive during the last fifty years of the nineteenth century.

A GREAT NORTHERN NO. 990

Henry Ivatt's Atlantic locomotive for the Great Northern Railway built in 1898. The firebox over the rear pair of carrying wheels will be noted. If desired, the width of the firebox could be increased without the constraint of fitting in between the driving wheels. The rear carrying wheels had outside axle boxes to keep the axle bearings away as far as possible from the heat of the fire.

B CITY OF TRURO

The Great Western Railway in England liked to build its locomotives with outside frames, hence the appearance of City of Truro designed by William Dean and built at Swindon in 1903. It is claimed that this locomotive reached a maximum speed of 102.3 mph (164.64 km/h), although some doubt has been cast on this and the actual speed was probably just below the 100 mph mark.

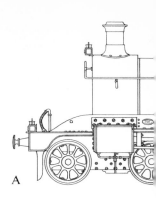

A

B

D

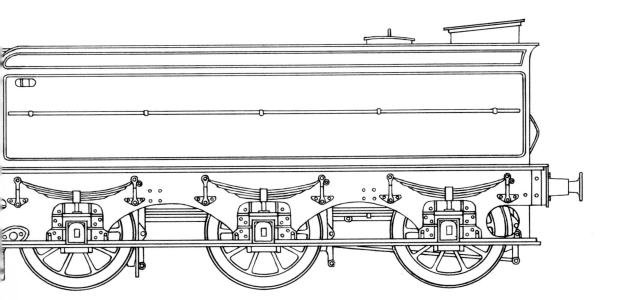

C DUNALASTAIR

The Dunalastair *built in 1897 and named after the otherwise undistinguished country house of a Caledonian Railway director. Apart from the rather larger diameter than usual of the boiler, the design epitomizes the standard British late nineteenth-century express locomotive, an inside-cylinder four-coupled machine with a leading bogie. The locomotive was the forerunner of many others for the Caledonian Railway, successive batches being built with larger and larger boilers.*

D LONDON & SOUTH WESTERN NO. 471

William Adams on the London & South Western Railway favored outside cylinders for his express locomotives, as in this example built in 1884. During this period British locomotive engineers prided themselves on the artistic appearance of their products, and in accordance with the taste of the time this locomotive has been acclaimed as one of the best. Apart from that it gave a very good performance when working trains.

A PRUSSIAN STATE P-8 CLASS 4-6-0
Nearly four thousand of this type were built between 1906 and 1924, and they were some of the first locomotives to be fitted with superheaters. An excellent straightforward two-cylinder mixed-traffic design, there are many still performing trojan work in Eastern Europe.

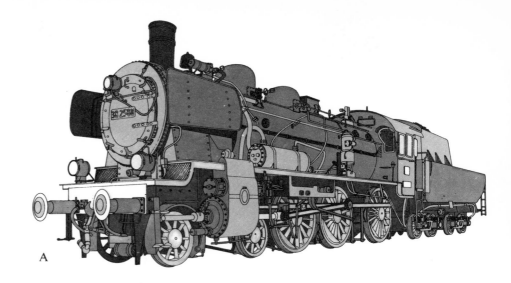

A

B ADRIATIC SYSTEM 670 CLASS
Giuseppe Zara designed this four-cylinder compound express locomotive for the Adriatic System in Italy in 1900. It was a Plancher compound with the two high pressure cylinders on one side of the locomotive and the two low pressure on the other. At that time the driver's view over the large diameter boilers then coming into use was worrying locomotive designers. For this reason the boiler of this locomotive was reversed on the frames and the driver's cab put at the front. Coal was carried in side bunkers and water in the tank wagon at the rear.

B

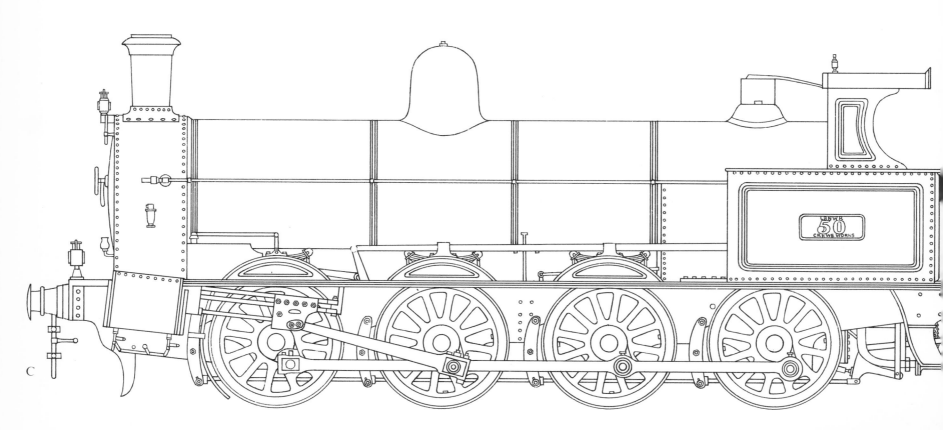

C

The four-coupled locomotive design was especially useful for hauling passenger trains, but it could also work freight trains readily and efficiently enough should the circumstances require it.

National design characteristics influenced the appearance of the various four-coupled locomotive types with a leading axle. Great Britain on the whole used inside frames combined with inside cylinders, although outside cylinder locomotive types were quite common, especially for export. In France the type had outside cylinders, inside frames, and usually had a long boiler. Following Crampton's practice, the valve gear was often outside the wheels. Germany, Austria, and Hungary followed the long boiler type as well, but the ancestry was quite different for their locomotives were derived from the Norris locomotives with a leading bogie. In Austria the bogies were actually removed from some American-built locomotives and a single leading axle substituted. From the 1860s outside frames were usual in Central Europe to improve stability on the track. Furthermore, it was not until the late 1870s that locomotives were built in quantity with the valve gear outside the frames. In this way locomotives that were built for much the same sort of service in the various countries differed radically in appearance.

The railway carriages for the earliest railways were adaptations of the road carriage. Indeed several lines provided flat wagons on which passengers' own road carriages were secured for a railway journey. Comfortable carriages proper were provided for first-class passengers, second-class passengers had a roof over their heads but as often as not the sides of the vehicle were open with perhaps a stout curtain to give protection from the weather. The luckless third-class got only benches in open wagons for their journeys. By the 1840s true railway carriages had evolved, closed in for all classes. Those in Europe were generally of the compartment type but in the United States the saloon coach was general. This was because such saloons could be heated by one or two stoves in winter and for the same reason the lower railway classes often had saloon coaches in Central Europe. Railway carriages in Europe were generally four-wheelers but again the United States differed. The very rough American tracks necessitated the development of eight-wheeled bogie coaches (on pivoted trucks). The *Victory* of 1836, built by Imlay in Philadelphia, was one of the first such coaches. Thus American "cars" quickly acquired a recognizable silhouette from the long body and the high clerestory.

During the 1830s lighting was provided by vegetable oil lamps in the compartments and a little later some heating was provided for the same compartments by the placing of near boiling cans of water on the floor. By the 1850s some six-wheel coaches were appearing in Europe and by the 1870s the bogie coach had crossed the Atlantic. From the 1830s trains travelled at night and some improvised sleeping arrangements were made. The first purpose-built sleeping-car was devised by George Pullman for the Chicago & Alton Railroad in 1859. Pullman sleepers of this sort came to Britain and Italy in 1873. The Great Western Railway of Canada appears to have run the first restaurant car in 1867 and such vehicles came to England in 1879.

The last mention of the British passenger locomotive was of the single-driver and of four-coupled locomotives with a leading pair of carrying wheels. The first express train four-coupled, inside cylinder, locomotive with a leading bogie was built for the North British Railway in 1871, the first of what was to become a characteristically British locomotive type. She was designed by Thomas Wheatley and she was the unlucky locomotive that dropped to the bottom of the Firth when the Tay bridge was blown down in 1879. She was salvaged and ran again until 1913. From the 1870s many British railways had the inside cylinder version of this wheel arrangement and a few the outside cylinder, the latter type being widely built for export.

Until the end of the nineteenth century locomotive boilers in Britain were of a comparatively small diameter, until the Caledonian Railway put the *Dunalastair* into service in 1897. Compared with the standards of that time she had a large boiler, although since then even larger diameter boilers have dwarfed this boiler to the modern eye. Besides running on the Caledonian Railway, locomotives of this John McIntosh design were also built for the Belgian State Railways. In the United States the standard American type was improved from 1894 by the addition of a trailing pair of carrying wheels, which allowed a much larger firebox to be carried. The type arrived in England on the Lancashire & Yorkshire Railway (with inside cylinders) and Henry Ivatt built the outside cylinder Atlantic type for the Great Northern Railway from 1898 on. A few years later in 1902 this great Northern design was improved by the application of a really large diameter boiler and the day of the massive express locomotive had arrived in Great Britain.

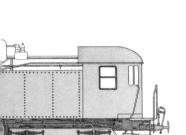

C WEBB'S COMPOUND

In the compound locomotive the steam exhausted from one cylinder (or cylinders) is diverted into another cylinder (or cylinders) for use a second time before being exhausted up the chimney. John Nicholson first tried the idea on two locomotives in England, 1851—1852, and Anatole Mallet built the first successful compound design in France in 1876. Francis Webb on the English London & North Western Railway was a champion of compounding and the freight locomotive shown here is a three-cylinder compound built at Crewe in 1893. Boiler steam was fed to the two outside cylinders and both exhausted into the large low pressure inside cylinder.

LATER LOCOMOTIVE DEVELOPMENT

A

Freight locomotives required a number of driving axles and smaller diameter driving wheels to give them the maximum adhesion and power for heavy loads. This was in contrast with passenger locomotives that had large diameter driving wheels in order to reduce the number of strokes made by the pistons each minute when traveling at high speed. Reducing the number of strokes made it easier for the steam to get into and out of the cylinders. Thus, an eight-coupled freight locomotive (the Q6 class of the London & North Eastern Railway in Britain) could not be made to run faster than 40 mph (64.4 km/h) on trial because steam could not get in and out of the cylinders quickly enough. Nevertheless, it was a highly satisfactory slow speed freight locomotive. During the last years of the steam locomotive the design of the steam passages to and from the cylinders was greatly improved and for this reason modern locomotives with small diameter driving wheels could run at much higher speeds than before.

The advance from four-coupled freight locomotives to six-coupled and eight-coupled has already been recorded. Ten-coupled locomotives became common in the United States at the end of the nineteenth century and a little later they became common elsewhere. The exception was the twelve-coupled locomotive, but in Russia there was a solitary fourteen-coupled locomotive with a carrying bogie at each end built in 1934 and not a success. Powerful locomotives require a large boiler to provide the necessary steam and another reason for many driving wheels was to enable the weight of the boiler to be spread over a greater length of the track. Many driving axles tended to increase the rigid length of the locomotive and there was difficulty in negotiating curves, hence the development of articulated locomotive types

in which the driving wheels were divided between two or more trucks. In America and continental Europe, the Mallet compound was the best known of the articulated locomotives while a wholly British type although mostly used outside Britain was the Garratt.

As railways spread far and wide over the world the men who built and operated them tended to come from Europe and the United States. Thus, it was quite common that home railway practice in every detail was simply transferred to a foreign land, especially in the colonial countries. A railway built by the French at the turn of the century in the Yunnan province of China would have been perfectly at home in Provence, solidly Dutch railways served Java, and an American-built line at a copper mine in Cyprus would have excited no comment in Colorado. This last American line had a junction with a British government railway, a line that could have served Scotland or Ireland equally well.

The great subcontinent of India had British railways throughout and even today in India and Pakistan the British steam railway practices of a bygone age linger on, just as both countries are the last home of former British social customs and practices. The first railway opened between Bombay and Thana in 1852, and was the start of the huge Great Indian Peninsula Railway system. The same year the East Indian Railway opened its first section at Calcutta and other lines soon followed. The gauge of the railways was 5 ft. 6 in. and British four-coupled locomotives with a leading axle were used, together with a few single-drivers. As British locomotive designs at home grew larger so did those for Indian railways. A famous Indian design built from the early years of the twentieth century was the Mail Engine, a six-coupled type with a leading bogie used by all the broad-gauge railways. For secondary rail-

A THE "WAGONS-LITS" BADGE
The symbol of the Compagnie Internationale des Wagons-Lits et des Grands Express Européens *was the sign of luxury and comfort in sleeping cars throughout Europe.*

B SLEEPING CAR, 1868
The great Cie. Internationale des Wagons-Lits et des Grands Express Européens *was founded by a Belgian named George Nagelmackers and shown here is one of his early sleeping cars, a vehicle that was exhibited at the* Paris Exposition *of 1868. Outside Germany (which has a similar company of its own) the Wagons-Lits people owned and operated sleeping cars, restaurant cars, and luxury vehicles on European railways for one hundred years or more.*

C SLEEPING CAR, 1970
A modern Wagons-Lits sleeping car is here shown as running today. The Wagons-Lits company ceased to own rolling stock in 1971, the existing cars being taken over by the various railways, and it now confines itself to supplying staff, food, and linen for their former property.

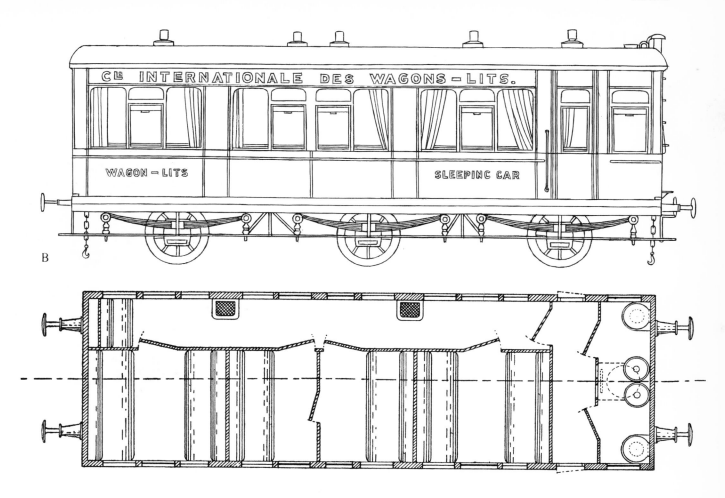

B

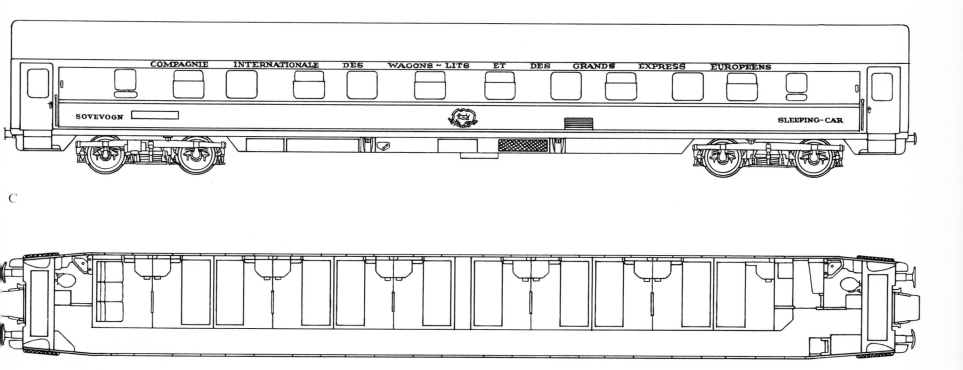

C

ways in India the meter gauge was used at first, for in the early 1870s when they were started all India was to change to the metric system. Later many meter-gauge lines developed into substantial railways in their own right and secondary railways came to be built with the even narrower gauge of 2 ft. 6 in.

Apart from some experimental or suggested battery-powered vehicles, the effective start of electric railways dates from 1879. In that year Werner von Siemens displayed a little electric locomotive (the driver sat astride the body) at the Berlin Trades Exhibition and used it to haul passengers about the grounds. In 1881 a Berlin tramway was run by electricity and in 1883 Volks Electric Railway opened along Brighton beach (it is still working) together with the Giant's Causeway & Portrush Railway in Ireland. The last line used water-generated electric power, using a modest fall of 24 ft. (c. 7 m) in the River Bush. Other little railways swiftly followed all over Europe and the United States. Among them was the world's first deep-level underground railway—the City & South London Railway opened in 1890. The line was only made possible by electric traction and it is now incorporated in London Transport's Northern Line. The Baltimore & Ohio Railroad in the United States opened the world's first main line electrification in 1895, through a short tunnel under the city of Baltimore.

All these early electric railways used low voltage direct current (300—650 volts) as the necessary apparatus was simple and cheap. On the other hand, it is most economical to generate and transmit electricity using three-phase alternating current at as high a voltage as possible. Attempts were made to use three-phase alternating current and the first line thus electrified was between Burgdorf and Thun in Switzerland in 1899. No less than 1,240 miles (1,996 km) of railway were later three-phase electrified in Italy, starting from 1901. There were difficulties: two overhead wires were needed (insulated from one another), while a three-phase electric motor by its nature will only run at a single constant speed after acceleration. This last difficulty was overcome by using two electric motors in each locomotive and varying the electric circuits so that two or four speeds were obtained for the locomotive.

Basically single phase alternating current is obtained by picking out two wires of the three in three-phase circuits. Experiments in using single phase for railway electrification started in Germany in 1901 and in the following year an experimental single phase rail-

A EAST AFRICAN GARRATT
A Garratt articulated locomotive of the East African Railways. In these locomotives the driving wheels are in two separate bogies at either end and the boiler is carried on a cradle between them. Jointed pipes carry the steam from the boiler to the cylinders and the exhaust back again to the chimney. The locomotives were particularly popular for curving and steeply graded lines in territories outside Europe and North America.

B UNION PACIFIC 9000 CLASS
These 9000 class twelve-coupled locomotives were built for the Union Pacific Railroad in the United States in 1926, and were the largest nonarticulated locomotives to be built there. They had three cylinders all taking boiler steam, for it would have been difficult to have found room for a pair of cylinders sufficiently large to deal with the high power output.

C RUSSIAN FREIGHT LOCOMOTIVE
The Soviet Union Railways Class E ten-coupled locomotive was the most numerous steam locomotive type in the world—over ten thousand were built with detail alterations over successive batches for forty years. Apart from all the Russian locomotive works, the class was also built by manufacturers in Sweden, Germany, and Hungary. The particular locomotive in the illustration was built in Sweden in 1920 and it shows the rugged nature of the design; many of the locomotives are still in service.

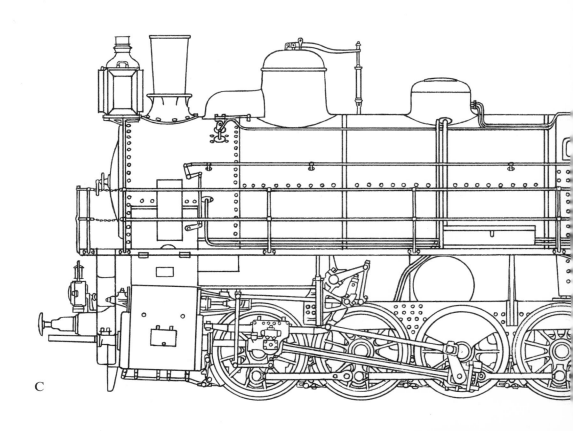

C

A

B

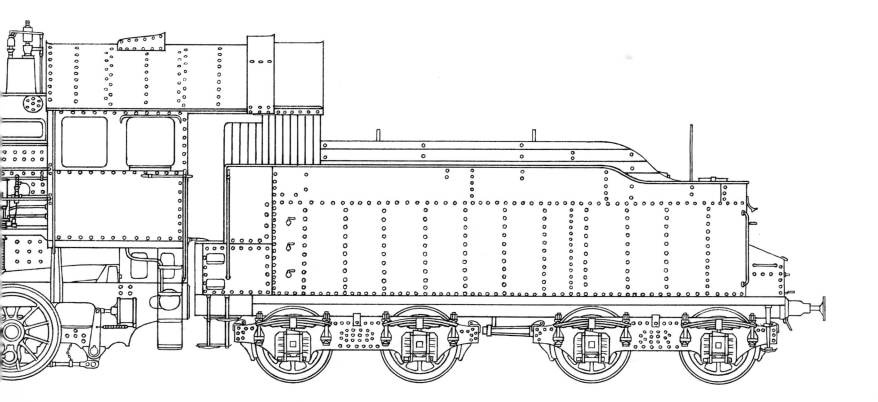

A

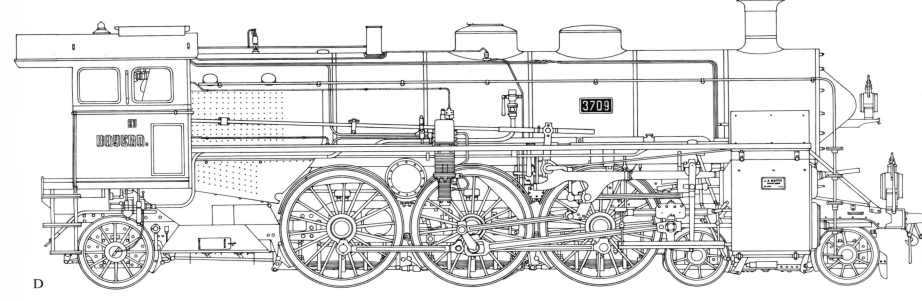

D

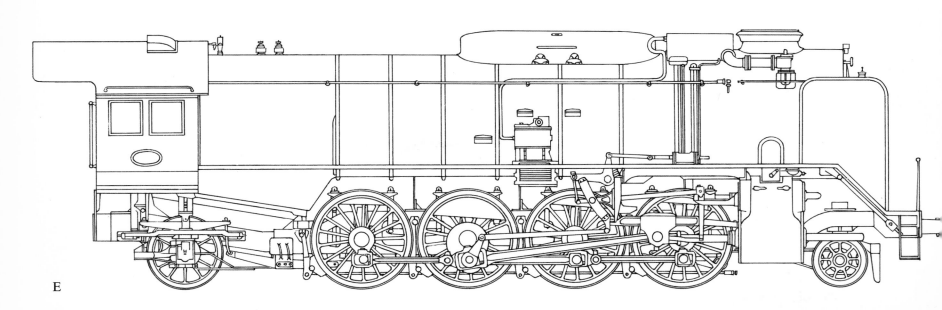

E

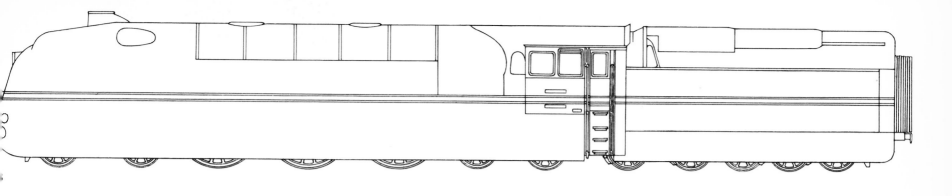

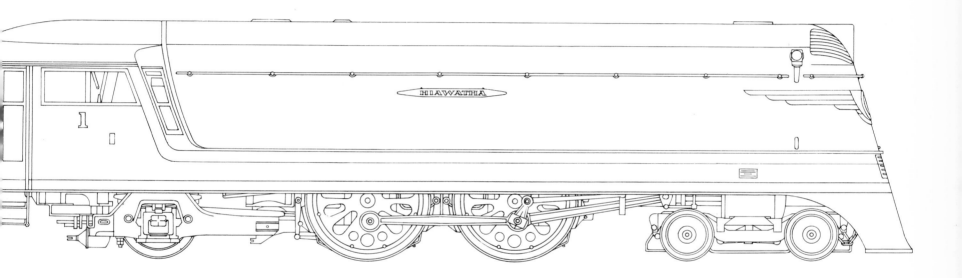

A SIR RALPH WEDGWOOD
The streamlined Pacific class A4 of the London & North Eastern Railway in England first appeared in 1937. Sir Ralph Wedgwood reached 100 mph (160 km/h). Later, another of the class Mallard *reached 126 mph (202.8 km/h), the highest authenticated speed reached by the steam locomotive.*

B GERMAN STATE HUDSON, 1935
Streamlining of locomotives also spread to continental European railways in the 1930s, as is demonstrated by this German State Railways locomotive. Two of these were built by Borsig and one of them achieved a speed of 124.5 mph (200.4 km/h).

C HIAWATHA
During the 1930s high-speed locomotives were given streamlined casings, or as in this example they were air-smoothed. The Chicago Milwaukee St. Paul & Pacific Railroad ran a train called the Hiawatha *hauled by these Atlantic locomotives, which regularly traveled at 100 mph (160 km/h) or over during the course of their duties. To aid high speed, the trains were light by American standards and thus within the capacity of the Atlantic type.*

D BAVARIAN STATE S 3/6
The S 3/6 class Pacific locomotive type of the Bavarian State Railways was first built in 1908, one of the earliest European Pacifics. The design was so successful

that more of them were built down to 1931, the last batches under the auspices of the German State Railways. The design was a four-cylinder compound and was unusual in Europe in having bar frames.

E BELGIAN STATE TYPE 5
On a previous page the first locomotive of the Mikado type was illustrated. Here is a European example built for the Belgian State Railways in 1930 to work passenger trains over the heavily graded main line from Brussels southeast to Namur and the Luxembourg border at Arlon. Unusual for a European locomotive, bar frames were provided, otherwise typical of American locomotive practice.

way electrification between Seebach and Wettingen in Switzerland was opened to traffic. Single phase alternating current quickly showed its superiority to three-phase for main line railway electrifications; for one thing unlike the latter, only a single wire was required above the track and the complications above points and crossings were avoided. The single phase electric motor provided for a variable range of locomotive speeds when required instead of being limited to at most four as with the three-phase system. On the other hand the traction motors were more complicated and required more maintenance, while supplying power was rather more expensive.

Overall single phase was cheaper than three-phase and it became the preferred electrification system for much of Europe, as well as for the Penn-Central Railroad in the United States. Today Austria, Switzerland, Germany, Sweden, and Norway all have single phase electrification systems. About 1915 a piece of apparatus called the mercury arc rectifier was developed to convert alternating three-phase current to direct current and as a result from about 1920 to about 1953 it was most economical to electrify main line railways with high voltage direct current, usually 3,000 volts or perhaps 1,500 volts for lines with very heavy traffic. Countries where railways were electrified with high voltage direct current are France, Belgium, Holland, Italy, Czechoslovakia, South Africa, and many others. It should be noted that the original low voltage direct current system still remained the most economical way of electrifying short railways not more than twelve miles (c. 19 km) long (it still is cheapest today) which is why all metropolitan and city underground railways use this system.

Single phase and three-phase electrified railways use alternating current of a special low frequency (frequency is the number of times the current alternates in each second). To convert from high industrial frequency (the frequency at which the current is generated) to railway frequency results in energy losses and hence greater operating expense. Before 1914 there had been one or two industrial frequency electrified railways of a tramway character, but they only worked because the locomotives were of very low horsepower. The problem of designing an industrial frequency locomotive for main line duties was taken up by Kálmán Kandó from 1917. He was a Hungarian who among other things had been responsible for introducing three-phase railway electrification into Italy from 1901. His first industrial frequency locomotive ran successful trials

outside Budapest in 1923. Between 1932 and 1934 the 116 miles (187 km) of rail from Budapest to the Austrian border at Hegyshalom were electrified at industrial frequency. Kandó's locomotives used electromechanical means to convert industrial frequency single phase current to three-, four-, and six-phase current for the traction motors. This was complicated and, although the system costs overall were cheaper than single phase, it could not compete with high voltage direct current electrifications.

The Germans started the search for improved industrial frequency locomotives in 1934, followed by the Russians in 1938 and by the French after the Second World War. The modern industrial frequency locomotive operating at 25,000 volts single phase, in which the alternating current is converted to direct current by a mercury arc rectifier that feeds the direct current traction motors, was perfected by the French by 1952. Industrial frequency is now the cheapest electrification method for main line railways and it is used in many countries. Since then many improvements have been made, among them the solid state electronic rectifier (first used by British Railways in 1955) and the electronic thyristor conversion and control of single phase current for direct current motors—used in both French locomotives and German motor coaches from 1970.

The internal-combustion engine in the form of the gasoline engine was first applied to rail motive power in the late 1880s and gasoline-driven railcars had a vogue in the early twentieth century, the largest vehicles running in the United States. The first commercial diesel locomotive was supplied by Richard Hornsby & Company of Grantham, England, to Woolwich Arsenal in 1896. As Rudolph Diesel, who developed his engine in Germany, worked for rivals of Hornsby, the machine was carefully called an oil engine locomotive and the word diesel as a description was not admitted by Hornsby's successors until fully seventy years later. The slow running diesel engine of the locomotive drove a flywheel and power to the wheels was transmitted through a gearbox. Gearbox transmission has been used for small locomotives and railcars ever since, but it is unsuitable for horsepowers much above 400 or so, even when assisted by modern fluid couplings to break the greater shocks from the wheels. Alternatively the diesel engine can drive a dynamo to provide direct current for electric traction motors. This type of transmission was pioneered on small gasoline railcars from the turn of the century and the first diesel application was in a small

railcar built for the Swedish State Railways in 1912. The electric transmission is now used by the majority of the world's diesel locomotives.

The diesel hydraulic appeared rather later and the first were built in Germany and Austria in 1924. They had what is known as hydrostatic transmission in which the diesel engine pumps oil round a circuit, and the oil drives a second pump in reverse, that in turn is connected to the wheels. The trouble was that very high pressures developed in the oil circuit and there were plenty of leaks. The hydrokinetic transmissions used today were developed in Sweden and Germany in the 1930s. The first German diesel-hydraulic shunting locomotive appeared in 1932 and their first main line locomotive in 1934.

In the conventional diesel-electric locomotive the diesel engine drives a dynamo that produces direct current for the traction motors. In France in 1965 two diesel-electric locomotives were built (the CC 70000 class), which generated alternating current that was then changed by an electronic rectifier to direct current for the traction motors. At first sight this looks like extra apparatus, but in fact a generator is cheaper to build than a dynamo and requires less maintenance so overall these locomotives are more economic. The French National Railways has had a number of 3,600 horsepower diesel-electric locomotives of this type since 1968, the CC 72000 class. In Britain the alternator 4,000 horsepower trial locomotive *Kestrel* was built in 1968 (since sold to Russia) and British Rail's 41 class appeared in 1972. The 2,700 horsepower alternator M63 class was built for the Hungarian State Railways in Hungary in 1971.

A trial locomotive *Hawk* was built in Great Britain in 1965 in which an electronic current inverter was installed. The current inverter was necessarily fed with direct current and the three-phase alternating output powered three-phase traction motors which are cheaper than the normal traction motor. A diesel engine was used to generate three-phase current which was changed to direct current by an electronic rectifier. The whole arrangement was cheaper than using the generated three-phase current straightaway in the traction motors. Unfortunately, the electronic current inverter was not satisfactory and the locomotive would not work. The Germans started to develop their own electronic current inverter in 1965 and in 1971 produced a 2,500 horsepower diesel-electric locomotive similar to the British attempt. This has been a success and three more have been built, known as the German Federal

A

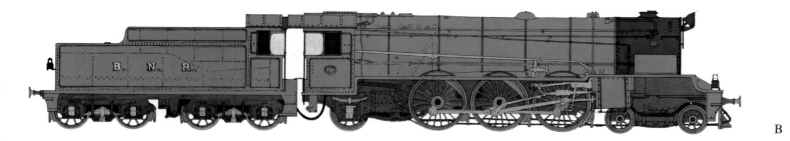

B

C

A RENFE 3100 CLASS
The largest freight locomotive of the Spanish National Railways System (RENFE) was the 3100 class introduced in 1943. They were three-cylinder ten-coupled locomotives with front and rear carrying axles. They were heavy with a maximum load on one axle of 21 tons, thus only certain lines were built solidly enough to carry them.

B DE GLEHN COMPOUND
This Pacific locomotive was built in Britain in 1936 for the Bengal-Nagpur Railway. Although it has a typically British appearance, it is a four-cylinder compound of the French de Glehn system and nothing like it ran on a British railway. About the same time a four-cylinder compound Pacific was designed for the London Midland & Scottish Railway, but this design was never built.

C BARSI LIGHT LOCOMOTIVE
Even the 2 ft. 6 in. gauge railways in India called for substantial locomotive designs and this six-coupled passenger locomotive with fore-and-aft bogies was built in England in 1940 for the Barsi Light Railway. This was the only 2 ft. 6 in. gauge locomotive design with this wheel arrangement in the world, although in both America and Europe impressive standard gauge express locomotives were of a similar type.

A

B

C

D

Railway 202 class. An advantage of both thyristor controlled electric locomotives and current inverter diesel locomotives is that they are fully automated; the driver uses only one lever to both accelerate and slow down. This automation helps experimental automatic train operation from the lineside without a driver on the locomotive.

The first experimental small locomotive powered by a gas turbine ran in Sweden from 1934. This was small enough for a mechanical transmission, but for all motive power of any size either an electrical or a hydraulic transmission is necessary. Switzerland was next with a gas turbine-electric locomotive in 1941 and during the 1950s half a dozen countries built large gas turbine locomotives for trial purposes. Only in the United States was the power mode taken up and the Union Pacific Railroad had a fleet of fifty-six gas turbine-electrics at one period. All the locomotives suffered from the same snag; the gas turbine is only fully efficient

at maximum output, whereas a locomotive only needs to work at maximum output for a small part of the time. The Union Pacific on the long grades of the Rocky Mountains and other mountain ranges pushed up the length of the periods of maximum output, but the other railways found that they wasted fuel in large amounts.

The gas turbine has one great advantage over the diesel engine—it produces far more power for a given weight of machinery. Railcar train sets for very high speeds must be light to reduce wear and tear on the track and the gas turbine was the choice for their power unit. In the United States the gas turbine-electric turbotrains produced in 1965 have had a rather checkered career; they have not lived up to their first promise. In France gas turbine-hydraulic train sets were built from 1970 with a maximum speed of 100 mph (160 km/h) which are running regularly on the Paris-Caen service. At the end of 1972 a French prototype gas turbine-

hydraulic train set went into service which has a designed maximum speed of 174.5 mph (280 km/h). Two gas turbine-electric train sets appeared during 1972 as well, British Rail's Advanced Passenger Train, and a French 185 mph (300 km/h) prototype train set that has reached 197.5 mph (317.8 km/h) during trials.

Almost as soon as the conventional railway established itself men were proposing alternatives. The monorail arrived over one hundred years ago and among later proposals are the Bennie monorail of 1920 in which the car was driven by an airscrew at speeds of up to 200 mph (322 km/h) and the Alweg monorail of the 1950s. This latter ran astride a concrete beam and a short Hitachi-Alweg line has been in operation between Tokyo and an airport since 1964. A tramway suspended monorail has been in successful operation in Wuppertal for nearly seventy years and it has recently acquired electronically-controlled rolling stock.

A SWEDISH STATE RC3 CLASS
The Swedish State Railways were the first to take single phase alternating current from the overhead wire and feed it to direct current traction motors through electronic thyristor circuits in 1965. The thyristors not only convert alternating current to direct current but also offer an easy way of controlling the current to regulate the locomotive's speed. Over one hundred of the thyristor locomotive type shown here are now in service in Sweden.

B CITY & SOUTH LONDON ELECTRIC
This locomotive was used on the world's first electrified city railway, the City & South London Railway opened in 1890.

The open cab for the driver on the locomotive was complemented by almost windowless passenger compartments, the argument being that the passengers could see nothing in the tunnels in any case. A conductor announced the names of the stations to each parlor car.

C SEEBACH-WETTINGEN NO. 1
Locomotive No. 1 of the Swiss Seebach-Wettingen experimental single phase electrified railway, 1902. Current from the overhead wire was used to drive an electric motor on the locomotive which in turn drove a dynamo to generate direct current for the traction motors. The locomotive worked well, but generating elec-

tric current twice in this manner, once in the power station and once on the locomotive, is inherently uneconomic and costly. Thus the method was abandoned and has been only rarely revived since.

D SIEMENS'S ELECTRIC
Werner von Siemens's pioneer electric locomotive for the Berlin Trades Exhibition in 1879. A very low voltage third rail was used to supply electric power. In later lines with a higher voltage the third rail electrified lines had to be fenced in or an overhead wire was used slung up out of harm's way.

A

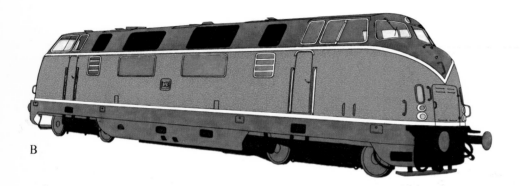

B

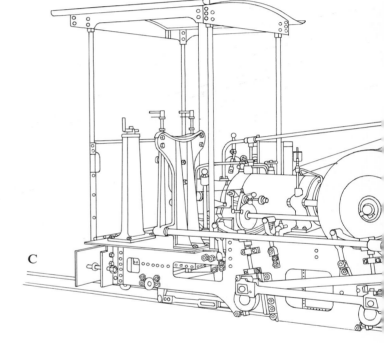

C

Today the hovertrain is proposed, in which the car is carried on a concrete beam by an air pad and is driven by a linear electric motor. Trial cars exist in Britain, France, and the United States but it now looks as if the idea will be uneconomical in practice. Even newer is the magnetic levitation mode in which the car is made to rise from the ground by the controlled force of opposed magnets and is then driven forward by a linear electric motor. Trial cars exist in Japan and Germany. Both these modes propose speeds of up to 300 mph (480 km/h) and both are made possible by the application of recent developments in technology. Unfortunately for the modes mentioned above the same new technology can be equally applied to the improvement of existing railways. British Rail has seriously proposed a 250 mph (400 km/h) railway between London and a new airport at Maplin, using their Advanced Passenger Train powered by a linear electric motor. Such a conventional line may very well be cheaper than the unorthodox modes for high speeds. Trains running on the earth's surface by the way will not run much faster than 300 mph (480 km/h) because of air resistance—any higher speed will call for so much extra power that it will not be worthwhile to do it.

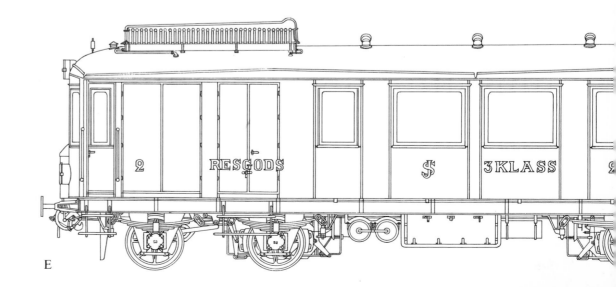

E

A NORTHERN PACIFIC V25C TYPE
A General Electric Co. (United States) heavy duty diesel-electric "hood" locomotive for freight and passenger work built in 1963. As was usual in America at this time it only has a 2,000 horsepower engine and two or more locomotives are put on a train in control of one driver if required. Nevertheless this same locomotive model was built in 1962 with a 2,500 horsepower engine and four-wheel bogies, a start to the gradual increase in power of American locomotives.

B GERMAN STATE V200 CLASS
This German Federal Railway V200 class (now 220 class) diesel-hydraulic locomotive was built in 1954 with two engines totaling 2,200 horsepower. A later version, the 221 class, is 2,500 horsepower and locomotives based on the design have also been built in Great Britain and in Italy for the national railway systems.

C HORNSBY'S DIESEL, 1896
The world's pioneer commercial diesel locomotive possessed a mechanical transmission and was built by Richard Hornsby & Co. of Grantham, England, in 1896. It worked (in fits and starts by all reports) at the army Woolwich Arsenal in London.

D GERMAN STATE 202 CLASS
The 202 class current inverter diesel-electric locomotive of the German Federal Railway built in 1971. The external appearance of the locomotive is explained because it was designed as a standard for export and the body will fit any railway with a gauge of one meter (39.37 in.)

upward. The buffer beams are readily detachable for example, and a different buffer beam with a center coupler can be quickly fitted.

E SWEDISH STATE DIESEL-ELECTRIC, 1912
This little pioneer diesel-electric railcar was built for the Swedish State Railways in 1912. A diesel engine and a dynamo were housed in a comparment of the coach body.

F KESTREL
The trial diesel-electric locomotive Kestrel built in Great Britain in 1968 by Brush Electrical Machines with a 4,000 horsepower diesel engine. After extensive running on British Rail the locomotive was sent to an exhibition in Russia and was then sold to the Soviet Union Railways. The Russians had built a twin diesel-electric locomotive with two 3,000 horsepower engines in 1971, also incorporating an alternating current generator as installed in Kestrel.

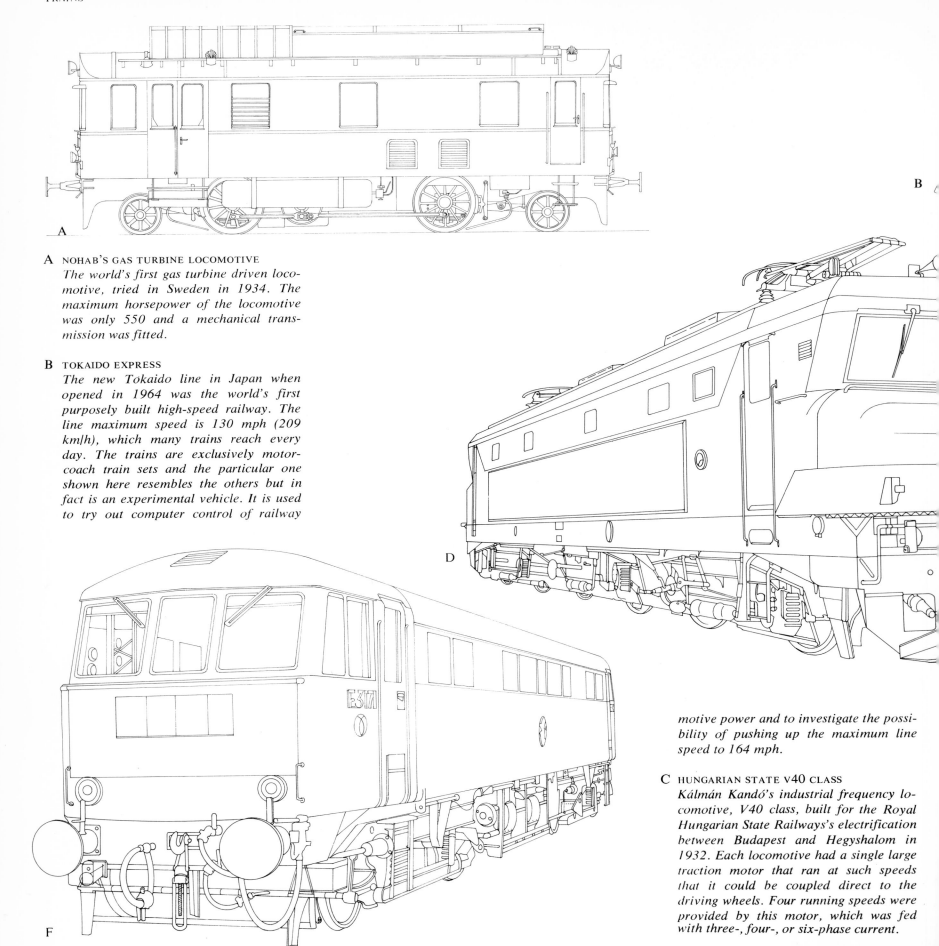

A NOHAB'S GAS TURBINE LOCOMOTIVE
*The world's first gas turbine driven loco-
motive, tried in Sweden in 1934. The
maximum horsepower of the locomotive
was only 550 and a mechanical transmission was fitted.*

B TOKAIDO EXPRESS
*The new Tokaido line in Japan when
opened in 1964 was the world's first
purposely built high-speed railway. The
line maximum speed is 130 mph (209
km/h), which many trains reach every
day. The trains are exclusively motor-
coach train sets and the particular one
shown here resembles the others but in
fact is an experimental vehicle. It is used
to try out computer control of railway*

*motive power and to investigate the possi-
bility of pushing up the maximum line
speed to 164 mph.*

C HUNGARIAN STATE V40 CLASS
*Kálmán Kandó's industrial frequency lo-
comotive, V40 class, built for the Royal
Hungarian State Railways's electrification
between Budapest and Hegyshalom in
1932. Each locomotive had a single large
traction motor that ran at such speeds
that it could be coupled direct to the
driving wheels. Four running speeds were
provided by this motor, which was fed
with three-, four-, or six-phase current.*

D BRITISH RAIL 86 CLASS

British Rail's class 86 industrial frequency electric locomotive is on the electrified railways northward from London to Liverpool, Manchester, and Glasgow. Many trains hauled by these locomotives have been running each day at the maximum permitted speed of 100 mph (106.9 km/h). This has led to increased track maintenance costs, and the development of both improved track and improved locomotive suspension is now in hand.

E NORTH AMERICAN TURBOTRAIN

One of the United States's turbotrains built from 1965 with gas turbine-electric propulsion. The coaches were in effect suspended from points near their roofs, so that when rounding curves they can swing out under centrifugal force and so cushion the curving effects for the passengers. Unfortunately, unpowered tilting of this sort is too slow to be fully effective and in trains built in other countries powered tilting was adopted.

F SOUTH KOREAN BO-BO ELECTRIC

A European group won the contract for the electrification at industrial frequency of part of the South Korean Railways. This is the locomotive design supplied to South Korea from 1972, in which thyristors provide for the conversion to direct current and for the current control. French and Belgian manufacturers built the locomotives.

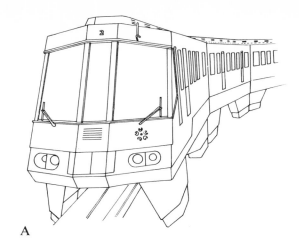

A

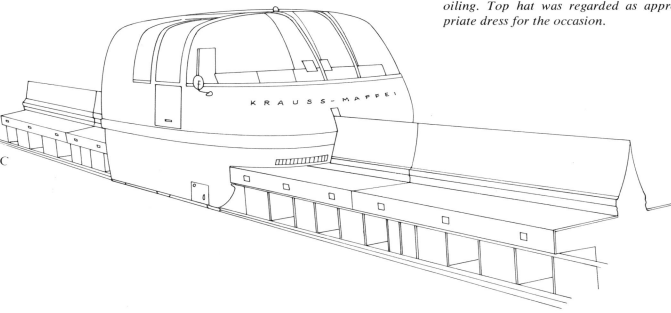

B

C

(Opposite)

A ROCKET

The directors of the Liverpool & Manchester Railway heard disquieting stories of the unreliability of the Stockton & Darlington's steam locomotives. Thus, they arranged a test of the latest steam locomotive types before their railway opened to traffic—the Rainhill trials of 1829. The winning locomotive design was the famous Rocket *built by Robert Stephenson & Co. She was the first locomotive with a multitubular boiler, with which was combined an exhaust steam blast up the chimney. Steaming of the boiler was vastly improved. When it was opened in 1830 the Liverpool & Manchester had eight locomotives of the* Rocket *type, the later ones improved in various minor ways.*

B WORKING ON THE NORTHUMBRIAN

George and Robert Stephenson, father and son, were undoubtedly the greatest railway and locomotive pioneers of their time. In this drawing (after Alexander Nasmyth) we see them working on the Northumbrian *shortly before the opening of the Liverpool and Manchester Railway. Robert is firing while his father is oiling. Top hat was regarded as appropriate dress for the occasion.*

A HITACHI-ALWEG MONORAIL

The Hitachi-Alweg monorail in Tokyo runs out to an airport. The car runs on driven rubber-tired wheels on top of a concrete beam and it is guided by further rubber-tired wheels bearing against the sides of the beam. The system is capable of high speed but on this particular line high speeds are not attempted.

B BRITISH HOVERTRAIN

The British hovertrain experimental vehicle. In this version of the hovertrain the car rests on an air pad on top of a concrete beam, and further air pads bear against the sides of the beam to guide the vehicle. A linear electric motor is used for propulsion.

C GERMAN MAGNETIC LEVITATION TRAIN

A German experimental magnetic levitation vehicle. Electromagnets on the vehicle draw the car upward toward the angle-iron rails—the vehicle in this case is light enough for this to be sufficient. Further magnets guide the car between the uprights of the rails and propulsion is by linear electric motor.

A

NORTHUMBRIAN

B

A *William Hedley believed in adhesion and after making experiments with a hand-driven model he built two locomotives in 1813 for a colliery plateway near Newcastle, England. Both the model and the first locomotive, the* Puffing Billy, *are in the Science Museum in London, while the second locomotive, the* Wylam Dilly, *is preserved in Edinburgh, Scotland.*

B *The first steam locomotive to be used commercially worked on the Middleton Railway, a colliery line, at Leeds, England. It was built by Matthew Murray and John Blenkinsop in 1812, the latter having doubts about adhesion. Surely, he thought, a smooth iron wheel pushing at a smooth iron rail would lose adhesion and slip should the haulage of heavy loads be attempted. So he devised a rack rail along which the locomotive propelled itself by means of a cogwheel.*

PUFFING BILLY

A

BLENKINSOP'S RACK LOCOMOTIVE

C This locomotive was the first to be built in the works of August Borsig in the Berlin suburb of Tegel in 1841. The design clearly shows the influence of the American Norris locomotives, except that a pair of carrying wheels has been added behind the drivers for steadier running. The locomotive worked on the Berlin-Anhalt Railway.

BORSIG NO. 1

B

C

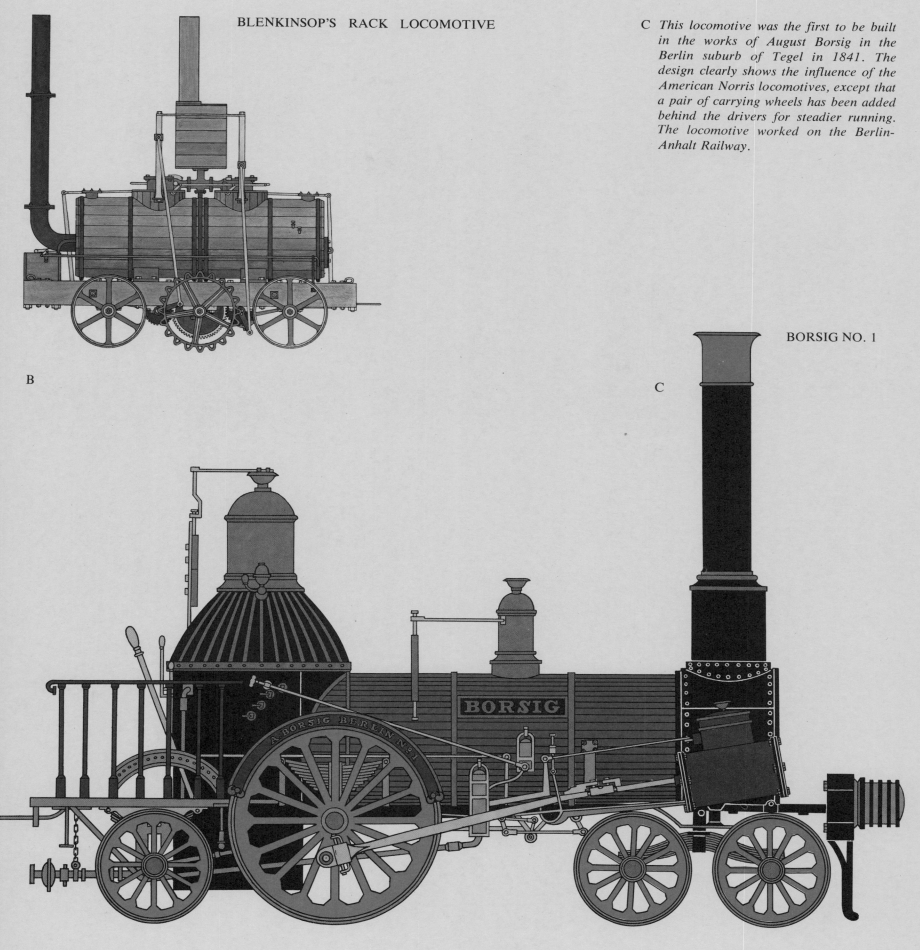

THOMAS ROGERS

A

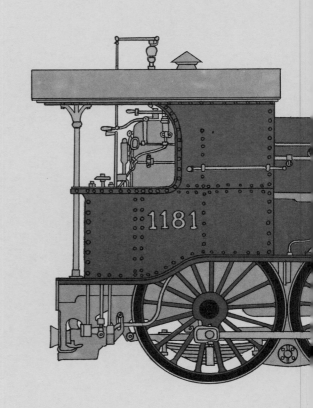

A *The American locomotive type in all its glory. Thomas Rogers was built by the Rogers Locomotive Works, Paterson, New Jersey, in 1860. Among other features typical of United States's locomotive practice, the sloped transition from the top of the boiler barrel to the top of the firebox may be noted—a locomotive boiler type known as the wagon top.*

B *This design was patented by M. N. Forney in 1866 and the example shown was built for the New York & Harlem Railroad about 1870. Tank engines were quite rare in the United States. Basically, this type is an 0-4-0 tender engine on a continuous rigid frame which also carried the tender, supported at the rear end by a bogie. Coal and water were carried in the tender portion, deferring to the standard American criticism of tank engines that their adhesive weight dwindled as the water was used.*

FORNEY 0-4-4-T

B

VITTORIO EMANUELE II

C

C Vittorio Emanuele II *was the first six-coupled tender locomotive with a leading bogie to run on a European railway. She was built by the Upper Italy Railways to work a 14$^1/_2$ mile gradient then building on a railway across the mountains behind Genoa. The date was 1884 and later on many more of the class were constructed. The type had long been known in the United States and it had been built previously in Europe for export.*

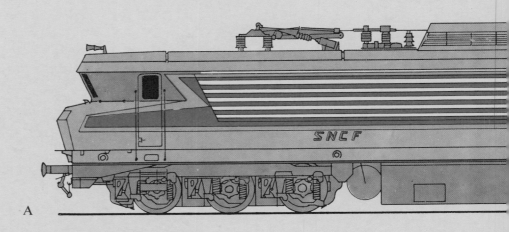

A

MIDI ELECTRIC

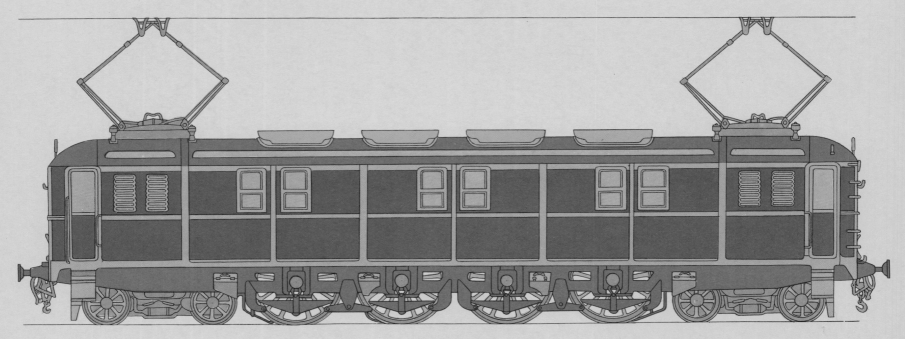

B

A *This is the latest French National Railways express locomotive for 1,500 volts direct current, built in 1968. No. CC 21001 is in fact arranged to run both on direct current and industrial frequency current as required, but there are many other locomotives of similar outward appearance for direct current only, No. CC 6501 upward.*

B *The French decided in principle to electrify suitable main line railways in 1917 and put their first 1,500 volts direct current electrifications into service in 1920. Here is an express locomotive for the Midi Railway built in 1923. The wheel arrangement is one that was widely used in France for thirty years afterward, but this particular design was not popular as it led to increased track maintenance.*

C *The world's first three-phase alternating current locomotive built for the Burgdorf-Thun Railway in 1899. The twin current collectors can be seen, one for each of the two overhead wires. Normally the two collectors were up together, the space between them bridging over the dead sections in the overhead wires where the latter crossed over each other above track points and crossings.*

SNCF NO. CC 21001

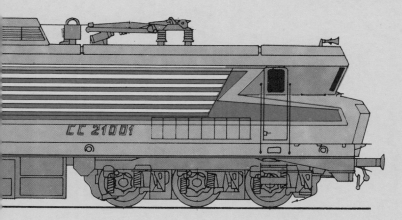

BURGDORF-THUN ELECTRIC

C

TGV 001

A The French National Railways prototype gas turbine-electric train set No. TGV 001 built in 1972. This train set has a designed maximum speed of 185 mph (297.7 km/h) and while on trial has reached 190.5 mph (306.6 km/h). The trial was made over a straight stretch of line for many miles south of Bordeaux where in 1955 an electric locomotive reached the world's record rail speed of 205.6 mph.

B British Rail's gas turbine-electric prototype Advanced Passenger Train built in 1972. The train is designed for a maximum speed of 155 mph (249.45 km/h) and possesses a tilting body. To maintain comfort a motorcyclist leans inward when rounding a curve and for the same reason this train has a powered lean for the coach bodies with respect to the trucks. This comes into action automatically as the train runs through curves.

A

ADVANCED PASSENGER TRAIN

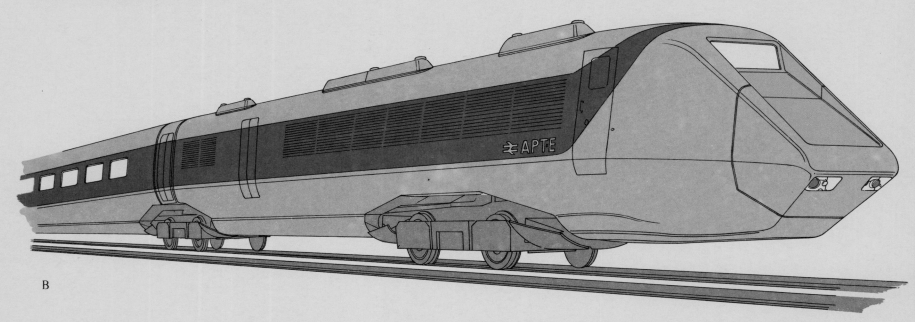

B

CARS

THE HORSELESS CARRIAGE

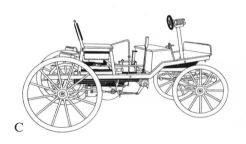

A

During the late eighteenth and early nineteenth centuries, travel by carriage and coaches became easier as better roads were built, and as the designers made lighter vehicles capable of going faster. Horse-drawn vehicles could only travel as fast as the horses could pull them, and teams of many animals were needed to move very heavy loads. The practical steam engine, invented by James Watt, a Scotsman, in the eighteenth century, was used for driving machinery and was developed later for the first railway engines. Many people tried to make steam road vehicles, but as they were very slow and heavy and the railways were so successful and popular, there was not much demand for mechanical road travel. One very early experiment in France was made by Nicolas Cugnot in 1770. His vehicle was designed to pull heavy guns for the army, but it could only travel at 4 mph (6.4 km/h), and it was very difficult to steer. William Murdock, who worked for James Watt, made a model steam car in 1784, but he did not perfect the idea. It was Richard Trevithick, a Cornish mining engineer, who built the first vehicle propelled by steam that was able to carry passengers, and he made at least two journeys on it in 1801. This very heavy carriage could travel at about 8 mph (12.8 km/h) on a straight, level road but, in common with all the early road vehicles, it was not very reliable.

Many more experiments followed and eventually the engines and the carriages were improved to such an extent that by 1832 Hancock was running his coach from London to Brighton, and journeys of over 100 miles (161 km) were becoming quite common. However, the cumbersome steam road vehicles were not very successful. They damaged the roads, were expensive to operate, relied upon the availability of coal and water along the route, and the cost to passengers

was more than the price for an equivalent journey by rail.

To make powered travel on roads really practical, a better, lighter engine was needed. It had to be one that did not have to carry a coal-fired boiler in order to raise steam, and it had to have a better power-to-weight ratio. This meant finding an engine that did not weigh so much that it only provided enough power to move itself and its carriage. From about 1860, some factory machinery had been driven by coal gas. This type of engine—the stationary gas engine invented and sold by a Frenchman named Etienne Lenoir—did not require its own boiler house to turn water into steam, it used coal gas from the local town supply which was piped to all streets and houses for lighting. Here was an engine which, if it could carry its own gas supply, would be better than a steam engine for driving vehicles on the roads.

Lenoir designed a surface vaporizer, or carburetor, which could convert liquid into gas by vaporization, and although he made a car, it was very slow and he did not develop the idea. Siegfried Markus, in Vienna, was one of the early pioneers, his gasoline-engined car of 1875 used a motor working on the 4-stroke cycle. Gasoline engines are really quite simple. To obtain the rotary motion necessary to drive the wheels of the vehicle, a piston, which is connected to a metal rod, travels up and down inside a cylinder. The end of the rod is attached to a crank on the shaft so that the movement of the piston can be converted into a circular motion. There can be up to twelve pistons all working on the same shaft, but most of the early motors had only one. Each movement of the piston up and down the cylinder completes a part of the cycle—suction, compression, explosion, exhaust. These four movements turn the shaft around twice.

C

A LENOIR'S GAS ENGINE
The picture shows a plan view of Lenoir's gas engine of 1860, which was the first to be a commercial success. A flywheel and crank on the left are joined to the piston by a jointed connecting rod. The engine was fairly quiet and did not require a boiler to raise steam, but only a means of connecting it to a gas supply. It is particularly important as being the type which Daimler was able to improve.

B DAIMLER, 1886
Gottlieb Daimler was born in Schorndorf on March 17, 1834. Like Benz, he had an aptitude for engineering and after thorough training in England and Germany he became a foreman of an engine building factory in Carlsruhe. In 1872

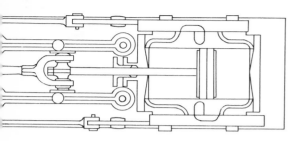

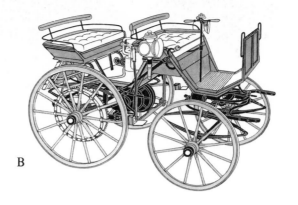

B

D

FM63

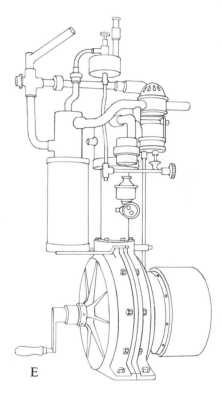

E

Daimler joined Dr. N. Otto who started a gasoline engine factory at Deutz after having invented his 4-stroke cycle. He left in 1882 to concentrate on building his own engine and developing a motorcycle. The first Daimler experimental car, built in 1886 by Daimler and Maybach at their factory in Cannstadt, was powered by a single cylinder water-cooled vertical motor and was really a horseless carriage. The horse and shafts were removed and replaced by a gasoline motor with its driving and steering gear. The first journeys in 1887 were at a top speed of 9 mph (14.5 km/h).

C MARKUS'S CAR, 1875
Siegfried Markus built four cars. The one illustrated still survives, and is possibly the first self-propelled gasoline-driven automobile. It had a 4-stroke engine with one cylinder giving only 3/4 horsepower at 500 revolutions, which is reputed to have given it a top speed of 5 mph (8 km/h). In fact, it was rebuilt to working order in 1949 and was driven at 8 mph (12.9 km/h) on a level road. It had a number of advanced features, including a low-tension magnetoignition system, mechanically operated valves, and a surprisingly modern type of carburetor.

D LOCOMOBILE STEAM CAR
Steam cars were developed alongside gasoline cars. They had the advantage of being silent, free from ignition trouble, and so flexible that they did not require a clutch or transmission. This particular steam car, the Locomobile, was designed by the Stanley brothers, great adherents of the steam principle. In America the steam car continued to be popular and it could be bought as late as the 1920s. The very light Locomobile used a gasoline burner to raise the steam, and although it was popular from about 1899 to 1903, it was too fragile and unreliable to remain a serious competitor to the gasoline car.

E DAIMLER ENGINE
Daimler was noted for his vertical high speed engine, the first of its type. Its speed was only high in comparison with other engines of the period—750 rpm.

B

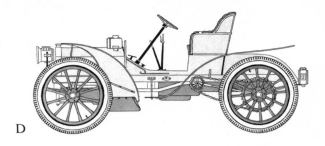

D

A

C

A BENZ, 1888

Carl Benz, the son of an engine driver, was born in Carlsruhe on November 25, 1844. He was an engineer as well as an inventor. He started a small business of his own in Mannheim with a view to building a self-propelled vehicle, his first idea being to fit a small gasoline engine into a low frame bicycle. This was not successful so he concentrated on a 2-stroke gasoline engine and began selling them in 1880. His first horseless carriage, still preserved in the Munich museum, was completed in 1885. Unlike Daimler, he used a horizontal engine lying flat over the rear axle. Like Daimler's engine, it had only one cylinder which gave $1^1/_2$ horsepower, and a gear with pulley, belt, and chain drive to the rear wheels. Ignition was by electricity rather than Daimler's hot tube and the engine was cooled by water that was in a storage tank and gradually boiled away.

B DURYEA, 1895

Inventors in America were slower to develop motor vehicles than the Europeans. The first vehicle, a Daimler motorcycle, was exhibited at the Chicago Exhibition in 1893 and this set the Americans to work in designing and building their own cars. Duryea was a great enthusiast for the three-wheeled car, but soon changed to four. This single cylinder phaeton won the first motor race in America, organized by the Times-Herald *in 1895.*

C PEUGEOT, 1893

Armand Peugeot, born in 1849, specialist in ironmongery and farm machinery, came to England to learn more about engineering and returned to France after the Franco-German war to set up a cycle factory. He favored steam cars at first, but soon changed over to gasoline engines. By 1893 his cars were using $2^1/_2$ horsepower twin cylinder Daimler gasoline motors. This one, now beginning

to look more like a car than a cart, had a cone clutch and a transmission with four forward speeds and reverse.

D FIAT, 1903

The Italian Fiat used a 24 horsepower 4-cylinder engine and had a top speed of 50 mph (80.5 km/h). Fiat stands for Fabbrica Italiana di Automobili Torino, and they began making cars in 1899, later using Mercedes ideas for their own models.

E VAUXHALL, 1904

Vauxhall was a British car both popular and reliable around 1904. It had a glass shield to keep some of the rain and wind off the driver and passenger. Steering on this version was still by a tiller handle; steering wheels came later.

F OPEL, 1900

The Opel brothers first built Darracq cars under license when they took over the Lutzmann factory in 1901. This car, prod-

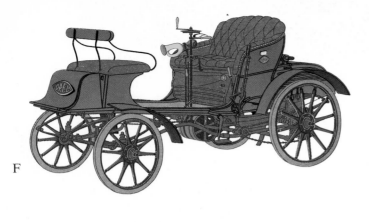

F

E

G

uced in 1900, was really a Lutzmann, which used the Benz design. It was capable of 14 mph (22.5 km/h).

G RENAULT, 1898
Louis Renault used a 2¹/₄ horsepower De Dion Bouton engine. All the other features of this odd car were designed by Renault himself, including the jointed propeller shaft and level gear rear axle. This was one of the first bodies to be completely enclosed.

H LITTLE SIDDELEY, 1904
This single-cylinder horizontal-engined Siddeley was a popular little car in Britain. It had a 6 horsepower engine with a three-speed and reverse transmission and pneumatic tires that made it both reliable and comfortable. Note the steering wheel that had replaced the tiller.

H

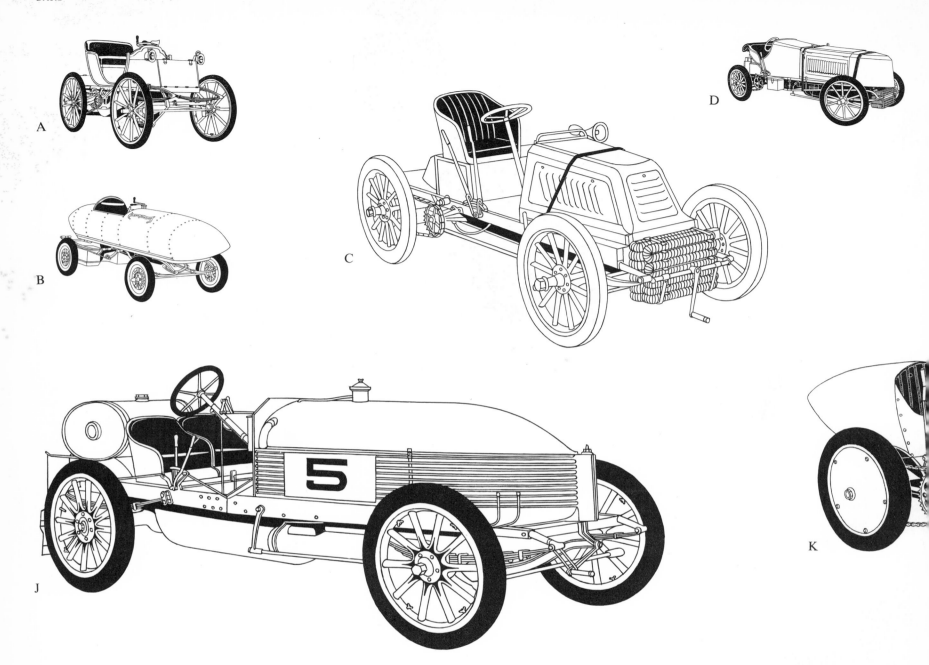

A JEANTAUD, 1899
Count de Chasseloup-Laubat achieved a record speed of 43.69 mph (70.3 km/h) early in 1899 at the first official world land speed record attempt in this car. It was powered by electric batteries and must have been very silent.

B JENATZY, 1899
This streamlined bullet-shaped Jenatzy electric car, known as La Jamais Contente, was driven by Jenatzy and was the first motor vehicle to exceed 60 mph (96.5 km/h). It did this in April 1899. Most of the early record breakers were powered by steam or batteries.

C MORS, 1902
The Mors was one of the fastest gasoline cars of its day. At the end of 1902 this one raised the world speed record to over 71 mph (114.3 km/h). It had a 4-cylinder 60 horsepower engine. At the front can be seen the grilled tube radiator.

D GOBRON-BRILLIE, 1903
Speeds rose very rapidly over the next year. This 100 horsepower Gobron-Brillié had an unusual 4-cylinder engine with eight pistons; in November 1903 it raised the land speed record to 84.73 mph (136.36 km/h).

E MERCEDES, 1904
In 1904 the 90 horsepower Mercedes broke the land speed record with a staggering 92.3 mph (148.54 km/h), to be followed in three months time with an increase to beyond 97 mph (156.11 km/h). The speed had been increased by 50 percent in five years.

F DARRACQ, 1904
Rigolly was the first to break the 100 mph record officially in July 1904, when he drove a Gobron-Brillié at 103.56 mph (166.66 km/h). The record held good for three months. Baras increased it another 1 mph in November on a Darracq.

E

G

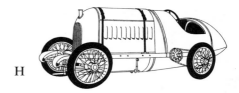

H

F

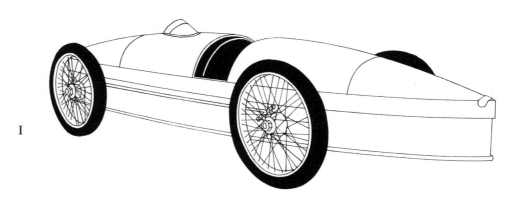

I

L

G DARRACQ, 1905

The 1905 Darracq went two better than the Napier with a V-shaped 8-cylinder motor of huge size that gave 200 horsepower. At the end of that year it reached nearly 110 mph (177 km/h) to be the world's fastest car.

H FIAT 300 GP

The "monster" racing car was still in evidence in 1911 when this Fiat lapped a controversial 154 mph (247.8 km/h) at Brooklands racing track in England. The engine capacity was no less than 28 liters.

I STANLEY, 1906

World records went to steam cars on two occasions. The second and last time was in 1906, when this American-built Stanley steamer was driven by Marriott at a speed just over 127 mph (204.4 km/h).

J NAPIER, 1905

This Napier was the first English car to hold the record early in 1905. Napier cars were noted for being robust and for having a 6-cylinder engine, which made them run very smoothly. The speed was over 104 mph (167.4 km/h).

K "BLITZEN"—BENZ

Barney Oldfield, the famous American racing ace, increased the record to 131.72 mph (211.98 km/h) in March 1910 with this 200 horsepower 4-cylinder Benz.

L GORDON BENNETT TROPHY

The prize presented by James Gordon Bennett, the New York newspaper magnate, to be competed for in the international races which bore his name.

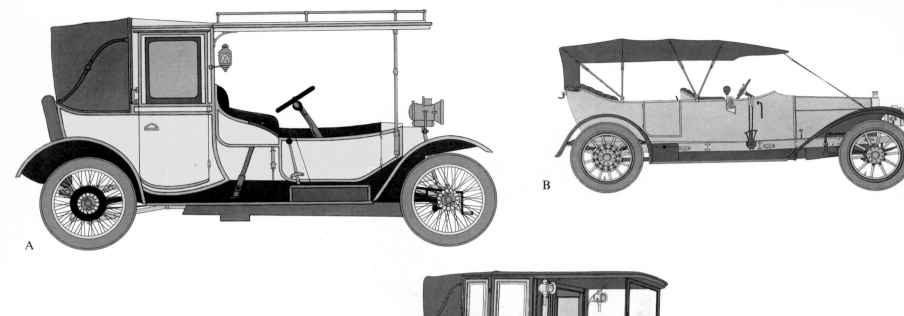

A LANCHESTER 28, 1910
An unconventional British car with a 6-cylinder engine and 3-speed transmission between driver and passengers. It used preselector epicyclic gears and a worm drive rear axle.

B ISOTTA-FRASCHINI, 1910
The Isotta-Fraschini was a high quality Italian car and was the equivalent in that country of the famous British Rolls-Royce. This example had a 4-cylinder 30 horsepower engine.

C RENAULT 12/16, 1910
This is a Renault doctor's coupé. It was designed for the owner/driver and pas-

sengers sat in the back, which could be opened to provide two extra seats. Not a car for the wet. It retains the rear-mounted radiator.

D LANCIA TYPE 51, 1908
Another famous Italian car, the Lancia, had open sides at the front with doors to the rear compartment only. Its top speed was over 50 mph (80 km/h) and it had a 15 horsepower engine. Note the gear and brake levers on the driver's right.

E RENAULT, 1906
The Renault of 1906 was popular as a taxi. As with all continental cars of the period, it has right hand drive. In this

C

D

H

I

car the radiator is at the rear of the engine, a hallmark of the model right up to the 1920s.

F MARCHAND LIMOUSINE, 1905
A car for the rich, with chauffeur isolated at the front, this Marchand was made in Italy in 1905. The 4-cylinder 22 horsepower motor worked with magnetoignition. The body style was known as a landaulet, the leather hood at the back being lowered in fine weather.

G WANDERER PUPPCHEN, 1911
This baby car, the Wanderer Puppchen, was Opel's answer to the Baby Peugeot, but unlike all other small cars that used

small single or 2-cylinder engines, it was powered by a small 4-cylinder unit.

H ROLLS-ROYCE "SILVER GHOST", 1908
The most elegant of all cars. So silent that it earned itself the name "Silver Ghost". It had a 6-cylinder engine and was in production virtually unchanged from 1906 to 1924.

I OAKLAND, 1912
This American Oakland had an enclosed two-door body designed for the owner/driver and was made like a miniature railway carriage. Mudguards covered the insides of the wheels to keep the mud off the body.

The car that Siegfried Markus had built in 1875 could never replace the reliable horse-drawn transportation of the day for short journeys, and could not have been demonstrated as a practical alternative to the railway train for covering long distances. Something both faster and more reliable had to be developed, and the idea was being considered by inventors all over the world. Carl Benz, a manufacturer of gas engines, started experimenting with cars in 1884. His gas engine was not sufficiently powerful, so he designed a gasoline-powered 4-stroke single cylinder motor that he used to power his first car, completed in 1885. This car had three wheels and a tubular framework with the engine placed horizontally at the back, driving the rear wheels through pulleys and chains.

At the same time, but without knowledge of the details of Benz's work, Gottlieb Daimler and his assistant, Wilhelm Maybach, designed and patented an engine that was capable of much higher speeds than any of its contemporaries, and this power unit was the ancestor of the engines in most of our modern vehicles. The single cylinder engine that he built in 1885 could reach speeds of 750 revolutions per minute (rpm) which compared with only 400 from the early Benz. By 1887, Benz had finished his third car, and he exhibited it at the Paris Exposition. Nobody seemed at all interested, until some time later Emile Roger from Paris visited the Benz works and decided to buy the car. He became the agent for Benz cars in Paris and the world's first automobile dealer. Anyone who wished to buy a car could now do so by ordering one either from Benz in Mannheim or Roger in Paris. As the demand increased, Roger built Benz cars under license. The motor industry had begun.

Up to this point in the story of the automobile car, the machines of the 1880s and early 1890s had been more experimental than practical. They were designed and built by the men who invented them, and were merely test beds on which they could make further developments and improvements. As they were uncomfortable and unreliable they appealed only to wealthy sportsmen and adventurers, and it was their efforts to gain more speed and reliability that hastened the adoption of pneumatic tires, better steering and more effective brakes. The cars of the late 1890s and early 1900s were still expensive both to buy and to operate, and, as well as being of interest to the mechanically-minded sportsman, they now began to appeal to other wealthy men who saw an automobile as a useful toy to park in a corner of the coach house.

Every journey was an adventure. The gentleman was usually driven by a chauffeur who had to be something of a mechanic to cope with the frequent mechanical problems. Broken chains, burst tires, electrical problems and gasoline leaks were some of the most frequent. There were no garages and gasoline had to be bought from the chemist or the ironmonger, and the only man who could help out with repairs was the village blacksmith. In the days before tarmacadam and concrete, roads were always muddy in winter and very dusty in summer. The early motorist was either covered in mud or enveloped in a cloud of fine white dust. People were frightened of these noisy, dirty, dangerous monsters that rushed along their roads killing chickens, narrowly missing children, and terrifying horses. Continued improvements, however, together with better roads, soon changed the pattern of travel and within twenty years the car had virtually replaced the horse.

Speed had to come. The inventors needed to test their vehicles to discover where improvements had to be made; many faults went unnoticed at low speed, but the early trials and endurance tests brought to light the need for better suspension and brakes, and pneumatic tires. Early motorists were just the sort of people who would be expected to travel fast. They were wealthy sportsmen who craved excitement at a time when every journey was likely to end up as a minor adventure. Automobile racing helped the manufacturers, too. Racing on the public highways in France became an accepted fact at a time when other countries viewed with suspicion all motorists who traveled on the roads. This enabled the French to dominate the automobile industry during the 1890s, because of the developments that had to be made to cars to enable them to win races. Only thirteen cars took part in one of the first races arranged by Giffard, a French newspaper editor. The distance of 79 miles (127 km) on roads between Paris and Rouen proved a grueling test of man and machine and the race was won at 11.6 mph (18.7 km/h) by the Comte De Dion. This event was so successful that the first French Grand Prix was arranged in the following year, this time much more ambitious with a distance of 732 miles (1,178 km) on a return run from Paris to Bordeaux. The winning car, driven all the way over two days by Emile Levassor, went almost nonstop at an average speed of 15 mph (24 km/h). This was a tremendous achievement for a car with a maximum speed of only 18 mph (30 km/h). By 1898 average speeds in these races between continental

A

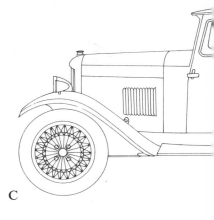

C

A AUSTIN 7 SEDAN, 1928
From about 1928 the tourer declined in popularity to be replaced by the sedan. This Austin Seven was known affectionately as the "Top Hat" and contained such refinements as an electric starter and a windshield wiper.

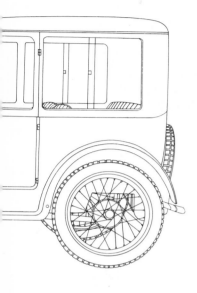

B

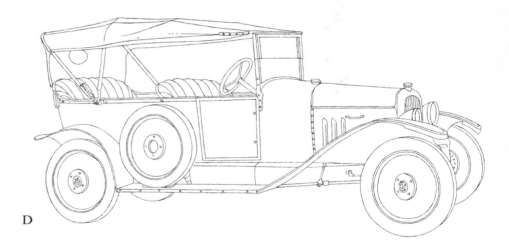

D

B LANCIA LAMBDA, 1925
In Italy, the Lancia Lambda was years ahead of its time. The body and chassis were combined, it had front-wheel brakes, and independent front suspension. This example used wire-spoked wheels for lightness and strength.

C RILEY 9, 1927
A dropped frame between the axles made the Riley 9 a low-set car, yet with ample headroom inside. It was much lower than the typical cars of the period, and had twin overhead camshafts.

D CITROËN TYPE A, 1919
Enclosed bodywork and pressed steel wheels were features of the first car to be made by André Citroën. The flush-sided body was typical of the design of the touring cars of the 1920s. Electric lighting was used, but it still lacked front-wheel brakes.

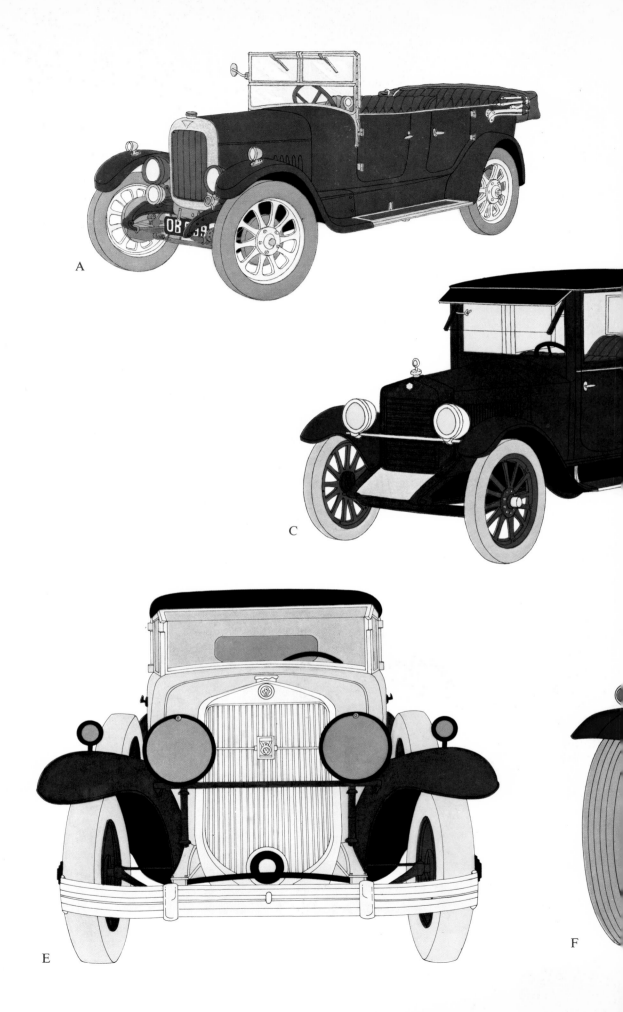

A ALVIS 12/50, 1926

The British Alvis 12/50 was one of the best sports tourers of the 1920s. They were highly reliable and economical and provided sports car performance with all the comfort of a standard touring car.

B CROSSLEY, 1929

The 15 horsepower Crossley, with its distinctive high radiator and 6-cylinder engine, was a popular good quality British car. This one had a sliding roof, a common feature in cars of the late 1920s.

C ESSEX COACH, 1922

The Americans continued to build cars during the 1914–1918 war and during those years they perfected the pressed steel body. This Essex was the first really cheap enclosed car; it still used wooden wheels which continued in use longer in America than in Europe.

D FIAT 9, 1930

This two-door Italian Fiat, the smallest model available from the company at the time, was mass-produced and the body was made by welding together pressed steel panels, a process that characterized cars in the 1930s.

E CADILLAC V8, 1928

American luxury cars like the V8 Cadillac were much larger than those in Europe. Its engine had eight cylinders mounted in V form and this, combined with a well-built body, made it a very smooth and quiet car.

F TYPE 30 BUGATTI, 1926

Ettore Bugatti's beautifully designed sports cars had, even by today's standards, exceptional performance. They were of more use for racing than for everyday motoring. One of his models had an 8-cylinder engine.

G BENTLEY 4½ LITER, 1929

Next to the Rolls-Royce, the Bentley was one of the best known quality cars. The 4½-liter model first appeared in 1927; it could reach 90 mph (145 km/h), provided that the occupants could stand the noise from the engine.

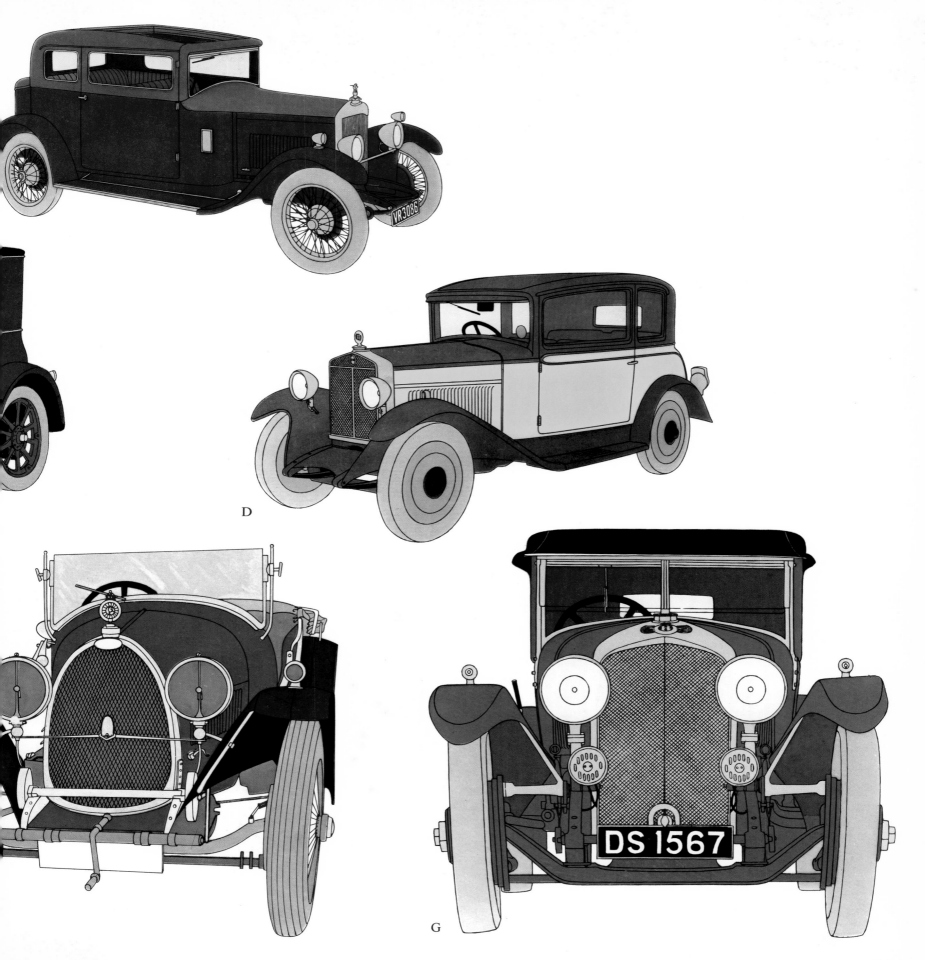

D

G

towns had almost doubled; they continued to be run until 1903, when the Paris to Madrid race was stopped at Bordeaux after a very bad accident in which about fifteen people were killed. After that, most racing took place on specially built racetracks such as Montlehery in France and Brooklands in England.

One of the most important racing events was instituted by James Gordon Bennett, owner of the *New York Herald*. To encourage the infant automobile industry, he presented a cup to be competed for annually by the automobile clubs all over the world. The first race was held in 1900 on a 352-mile (566.5 km) course between Paris and Lyons, and was won by Charron in a Panhard-Levassor in 9 hours, 9 minutes, an average speed of 38.6 mph (62.12 km/h). In fact, his car was the only one to finish, those from Belgium, Germany, and America putting up what were regarded as disgraceful performances even in those days. Opposition to the competition came from the French automobile industry, which considered themselves as having a monopoly, and from the public in general who were in opposition to the idea of road racing because of the danger to spectators and other road-users. After that, the challenge race for the cup was run in conjunction with an open motor race.

Girardot, again the only one to reach the finish on time, won the second race in 1901, which was run between Paris and Bordeaux. If nothing else, this proved the reliability of his Panhard car and the tires that he used. The British Club issued a challenge on behalf of Wolseley and Napier cars in 1902, the Wolseleys started in the open race, but S. F. Edge ran his Napier on the third Gordon Bennett course from Paris to Innsbruck and, much to everyone's surprise, won at an average speed of 31.8 mph (51.18 km/h). This meant that the 1903 event took place over a circuit in Ireland and it was won by Jenatzy on a Mercedes at nearly 50 mph (80 km/h). Two more races in 1904 and 1905 were won by Théry on a Brasier and after that the Grand Prix races replaced the Gordon Bennett events that later degenerated into balloon races.

By now everyone who was anybody in America and Europe wanted to own an automobile. They were completely reliable, but still journeys were inclined to be adventurous, and long journeys were often undertaken with a chauffeur-mechanic who could both drive and repair the car if it broke down. Open touring bodywork was still the most popular, but the Americans were already making some enclosed sedans in which driver and passengers were in the same compartment. The larger sedan, or landaulet, bodies had a separate body for the passengers and the driver had to sit in the front, often separated from the passengers by a glass screen. He sat on leather upholstery whilst the owners sat in the back in the luxury of well padded cloth of the highest quality. Directions and orders to the chauffeur were passed by a mechanical telegraph system or a microphone. Expensive cars, which meant almost all those available at the time, were bought as chassis. All the working parts, including hood, radiator, and fenders, were built onto the chassis and the new owner had the bare chassis delivered to his body-builder. A wide selection of body styles existed and each was built onto its chassis using the best ash covered in sheet metal, all beaten to shape by hand. The job could take months to finish. Next it went to the upholsterer who would need another two weeks before the finished car was ready to go to the coach painter. All the old skills of the horse-drawn coach building trade were employed and only the very highest standards were accepted, everything being done by hand, for each car was treated as a new separate job. The painters applied dozens of coats of paint before finishing in the final color and varnishing, and a car had to spend many weeks with the coach painters.

Although most of the cars made before 1914 were large, there were some exceptions. The market for expensive individually built vehicles was quite large, but many manufacturers saw an even bigger future for cheaper, smaller models. Only very few cars had brakes on the front wheels; no one had quite worked out how to combine braking with steering. The result of applying rear-wheel brakes suddenly was an inevitable skid on wet roads and a fair amount of skill was needed on the part of the driver. He also had to manipulate a fierce clutch and a crash transmission. It was not possible to slide the gear lever from one position to another without the most precise judgment of both road and engine speeds.

Toward the end of this period there were some cars with electric lighting, but the majority used paraffin lamps for side and tail, and acetylene gas lamps for headlights. All these were quite likely to blow out, and lighting them with matches on a wet and windy night was well nigh impossible.

However, many problems had been overcome. Cars were both comfortable and reliable, roads had been improved, and the automobile was accepted in most civilized countries as a familiar part of the daily scene which had come to stay. People like Henry Ford had seen the enormous potential and there were already thriving automobile industries in the United States, Britain, France, Germany, and Italy. Now the market had to be expanded either by exporting to foreign countries or by making cheaper cars with a wider appeal. Everything stopped in 1914 when the Great War began, and everyone's attention in the automobile trade was turned to making munitions. The building of private cars virtually stopped until 1919.

As soon as the war was over the car-producing countries got down to the serious job of satisfying the increasing demand for motor vehicles. At first they had to be imported from the United States and when the Europeans started again they followed many of the prewar designs. By 1922, however, there were a number of important changes. Customers required greater comfort, improved reliability and, above all, cheaper cars. In Great Britain, Sir Herbert Austin and William Morris both decided to follow Henry Ford's example and to make cars that could be bought by people of limited means for about $500 (approximately £200). Coupled with this low initial cost had to come low running costs, fifty miles per gallon, and "motoring at tram fares". These little cars could be run for as little as a penny a mile.

In order to make a cheap car it was necessary to keep down the cost by using cheap materials. Leather cloth, steel pressings in place of machined castings, and four-seaters with two doors were some of the methods employed. Labor costs were kept to a minimum by adopting what was known as mass production. In this process it was first of all necessary to concentrate on the greatest accuracy in making the individual parts so that any piece could be picked up at random and be fitted to its mating part without the need for hand filing or drilling. All the components came together on an assembly track and could be put together by semiskilled labor. Painting was done by spray, and in the early part of the decade the slow drying oil-based paints were still used, but these were replaced by the harder wearing cellulose enamels in about 1927, and they dried in a matter of hours rather than days.

The Volkswagen does not look as if it has much in common with the Model T Ford, and yet there is one important similarity. They both exceeded a production run of over 15 million without requiring any major basic design changes. The Model T had achieved this astonishing figure when manufacture ceased in 1927, less than twenty years after it was first introduced. It was the first car to be built on mass-produced lines; components were cheap, simple, and accurately made for quick and interchangeable assembly. Parts were put together in small production lines and assembled on a long moving line where workmen became skilled and quick at doing the particular tasks assigned to them. The choice of model, color and specification was restricted enabling the cost to be kept to a minimum and the real success of these methods showed up with large-scale production created by the demand for a reliable economy car. It had a large engine by European standards because fuel was much cheaper in the United States and a great proportion of the cars were sold there, unlike the much more economical Volkswagen of a later era that has been exported so successfully all over the world.

The Model T became a legend, and in spite of the fact that it was called the Tin Lizzie, it was always described with affection, and a whole generation of Americans grew up with it and learned to drive on it. It lacked elegance, and was more often than not painted black with black painted fittings and it was cheap without being too nasty.

By 1927 the cost of producing it was only one third of its selling price when first introduced in 1908, in spite of increasing costs brought about by inflation during World War I. This was achieved by a continued increase in the demand and the fact that mass production reduced labor costs to a minimum and allowed raw materials to be bought very cheaply.

Cheapness and economy were important but were only half the story of the twenties. The large, beautifully finished expensive cars were still very popular. Although the middle classes had achieved greater purchasing power, by far the greatest proportion of the wealth of Europe and America was held by the increasing number of the newly rich, such as men who had made fortunes during the war and from the boom in consumer spending directly after it. These men demanded cars of the highest quality. With the exception of the cheaper cars pressed out and assembled in great quantity, the tradition of hand-built cars with individually fitted components upholstered and painted by hand still persisted.

A number of important changes were made in car design during the 1920s. Gear levers moved from the old right-handed position to the center, four-wheel brakes were the rule after about 1924, and the sedan body predominated after 1928. Magnetoignition systems began to be replaced by battery and coil methods from 1929, and electric starters were common from 1921. Tires saw very noticeable advances; the high pressure beaded edge type pneumatic tires that lasted for only some 6,000 miles (c. 9,660 km) were superseded, by the well-base balloon tires after 1926, and these gave added comfort, greater freedom from punctures and longer life. Cars were now commonplace, they were available to suit all incomes, the cheapest being as little as $235 (about £100). The automobile industries of America and the major countries in Europe were becoming a vital part of the economy, but they had to be made in greater quantities and at cheaper prices. These were the factors that were most important in the next decade.

THE POPULARIZATION OF THE CAR

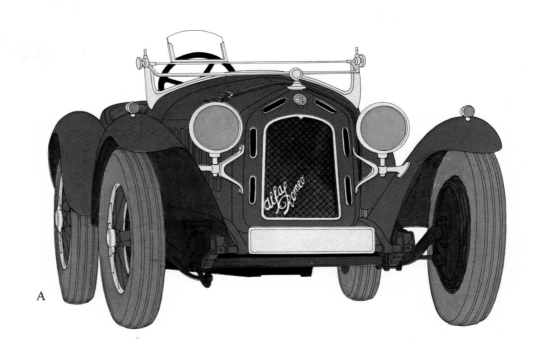

A

By 1930 the world annual demand for passenger cars had reached 5 million. There were a number of reasons for this figure having doubled in ten years: increased prosperity in Europe, better road systems, the need for greater speed and comfort than could be provided by horse-drawn transportation, cheaper fuel, and above all cheaper cars. Economy of scale applies as much in car production as in any other industry. A hundred workers may produce ten cars a year, but it does not follow that a thousand men can make only a hundred, for by using a large work force techniques can be adopted that make it possible to increase output tenfold. Of course, style and design have to be adapted for convenience of production, and this is what happened in the 1930s.

It was no longer practical to use highly skilled craftsmen working by hand on each individual car; body-building, painting, upholstery, wooden-wheel building all took time and all these processes had to be adapted for greater output. The customer may have had to accept lower standards, but he could still have the higher standards if he wished to pay the price. During the 1920s most of the small car factories had either gone out of business or been bought out by the big firms, but those who remained like Rolls-Royce and Daimler were still able to sell their expensive high quality cars at a profit. To make a car to sell for about $250 (approximately £100) called for a great deal of ingenuity, but with a profit margin to the manufacturer of about $25 (£10) savings had to be made somehow. This was done only by very large quantity production. If a firm could make 20,000 cars a year, it could buy its materials at a very cheap rate, but it also had to find other ways of reducing production costs and yet still turn out a reliable product.

Body styling had to follow lines dictated by production methods. No longer were bodies constructed from handmade timber frames covered with hand-beaten sheet metal; they were made from sheet metal sections which were pressed to the required shape by machines and welded together onto

A ALFA ROMEO MILLE MIGLIA, 1933
Alfa Romeos with their exciting sporty appearance lived up to their looks. This Mille Miglia model of 1933 had a 2.3 liter straight 8-cylinder engine that developed 130 horsepower and had a top speed of well over 100 mph (160 km/h). The body style has lost the square edges of the MG and everything slopes to cut down wind resistance.

B CITROËN TRACTION AVANT, 1934
Up to 1933 Citroën cars were typical and conventional, although well made and reliable, but the new Traction Avant model introduced in 1934 was years ahead of its time. It used independent suspension on all wheels and the engine drove the front wheels. The body was low and built in one unit with the chassis. Cars like this, which were produced from advanced designs, were expensive to introduce but had the advantage of being able to remain in production for a long time, allowing the high initial cost of tooling to be written off over an extended period. The model was built for over twenty years and was always popular.

B

C

D

C CHEVROLET MASTER SEDAN, 1935

This American Chevrolet was typical of the design in the United States in the 1930s. The large pressed steel body was still very square at the back to allow for headroom for the passengers, but the windshield and radiator are sloped back slightly more than they were in the 1920s.

D LANCIA APRILIA, 1939

Another unconventional car of the period, the famous Lancia Aprilia. It had a small narrow V-4 engine, which kept down the weight and dimensions of the car. Notice how the two doors open from the center; this was done by designing the body so as not to need support from a central pillar in the structure.

prefabricated metal supports that were built into the body. Just as earlier methods had created their styles, so the pressed steel techniques created theirs. The resulting cars were not particularly handsome, but they were cheap and functional, almost a metal box on wheels. But not quite a complete box because the hood containing the engine still protruded well in front of the body and the fenders were still separate. Wheels were being made smaller, the 20- and 21-inch types of the late 1920s giving way to 16- and 18-inch sizes. Another feature of the decade were chromium-plated bumpers at the front and rear of the car to protect the body from minor dents and scrapes.

In all but the cheapest cars, upholstery was still in leather; it was not padded and pleated as it used to be and was often in the form of separate sections stretched onto a metal frame, rather than being fixed direct to a wooden structure and upholstered like furniture. This all helped to reduce costs and made the car interior very comfortable. Some manufacturers tried pneumatic cushions under the upholstery, but they punctured and were not successful. Electrical equipment had become very sophisticated, but the car heater had not yet been introduced and a long journey in the winter could be as uncom-

fortable in a 1939 car as it was in a 1924 sedan. Traveling rugs were essential for the passengers in the back.

With large quantities, a small saving on each car is magnified. If it is possible to reduce the thickness of metal, the length of a screw, or the thickness of a bolt, then noticeable savings can be made. The other way to cut costs is to reduce the labor force by simplifying the processes of manufacture and assembly. In the cheap cars of the 1930s many new production methods were introduced. Cars still consisted of two major parts, the chassis and the body. All the cast, forged, and pressed metal parts of the major components, such as the engine and transmission, were machined and assembled using as many automatic methods as could be devised. One man could supervise a number of semiautomatic machines, just fitting the component on and taking it off after the process was completed, and even such jobs as tightening down nuts could be speeded up by using the right type of machinery rather than by having one man do it with a spanner. This meant that a very high initial cost was involved when tooling up for a new model and it was desirable to continue without any major alterations in design for as long as possible.

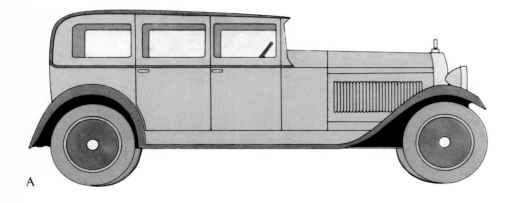

A

B

D

E

A DELAGE, 1929

The Delage of 1929 is a typical example of the large 6-cylinder sedan of the late 1920s, with a radiator still noticeable as a separate part and a distinct division between the engine compartment and the passenger body. No attempt was made to streamline the shape, the edges are square, and there is no slope to the windshield.

B PIERCE-ARROW SILVER ARROW, 1933

The Pierce-Arrow Silver Arrow was much more streamlined than its American contemporaries. In this body the head lamps have already been contained in the wing shape. It had a large V-12 engine and was expensive. Unlike other cars of advanced design, it did not last for long because the manufacturers got into financial difficulties.

C FIAT 500, 1938

Cheap, small economy cars filled the roads in the 1930s and brought the pleasures of driving to a very wide public. This Fiat was called the Topolino and was powered by a tiny 4-cylinder 570 cc engine, which gave it a top speed of 55 mph (88.5 km/h) and a fuel consumption of 50 miles (80 km) per gallon.

D MG TYPE M, 1930

There was still a small demand for the open touring type of bodywork, but mostly in the sports car field. MG cars were remarkable in that they managed to achieve surprisingly good performance by adapting the standard Morris car engine and tuning it up for speed. It was really a modified Morris Minor.

E FRAZER NASH LE MANS REPLICA, 1934

A small demand for fast cars for sporting purposes has always existed. The Frazer Nash was not based upon a standard production car as were so many other so-called sports cars; it was built for sports driving. For some reason its final drive to the rear wheels was by chains.

F DKW, 1938

The German Auto Union Company made this advanced DKW car in 1938. Unlike most other vehicles it was powered by a twin-cylinder two-stroke engine, which had only five moving parts. It had front-wheel drive and was very economical with a fuel consumption of 55 miles (88.5 km) per gallon.

C

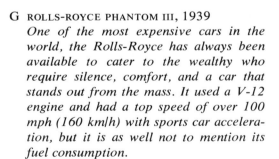

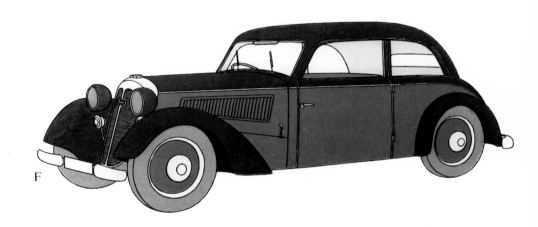

F

G ROLLS-ROYCE PHANTOM III, 1939
One of the most expensive cars in the world, the Rolls-Royce has always been available to cater to the wealthy who require silence, comfort, and a car that stands out from the mass. It used a V-12 engine and had a top speed of over 100 mph (160 km/h) with sports car acceleration, but it is as well not to mention its fuel consumption.

G

A S.S. JAGUAR, 1939

This 3¹/₂-liter 25 horsepower model had a 6-cylinder overhead valve engine that had ample power to cope with a spacious and very comprehensively equipped body. It could reach a speed of over 90 mph (145 km/h).

B LANCIA AURELIA GT, 1952

Pinin Farina designed the body of this fine model. Its narrow-angle V-6 engine could attain over 110 mph (177 km/h) and was separated completely from the clutch, transmission, and inboard-mounted rear brakes, which were grouped at the back.

C AUSTIN A40, 1947

The newly designed Austin A40, which was first introduced in October 1947, was a very popular car. It had an overhead valve 4-cylinder 1200 cc engine and independent front suspension, and could be obtained as a two-door sedan called the Dorset or four-door called the Devon. Some 300,000 were made before the body was completely redesigned in 1952.

D CISITALIA, 1947

The very simple, clean lines of the Cisitalia were very advanced for 1947. The designer was Pinin Farina, a man who was to influence the shape of the European car for more than a decade.

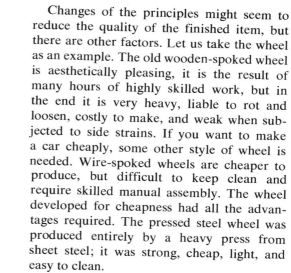

E FORD V-8, 1945

The Ford V-8, still prewar in character, had the typical Ford characteristics of rugged reliability and a low price. Its inconvenient divided windshield was soon to be replaced by the curved single shield, but this was not yet possible as the safety glass of the period had to be made in flat sections. The rather fussy chromium-plated additions seen around the grille were features demanded by the American buyer.

Changes of the principles might seem to reduce the quality of the finished item, but there are other factors. Let us take the wheel as an example. The old wooden-spoked wheel is aesthetically pleasing, it is the result of many hours of highly skilled work, but in the end it is very heavy, liable to rot and loosen, costly to make, and weak when subjected to side strains. If you want to make a car cheaply, some other style of wheel is needed. Wire-spoked wheels are cheaper to produce, but difficult to keep clean and require skilled manual assembly. The wheel developed for cheapness had all the advantages required. The pressed steel wheel was produced entirely by a heavy press from sheet steel; it was strong, cheap, light, and easy to clean.

Once again, just as in 1914, European and American car production came to a virtual standstill in the early 1940s to make way for the manufacture of military vehicles and armaments. When the war ended in 1945, the factories in Germany and in most of the countries that had been occupied were destroyed or badly damaged. The people of Europe concentrated on rebuilding their towns and cities and on providing food; consequently it was some time before raw materials and the means of converting them into automobiles were available. Britain, where the industrial centers were still intact, was able to turn to car production again much more quickly, and this gave her a considerable advantage in being able to build up an export trade once again.

The car factories, and all the subsidiary industries that were necessary to provide steel, aluminum, electrical equipment, tires, and fuel, had become a vital part of the economy, which accounted for more capital and employed more people than any other industry. One of the problems with becoming a car producing economy is that the nation involved becomes dominated by the industry. Luckily, the demand for cars was so great after the war that Britain was able to export all the cars that could be produced. In design and appearance, not very much progress had been made. Bodies were still of pressed steel design and in most cases they were built up onto steel chassis that contained the major components. Fenders were still separate attachments, although the running boards of the previous decade had disappeared. Wheels were slightly smaller and the frames were slung lower and closer to the ground, enabling the overall height of the vehicles to be reduced. Generally, although reliable and quite well made, the popular cars of the period were uninspiring.

E

129

A PACKARD, 1940

An American car, something like the La-gonda in appearance, but with an engine having only eight cylinders—it was called the Super 8. The high quality body was not standard to Packard and was made by a specialist coachbuilder named Dar-rin. Head lamps and sidelights have yet to be merged into one unit and the fend-ers still retain the appearance of being added rather than being built into the body shape.

B CITROËN DS19, 1956

This DS19 followed the highly successful Citroën with front-wheel drive. It is un-conventional both in appearance and in some of the principles that it employs.

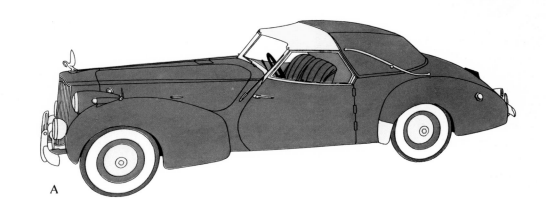

A

B

D

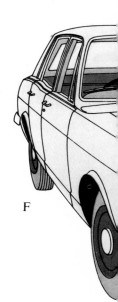

F

E

HWK 315

Hydraulic operation of the brakes, steer-ing, and the unique self-balancing sus-pension system are features of the DS19.

C CHRYSLER IMPERIAL, 1963

American cars like the Chrysler Imperial were still large, and had power-assisted steering and brakes and automatic trans-mission. This had a 400 cubic inch V-8 engine and was a very easy and pleasant car to drive.

C

G

D V-12 LAGONDA, 1940
W. O. Bentley joined the Lagonda firm in 1935 and the first car that he designed for them entirely to his own specifications was this fabulous V-12 Lagonda car. It had independent suspension on the front wheels and a body of very clean and classic lines; it was still a car of the late 1930s in general appearance, but was a low streamlined elegant sportsman's sedan, the fastest of its type in Britain. The engine was of $4\frac{1}{2}$-liter capacity.

E RILEY $2\frac{1}{2}$ LITER, 1946
In 1946 the $2\frac{1}{2}$-liter Riley was one of the first new postwar cars in Europe that was not a continuation of a 1939 model. It had a very efficient overhead valve engine and independent suspension on the front wheels, which gave it excellent performance even over rough roads.

F FORD ZODIAC, 1966
In 1966 the Ford Zodiac was just about the largest mass-produced British car, its

top speed from the V-6, 3-liter engine was 100 mph (160 km/h). It was comfortable, and carried five passengers in its roomy body.

G MORRIS 1100, 1964
The British Leyland 1100, still a current model, uses a transverse engine to drive the front wheels and has proved very reliable and economical. Body styling was by Pinin Farina and the car was designed by Alec Issigonis.

A ROLLS-ROYCE CORNICHE

An 8-cylinder 6-liter two-door sports version of the world's most elegant and expensive car. It costs £10,000 (approximately $23,500), does over 120 mph (193 km/h), with a fuel consumption of 15 mpg.

B VAUXHALL VX 4/90

Vauxhall is a part of General Motors and Britain's third largest manufacturer, with a production of about 200,000 cars a year. The VX 4/90 has a 4-cylinder 1,975 cc engine, a maximum speed of 99 mph (159 km/h), and a fuel consumption of 26 mpg (42 km/g).

C PONTIAC GRAND PRIX

Pontiacs are made by the world's largest automobile corporation, General Motors, which makes half a million of this make each year. It has a typical large 8-cylinder engine of about 406 cubic inches with a top speed of 110 mph (177 km/h).

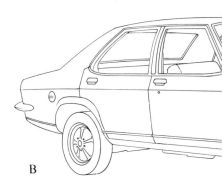

G TOYOTA CORONA

The Toyota Corona comes with a variety of engines from 1,600 to 1,900 cc. The smallest has a top speed of 91 mph (146 km/h) in fourth and 109 (175 km/h) in fifth gear, with a fuel consumption of 28 mpg (45 km/g).

D MOSKVICH 412

AZLK of Moscow make the Moskvich, a rugged car of simple traditional appearance with a 1480 cc engine, reputed to have a top speed of 93 mph and fuel consumption of 32 mpg (51.5 km/g).

E VOLVO 164

Over 200,000 Volvos are made each year, and they are exported to most European countries. The 164, a well made, heavy, robust car, has a 6-cylinder 3-liter engine and is capable of 110 mph (177 km/h).

F SKODA 110R COUPÉ

Tatra and Skoda cars are made in Czechoslovakia. The first Skoda was made in 1905; now about 125,000 are produced each year. The 110R coupé has a 1107 cc engine with a fuel consumption of 36 mpg (58 km/g).

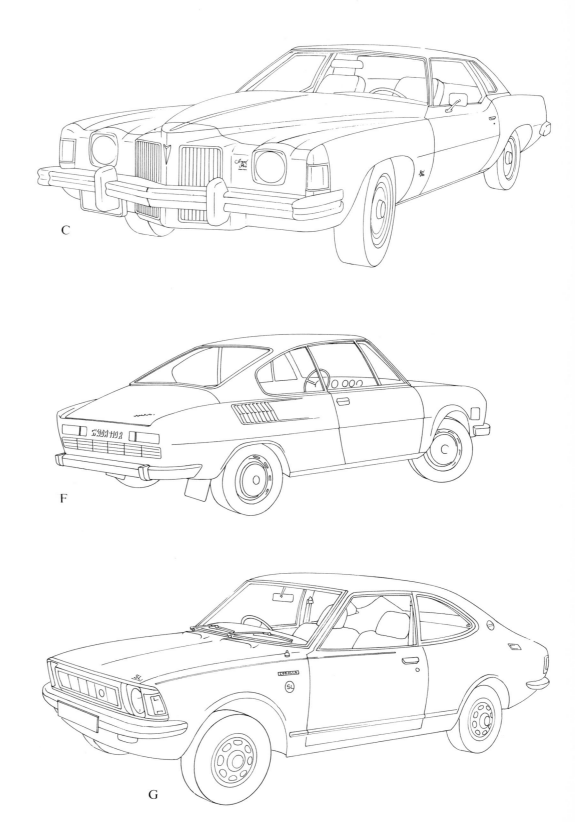

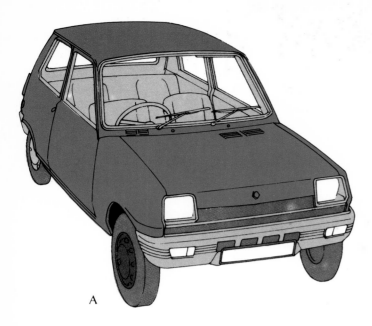

A

B

C

A RENAULT 5

Renault produces a wide range of cars, the smallest having an engine of less than 1 liter in capacity. It is conventional, but cheap, popular, and economical. Renault is a nationalized firm and is the largest automobile manufacturer in France, producing over a million cars a year.

B MASERATI BORA

The Maserati Bora does not look the most comfortable of cars, but it is designed for speed and performance, which make the low-slung style necessary. It has a V-8 engine of 4.7 liters and a top speed of 174 mph (280 km/h) in fifth gear.

C BMW 3.0 CSL

An elegant and fairly expensive sedan, the BMW 3.0 has a 2985 cc engine and a top speed of 127 mph. Fuel consumption is 25 mpg, which is very good for an engine of 3 liter capacity.

D FORD CAPRI

The British Ford Capri is a two-door four-seater coupé available with a wide range of engine sizes, 1300, 1600, 2000, and 3000, the 3000GT having a top speed of 122 mph (196 km/h).

E FIAT 128 COUPÉ

Fiat, Fabbrica Italiana di Automobili Torino, was founded in 1899 and now makes over 1 1/2 million cars a year and employs nearly 200,000 people. The 2-door 128 Giannini has a 4-cylinder engine, top speed of 100 mph (160 km/h), and a fuel consumption of 35 mpg (56.3 km/g).

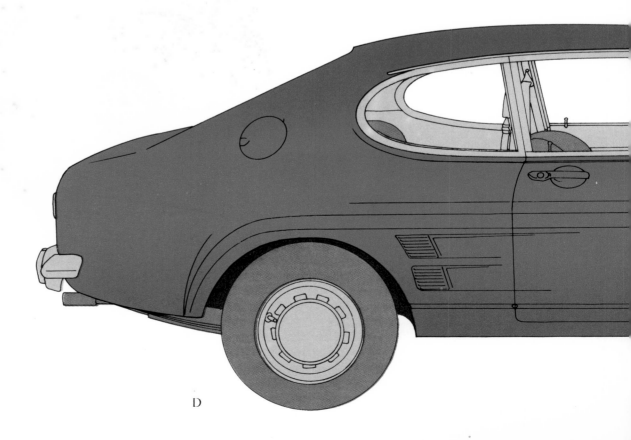

D

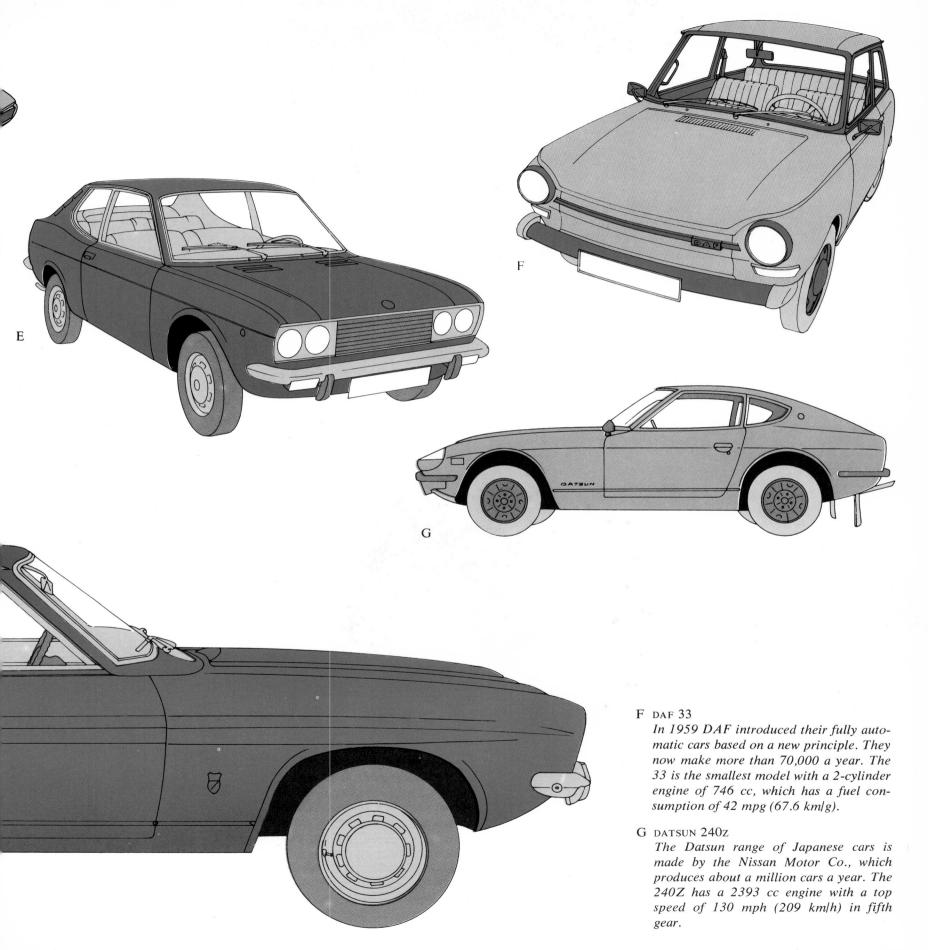

E

F

G

F DAF 33

In 1959 DAF introduced their fully automatic cars based on a new principle. They now make more than 70,000 a year. The 33 is the smallest model with a 2-cylinder engine of 746 cc, which has a fuel consumption of 42 mpg (67.6 km/g).

G DATSUN 240Z

The Datsun range of Japanese cars is made by the Nissan Motor Co., which produces about a million cars a year. The 240Z has a 2393 cc engine with a top speed of 130 mph (209 km/h) in fifth gear.

A

B

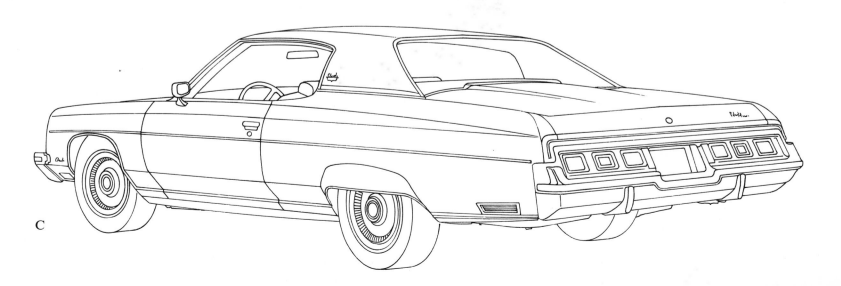

C

A ASTON MARTIN V8

The DBS V8, costing £7,000 (about $16,500), is a car for the wealthy enthusiast. It has an 8-cylinder 5.3-liter engine that uses fuel at the rate of 13 mpg (21 km/g), but gives a top speed of 136 mph (220 km/h).

B AUDI 80

The Audi can be obtained with a conventional 1500 cc piston engine, as an alternative to the Wankel rotary type. It uses front-wheel drive and is very economical with a fuel consumption of 32 mpg (51.5 km/g).

C CHEVROLET IMPALA

Two-door cars even spread to America, and the Impala can be obtained with a coupé body. It uses a large 6-cylinder 4-liter engine giving a top speed of over 90 mph (145 km/h). Fuel consumption of 18 mpg (29 km/g) is quite good for such a large engine.

D ALFA ROMEO ALFETTA

Alfa Romeo, the Italian firm, was founded in 1910 and is the second largest manufacturer of cars in that country with an annual production in excess of 100,000. Their cars do very well in international competitions.

D

E

F

The Volkswagen Beetle has been as successful as the Model T Ford; during 1971 the total production figure exceeded 15 million, the first single car type to exceed the previous record set by Henry Ford's Model T in 1926. Although it was an entirely different car from its famous predecessor, it has several things in common; it has not changed its basic shape since it was first introduced, it is cheap and reliable, and although in some respects unconventional—for example its rear-mounted air-cooled engine—it has been one of the world's most popular cars for more than twenty years.

The brilliant Austrian engineer Ferdinand Porsche first considered producing a cheap "people's car" during the 1920s, but could not find anyone to back him. He made three prototypes in 1936 and by 1938 people in Germany were given the opportunity of making advance payments to enable them to buy the new "people's car" by a sort of advance payment hire purchase scheme. In May 1938 work began on building a factory in Lower Saxony, and the car was to be known as the KdF-Wagen or the "strength-through-joy-car". There was no joy, because a year later, after only a few cars had been completed, the war intervened. For the next four years the output of the new factory consisted of armaments and military vehicles based on the KdF principles. Toward the end of the war the factory was completely destroyed by bombing, and later on the ruins were taken over by Professor Heinz Nordhoff, who transformed the rubble into a huge new factory surrounded by its own town—Wolfsburg—to house the 95,000 workers and their families.

The sports car could never be called a "people's car" although it has always been popular. It has been defined as a car in which performance takes precedence over carrying capacity, and it is not surprising that many cars designed to take part in auto sport and auto racing are quite unsuitable for daily use on the roads. There are notable exceptions such as the MGs of the 1920s and 1930s and the E-type Jaguars of today. Sports cars before 1914, like the racing cars of the period, relied upon engine capacity for their speed and performance. They used massive aeroengines to achieve results and must have been both exciting and frightening to drive.

Many of the developments first introduced into sports cars, such as four-wheel brakes, have become standard in sedans, having been proved under the stress of speed and high performance. Higher engine speeds were necessary for wartime aeroengines and it was

E AUSTIN MAXI
The Austin Maxi, made by British Leyland, was the first British car with a fifth door at the back. It has a transverse engine at the front and uses front-wheel drive. Capacity is either 1500 or 1750 cc.

F CITROËN SM
Citroën makes more than half a million cars a year and employs over 80,000 people. They make the little 2CV with a twin-cylinder 435 cc engine and this less conventional SM with a V-6 2.6-liter engine having a top speed of 137 mph (220 km/h) in fifth gear.

A

B

D

E

A VAUXHALL 30/98, 1920
One of the first sports cars to be introduced after the war, the 30/98 Vauxhall used a pre-1914 side valve 4½-liter engine and was based on the chassis used for a military staff car. It was very flexible and could be driven in top gear at under 10 mph (16 km/h), with a top speed of more than 80 mph (129 km/h).

B MERCEDES-BENZ SSKL, 1931
The monster Mercedes in its ultimate form, with 7-liter 6-cylinder engine and overhead camshaft and top speed of 130

mph (209 km/h), was one of the last giant sports cars. Its chassis alone weighed well over a ton.

C JAGUAR XK 120, 1949
The XK 120, first of a line of elegant, fast, and relatively cheap sports cars of character that were exported all over the world. It was the first time a twin-cam 160 brake horsepower engine capable of 120 mph (196 km/h) had been offered at such a modest price.

D BUGATTI BRESCIA, 1923
Ettore Bugatti's little 1500 cc 1923 Brescia model had a 4-cylinder engine with an overhead camshaft. The top speed was about 75 mph (120 km/h). It had no front-wheel brakes, was noisy and uncomfortable, but exciting to drive.

E ALFA ROMEO 8C-2300, 1932
An 8-cylinder 2300 cc supercharged engine with twin overhead camshafts capable of 110 mph (177 km/h) made it possible for these Italian sports cars to win four Le Mans and three Mille Miglia.

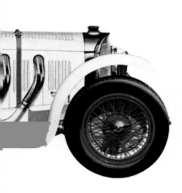

C

F

F FERRARI 250 GT, 1959
   *A 3-liter V-12 racing car for the very
   wealthy enthusiast. The twin overhead
   camshaft engine of 270 brake horsepower
   gave this, one of the most desirable and
   beautiful cars of all time, a top speed of
   140 mph (225 km/h).*

G LOTUS ELAN, 1966
   *1558 cc, 4 cylinders, twin overhead cam-
   shaft Ford-based engine. 105 brake horsepower and 115 mph (185 km/h). Backbone frame, disk brakes on all four
   wheels, and retractable head lamps.*

G

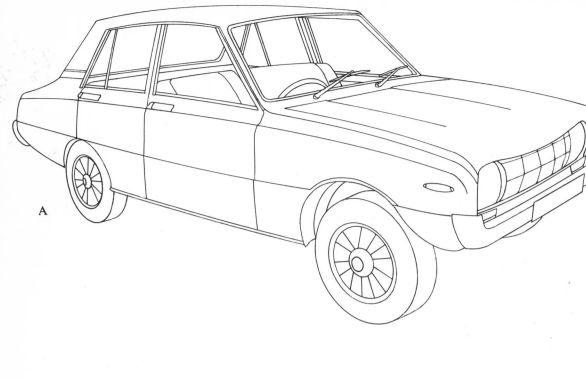

A

B

C

D

A MAZDA R100

The less sporting R100 can travel at 112 mph (180 km/h) using the water-cooled two-rotor 491 × 2 cc rotary engine, which gives 110 horsepower at 7,000 rpm.

B MAZDA R130

The R130, one of the more expensive types, uses a bigger engine with each rotor having 655 cc, giving the car a top speed of 118 mph (190 km/h) and a fuel consumption of 23,5 mpg (37.8 km/g).

C MAZDA SAVANNA GS II

Although the Savanna GS II coupé uses the 491 × 2 cc rotary engine with a top speed of 112 mph (180 km/h), and has only two seats, it has a very sporty appearance.

D NSU RO80

The German NSU Ro80 has been among the most successful rotary engined cars. It uses a twin-rotor engine of 497 × 2 cc, which gives it a top speed of 112 mph (180 km/h) and a fuel consumption of 25 mpg (40 km/g).

the use of aluminum pistons that made this possible, and by the mid-1920s just about every car manufacturer had discarded cast-iron pistons. Again, in the early twenties, only a few sports cars used overhead valves for increased performance with a given size of engine, and by 1930 more than half the current production sedans had them.

There were no real sports cars built in America during the height of the sports car boom in Europe. The lack of races for sports cars and the overcrowded roads were the main reasons for this, but American manufacturers did make the speedsters, cars of sporting appearance that appealed to the younger generation and as second cars for use on weekends. In the 1930s there was great interest in the cheap sports cars, tuned-up versions of the better family sedans of the period, a British peculiarity that still exists and examples of which are exported all over the world.

After the dull cars of the 1940s and 1950s, a pleasant change occurred in the next decade. Even in America, the flashy, chromium image gave way to elegant styling, which came from the adoption of some of the ideas that had originated in Italy. Pinin Farina was one of the major stylists whose designs influenced the shape of car bodies.

In Britain the Mini and the 1100 made by the combined Austin-Morris group which had joined to form the British Motor Corporation in 1952, were completely new concepts in automobile design. Driver and passengers were housed in a small box that was surprisingly roomy, and all the mechanical parts were under the hood at the front. The engine was mounted across the width of the car with the transmission and axle beneath it, with drive through to the two front wheels. This provided both comfort and unbelievable road-holding characteristics. One feature of both the Mini and the 1100 was their long production runs, which enabled the high cost of development and the tooling charges to be absorbed in the millions of cars that were made. Changes are made from time to time to keep the models up-to-date, but the basic shapes have not been altered. These two factors, keeping up-to-date with technical advances and keeping the price down, allow the cars to remain competitive.

By the end of the 1960s all European cars were provided with heaters, defrosters, and windshield-washers, and even seat belts were becoming popular. Comforts such as these were made necessary by the increase in the number of highways being built, which made it possible to undertake much longer journeys by car than had been possible before.

A VOLKSWAGEN SAFETY CAR

Volkswagen's experiments were based on the principle of the strong central passenger box. Front and rear telescopic bumpers are fixed onto the box and in an accident the front or rear portions crush, but the central compartment remains rigid.

B GM 512 URBAN CAR

Automobiles are not suited to towns where high speeds are not needed and parking is an increasingly difficult problem. A small low-speed car driven by electric batteries has distinct advantages, but batteries give a limited range and the weight of the lead-acid battery also presents problems. General Motors are attempting to solve these problems with this gasoline/electric experimental car.

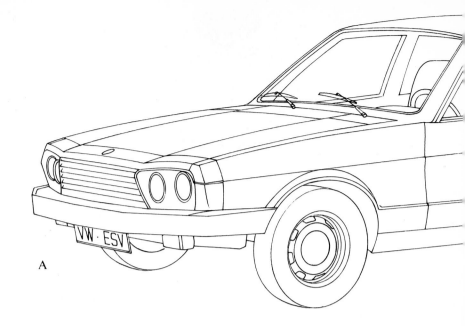

A

B

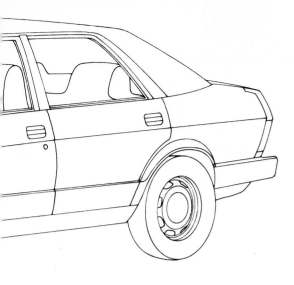

Although the modern car bears very little resemblance to those horseless carriages of the nineteenth century, the principles of operation of the modern gasoline engine are the same as they have been for nearly a hundred years. The power from the explosion still drives pistons down cylinders, takes that power by connecting rod to a crank, where it is converted into rotary motion to be passed to the driving wheels. This is not an efficient means of producing power, because so much is wasted in friction in the bores and on the bearings of the crank, and the present engine has been developed just about as far as it can be.

Dr. Felix Wankel, a German engineer, has spent many years studying the principle of the rotary piston engine. In 1951, in collaboration with the NSU company, he made an experimental engine and spent eight years on its development, finally patenting the idea all over the world. It now seems likely that over the next few years this type of engine will gradually replace the conventional piston engine. In the early stages Wankel met with a number of problems. It was difficult to seal the edges of the rotor, which takes the place of a piston in a conventional engine, and a great deal of work has been done to perfect this. Another early fault was the rapid wear to the rotor blades—the piston rings of a rotary engine—but with modern materials these early difficulties have now been overcome. In a rotary piston engine, one revolution of the rotor is equivalent to three revolutions of an ordinary piston engine and the resultant advantages are that the engine is quieter, vibrates less, and is capable of giving a much better power-to-weight ratio.

With the importance of the automobile industry in a nation's economy, it is essential for a manufacturer to remain competitive. If production has to be limited because of the inability of a company to expand, bearing in mind that profits are greater and sales higher if an increasing volume can be maintained, that company will either go out of business or it will have to amalgamate with others. Failing this, it is likely to be taken over by a competitor as a means of removing competition and increasing his own output. America has never bothered about direct exports outside of North America. Distances to its potential markets are very great and the cars that it makes for home consumption would not be suitable in Europe. They are too big and are too expensive to run. This does not mean that American companies do not interest themselves in foreign trade; they do, by taking over firms in their home countries. Only one large British manufacturer is still free from American domination; Ford and General Motors also have controlling interests in European and Australian firms. They do not have to export, they simply manage, control, and take a part of the profits. The countries themselves gain advantages. American capital is always available for expansion and for the introduction of new models, and employment of the local population is maintained.

Recent years have seen the rise of a new car-producing nation—Japan. A small industry existed there before the war and they made only 110 cars in 1946. Within eighteen years this had risen to half a million and it reached 2 million in 1968. Their achievement has been in increasing the number of cars in use in Japan and they have begun to make a significant impact on exports into the United States and Europe.

The shape of the current European car has become more or less standardized. Exceptions are still to be found, for example, in the British Leyland Mini and 1100—1300 ranges, in which there is no trunk protruding in the rear, or in the Volkswagen, which has the engine in the rear. All others have fairly large trunks in the back with engines and transmissions in the front with drive onto the rear wheels. Fenders have disappeared and wheels are contained within the body shapes and cars are built on the principle of unitary construction. In this principle the body is combined with the chassis, or undercarriage, and constructed into a single welded metal box of great strength. Axles are hung underneath on strong subframes to which the body is bolted.

A great demand exists for the two-door car with an engine of from 850 to 1200 cc; it is relatively cheap to buy and, being capable of 40 mpg, cheap to run. With the current fuel situation, more and more small cars will be used. About a million a year are sold throughout Europe and with a useful life of about five years it seems that this type of market will always need to be catered to. The slightly larger 1300—1700 cc range of four-door sedans also has a very large following, while there is a limited requirement for two-door semisports cars like the Ford Capri and a fringe demand for the larger cars and the specialized luxury cars, still made by some of the smaller manufacturers and costing up to $24,000 (£10,000) each. Station wagons, or estate cars, are another variant, to cater to the owners who require extra luggage space and interior carrying capacity. A new development has been the five-door sedan, with an extra door built into the back of a sedan body to enable it to be converted into a two-seater station wagon when required.

As labor costs represent such a high proportion of the total cost of car production, new methods are constantly being sought to keep the man hours for any operation down to a minimum. Painting was done by hand with cellulose enamel, and the process has been simplified by automation, but even this requires a certain amount of labor. The latest idea is to use electrostatics for paint application. Vehicles are run into a compartment filled with electrically charged paint particles, that are attracted evenly to the metal of the bodywork. The particles take up all the shapes and curves and no labor is required. Glass fiber has been used in body production for a number of years and it can be colored in manufacture making painting unnecessary; although it shatters when damaged, it can be repaired easily.

There are other plastics with greater strength, but they have not yet been used extensively in the automobile trade. New shapes, new developments, and new ideas continue to evolve. Some are introduced in order to provide greater comfort, economy, longer life, and maximum reliability, all things demanded by the modern motorist who has grown up to expect a great deal from his car. All European manufacturers are seeking to extend their production because it is from increased numbers that the greatest profits are to be earned. Germany, France and Italy have each already been able to achieve between 25 and 30 percent penetration of one another's markets, with Britain only managing in the past to capture a mere $1\frac{1}{2}$ percent of total continental sales and having to accept that a quarter of its own demand is met by imports. The future will see constant battles for sales all over Europe, with an increasing interest being taken in European markets by America, who will invest in existing companies in Europe and take profits without having to export home-built cars across the Atlantic.

It is impossible to predict the future as far as the automobile is concerned, but some factors likely to affect future design include a greater utilization of plastics and growth of the use of automatic transmissions. It is unlikely that many cars will use the conventional clutch and transmission in the 1980s, and the same applies to the reciprocating piston engine.

In spite of continued revival the use of steam power will probably remain an enthusiast's dream, and all cars will adopt the rotary engine working on the Wankel principle. Servicing after every 3,000 or 5,000 miles will become less necessary with the increasing use of sealed components with quite long predetermined lives. As each part reaches its mileage, a light will flash on the dashboard to inform the driver that the car should be taken to a garage for a replacement component.

Spare wheels will be a thing of the past. There is already a tire that will not deflate fully when punctured. It can be driven for up to a hundred miles and repaired at the end of the journey. Cars with these new tires will be available in 1974 or 1975 and could well be the standard tire by 1980.

It is estimated that over 130,000 people are killed on the roads each year and more than another 2 million receive disabling injuries. In 1972, in the United States alone, 56,000 people died in road accidents. These staggering totals increase each year and every effort is being made to modify the design of cars to make them safer. Sliding doors, double-braking systems that are designed to prevent skidding, padded interiors, non-crushable compartments, headrests, seat belts, and impact-absorbing protrusions will all help. So will speed limits and other restrictions, but in the end, however well a driver is trained and examined, the answer lies in the common sense, skill, and care of the motorist.

CUGNOT'S MACHINE

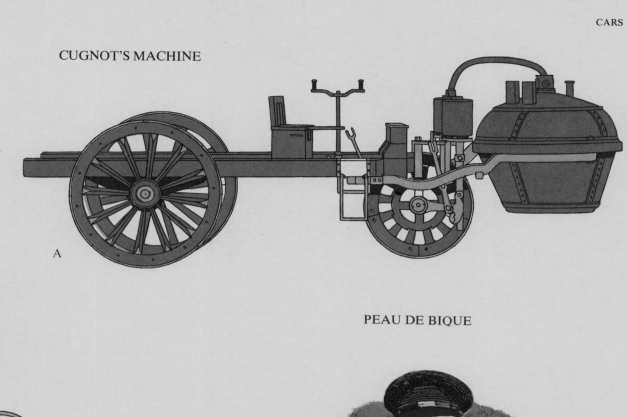

A

TREVITHICK'S STEAM CARRIAGE

PEAU DE BIQUE

B

A Joseph Cugnot's machine is still preserved in Paris. Its main fault was that the weight of both the boiler and the engine was over the front wheel, which was driven by the engine and was also used for steering. The invention of 1769—70 was not developed owing to a lack of money from the government.

B In 1803 Richard Trevithick made his "London" steam carriage. It ran very well, but was far in advance of its time and the inventor was unable to develop it through the lack of financial support.

C The goat-skin coat as worn by the Chevalier René de Knytt and other pioneer motorists.

C

FORD, 1896

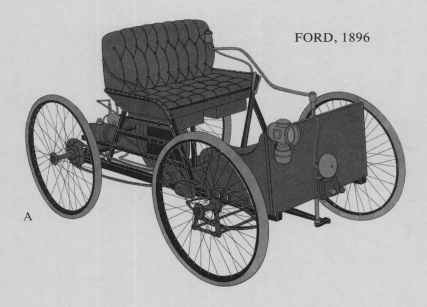

A

B

MODEL T FORD, 1908

A *Henry Ford was born in America in 1863. The son of an Irishman who had emigrated as a farmer, he always wanted to be a mechanic. When he left school at 16 he started work in a small factory and later learned how to repair steam-driven farm machinery. He made his first quadricycle in 1896, powered by a 2-cylinder rear-mounted engine, and gave up his job in 1899 to start up a business on his own. By 1910 his name was a household word. Henry Ford became one of the richest men in the world from his success in making motoring possible for almost everybody in America. His policy was "reliability and low cost", a proud boast of the vast international organization that now bears his name.*

B *The first Model T Ford tourer, distinguished by its brass radiator, later to be replaced by a cheaper black painted steel cowl, was as good on hills as on level ground and as good cross country as on a local road. The Model T Ford was reliable and very easy to drive. Spare parts were easily obtainable, cheap, and comparatively easy to fit, either by the owners or by the farm mechanics in the country. There was no gear lever, the only hand controls were the brake and the throttle, and there were three foot pedals. One was a brake, another for the two forward speeds, and the third for reverse.*

C *Only a few body styling refinements were made in twenty years of production. The windshield has been given a backward slope and the body has a more flush-sided appearance, but the traditional Ford transverse suspension still persists.*

D *The demand for a sedan body was catered to by 1927, but the design was beginning to age. Rather than alter the existing model, Ford decided to withdraw it and replace it with the completely new Model A, which was not nearly so successful.*

MODEL A FORD, 1927

D

MODEL T FORD, 1924

C

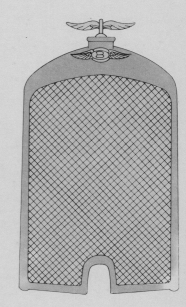

BENTLEY

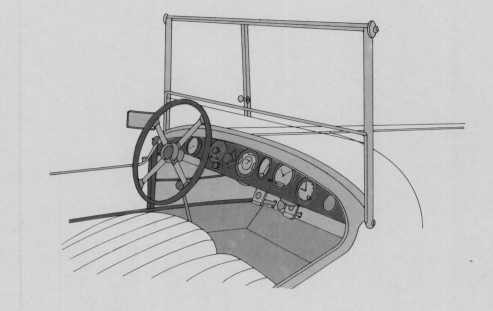

W. O. Bentley was a partner in a London agency for the French D.F.P. cars. He tuned up a 12/15 horsepower D.F.P. 2-liter tourer and entered it for the 1914 Tourist Trophy. Twenty-two cars started this two-day race, but only six finished. Bentley's D.F.P. was the sixth. This great designer had worked on two very successful rotary airplane engines with T. F. Burgess during the First World War. Burgess had been involved in the design of the 1914 T. T. Humber and the two men joined in partnership in 1919 to start work on a new sports car. A 3-liter Bentley first appeared in 1919 and was a sporting car for road rather than track use, based on the designs of the prewar light racing cars. It had very good acceleration and a comparatively high top speed, the first models producing 65 brake horsepower at 3,500 rpm. The 3-liter cars were much improved during their life; in 1924 they were given front-wheel brakes, and the engines were developed to give up to 88 brake horsepower by 1926. Altogether 1,620 were built. By that time the 3-liter Bentley was being outclassed in performance by Sunbeam and Bugatti cars of similar capacity, so Bentley designed a faster, smoother, larger $4^1/_2$-liter car in 1927 (illustrated). It produced 110 brake horsepower and was capable of a top speed of 92 mph (148 km/h), and apart from a major clutch modification was not altered during its production life. One of these cars won the 24-hour race at Le Mans in 1928. In 1930 a supercharged model was made that gave the car a maximum speed of 100 mph (160 km/h), but only 50 of these were made against 662 standard cars, until the large 4-cylinder sports cars were superseded in 1931 by the 6-cylinder version.

B

C

D

A

E

F

A *This is the 1937 Volkswagen prototype which was produced for Dr. Porsche by the Daimler Benz factory.*

B *The 1939 KdF-Wagen ("Strength-through-Joy" car) which was the forerunner of the Volkswagen Beetle. Only 210 were completed before the factory was changed over to war production.*

VOLKSWAGEN K70

G

KARMANN-GHIA COUPÉ

H

C The 1932 Porsche Type 12 design upon which Dr. Ferdinand Porsche based the Volkswagen Beetle. Only three prototypes were built.

D By 1935 Dr. Porsche had developed this experimental car from the Type 12 but it never went into production.

E Although this 1971 Volkswagen Super Beetle has changed very little in outward appearance from the original prewar design, all the engine parts and other details have been changed.

F Like the K70, this Volkswagen 412LE is different from the traditional Beetle with a lot more space in the back.

G The K70 has a top speed of nearly 100 mph (160 km/h). The 1605 cc in-line engine is at the front and drives the front wheels. The car has four doors and is a complete breakaway in style from the original Volkswagen.

H Built to use the 1584 cc engine, the sporting coupé with the Karmann-Ghia body satisfied the demand for a two-seater Volkswagen with a faster look.

A *In outside appearance the prototype ESFO5 safety car made by Mercedes-Benz looks like a conventional sedan. Safety features include the large "bellows" bumpers, headlight wipers, and nonburst door locks. The Germans have rejected as being too costly for Europe the American idea of a "strongbox", a rigid passenger compartment that will remain intact even in the most severe accident.*

A

B *The American General Motors safety car attempts to increase the rigidity of the body by having fixed side windows, with only one small section that opens on the driver's side. Thick padding is applied to the interior and the front and back ends of the car are designed to crush on impact.*

GENERAL MOTORS SAFETY CAR

B

AIRCRAFT

THE CONQUEST OF THE AIR

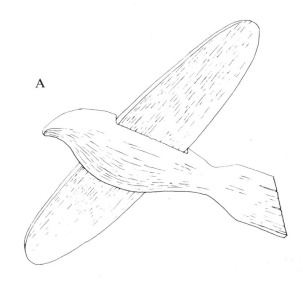

A

From the dawn of history, the flight of birds has inspired men with a longing to fly. But thousands of years and countless lives were wasted in trying to imitate the birds. In the eleventh century A.D., the so-called "Saracen of Constantinople" was killed when he tried to fly with a stiffened cloak. Almost five hundred years later, in 1507, Abbot Damian of Tungland was injured in an attempt to fly with wings from the walls of Stirling Castle in Scotland. Countless others, whose exploits history has failed to record, built themselves wings that were far too small and tried to flap them with arms that were far too weak. The result, usually, was death or serious injury. These brave and foolhardy men are often regarded as pathetic, comical figures but it was they who kept alive the dream of, one day, flying through the air. In the late fifteenth century, Leonardo da Vinci suggested augmenting muscle power with levers and pulleys, but the results were clearly not good enough, and there is no evidence to show that anyone tried to build or fly a Leonardo flapping-wing machine. In 1680, Giovanni Borelli, an Italian physiologist, demonstrated the total inadequacy of human muscle-power for ornithopter flight and this diagnosis has held good until very recently when, with the aid of modern ultra-light materials, brief man-powered flights have been made.

When men finally did leave the ground it was in a craft almost as frail and fickle as a bubble. Some claim that, in the thirteenth century, Roger Bacon, the English monk, scholar, and scientist, first pointed the way to lighter-than-air craft when he wrote about "a large hollow globe of copper or other suitable metal, wrought extremely thin in order to have it as light as possible . . . filled with etherial air or liquid fire".

For nearly five centuries, the idea of flotation in the air vied with flapping wings as a potential method of getting airborne. During this period, monasteries were the centers of science and learning, so it is not surprising that most of those whose theories survive, with the exception of Leonardo, were monks or priests. Francisco di Mendoza, who died in 1626, suggested that a wooden vessel would float through the air if it was filled with what he called "elementary fire". Not long afterward, the Bishop of Chester, John Wilkins, described Bacon's ideas in more scientific terms when he stated that since the air of the upper atmosphere was known to be of lower density than the lower air, a container filled with air from the upper atmosphere would rise. Unfortunately, he omitted to explain how one was supposed to get up to the upper atmosphere in order to fill the container!

Francesco de Lana-Terzi, an Italian Jesuit, decided that the real answer was to have nothing at all inside the containers. In 1670, he published in his *Prodromo* a design

B

A EGYPTIAN MODEL "GLIDER"
This wooden model of a bird, with 7 inch (18 cm) span wings, came to light in 1972 in a storeroom at the Cairo Museum. It may have been no more than a weather vane, but its design leads some historians to believe that the Egyptians may have been making and flying model gliders as early as the third or fourth century B.C.

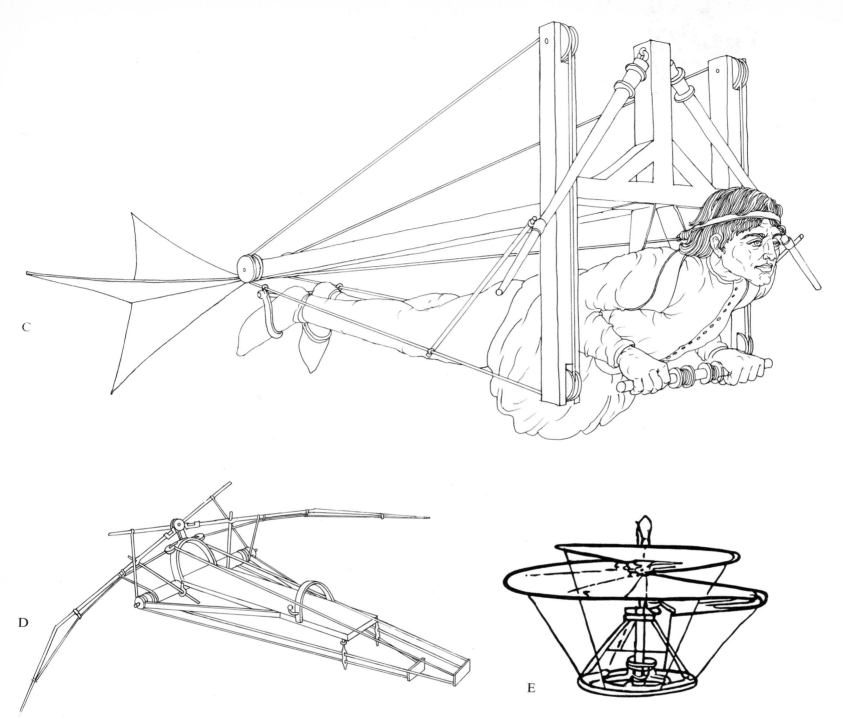

C

D

E

B ALEXANDER THE GREAT
So awe-inspiring were the achievements of Alexander the Great (356—323 B. C.) that legend even credited him with the ability to fly. This ancient print depicts his vehicle as a kind of cage, lifted by four griffons.

C LEONARDO'S "HEADBAND" ORNITHOPTER
Another of da Vinci's historic designs for an ornithopter (flapping-wing machine). This one utilized movements of the pilot's head, by connecting the movable tail surfaces to a headband.

D LEONARDO'S PRONE ORNITHOPTER
One of the flapping-wing aircraft designed by Leonardo da Vinci. Realizing that man could not fly by using arm muscles alone, he produced drawings of machines worked by both arm and leg movements. Altogether, da Vinci's notebooks contained about 150 sketches of flying machines of various types.

E LEONARDO'S HELICAL SCREW
This sketch, made by da Vinci in 1490, shows a flying device intended to screw itself vertically up into the air. Da Vinci called it a helix, the Greek word for screw which forms part of our modern word helicopter; of it he said: "If this instrument is made well the helix is able to make a screw in the air and to climb high."

for a "flying ship" which would be raised by four vacuum spheres. A near vacuum, made practicable by the invention of the air pump by Otto von Guericke in 1650, was clearly lighter than any kind of air or other lifting agent. So all one had to do was to make some thin copper spheres, extract the air, attach the spheres to a boat-shaped carriage, and take off—strange that nobody at this period seems to have given any thought to how they would get the "flying ship" down again! Unfortunately, de Lana soon discovered that, if the copper skin of the globes was made thin and light enough to become lighter than air when evacuated, the atmospheric pressure would crush the globes as the air was extracted. Nonetheless, de Lana was the first to design a lighter-than-air craft based on definite scientific principles.

Who finally discovered that the lifting force that everyone sought was available in their own homes? Evidence seems to confirm that it was a Brazilian priest, Bartolomeu Laurenço de Gusmão. A contemporary account of one of his experiments, made before the King of Portugal, tells how, on August 8, 1709, Gusmão lit a fire under a model balloon, that took off and traveled through the air. Gusmão has hitherto seldom been rated very highly as a pioneer of flight, because the usually published drawings of his *Passarola* (Great Bird) show a ridiculous contraption with a parachute, flapping wings, rarefied air, magnets, and rockets—every conceivable kind of lifting agent. In fact, the drawings were probably produced by an imaginative artist who learned secondhand of Gusmão's experiments and put down his own interpretation of the design. When the drawings are stripped of the probably imagined features, it is possible to see how sufficient hot-air lift might have been produced under the parachute "sail" to raise a light model into the air. An alternative possibility is that the *Passarola* was only a carriage, intended to be suspended beneath a full-sized hot-air balloon.

The year in which man finally got off the ground was 1783. Two French papermakers, Joseph and Etienne Montgolfier, noting the way that smoke from a fire whisked upward pieces of charred paper, began experimenting with paper bags. They held large bags, open end downward, over a fire for a while and then released them. The bags promptly rose to the ceiling. Here was the lifting force for which would-be fliers had been waiting. They did not realize that their "Montgolfier gas" was no more than hot air which, being rarefied, was lighter than the colder surround-

A

A THE FIRST HUMAN AERIAL VOYAGE
The brothers Montgolfier were the first to design an entirely successful man-carrying balloon. After a test flight on September 19, 1783, with an animal payload, the first human journey was made on November 21 of the same year by Pilâtre de Rozier and the Marquis d'Arlandes, in a flight across Paris.

B THE FIRST HYDROGEN BALLOON
Of more practical value in the quest for flight was the hydrogen balloon, the invention of Professor J.A.C. Charles, which appeared very soon after the first Montgolfier craft. On December 1, 1783, Charles, with Marie-Noël Robert as passenger, made the first man-carrying flight—also across Paris—in a balloon of this type.

C PASSAROLA
Gusmão's Passarola *(Great Bird), depicted in this undoubtedly fanciful artist's impression, was thought to be a complete design for a flying machine. It now appears more likely that it was only a passenger-carrying nacelle, intended to be suspended beneath a hot-air balloon. A*

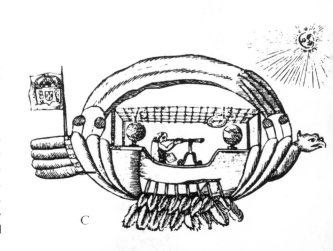

C

B

remarkably similar carriage formed part of an 1843 design for a convertiplane by Sir George Cayley. Recent historical research has established that Gusmão, on August 8, 1709, became the first man successfully to demonstrate a model hot-air balloon, 74 years earlier than the first such demonstration by the Montgolfier brothers.

D TWO HISTORIC JOURNEYS
The first two historic man-carrying flights, both in lighter-than-air aircraft, are shown in the map on the right. The route in blue is that taken by de Rozier and the Marquis d'Arlandes on November 21, 1783. Taking off from the Château de la Muette, they landed at Butte-aux-Cailles some 25 minutes later, having covered a distance of about 7 1/2 miles (12 km) and reached a height of over 3,280 ft. (1,000 m). As can be seen from the map, the journey of the Charles hydrogen balloon on December 1, 1783 (shown in red), improved considerably upon the distance flown by the montgolfière ten days earlier. In fact, its cross-country flight covered a distance of some 27 miles (43 km).

D

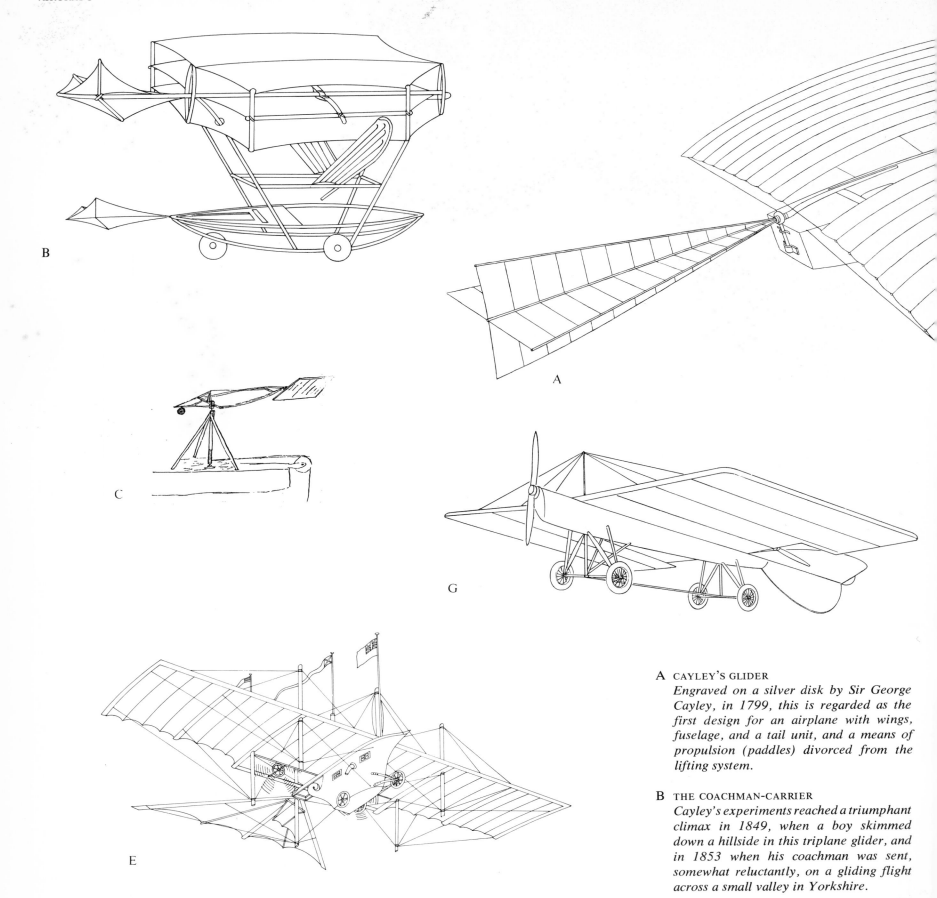

B

A

C

G

E

A CAYLEY'S GLIDER
Engraved on a silver disk by Sir George Cayley, in 1799, this is regarded as the first design for an airplane with wings, fuselage, and a tail unit, and a means of propulsion (paddles) divorced from the lifting system.

B THE COACHMAN-CARRIER
Cayley's experiments reached a triumphant climax in 1849, when a boy skimmed down a hillside in this triplane glider, and in 1853 when his coachman was sent, somewhat reluctantly, on a gliding flight across a small valley in Yorkshire.

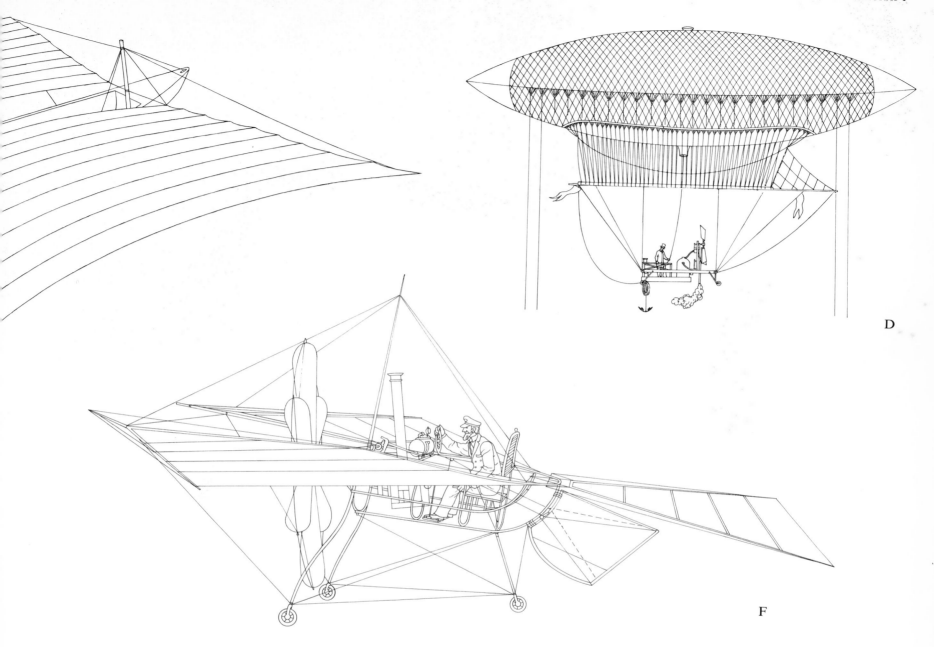

C CAYLEY'S WHIRLING ARM
True heavier-than-air research dates from 1804, when Cayley built a whirling arm device, spun by a weighted cord, to measure the lifting power of a wing surface. In the same year he flew the first successful model airplane, consisting of a kite-shaped wing mounted on a pole, with a universally jointed tail unit.

D THE FIRST AIRSHIP
The first attempt to produce a dirigible (steerable) lighter-than-air aircraft was this steam-powered airship built by Henri Giffard in 1852. In it, Giffard flew 16³/₄ miles (27 km) from Paris to Trappes on September 24 of that year, but its 3 horse-power engine gave it an average speed of
only about 5¹/₂ mph (9 km/h) and it was not fully controllable.*

E AERIAL STEAM CARRIAGE
Henson's inspired and prophetic design provided a major stepping-stone between the theories of Cayley and the reality of flight some sixty years later. A 20 ft. (6.10 m) span model was tested between 1844–1847; it did not fly, but the design lacked only wing dihedral and a suitable power plant to have had all the essential ingredients for success.

F DU TEMPLE'S MONOPLANE
In about 1874, Félix du Temple's monoplane, fitted with a hot-air engine, became the first powered heavier-than-air
aircraft to leave the ground with a pilot on board, though it made only a short hop after gaining speed down an inclined ramp. Its three-wheel landing gear was fitted with shock absorbers and was designed to be retracted in flight.*

G MOZHAISKI'S STEAM MONOPLANE
Another airplane that made a short flight after taking off down a slope was the huge (74 ft. 9¹/₂ in; 22.80 m) span monoplane of Alexander Mozhaiski, in Russia in 1884. This was creditable, as the aircraft weighed nearly a ton and was powered by two small British-built steam engines giving a total of only 30 horse-power.

A

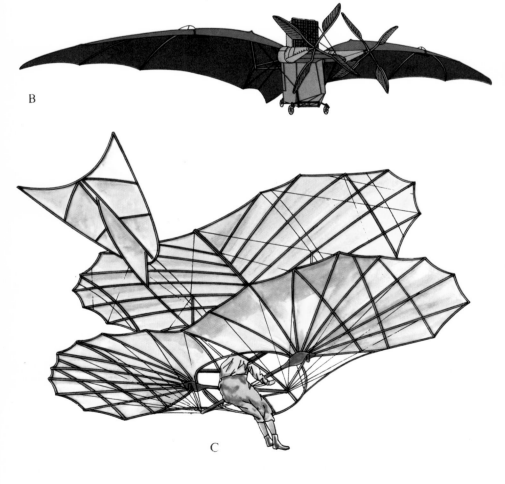

B

C

ing air and consequently rose. Not that this mattered. On October 15, 1783, Pilâtre de Rozier became the first man to leave the ground, in a tethered Montgolfier balloon of paper-lined linen. On November 21, the same man, accompanied by the Marquis d'Arlandes, flew over Paris in another Montgolfier hot-air balloon—and flying had become practicable.

However, the hot-air balloon was a somewhat dangerous contraption, as the brazier that maintained the supply of hot air in flight tended to set light to the fabric. Far better was the completely enclosed spherical balloon invented in the same year by the French physicist J. A. C. Charles, which used as its lifting force "inflammable air", or hydrogen, discovered by Henry Cavendish in 1766. But even the hydrogen balloon was a mere plaything of the elements, capable of no more than a one-way, downwind flight. The irritating inability to steer balloons in flight, however, led to the beginnings of aerial propulsion, and to the invention of the airscrew which was to become the forerunner of the propeller.

It was Yorkshire-born Sir George Cayley who discovered the basic principles on which the modern science of aeronautics is founded. At the age of twenty-six, in 1799, he understood the problems well enough to produce a diagram showing the forces of lift, thrust, and drag acting on a wing, and to design an airplane with a fixed wing, tail surfaces, and two propulsive paddles. Then, realizing that the kite held the key to heavier-than-air flying, he mounted a kite wing, with its leading edge raised to a 6-degree angle of incidence, on a 5 ft. (1.52 m) stick "fuselage", and attached a movable tail unit; he could control the direction of flight, and make the model climb or dive, by adjusting the tail's position.

This model flew successfully in 1804, marking the true beginning of the fixed-wing airplane. By 1809 he had scaled up the design into a glider big enough to carry a boy. With his eightieth birthday approaching, he completed a triplane glider, had it carried to a hillside, and ordered his coachman on board. That first reluctant pilot made a brief, comparatively uncontrolled glide across the valley—and resigned immediately afterwards!

Anyone taking full advantage of Cayley's theories might have built and flown a practical glider: to do more was not possible without a suitable lightweight power plant. William Samuel Henson, who first described Cayley as the "Father of Aerial Navigation", produced in 1842 one of the most remarkable designs in early aviation history. His "Aerial Steam Carriage", or "Ariel", was to be a huge monoplane, driven by a steam engine in the fuselage and spanning 150 ft. (45.72 m), with cambered, double-surface wings, tail control surfaces, a tricycle landing gear, and an enclosed passenger cabin. With John Stringfellow, he built a model of the "Ariel" in an effort to prove his claims for the imminence of international air travel. When tested, it achieved no more than a "descending glide", weighed down by its engine. So died a project that, given a lightweight engine, might have saved a further half century of wasted effort.

To offset the shortcomings of the power plants then available, the pioneers who followed Henson employed assisted takeoff in the form of a downward sloping launching ramp. Félix du Temple, a French naval officer, was—so far as we know—the first to fly a powered model airplane, in about 1857. By 1874 he had built a full-scale airplane on similar lines, powered by a hot-air engine. This made a short hop, after running down a ramp, in about 1874—the first known hop by a man-carrying powered airplane. In 1884 similar hops were made in Russia in a large steam-powered monoplane designed and built by Alexander Mozhaiski.

Meanwhile, some progress had been made with lighter-than-air aircraft. The balloon offered only lift, without power or control. What was needed was a self-propelled, steerable balloon—a true "airship". Cayley, in 1837, drew up a design for a really practical airship, with a streamlined envelope and steam-driven propellers for propulsion and steering.

Theories were translated into reality by a Frenchman, Pierre Jullien, who flew a clockwork-powered model airship named *Le Précurseur* in 1850. It paved the way for the first full-size airship, in which Henri Giffard flew from Paris to Trappes two years later. Giffard's airship was powered only by a 3 horsepower steam engine, and lack of a really suitable lightweight power plant continued to hamper progress for the remainder of the nineteenth century.

The first completely successful airship, able to be steered in flight back to its starting point, was the electrically driven *La France*, built by Renard and Krebs in 1884. By then, however, the internal-combustion engine had been evolved. The little Brazilian pioneer, Alberto Santos-Dumont, proved its capabilities by fitting a gasoline engine to one of his airships in 1898 and, later, by circling the Eiffel Tower in Paris—a feat that earned him 100,000 francs.

It was left to the Germans to find a practical use for the first really satisfactory craft. Graf Ferdinand von Zeppelin began to plan a series of giant military airships as early as 1874. They were not merely elongated balloons but real flying ships, built around a rigid metal framework, and were destined to become among the most feared, and later most respected, aircraft ever flown.

Almost without exception, the birdmen had tried to fly by flapping artificial wings as they fell. None of the early would-be fliers appear to have thought of using easier-to-make fixed wings. They studied the flight of birds, yet do not seem to have appreciated that many birds wheel and soar without needing to flap their wings.

A French sea captain named Jean-Marie Le Bris appears to have been one of the first to attempt a fixed-wing soaring flight in 1857, but it was the German Otto Lilienthal who became the first great exponent of gliding. From an artificial hill, he made some 2,500 successful glides in graceful, birdlike craft. He improved his designs gradually, until he could cover distances of around a quarter of a mile (400 m) at heights up to 75 ft. (23 m) above the ground. Unfortunately, he relied on movements of his body in the air—by swaying fore and aft and to each side—to control the aircraft's flight. On August 9, 1896, he lost control, crashed, and died soon afterward.

The great achievement of Lilienthal was that he proved beyond doubt that heavier-than-air flight was entirely practicable. It was clearly only a matter of time before somebody made a proper powered, controlled, and sustained flight, but meanwhile other "hoppers" continued to make news. Clément Ader of France claimed to have covered some 164 ft. (50 m) in his bat-like, steam-powered *Éole* monoplane, on October 9, 1890, and Karl Jatho of Germany made a number of hops and short flights of up to 200 ft. (61 m) between August and November 1903. Dr. Samuel Pierpont Langley, eminent astronomer and secretary of the Smithsonian Institution, designed a series of tandem-wing "Aerodromes", the first of which was a steam-powered model spanning 14 ft. (4.27 m); it flew well over three-quarters of a mile (1.2 km) at 25 mph (40 km/h) in 1896. A full-size "Aerodrome", piloted by Charles Manly—who had built its very advanced 52 horsepower radial gasoline engine—was catapult-launched from a house-boat on the Potomac River on October 7, 1903. Unfortunately, it struck a post on the launch-gear and plunged into the water. The same thing happened in a second attempt on December 8.

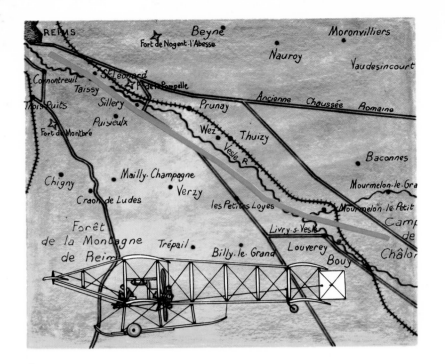

A

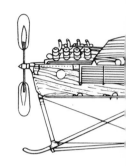

B

D

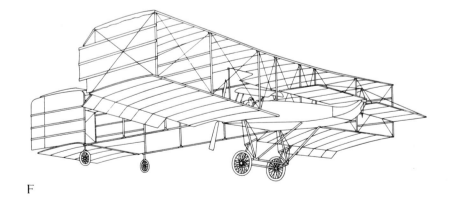

F

G

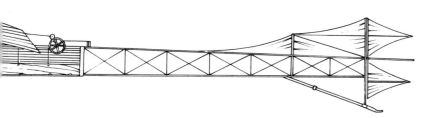

C

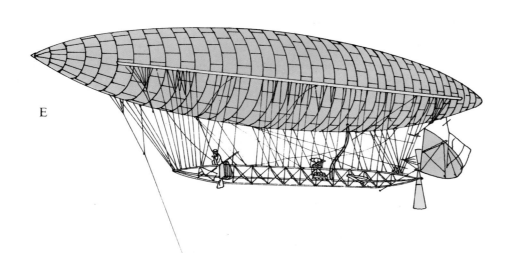

E

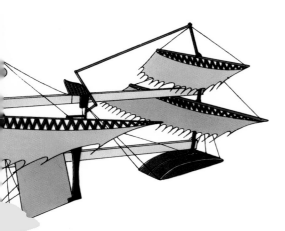

after he had fitted his aircraft with ailerons and a more powerful engine.

B ANTOINETTE MONOPLANE
A projecting front skid was also a feature of the handsome Antoinette monoplane of 1909, perhaps the most elegant of all the early European monoplane designs. Purpose of the skid was to prevent the aircraft from tipping over onto its nose.

C SANTOS-DUMONT BIPLANE
Already celebrated for the success of his airships, Alberto Santos-Dumont in 1906 made the first officially observed and recognized powered flights in Europe in his tailfirst 14-bis biplane. In making this flight, on October 23, 1906, he set up the first world airspeed record of 25.65 mph (41.28 km/h). The cellular wings and tail of the 14-bis were based on the box-kite invented by Lawrence Hargrave in Australia.

D FARMAN-VOISIN BIPLANE
Henry Farman was a great innovator as well as a great pilot. This illustration shows some of the improvements that he made to the standard Voisin biplane: the elimination of wing and tail "side curtains", the use of movable rudder surfaces, and a wheel-and-skid landing gear. When fitted with the new Gnome rotary engine in 1909, one of these Farman biplanes won the distance prize at the Reims air meeting with an outstanding flight of 112 miles (180 km).

E SANTOS-DUMONT'S AIRSHIP
The completely practical airship was born in 1898 when Santos-Dumont fitted a gasoline engine for the first time. Altogether, Santos built 14 airships, of which the one illustrated is typical, and gained worldwide fame on October 19, 1901, by flying the sixth one around the Eiffel Tower in Paris.

F VOISIN BIPLANE
Far more practical than either the Wright biplane or European designs like the 14-bis were the Voisin biplanes that began to make a name for themselves in France in 1907.

G THE FIRST SEAPLANE
The first successful flight of a powered seaplane was made by Henri Fabre, at Martigues, France, on March 28, 1910. His strange-looking tailfirst aircraft had a 50 horsepower Gnome engine.

A FARMAN'S CROSS-COUNTRY ROUTE
Henry Farman's first closed-circuit flight of more than 1 km was made on November 9, 1907, but since official observers were not present he had to repeat the performance on January 13, 1908, in order to go into the record books. The map shows a cross-country flight of 16³/₄ miles (27 km) made on October 30, 1908,

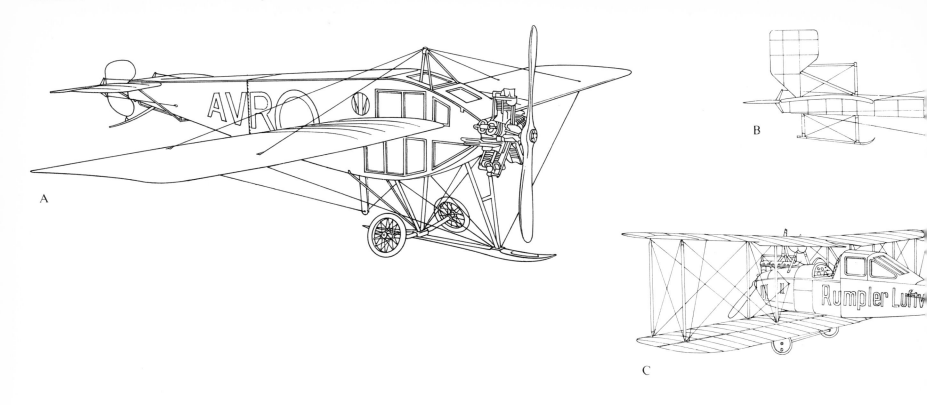

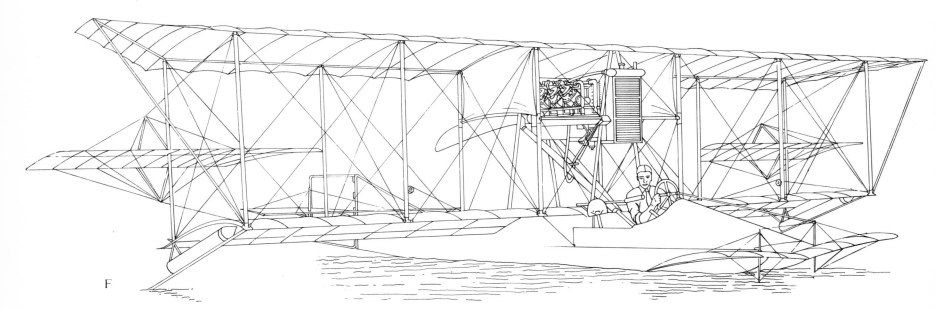

A A.V. ROE TYPE F

In 1912 Roe produced his Type F mono-plane, the first airplane with totally en-closed accommodation to fly anywhere in the world.

B RUSSIAN KNIGHT

Some designers "thought big" from the start—though by no means all of them successfully. One design, which was am-bitious and outstandingly successful for its time, was the "Russian Knight" bi-plane (also known as Bolsche or Le Grand: "The Big One") designed, built, and

flown by Igor Sikorsky in Russia in 1913. It was the first four-engined airplane to fly.

C RUMPLER C.I

Surprisingly, perhaps, the first postwar passenger air services were operated by the recently defeated Germans in 1919. The aircraft used were converted Rumpler C.I two-seat reconnaissance biplanes, with a crude cabin over the rear cockpit for the two passengers.

D SOPWITH SCHNEIDER

The first seaplane able to outperform most contemporary landplanes was the Sopwith Schneider. Powered by a 100 horsepower Gnome engine, it won the contest for the important Schneider Trophy at Monaco in 1914 at a speed of 86.78 mph (139.66 km/h).

E SACHSEN

Count Ferdinand von Zeppelin conceived the rigid airship as a large military ve-hicle, and in due course his ideas came to fruition in the 1914–1918 war. Be-

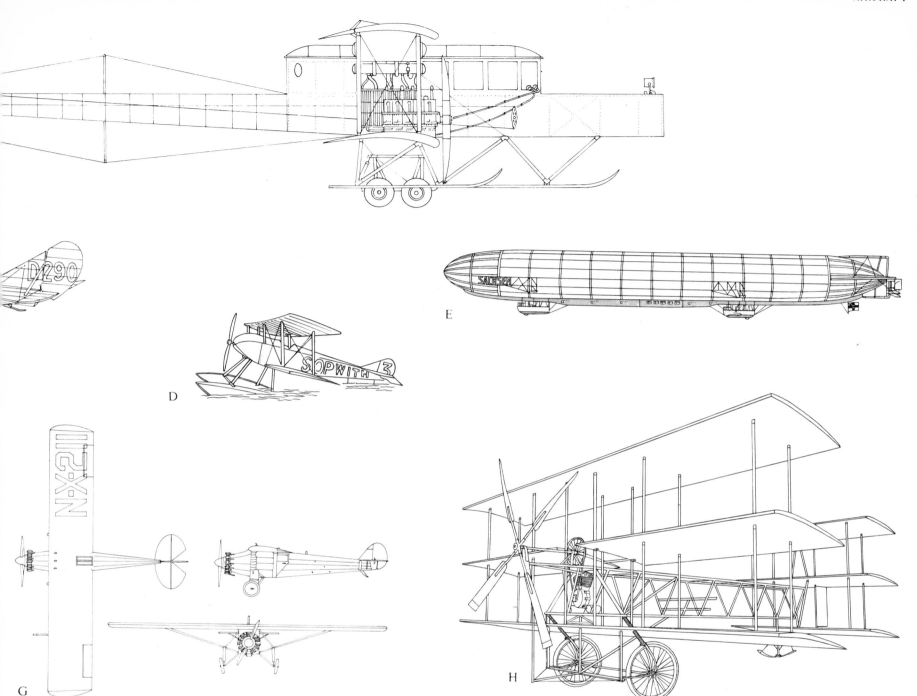

E

D

G

H

fore then, however, six of these metal-framed giants had, between 1910 and 1914, operated the world's first regular passenger airline service. During those four years Delag, as the airline was known, flew a total of 170,000 miles (273,600 km) and carried 35,000 passengers without a single injury.

F CURTISS FLYING BOAT
Fabre's seaplane, although successful, was hardly a realistic vehicle. The great pioneer of waterborne aircraft was Glenn Curtiss of America, whose seaplanes and

flying boats were far more practical than that of Fabre. The first Curtiss flying boat flew for the first time on January 10, 1912; he had flown a float-fitted development of his Golden Flyer land biplane a year before this, on January 26, 1911.

G SPIRIT OF ST. LOUIS
Charles Lindbergh, like Blériot, became a world hero when, on May 20–21, 1927, he made the first solo Atlantic crossing, all the way from New York to Paris, in the little 220 horsepower Ryan

monoplane Spirit of St. Louis. The 3,600 mile (5,790 km) flight was made in 33½ hours.

H A. V. ROE TRIPLANE
The first officially recognized flight by a Briton in the United Kingdom was made by A. V. Roe in 9 horsepower paper-covered triplane om July 13, 1909. Greatest of the British pioneers, Roe later founded the famous Avro company.

There was no longer any effective competition for Wilbur and Orville Wright, the bicycle-manufacturing brothers of Dayton, Ohio, who were already preparing their tail-first biplane for flight on the sand dunes of Kitty Hawk, North Carolina.

They deserved success. For more than four years they had been experimenting, first with a 50 ft. (15.24 m) kite to prove their wing-warping control system, then with full-size piloted gliders. They had evolved their own wing sections with the aid of a homemade wind tunnel, and had built their own 12 horsepower gasoline engine to power their biplane. On December 17, 1903, their first *Flyer* made four flights. The air age had come at last.

How great was the Wright brothers' achievement? The first flight, by Orville, covered only 120 ft. (37 m) and consisted of a series of dives and climbs until one slightly bigger dive brought the twelve second hop to an abrupt end. Even the fourth flight, by Wilbur, covering 852 ft. (260 m), was not terribly impressive.

If the Wrights had decided to rest on their laurels at that point, they would hardly be remembered today. But they did not. They went home to Dayton and began work on a better *Flyer* and a falling-weight catapult to speed its takeoff. A more powerful engine was fitted. Stability and control were improved. At last they felt that their airplane was good enough to offer to the United States Army—only to be told, on October 24, 1905, that "the Board...does not care to formulate any requirements for the performance of a flying machine or take any further action on the subject until a machine is produced which by actual operation is shown to be able to produce horizontal flight and to carry an operator." Yet only nineteen days earlier they had covered 24 1/2 miles (39 1/2 km) in 38 minutes, 3 seconds, in their best flight of the year!

Even in 1908 the Wrights were still unchallenged masters of the air, but already the limitations of their aircraft were becoming clear; in particular, the front-elevator design was much inferior to the tail-at-the-rear layout suggested by Cayley and Henson. But they proved the value of a scientific, rather than a "build-it-and-see" approach to flying, and their example inspired others to build better "go-anywhere" airplanes.

Those better airplanes did not emerge overnight. The "14-bis" biplane in which Santos-Dumont made the first officially recognized powered flight in Europe, three years after the Wrights's early success, was less advanced than even their original *Flyer*,

but a hint of future possibilities was given by the neat little triplane that A. V. Roe flew in July, 1909, and the businesslike Type XI monoplane in which Louis Blériot flew across the English Channel on July 25, 1909. With Blériot's great flight the airplane showed, for the first time, its ability to overcome natural and political barriers.

France, the acknowledged center of world aviation from about 1907 onward, was inevitably the first country to establish an airplane industry. The Voisin brothers set the lead by building box-kite biplanes for anyone with money and courage to buy them. Antoinette and Blériot monoplanes were also bought by sporting fliers. In 1909 there appeared a revolutionary little aeroengine named the Gnome, invented by Louis and Laurent Seguin; its crankshaft had to be bolted to the aircraft structure, so that the seven cylinders and the propeller rotated around it, and it gave an honest 50 horsepower for a weight of only 165 lb. (75 kg).

During Louis Blériot's historic flight from France to England, the 25 horsepower Anzani engine of his monoplane began to overheat. Just as he was about to brace himself for a ditching in the sea, a fortuitous shower of rain cooled the cylinders and enabled him to complete the trip.

His great rival for cross-Channel honors, Hubert Latham, was not so lucky, and twice came down in the water in his Antoinette monoplane. Fortunately the aircraft was buoyant enough to remain afloat until he was rescued, but clearly there was a future for airplanes deliberately designed to land on, and take off from, water. Blériot himself had experimented with floatplanes in 1906, in collaboration with Gabriel Voisin. Even the Wrights had tested a set of hydrofoils on the Miami River at Dayton in 1907, when they began to realize the limitations of their wheelless *Flyers*. Inevitably, designers in several countries began to look more closely at the possibilities of flying from the water in 1909—1910.

The first powered airplane to take off successfully on floats, on March 28, 1910, was an incredible contraption built in France by Henri Fabre. It utilized a special lattice type of wing spars, which had the same depth and strength as a solid spar but did not create nearly so much drag. Perhaps the best part of the aircraft was the float landing gear, for long after the airplane itself had ceased flying—to become eventually an exhibit in the French Musée de l'Air—Fabre was still turning out similar floats for some of the very efficient seaplanes of the 1912—1914 era.

A

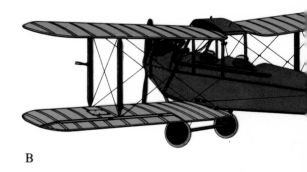

B

D

A GRAF ZEPPELIN
Last of the great passenger airships were the Graf Zeppelin *and her sister ship* Hindenburg, *which could fly from Frankfurt to New York in 52 hours carrying up to 100 passengers. Their luxurious accommodation has yet to be surpassed by a heavier-than-air aircraft, but when* Hindenburg *caught fire after arriving in America on May 6, 1937, it marked the end of the airship as a commercial passenger carrier.*

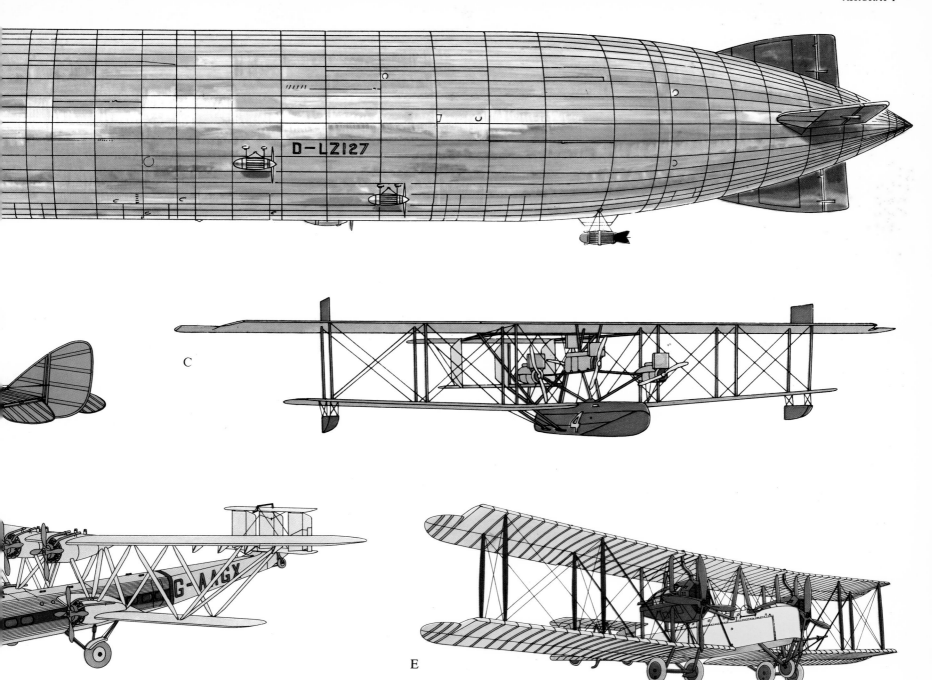

B DE HAVILLAND MOTH
Flying, for so long the prerogative of military or rich or adventurous private pilots, suddenly came within reach of ordinary people in 1925 with the appearance of the Moth, a cheap two-seat lightplane designed by Geoffrey de Havilland, which marked the start of flying clubs the world over.

C CURTISS NC-4
First airplane crossing of the Atlantic was made in stages by airmen of the United States Navy, who left Newfoundland on May 16, 1919, in three NC (Navy-Cur- *tiss) flying boats: NC-1, powered by three 400 horsepower Liberty engines, and NC-3 and NC-4, each with four engines. Only NC-4, after an intermediate stop at the Azores, reached Lisbon thirteen days later.*

D HANDLEY PAGE H.P. 42
Only eight of these aircraft were built. They carried more passengers between London and Europe in the 1930s than all other types of airliner combined—and did so with a 100 percent safety record. Among the last of Imperial Airways's biplane airliners, they offered Pullman-class *comfort for the passengers and an enclosed cabin for the crew.*

E VICKERS VIMY
Outstanding though NC-4's achievement was, it was eclipsed on June 14–15, 1919, when Captain John Alcock and Lieutenant Arthur Whitten-Brown flew nonstop in this converted Vimy bomber from St. John's, Newfoundland, to Clifden in Ireland in $16\frac{1}{2}$ hours—one of the greatest trailblazing flights in history.

The great pioneer of marine flying was Glenn Curtiss of America. During the winter of 1910—1911 he fitted floats to one of his sturdy pusher biplanes and flew this off water for the first time on January 26, 1911. It was the first really practical seaplane, and Curtiss followed it with the first flying boat on January 10, 1912. This latter aircraft differed little from the seaplane, except that the central float was enlarged sufficiently to accommodate the pilot and controls; but from it was evolved the whole long line of great and gracious flying boats that played such a big part in the progress of civil and military flying.

From the start the power plant held the key to progress in flight. Little progress at all had been possible until the advent of the lightweight, efficient gasoline engine. Now that the art of flying had been learned, designers became insatiable in their demands for more powerful and more reliable engines. The Seguins mounted two Gnomes together in 1913 to produce a 14-cylinder two-row engine giving 160 horsepower. But reliability suffered and designers began to prefer a number of small engines to one big one. The Short brothers, in England, with their "push-and-pull" Tandem Twin of 1911, had built the world's first twin-engined airplane, but the person with the best idea, because it was the simplest, was Igor Sikorsky. When, in 1913, he completed the world's first four-engined airplane, named appropriately *Le Grand*, he simply mounted the engines in a row on the lower wings, driving tractor propellers, and set the fashion that has lasted to the present day.

It is often claimed that the 1914—1918 war advanced aviation progress to an unprecedented degree, but such an assessment depends on the terms by which we measure progress. In the field of aeroengine design and manufacture, certainly, the war had brought significant progress. Even an attempt to fly the Atlantic seemed less fearful now that aircraft could be fitted with engines like the superb 360 horsepower Rolls-Royce Eagle, and several British crews made their way to Newfoundland with aircraft that they considered adequate for such a flight.

They were forestalled by airmen of the United States Navy, who left Newfoundland in three Curtiss flying-boats on May 16, 1919, to attempt the first transatlantic flight via the Azores. Every possible safety precaution was taken, to the extent that warships were spaced out along the route to assist the airmen in an emergency. In spite of all this, of the three flying boats only NC-4 succeeded in reaching Lisbon.

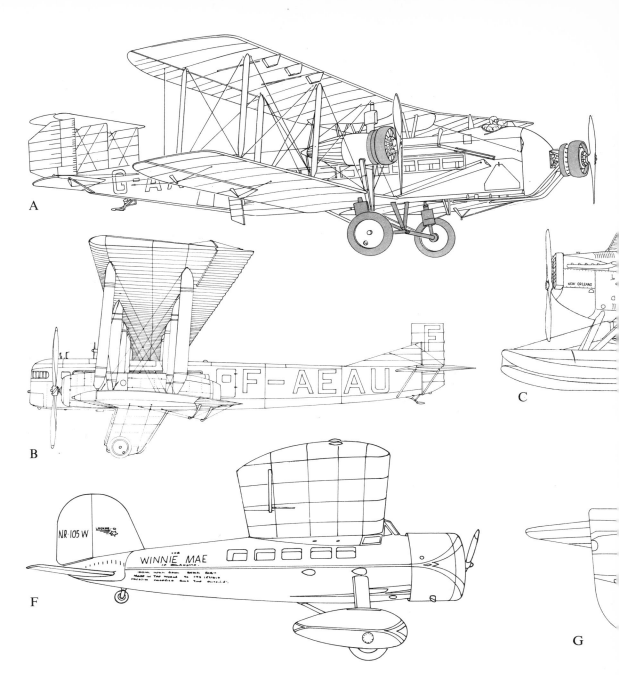

A ARMSTRONG WHITWORTH ARGOSY
The three-engined Armstrong Whitworth Argosy airliner introduced the first luxury "named" service—Imperial Airways's London—Paris "Silver Wing" service of 1927. In contrast to the comfort inside the cabin, the crew sat in an open cockpit.

B FARMAN GOLIATH
The aircraft with which French airlines opened up their first international services in 1919 were Farman Goliaths. Developed from a wartime bomber design, and with wings "built by the mile and cut off by the yard", they carried 12 passengers in two cabins. Cruising speed was 75 mph (120 km/h).

C DOUGLAS WORLD CRUISER
First successful round-the-world flight, in stages, was made by two of four special Douglas World Cruisers, flown by pilots of the United States Army Air Corps, which left Seattle on April 6, 1924. They arrived back on September 28, after a 175-day journey in which they flew some 28,000 miles (45,060 km) and used up no fewer than 29 engines between the four aircraft.

D BREGUET XIX
Several long-distance flights were made in the mid-1920s in the French Breguet XIX, of which one of the most notable was that from Paris to New York nonstop on September 1–2, 1930, by Captain

Within little more than two weeks, NC-4's feat was overshadowed completely by the nonstop Atlantic flight of Alcock and Brown in a converted Vickers Vimy bomber with two Eagle engines.

The Atlantic continued to challenge pilots throughout the 1920s and 1930s. Charles Lindbergh became a world hero in 1927 by making the first solo crossing, all the way from New York to Paris, in the Ryan monoplane *Spirit of St. Louis* with only a single 220 horsepower engine. General Italo Balbo, Italy's air minister, stirred the imagination of his countrymen by leading two mass flights of Savoia-Marchetti flying boats over both the South and North Atlantic.

Less publicized, but more significant, were the crossings made by men like Jean Mermoz of France. By opening a mail service across the great oceans, they paved the way for the passenger airliners that were to follow.

To Germany goes the distinction of having operated the world's first airline services. The year was 1910, the aircraft a huge Zeppelin airship named *Deutschland II*. With her sisters, she carried 35,000 passengers a total of 170,000 miles (273,600 km) between Lake Constance, Berlin, and other cities, before the outbreak of war gave the Zeppelins more sinister tasks to perform. This was not the end of the Zeppelin as an airliner. In the late 1920s and 1930s the *Graf Zeppelin* and *Hindenburg* operated the first passenger services across the Atlantic; but by then the airship was beginning to be outclassed by the faster airplane, and when the *Hindenburg* was lost, with thirty-five passengers and crew members, while landing at Lakehurst in America on May 6, 1937, the whole concept of lighter-than-air commercial airliners died with her.

A flying boat service was operated briefly by the St. Petersburg and Tampa Airboat Line in America in 1914. One passenger at a time could be carried across the Bay of Tampa, the twenty-three minute flight costing five dollars. Then war halted progress for five years. When international airline flights did begin in August 1919, the best that could be offered to passengers was a wicker chair inside the drafty cabin of a converted bomber. Forced landings were frequent and, in the days before radio was fitted, pilots had to rely on familiar features such as straight roads and railways to guide them to their destination.

Serious accidents were surprisingly rare. One of the worst occurred when the pilot of a Paris-bound airliner, following a main road in France, failed to spot a London-bound airliner following the same road at

Dieudonné Costes and Maurice Bellonte in the Point d'Interrogation.

E LATÉCOÈRE 28

Commercial airplane flying over the Atlantic was pioneered by Jean Mermoz of France. On May 11, 1930, he took off from Dakar, West Africa, in a Latécoère 28 floatplane and flew through the night to land at Natal, Brazil, 19½ hours later. The airmail he carried reached Buenos Aires four days after leaving France, instead of the usual eight days. Not until four years later was a regular transatlantic mail service inaugurated to South America, by the German company Deutsche Lufthansa.

F LOCKHEED VEGA "WINNIE MAE"

Lockheed's 5-seat, 220 horsepower transport monoplane Vega appeared in 1927. Six years later, in the specially modified Vega Winnie Mae, *Wiley Post achieved the ultimate flying ambition: a solo flight around the world, completed in 7 days, 18 hours, 50 minutes.*

G DORNIER DO X

The largest number of engines ever installed in an airplane were the 12 that powered the Dornier Do X flying boat of 1929. Although it once flew with no fewer than 169 people on board, neither its engines nor their form of installation were satisfactory.

A BOEING 247

Although the 1930s are remembered chiefly as the golden age of flying boat airliners, a major revolution in landplane airliner design had appeared in the Boeing 247 of 1933. A cantilever, all-metal monoplane, with retractable landing gear, it could cruise at 189 mph (304 km/h), carry 10 passengers and their baggage over a 750 mile (1,207 km) range, and climb under full load on one engine. It was the first really cost-effective airliner in the modern idiom.

B SHORT "C" CLASS

Designed to the requirements of Imperial Airways for the delivery of all Empire airmail, the Short "C" (or "Empire") class flying boat entered service in October 1936, and eventually flew routes from the United Kingdom to East and South Africa, India, and Australia, establishing a new standard of comfort for both crew and passengers. It was also used in 1939, with experimental in-flight refueling techniques, to pioneer Imperial Airways's attempt to inaugurate a regular nonstop service across the North Atlantic.

C BOEING 314

First to establish a regular passenger service across the Atlantic, starting on June 28, 1939, were the Boeing 314s of Pan American Airways. Seating up to 74 passengers, they were powered by four 1,500 horsepower double cyclone engines and carried a 4,200 United States gallon (15,900 liter) fuel load. With a 40-passenger payload, they had a range of 3,100 miles (4,990 km) and were among the first really practical transoceanic transport aircraft.

D SIKORSKY S-42

Igor Sikorsky, having left Russia after the 1917 Revolution, began his second career in aviation when he formed a new company in the United States in early 1923. Here he resumed his development of large fixed-wing aircraft, devoting his attention chiefly to flying boats and amphibious designs. These were very successful in both military and civil markets between the wars; typical of the genre was the S-42, an all-metal monoplane with four 750 horsepower Pratt & Whitney engines that could seat up to 32 passengers.

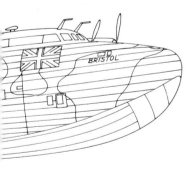

the same height but in the opposite direction. They met head-on.

Gradually, new standards of comfort and safety were achieved. By the late 1920s machines like the Fokker F.VII-3m trimotor were offering a combination of metal construction, multiengined reliability, and the luxury of an enclosed cabin. On some services passengers even received full-course meals in flight, served by a smartly uniformed steward.

The switch to all-metal low-wing monoplane design, with refinements such as a retractable landing gear, control surface trimtabs, variable-pitch propellers, an automatic pilot, and deicing equipment, made the Boeing 247 airliner of 1933 quite revolutionary in a largely biplane age. Its maximum speed of 200 mph (322 km/h) made it as fast as many single-seat fighters of its day, and it reduced the traveling time on United States transcontinental airline services to under twenty hours, carrying ten passengers.

Such aircraft brought to an end the long reign of the biplane. Its traditional advantage of combining great strength with small span

and weight was less significant now that designers could build their airplanes of high strength metals. In any case, the cleanest possible aerodynamic shape was essential if advantage was to be taken of new features like retractable landing gears and the greater power of new aeroengines.

Good as the Boeing 247 was, it was completely eclipsed by the new low-wing monoplane airliners introduced by the Douglas company soon afterward. First of these was the DC-1 prototype, from which were evolved the DC-2 and DC-3. The latter had already gained worldwide acceptance when World War II brought a demand for huge numbers of military transport aircraft. No type met the requirement so well as the DC-3, and more than 10,000 were built. When the war ended, they were sold to civilian airlines to rebuild war-shattered networks of passenger services. They did the job so well, and were so unrivaled as moneymakers in their class, that thirty years after the first of them flew, in 1935, DC-3s still outnumbered any other type of airliner in worldwide service.

FROM JET TO SPACE ROCKET

Back in 1928, when RAF fighters were flying at around 150 mph (240 km/h), a young RAF cadet named Frank Whittle wrote a thesis on *Future Developments in Aircraft Design*, which looked forward to the time when speeds of 500 mph (800 km/h) would be attainable, at heights where the air is far "thinner" than at sea level. Propellers and pistons would be no good, and he suggested the use of rockets or gas-turbine engines.

There was nothing new in the basic idea. Gas turbines, or jet engines, for aircraft had been proposed in the pioneer days, but serious work had to await a time when somebody produced metals capable of withstanding the intense heats and stresses involved. Believing that the time was approaching, Whittle patented his ideas for a jet engine in 1930 and began translating theories into hardware, with the grudging approval of the Air Ministry. Despite difficulty and discouragement, he completed the first practical aircraft jet engine and tested it successfully on April 12, 1937.

Unknown to Whittle, another young man named Pabst von Ohain was working on similar types of power plants in Germany. He ran his first engine, the He S1, in September 1937, and, having rather better financial support than Whittle, was the first to install a jet engine in an airframe—the Heinkel He 178. It was not a very inspiring or very successful aircraft, but it was the first jet-plane to fly, on August 27, 1939. The Heinkel company thus achieved a unique "double" during that year, for on June 30, the first flight had been made by the He 176, the world's first airplane to fly solely on the power of a liquid-fuel rocket engine.

The world's second jet aircraft, Italy's Caproni-Campini N.1, was rather a side-track design. The compressor of its engine was driven by an ordinary piston engine and top speed was a mere 233 mph (375 km/h).

When Britain's first jet aircraft, the Gloster E.28/39, took off for the first time on May 15, 1941, powered by a Whittle W.1 turbojet, it was far more impressive. Top speed was 338 mph (544 km/h), although the engine's output was equivalent to only 688 horsepower at that speed. In other words, the E.28/39 flew nearly as fast as some of the first-line piston-engined fighter aircraft of its time on only half their power. When fitted with a more powerful turbojet, it achieved 466 mph (750 km/h).

While all this was going on, other pioneer aircraft designers were busy in another promising field of aviation endeavor. Thomas Alva Edison, unimpressed by the Wright biplane, once commented sourly: "The airplane won't amount to a damn until it can fly like a hummingbird, go straight up, straight down, hover like a hummingbird." History has shown that he was far from correct in his assessment of the fixed-wing airplane, but there has never been any doubt that aircraft able to take off and land vertically would offer many advantages compared with those that operate conventionally.

Helicopter toys, in which a small rotor is spun up into the air by pulling on a cord, are almost as ancient as kites. Two primitive man-carrying helicopters, one built by Paul Cornu and one by the Breguet brothers, flew in France as long ago as 1907; but the first practical machines of this type did not appear until the mid-1930s. These were the Breguet-Dorand helicopter, tested in 1935—1936, and the German Focke-Achgelis Fw 61, which made flights of over an hour, and reached a height of 11,243 ft. (3,427 m) and a speed of 76 mph (122.5 km/h) between 1937 and 1939. These designs were followed in 1938 by the Weir helicopter in Britain; but the helicopter was only developed into a fully practical vehicle, capable of doing a true job of work, by Igor Sikorsky—the same Sikorsky who had built the world's first four-engined airplane back in 1913.

After an early flirtation with a coaxial rotor design, built in Russia in 1910, Sikorsky, who later emigrated to America, then concentrated on the "single-rotor" configuration. His little VS-300 prototype of 1939 was not immediately successful when tested in tethered form in that year, but after much experiment and modification it finally became, in 1942, the first entirely practical and successful helicopter. From it, all modern "single-rotor" helicopters have descended.

However, although the major credit goes to Sikorsky, his machine embodied important features developed much earlier by the Spanish engineer Juan de la Cierva, who in 1923 produced the first successful Autogiro—the important feature of which, so far as subsequent helicopter development was concerned, was the "flapping" hinges incorporated in the rotor blades. These neatly solved the control problems that had defeated all earlier rotorcraft designers by allowing the advancing rotor blade to pivot, or "flap", upward as its lift increased. The retreating blade's own weight and centrifugal force brought it down again, and lift was thus just about balanced out on each side.

It was not long before the higher speeds made possible by the advent of the jet engine brought their own problems to the designers of fixed-wing aircraft. Even the faster piston-engined fighters sometimes ran into trouble during high-speed dives, losing wings or tails for no apparent reason. Designers knew that their enemy was the invisible, seemingly harmless air, which became so compressed by the speeding aircraft that it formed shock waves which hammered the structure until it broke up. By sweeping back the wings of their aircraft and making them thinner, they managed to delay the shock-wave effects and gain a few extra miles per hour; but many experts doubted that airplanes would ever be able to fly above the speed of sound—past the so-called "sound barrier".

To discover if a specially designed aircraft with a very powerful engine could pen-

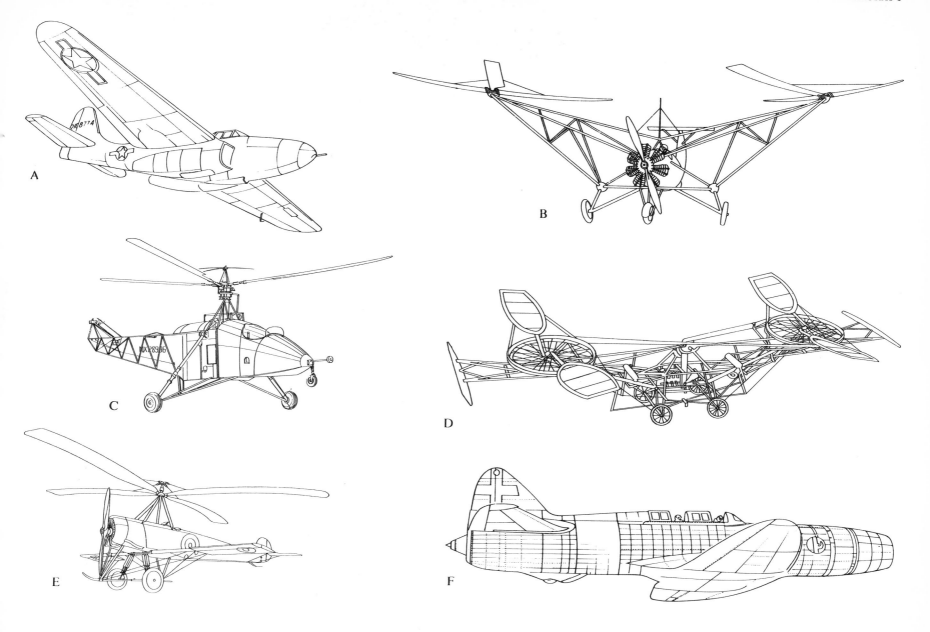

A BELL XP-59A AIRACOMET
America's first jet plane flew on October I, 1942. Powered by two 1,760 lb. (798 kg) st General Electric I-A turbojets, based on the Whittle W.2B, it was later built in small numbers for training, the final production version having a top speed of 413 mph (665 km/h).

B FOCKE-WULF FW 61 HELICOPTER, 1936
This was the first fairly practical VTOL aircraft. A larger helicopter of similar layout, the Fa 223, flew in 1940 and was put into production.

C SIKORSKY VS-300, 1940
The first practical "single-rotor" helicopter. It is from this machine, in its final 1942 form, that all modern helicopters of this configuration have descended.

D CORNU HELICOPTER
First heavier-than-air aircraft to take off vertically in free flight, carrying a pilot, was this twin-rotor helicopter built by Cornu, on November 13, 1907.

E DE LA CIERVA AUTOGIRO
The greatest name in early rotating-wing design was Juan de la Cierva. The principles he evolved with his Autogiros, using unpowered rotors, made possible the modern helicopter.

F CAPRONI-CAMPINI N.1
Italy's first jet airplane, the Caproni-Campini N.1, used an ordinary piston engine to drive its compressor and was not very efficient. It was, however, the first jet aircraft to make a proper cross-country flight, from Milan to Rome, on November 30, 1941. Test flights of the He 178 had been limited to the vicinity of the airfield.

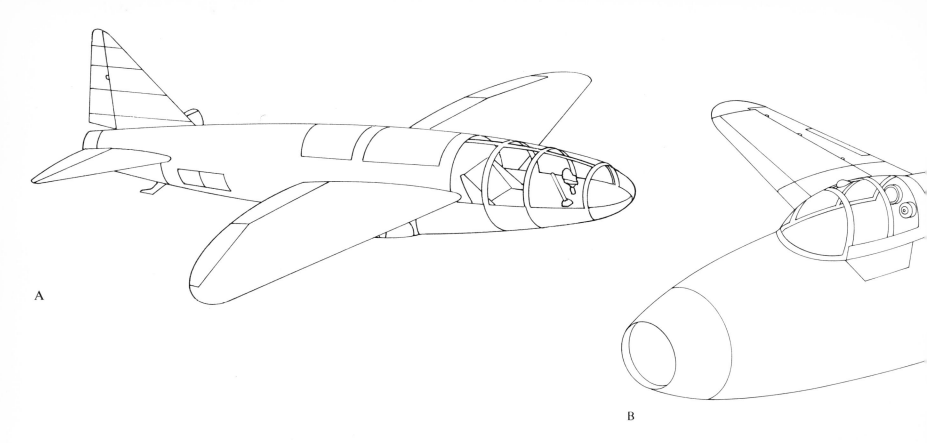

A

B

etrate this barrier, the British government ordered a bullet-shaped research monoplane from the Miles company, but canceled the project before it had a chance to fly.

In the United States, work continued on a small rocket-powered research aircraft known as the Bell XS-1 (later X-1), intended for a similar purpose. The pilot chosen for the attempt to achieve supersonic speed was Captain Charles "Chuck" Yeager; to conserve fuel, it was decided to drop the X-1 from a converted Superfortress mother plane at a height of around 30,000 ft. (9,100 m), instead of taking off normally.

Each time he flew, Yeager approached a little nearer to the speed of sound. Eventually he reached Mach 0.94 (94 percent of the speed of sound), and felt the aircraft bucking under the blows of shock waves that would have smashed anything else in the air at that time. But finally, on October 14, 1947, he opened up the four-chamber rocket engine fully for an all-out attempt. Fighting to keep control, he watched the needle on the Machmeter swing past Mach 0.94, on to 0.96, 0.98...then, suddenly, the hammering stopped. Yeager had become the first man to fly into the calmer conditions that lie beyond the sound barrier. In doing so he had proved that the barrier does not really exist.

By August 1955, the North American F-100C Super Saber fighter, powered by an ordinary jet engine, was able to demonstrate, by setting up the first official supersonic world airspeed record of 822.135 mph (1,323.095 km/h), that a properly designed airplane can approach and pass the speed of sound with no more noticeable effect than a flicker of needles on the cockpit instruments as it does so. From that moment it became only a matter of time before airliners were designed to carry passengers at supersonic speed.

Nor has there been any slackening in research that will lead one day to even higher performance for military and commercial airplanes. The rocket-powered North American X-15A has already carried pilots well beyond 4,000 mph (6,440 km/h), and who can doubt that, one day, passengers will fly from A to B at the kind of speeds experienced so far only by astronauts?

After World War II, Britain led the world in the new science of jet propulsion. Engines designed in Great Britain were being built under license in the United States. Russia bought some Rolls-Royce Nene turbojets which it stripped down, copied, developed and put into production, without license, to power a whole generation of combat aircraft such as the MiG-15 fighter.

A HEINKEL HE 176
Built by the Heinkel company to flight test the Walter rocket engine, the project received no support from the German government and only this open-cockpit, fixed-undercarriage prototype ever flew. It was intended for low-speed trials only, and achieved 171 mph (275 km/h) on its first flight on June 20, 1939.

B GLOSTER E38/39
This was the first British jet to fly, on May 15, 1941, powered by an 860 lb. (390 kg) thrust Whittle W.1 turbojet. With this engine it reached a speed of 338 mph (544 km/h), and when fitted later with a 1,700 lb. (770 kg) st W.2/500 engine reached approximately 450 mph (724 km/h).

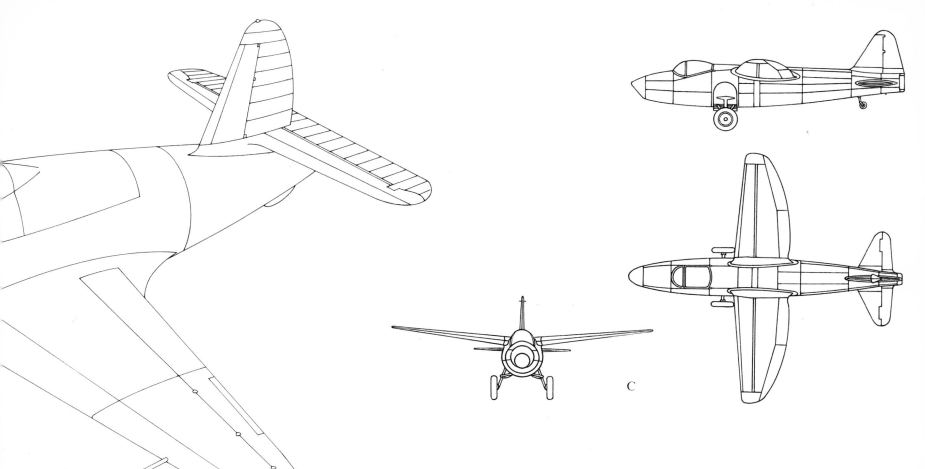

C HEINKEL HE 178

Flugkapitän Erich Warsitz, who tested the He 176, was also the pilot on August 27, 1939, of the first jet-powered aircraft to fly: the Heinkel He 178. The aircraft's main wheels, although designed to retract into the fuselage, were fixed in the "down" position for the early flights and blanking plates fitted over the wheel wells. The second prototype He 178, which never flew, had straight-tapered wings of greater span still.

Britain had no such lead, however, in airliner design, at least to begin with. America had been the source for the large numbers of wartime transport aircraft needed by the Allies, leaving Britain's industry free to concentrate on building combat and training machines. When the war ended, therefore, Britain had no airliners of her own to match the DC-4s, Constellations, Stratocruisers, and Convair passenger liners from across the Atlantic.

The scale of wartime airlifts of supplies and equipment also led many to expect a worldwide boom in air freighting once the war was over, but this did not in fact reach major proportions until the middle and late 1950s, when large piston-engined passenger transports that might otherwise have become obsolete were turned into freighters once their future was overshadowed by the new jet airliners. Today, most of the well-known jet airliners themselves exist also in freight-carrying versions, and many of the best-known "passenger" airliners actually rank higher in the table of freight ton-miles flown per year than in terms of human transportation.

One early postwar type that did carve a special niche for itself, however, was the Bristol Freighter, a short-range "flying boxcar" whose existence enabled Silver City Airways to operate the world's first and longest running car ferry service by air, across the Channel between England and Europe. Opened in 1948, it ran until 1970 before the Freighters' age made it necessary to retire them. Thanks to the Freighter's large nose-loading doors, which opened like a pair of huge jaws, cars could be driven straight into the hold, flown across the Channel in twenty minutes and driven out onto French soil. Tens of thousands of cars, as well as many other kinds of air freight, were transported by the Freighter fleet, and their job is still being carried on by the larger Aviation Traders Carvair, a specially modified car-carrying adaptation of the DC-4 airliner.

Meanwhile, although Britain's two state-owned airlines (BOAC and BEA) had to make do temporarily after the war with airliners based on wartime bombers, supplemented by a few long-range airliners bought from America, prototypes of the turbojet-powered de Havilland Comet and turboprop-powered Vickers Viscount were flying less than four years after the war's end. They soon proved that the greater speed and cruising height of turbine-powered airliners offered not only a saving in journey time but a smoother ride for their passengers, by climbing above most of the rough weather.

A VICKERS VISCOUNT

An airplane which revolutionized air transport and entered scheduled service with British European Airways on April 17, 1953. First turboprop airliner in the world, it not only offered new standards of performance but carried its passengers in vibrationless comfort above most of the "bumpy" weather that had previously induced airsickness.

B NORD GRIFFON

France's Nord Griffon had a turbojet mounted in the center of a huge ramjet.

Takeoff and climb power was provided by the turbojet, which also started the ramjet at a predetermined speed and height.

C BELL X-1

On 14 October 1947, Captain Charles Yeager of the United States Air Force proved that airplanes could fly beyond the speed of sound by accelerating the Bell X-1 rocket-plane to supersonic speed. The X-1 was launched from the B-29 mother plane at a height of 30,000 ft. (9,100 m) to save the fuel that would

otherwise have been expended during takeoff and climb.

D FAIREY DELTA 2

In this research aircraft, test pilot Peter Twiss reached 1,132 mph (1,822 km/h) on March 10, 1956, to raise the world airspeed above 1,000 mph (1,609 km/h) for the first time.

E LOCKHEED CONSTELLATION

Designed as a civil airliner in 1939, the Lockheed Constellation was first used as a wartime transport. Seating up to 64

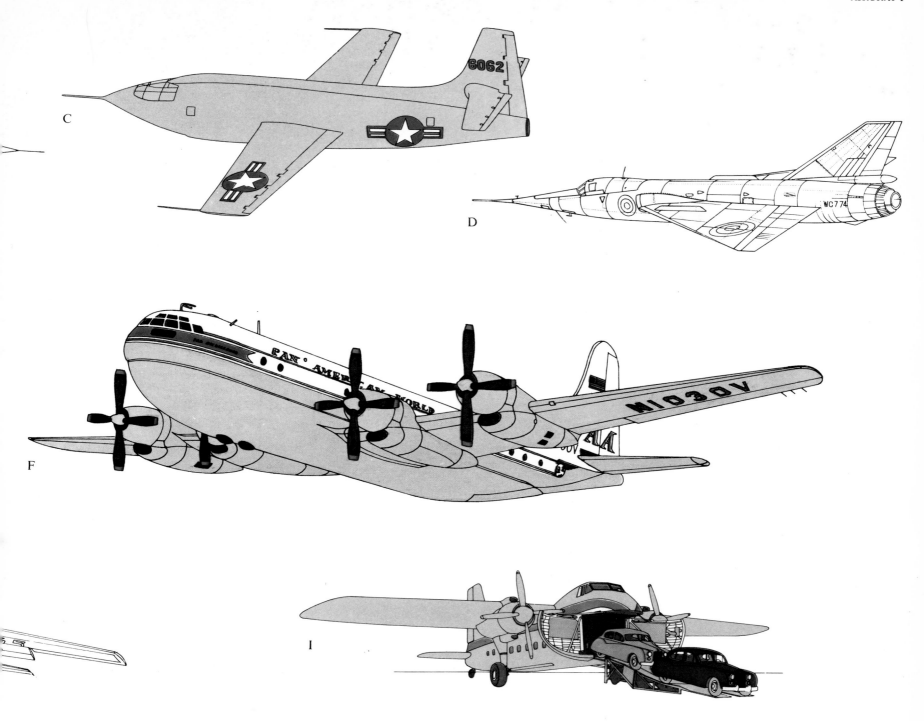

passengers, it entered airline service shortly after World War II, to be followed by
the 94-seat "stretched" Super Constellation and the very long-range Starliner.

F BOEING STRATOCRUISER
*The unique interior layout of this airliner
enabled passengers to relieve the monotony of long flights by getting up and
walking around or visiting the lower-deck
lounge which was reached by a spiral
stairway from the main passenger cabin.*

G CARAVELLE
*A completely new fashion in jet airliner
design was set by the French Caravelle,
which had its two Rolls-Royce Avon turbojets mounted on the sides of the rear
fuselage. Offering reduced cabin noise,
easier maintenance and a "clean" wing,
the rear-engine layout became standard
for many years.*

H TUPOLEV TU-104
*Evolved from the Tu-16 twin-jet bomber,
this was the second jet transport to enter
scheduled service. Operation on Aero-*

*flot's network began on September 15,
1956, initially in a 50-seat configuration.*

I BRISTOL FREIGHTER
*The large nose doors of the Bristol Freight-
er, providing full-width loading directly
into the cargo compartment, helped to
keep this early postwar aircraft in useful
service long after most of its contemporaries had been retired. Some were still
carrying out regular duties in the early
1970s.*

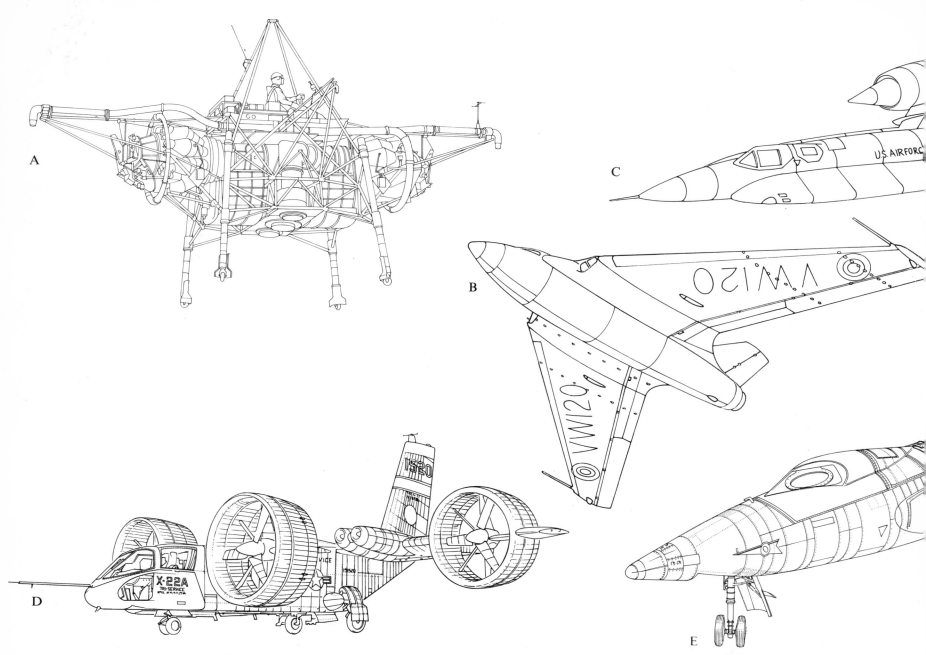

A ROLLS-ROYCE TMR

The Rolls-Royce Thrust Measuring Rig, more usually known by its nickname of "Flying Bedstead", heralded one of the most important advances in aviation history. By using the diverted thrust of two 5,000 lb. (2,268 kg) Nene turbojet engines to lift it into the air, and sustain it in flight, it made possible an entire new generation of rotorless, high-speed VTOL aircraft.

B D.H. 108

Test pilot Geoffrey de Havilland, son of the famous aircraft designer, was one who lost his life in the cause of progress. The shock waves hammering his little D.H. 108 during a high-speed flight in 1946 caused it to break up in the air—one of the first casualties in man's attempt to break through the so-called "sound barrier".

C LOCKHEED YF-12A

This remarkable aircraft had to cruise at Mach 3 for long periods at heights where there is little air for its engines to breathe. To enable the aircraft to withstand the sustained thermal "soaking" that such flights involve, raising the temperature of parts of the airframe to 1,000° F (538°C), the YF-12A is built almost entirely of a special titanium alloy. It was a YF-12A that, on May 1, 1965, shattered the world airspeed record with a new figure of 2,070.102 mph (3,331.507 km/h)—a record that remains unchallenged, to this day.

D BELL X-22A

Bell Aerosystems's X-22A research aircraft was produced to explore the mechanical and aerodynamic characteristics of the dual-tandem, ducted-propeller V/STOL concept. The engine nacelles each house two General Electric T58 turbines, which exhaust at 65° to the horizontal, thus providing additional takeoff thrust. Shafts extend from the rear of the engines to the transmission system, which embodies interconnecting shafts so that all four propellers are driven even after the failure of one or more engines.

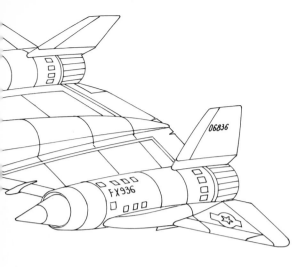

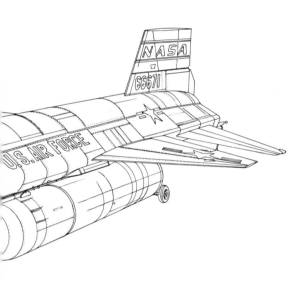

E NORTH AMERICAN X-15A
Fastest piloted airplane yet flown, this aircraft was powered by a liquid-propellant rocket engine of 57,000 lb. (25,855 kg) thrust, which enabled it to reach speeds of up to 4,534 mph (7,297 km/h) in short bursts. It was launched in mid-air from a mother plane, landing on a twin nosewheel and twin skids at the rear of the fuselage. The large external fuel tanks were jettisoned when empty. As well as contributing valuable data to the American space programs, experience gained with the X-15A has helped in evolving materials for the construction of ultra-high-speed conventional aircraft.

Thus, in the early 1950s, Britain's aircraft industry felt on top of the world. Nobody else could offer the airlines such fast comfortable transports, and operators lined up to buy them. Then disaster struck the Comet. Constant pressurizing and depressurizing of its cabin produced minute cracks, due to the then little understood phenomenon of metal fatigue. Two Comets fell out of the sky over the Mediterranean, with the loss of all on board, and the graceful flagship of Britain's civil air fleet was grounded.

There followed one of the most skillful detective stories in aviation history. Using the latest techniques of television and salvage, the Royal Navy recovered from the floor of the Mediterranean almost the entire remains of one of the lost Comets. Scientists at the Royal Aircraft Establishment studied and analyzed the shattered evidence and—to their eternal credit—made their findings available to the aircraft industries of the world to avoid any possible repetition of the disasters. By so doing they gave away Britain's leading position as a supplier of modern transportation aircraft to the airlines of the world.

By the time the entirely new Comet 4 was in service, and operating the first jet transatlantic passenger services in October 1958, the Soviet Tupolev Tu-104, based on a jet-bomber design, was already in large-scale operation. Within weeks the first big Boeing 707s followed the Comet across the Atlantic and, with Douglas's DC-8, became the standard types used on long-range services in the West.

The Viscount continued to sell in large numbers, and for many years it had no counterpart elsewhere. Similarly, when France produced its unique engines-at-the-rear Caravelle short-haul jetliner, this also found a ready market, but it is doubtful if Europe will ever again rival America as a producer of the biggest types of airliner, as the cost of developing aircraft that sell for $20 to 50 million apiece is beyond its financial resources.

Sizes have continued to increase to cope with the demands of an ever-growing mass-travel market. Boeing's Model 747, first of the new generation of jumbo-sized jets, can accommodate up to 500 passengers, and the trijet Lockheed TriStar and McDonnell Douglas DC-10 are not so far behind with 400 and 380 respectively. Instead of attempting to match them, the aircraft industries of Britain and France, while "keeping their hand in" with the smaller twin-engined A 300B European Airbus, have taken a much bolder step forward by producing the Concorde, the West's first supersonic airliner.

Not to be outdone, the Tupolev design bureau in Russia has produced a Soviet counterpart in the Tu-144, which first flew on December 31, 1968, some nine weeks before the Concorde. Both types are due to enter regular service in the mid-1970s and, if they are not unacceptably cramped in their operations by legislation against their supersonic "bangs" or alleged pollution dangers, will bring a revolution in traveling times between continents as great as that effected between cities by the Boeing 247 and the Douglas DC-3 in the 1930s. America, after commissioning prototypes of its own SST (SuperSonic Transport) from Boeing at the end of 1968, found the project canceled by the narrowest of congressional voting margins in the spring of 1971, and is still a nonstarter in the supersonic airliner stakes. Most people believe, however, that she will not allow herself to be out of the race for longer than she can help, and we may be sure that her aircraft designers are continuing to prepare for the day when she will again take her place in the forefront of modern airliner design.

In this modern age of "swinging" wings, supersonics, and jumbo jets, when orders for airliners are counted in tens or hundreds, it is easy to forget that by far the great majority of the aircraft flying in countries all over the world are small and usually simple machines that can be numbered in tens or hundreds of thousands. In the United States, for example, privately owned small airplanes, ranging from simple "home-builts" constructed by amateurs from plans and material kits to sophisticated family tourers with twin engines, retractable landing gears, pressurized cabins and airliner-type comforts and controls, outnumber the recognized airliners by about 100 to 1. In May 1972, Cessna, one of America's Big Three manufacturers of ready-made private aircraft (with Beech and Piper), itself completed the 100,000th aircraft to roll off its assembly lines; and at that time it had in production no fewer than forty-three models of commercial aircraft, in addition to several military types. Over a period of nearly twenty-five years, the industries of Russia and Poland have turned out some 10,000 examples of the Antonov An-2 biplane, a maid-of-all-work aircraft that performs all manner of jobs imaginable (and probably a few unimaginable ones!) in some two dozen countries. These figures are exceptional, but there is no doubt that the market for such light and "general aviation" aircraft has risen dramatically during the past quarter of a century, and we show a small selection of the range available on pages 180—181.

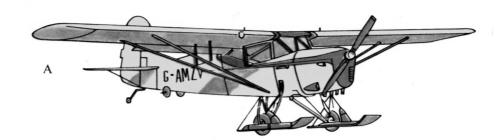

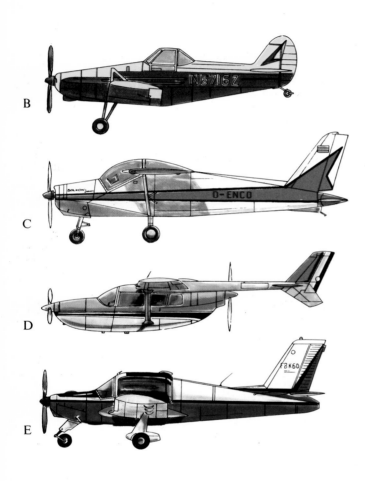

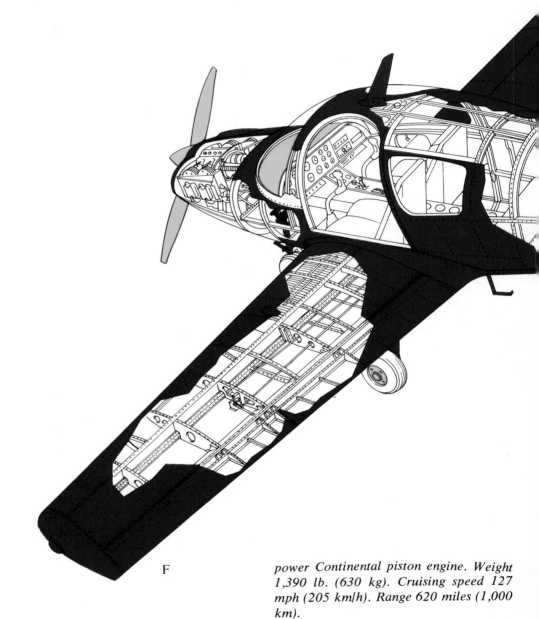

A AUSTER
   The Auster family of light planes, developed from the prewar Taylor Cub, were among the most popular European private aircraft of the early postwar years.

B PIPER PAWNEE C
   Single-seat agricultural aircraft. 235 horsepower Lycoming piston engine. Weight 1,488 lb. (675 kg). Cruising speed 105 mph (169 km/h). Range 270 miles (434 km).

C MBB BÖLKOW JUNIOR
   2-seat aerobatic light aircraft. 100 horse-

F

power Continental piston engine. Weight 1,390 lb. (630 kg). Cruising speed 127 mph (205 km/h). Range 620 miles (1,000 km).

D CESSNA SKYMASTER
   4/6-seat light aircraft. Two 210 horsepower Continental piston engines. Weight 4,630 lb. (2,100 kg). Cruising speed 190 mph (306 km/h). Range 755 miles (1,215 km).

E SOCATA RALLYE COMMODORE
   4-seat light aircraft. 150 horsepower Lycoming piston engine. Weight 2,160 lb.

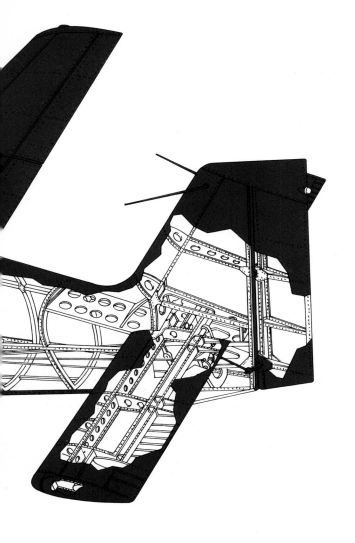

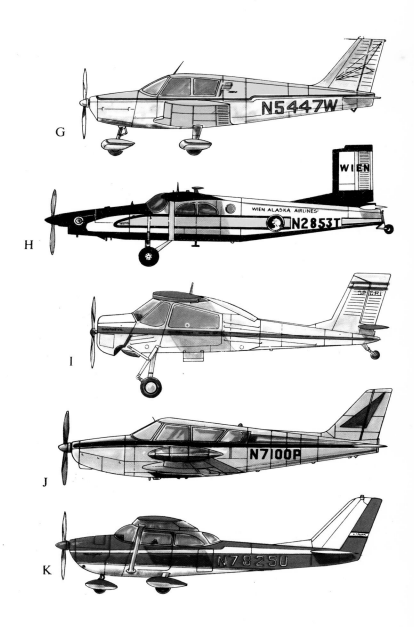

(980 kg). Cruising speed 124 mph (200 km/h). Range 590 miles (950 km).

F BEAGLE PUP

A 2- or 4-seat light aircraft. 100 horsepower Rolls-Royce Continental or 150 horsepower Lycoming engine. Cruising speed 112 or 147 mph (180 or 236 km/h). Range 540 or 760 miles (870 or 1,223 km).

G PIPER CHEROKEE 180

4-seat light aircraft. 180 horsepower Lycoming piston engine. Weight 2,400 lb. (1,089 kg). Cruising speed 143 mph (230

km/h). Range 725 miles (1,165 km).

H PILATUS TURBO-PORTER

8/12-seat STOL utility transport. 550 shp Pratt & Whitney (UACL) turboprop engine. Weight 4,850 lb. (2,200 kg). Cruising speed 161 mph (259 km/h). Range 634 miles (1,020 km).

I PZL-104 WILGA 3P

4-seat general-purpose aircraft. 260 horsepower Ivchenko AI-14R piston engine. Weight 2,711 lb. (1,230 kg). Cruising speed 120 mph (193 km/h). Range 410 miles (660 km).

J PIPER COMANCHE

4-seat light aircraft. 260 horsepower Lycoming piston engine. Weight 3,200 lb. (1,451 kg). Cruising speed 185 mph (298 km/h). Range 735 miles (1,180 km).

K CESSNA 172

4-seat light aircraft. 150 horsepower Lycoming piston engine. Weight 2,300 lb. (1,043 kg). Cruising speed 131 mph (211 km/h). Range 615 miles (990 km).

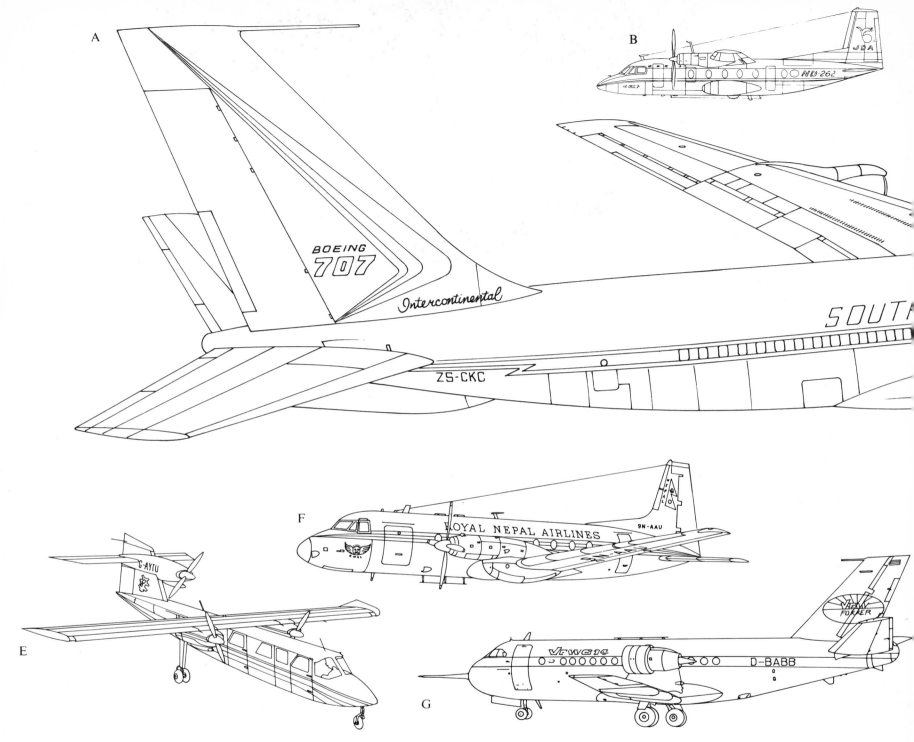

A BOEING 707
First off the mark with a jet transport in the United States, Boeing has since reaped a huge reward with a whole family of jet-liners. First to appear was the Model 707, which entered service in 1958. By early 1971, Boeing designs accounted for 2,200 of the 3,600 jet airliners then in service throughout the world.

B AÉROSPATIALE N 262
Up to 29 passengers. Two 1,080 ehp Turboméca turboprop engines. Weight 23,370 lb. (10,600 kg). Cruising speed 233 mph (375 km/h). Range 605 miles (975 km).

C BRITTEN-NORMAN ISLANDER
Up to 9 passengers. Two 260 horsepower Lycoming piston engines. Weight 6,300 lb. (2,857 kg). Cruising speed 160 mph (257 km/h). Range 717 miles (1,153 km).

D SHORT SKYVAN
Up to 19 passengers. Two 715 shp AiResearch turboprop engines. Weight 12,500 lb. (5,670 kg). Cruising speed 195 mph (314 km/h). Range 694 miles (1,115 km).

E BRITTEN-NORMAN TRISLANDER
Up to 17 passengers. Three 260 horsepower Lycoming piston engines. Weight 9,350 lb. (4,241 kg). Cruising speed 180 mph (290 km/h). Range 1,000 miles.

H SWEARINGEN METRO

Up to 20 passengers. Two 940 shp Ai-Research turboprop engines. Weight 12,500 lb. (5,670 kg). Cruising speed 294 mph (473 km/h). Range 500 miles (804 km).

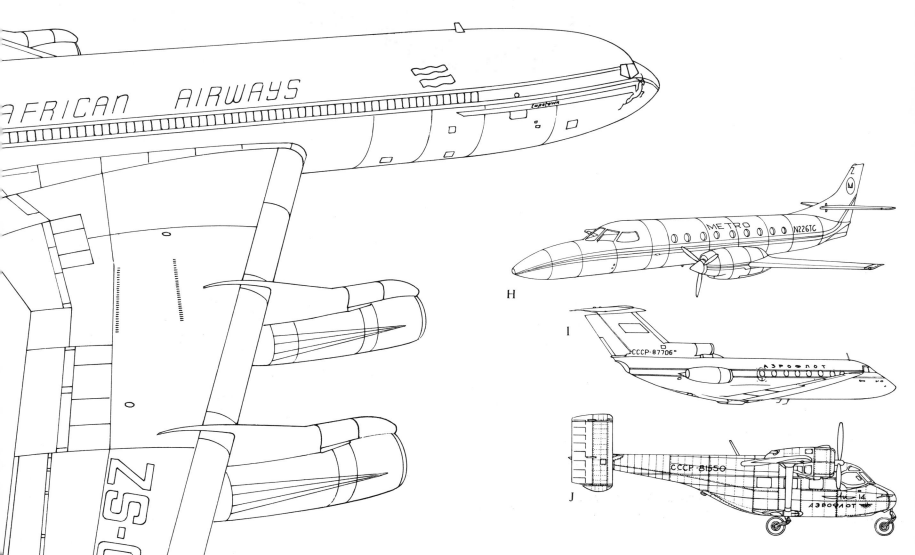

F HAWKER SIDDELEY 748

Up to 58 passengers. Two 2,280 ehp Rolls-Royce turboprop engines. Weight 44,495 lb. (20,182 kg). Cruising speed 278 mph (448 km/h). Range 1,987 miles (3,150 km).

G VFW-FOKKER VFW 614

Up to 44 passengers. Two 7,480 lb. (3,393 kg) st Rolls-Royce/SNECMA turbofan engines. Weight 41,000 lb. (18,600 kg). Cruising speed 449 mph (722 km/h). Range 414 miles (667 km).

I YAKOVLEV YAK-40

Up to 34 passengers. Three 3,300 lb. (1,500 kg) st Ivchenko turbofan engines. Weight 36,375 lb. (16,500 kg). Cruising speed 342 mph (550 km/h). Range 807 miles (1,300 km).

J ANTONOV AN-14

Up to 8 passengers. Two 300 horsepower Ivchenko piston engines. Weight 7,935 lb. (3,600 kg). Cruising speed 118 mph (190 km/h). Range 423 miles (680 km).

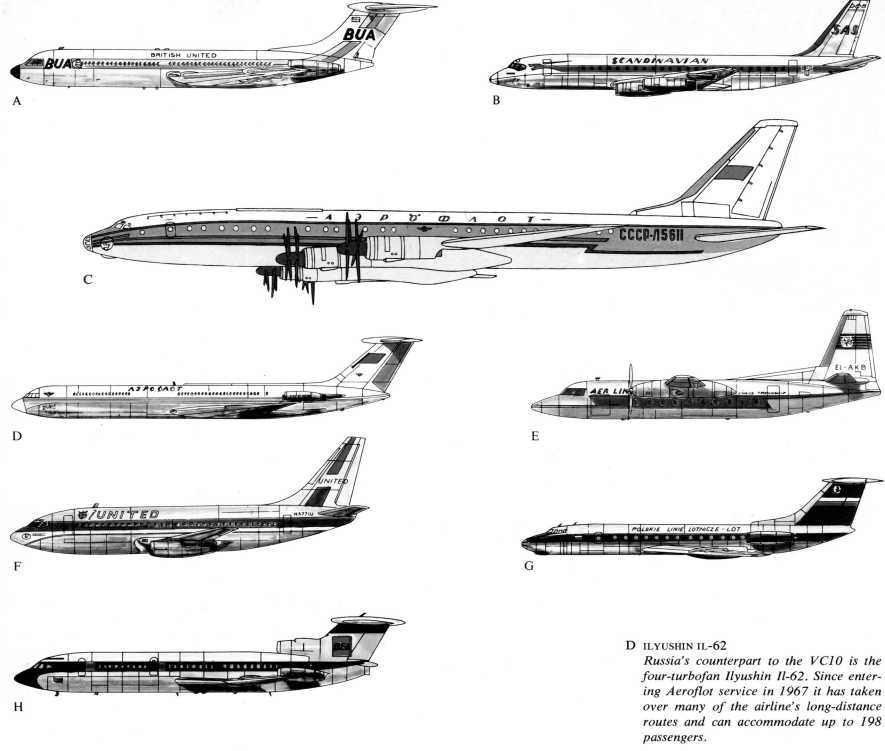

A

B

C

D

E

F

G

H

D ILYUSHIN IL-62

Russia's counterpart to the VC10 is the four-turbofan Ilyushin Il-62. Since entering Aeroflot service in 1967 it has taken over many of the airline's long-distance routes and can accommodate up to 198 passengers.

E FOKKER FRIENDSHIP

The Dutch Fokker company, renowned for its prewar transport airplanes, re-entered this market after World War II with the twin turboprop Friendship. Some 15 years after first deliveries began in 1958, this popular 40/48-seater was still in production, its total sales of nearly 600 making it easily the best-selling turboprop airliner ever built.

A BAC VC10

Placing of the four Conway turbofan engines at the rear of the fuselage, Caravelle-fashion, contributed to the considerable passenger appeal of the BAC VC10—an appeal that was not, unfortunately, matched by large-scale orders from airlines.

B DOUGLAS DC-8

First to point the way toward the high capacity jumbos of today were three "stretched" versions of the McDonnell Douglas DC-8, which appeared in the mid-1960s. Known as the Super Sixty series, they can seat 189 or 259 passengers.

C TUPOLEV TU-114

This was the world's largest and fastest turboprop transport, when it appeared in 1957, with a weight of around 170 tons and seats for up to 220 passengers.

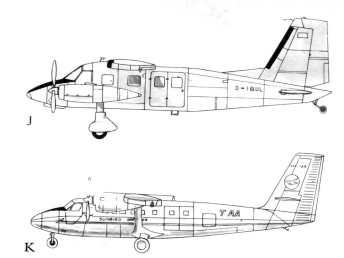

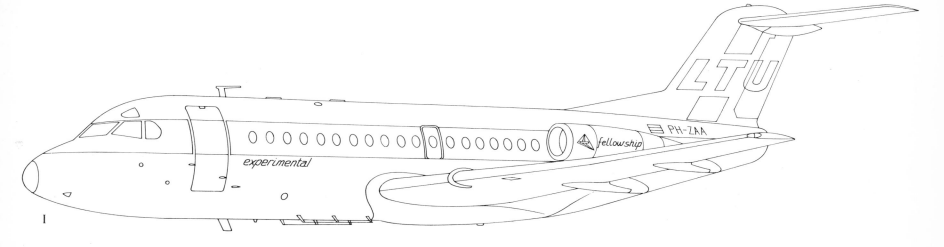

F BOEING 737

The smallest member of the Boeing jet transport family is the short-haul Model 737, but even this "baby" can seat up to 130 passengers and has a range of more than 2,000 miles (3,220 km).

G TUPOLEV TU-134

Developed from the Tu-104, with a "T" tail and rear-mounted turbofan engines, the Tu-134 medium-range jetliner entered service in Russia in 1967.

H H.S. TRIDENT

First western jetliner to be sold to the Chinese People's Republic, the Hawker Siddeley Trident, designed originally to BEA requirements, was also the first to adopt a three-engines-at-the-rear layout and the first to make a "hands-off" automatic landing during a commercial airline flight.

I FOKKER-VFW FELLOWSHIP

Up to 65 passengers. Two 9,850 lb. (4,468 kg) st Rolls-Royce turbofan engines. Weight 65,000 lb. (29,485 kg). Cruising speed 528 mph (849 km/h). Range 1,208 miles (1,945 km).

J DORNIER SKYSERVANT

Up to 14 passengers. Two 380 horse-power Lycoming piston engines. Weight 8,050 lb. (3,650 kg). Cruising speed 178 mph (286 km/h). Range 1,125 miles (1,810 km).

K DE HAVILLAND CANADA TWIN OTTER

Up to 20 passengers. Two 652 ehp Pratt & Whitney (UACL) turboprop engines. Weight 12,500 lb. (5,670 kg). Cruising speed 210 mph (338 km/h). Range 794 miles (1,277 km).

A DASSAULT MYSTÈRE 20/FALCON 20
Up to 14 passengers. Two 4,315 lb. (1,960 kg) st General Electric turbofan engines. Weight 28,660 lb. (13,000 kg). Cruising speed 536 mph (862 km/h). Range 2,220 miles (3,570 km).

B NORTH AMERICAN ROCKWELL AERO COMMANDER
Up to 7 passengers. Two 290 horsepower Lycoming piston engines. Weight 6,750 lb. (3,062 kg). Cruising speed 203 mph (326 km/h). Range 901 miles (1,450 km).

C HAWKER SIDDELEY 125
Up to 12 passengers. Two 3,360 lb. (1,525 kg) st Rolls-Royce turbojet engines. Weight 23,300 lb. (10,568 kg). Cruising speed 508 mph (818 km/h). Range 1,865 miles (3,002 km).

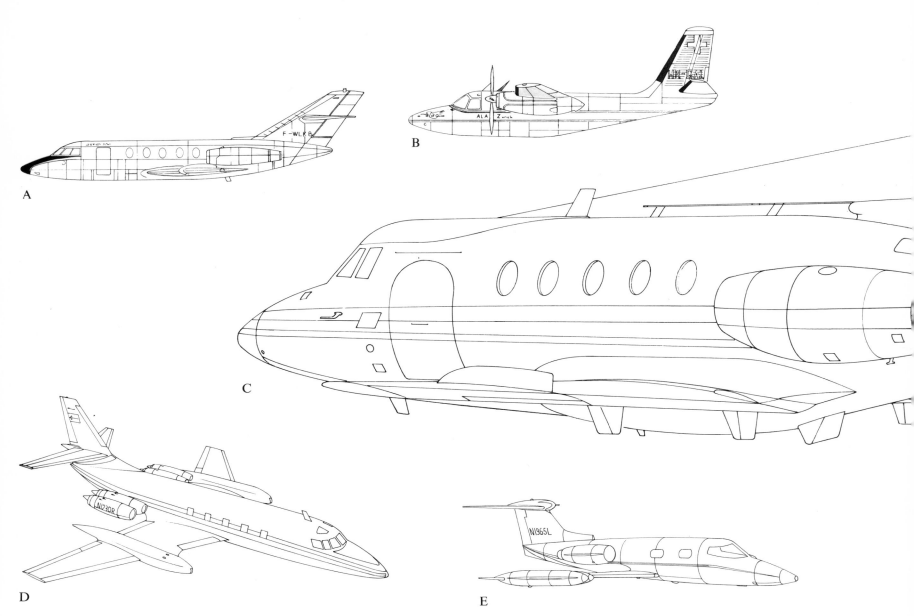

E GATES LEARJET 24D
Up to 7 passengers. Two 2,950 lb. (1,340 kg) st General Electric turbojet engines. Weight 13,500 lb. (6,124 kg). Cruising speed 534 mph (859 km/h). Range 2,020 miles (3,250 km).

F BEAGLE B.206
Up to 7 passengers. Two 340 horsepower Continental piston engines. Weight 7,499 lb. (3,401 kg). Cruising speed 218 mph (351 km/h). Range 1,600 miles (2,570 km).

G PIPER AZTEC
Up to 5 passengers. Two 250 horsepower Lycoming piston engines. Weight 5,200 lb. (2,360 kg). Cruising speed 210 mph (338 km/h). Range 1,080 miles (1,738 km).

H SCOTTISH AVIATION/HANDLEY PAGE JETSTREAM
Up to 18 passengers. Two 850 eshp Turboméca turboprop engines. Weight 12,500 lb. (5,670 kg). Cruising speed 306 mph (493 km/h). Range 1,900 miles (3,058 km).

I MBB HFB 320 HANSA
Up to 7 passengers. Two 3,100 lb. (1,406 kg) st General Electric turbojet engines. Weight 20,280 lb. (9,200 kg). Cruising speed 513 mph (825 km/h). Range 1,472 miles (2,370 km').

J BEECHCRAFT QUEEN AIR B80
Up to 5 passengers. Two 380 horsepower Lycoming piston engines. Weight 8,800 lb. (3,992 kg). Cruising speed 224 mph (360 km/h). Range 1,550 miles (2,494 km).

D LOCKHEED JETSTAR
Up to 10 passengers. Four 3,300 lb. (1,497 kg) st Pratt & Whitney turbojet engines. Weight 42,000 lb. (19,051 kg). Cruising speed 570 mph (917 km/h). Range 2,120 miles (3,410 km).

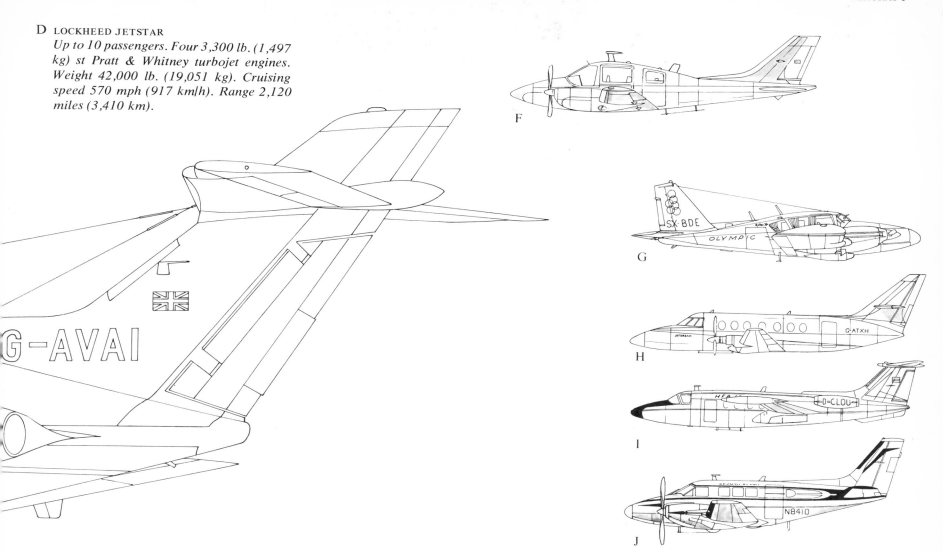

Completing the spectrum of transportation types, between the smaller general aviation aircraft and the third level, or feeder, type of miniairliner, come the range of aircraft that fulfill the needs of business aviation. This area of activity, too, has undergone a significant rise in both scope and importance during the past twenty years or so, and today represents a major industry in its own right. Any sizable company whose management executives need to travel—and this means most of them—can find the operation of its own aircraft both useful and profitable. There are aircraft of the right size and price for almost any company's budget, ranging from the superexecutive for people like Playboy chief Hugh Hefner, who can afford his own personal DC-9, down through smaller twinjets like the Dassault Falcon, Gates Learjet and Hawker Siddeley 125 to the more widely used business twin piston-engined light aircraft seating about four to six people. Over distances of 1,000 miles (1,600 km) or so these can offer travel on terms, and at speeds, that compare favorably with

those of regional airlines. They have the added advantages that they can use either established airports or smaller airfields where the larger airliners cannot go, and, of course, the executive is not tied to the limitations of airline timetables.

At the upper end of the size scale, such aircraft begin to overlap the airliner market with types such as the Scottish Aviation Jetstream, Mitsubishi MU-2, the Aero Commanders, and the larger of the Beech, Cessna, and Piper twins, some of which can seat up to twenty people. At the opposite end of the scale is a wide range of helicopters such as the Fairchild FH-1100 and Bell Jet Ranger, which need only a small "pad" of concrete or grass, or a rooftop, as their operating base.

It was Sikorsky's R-5, and its civil counterpart, the S-51, which really ushered in the long-delayed era of the helicopter. It led to the larger S-55, which distinguished itself particularly in the Korean War on rescue, ambulance, and supply duties. In three years (1950—1953) the "choppers" carried more than 23,000 casualties, half of whom, it has

been estimated, would otherwise have died. Since then helicopters have proliferated—not quite to the extent anticipated, but given a big impetus by the development of turboshaft (shaft-turbine) engines. Designers quickly found that they could more than double the payload of a helicopter by exchanging its bulky piston engine, mounted in the fuselage, for one or more turboshaft engines mounted above the cabin. This has helped considerably to mitigate one of the helicopter's major disadvantages in relation to fixed-wing airplanes: its high cost of operation; and has made feasible the design of huge payload-carrying vehicles like Sikorsky's S-64 Skycrane and the massive four-engined, twin-rotor Mi-12.

Unfortunately, helicopters cannot as yet fly as fast as fixed-wing airplanes. This has led designers to investigate many different techniques for vertical takeoff and landing (VTOL). An entirely new form of flight emerged in 1954, when Rolls-Royce flew its fantastic "Flying Bedstead" VTOL research machine, which was lifted off the

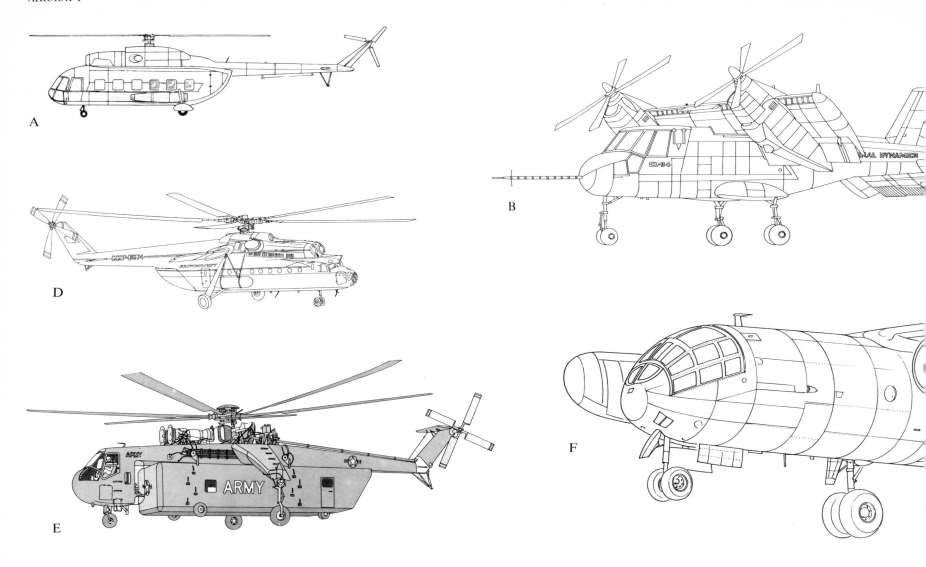

ground by the thrust of two vertically mounted jet nozzles.

From the "Flying Bedstead" has evolved an incredible variety of different VTOL concepts. One of the first to be tried was the "tail-sitter" type of aircraft, represented by the Convair XFY-1 and Lockheed XFV-1, but such a configuration presents various difficulties and has not been pursued seriously. Several aircraft of the tilt-rotor concept, such as the Bell XV-3 of 1958, have been or are being tried out. An alternative approach favors tilting not only the propeller but the engines and complete wing for vertical flight. In normal flight, with the wings and engines horizontal, such machines are virtually conventional aircraft in all respects. The biggest example of this type of VTOL aircraft yet flown is the LTV-Hiller-Ryan XC-142A of the late 1960s, and tests are continuing with Canadair's smaller CL-84 built to the same concept.

Promising as the tilt-wing idea seems, perhaps the strongest school of thought is that which favors using pure jet thrust, as in the

"Flying Bedstead" of twenty years ago. Certainly this view can be supported by the Hawker Siddeley Harrier, a tactical V/STOL (Vertical and Short Take-Off and Landing) strike aircraft that in 1974 was still, after four years, the only nonrotorcraft type of VTOL aircraft actually in full-scale service anywhere in the world. The thrust of its single Pegasus turbofan engine can be directed downward for V/STOL operation or rearward for conventional flight. In due course, history will accord the P.1127, the prototype of the Harrier, a place ranking with those held by the Wright *Flyer* and the Sikorsky VS-300 helicopter. The biggest multiengine jet-lift VTOL aircraft to reach the hardware state so far is the German Dornier Do 31 experimental transport, powered by two Pegasus lift/cruise engines, with the exhaust ejecting through four rotatable nozzles as on the Harrier, and two wing-tip pods each containing four lift jets.

Mention has already been made of the ultrahigh speeds achieved by the North American X-15A rocket-powered research air-

craft. This unique airplane, first flown as early as June 1959, in October 1967 reached a fantastic 4,534 mph (7,297 km/h)—nearly seven times the speed of sound. Nor was this by any means the only great feat by this remarkable airplane, which two weeks later flew to an unprecedented and still-unequaled altitude of 277, 000 ft. (84,430 m)—a height of more than 50 miles (80 km), which was so far above the earth's surface as to qualify its pilot, Major Pete Knight, for a pair of astronaut's "wings". By flying to the very fringe of the earth's atmosphere, the X-15A pointed the way toward a project that, in the very near future, will play a large part in increasing man's exploitation of his newly found ability to travel in space.

We are all familiar, through television, with the dramatic blast-offs of the gigantic rockets that have sent American and Soviet astronauts into space. But, when you fire a rocket you lose a rocket, and this has been one of the principal reasons why adventures like the Apollo man-on-the-moon program have been so cripplingly expensive. Much

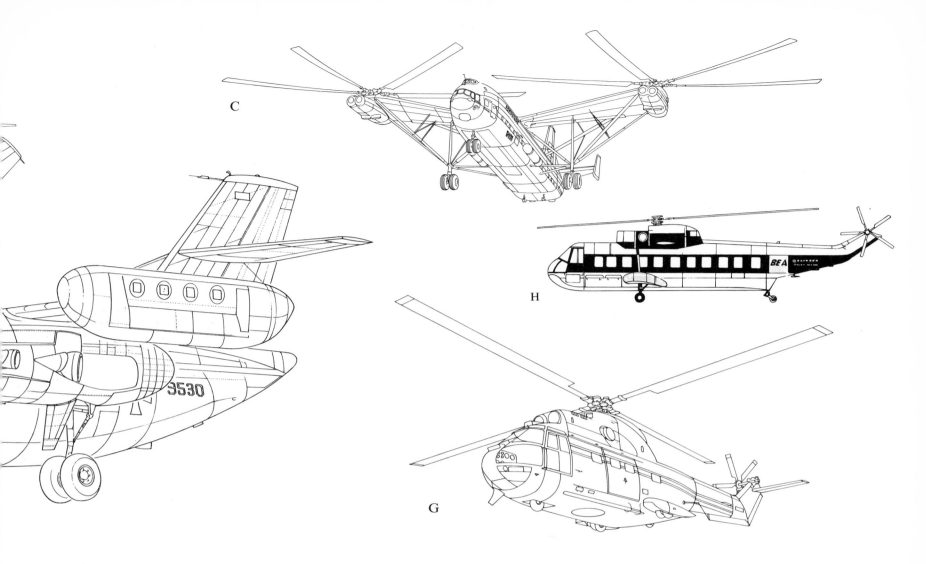

A MIL MI-8
The 28/32-passenger Mi-8 is used widely by Aeroflot, the Soviet airline, and many of the world's air forces. But even this helicopter can carry more people than some of the smaller fixed-wing airliners shown on earlier pages.

B CANADAIR'S CL-84
This experimental tilt-wing aircraft not only represents one line of development in the quest for higher cruising speeds from VTOL aircraft: its special tail rotor is also of interest as an example of a rotating wing designed to be stopped and restarted in flight.

C MIL MI-12
The world's biggest helicopter, by a considerable margin, is Russia's Mil Mi-12, which is powered by four turboshaft engines, each of 6,500 shp, driving twin 5-blade rotors whose diameter is almost 115 ft. (35 m). It can lift a payload that

is greater than the entire loaded weight of the Sikorsky Skycrane.

E SIKORSKY CH-54A
This is basically a "skeleton" helicopter airframe to which can be attached cargo containers or "people pods", the latter seating up to 67 persons.

D MIL MI-6
The advent of gas-turbine power made possible the production of very large helicopters able to lift substantial payloads, such as Russia's Mi-6, which can carry up to 65 passengers or troops.

F DORNIER Do 31
This experimental VTOL transport combined the techniques of deflected thrust and direct jet lift. The underwing pods each contain a Rolls-Royce Pegasus vectored-thrust lift/cruise turbofan engine, while in each wing-tip pod are four Rolls-Royce RB.162 lift jets. Its fuselage was

designed to accommodate up to 36 passengers.

G SA 330 PUMA
An important Anglo-French program conceived in 1967 was for design and co-production of a trio of multipurpose helicopters, of which the largest is the SA 330 Puma. Although designed initially for a military role, it is being built also in a 20-passenger commercial transport version.

H SIKORSKY S-61L
The first helicopter to take full advantage of the new economics promised by gas-turbine propulsion was the Sikorsky S-61L, an elongated passenger-carrying version of the Sea King antisubmarine helicopter. It entered service in late 1961 with Los Angeles Airways. The S-61N is an amphibious version.

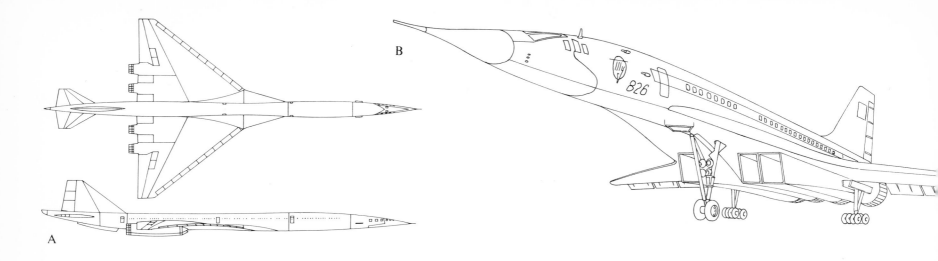

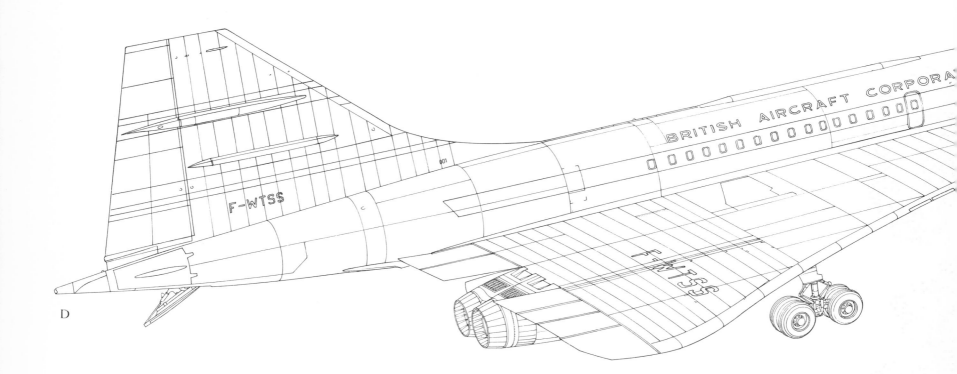

work has, therefore, been devoted toward evolving craft that can carry out a mission in space, return with their human or other cargo through the earth's atmosphere, land like a conventional aircraft, and be refueled and used over and over again.

Representing, as it were, the "Wright *Flyer*" stage in this evolution have been strange craft like the Martin X-24 and Northrop HL-10, known as "lifting-body reentry vehicles" because, for flight within the atmosphere, they derive their lift from aerofoil-shaped bodies instead of conventional wings. These craft are the trailblazers for a much more ambitious vehicle, the space shuttle,

which, as its name implies, will be able to shuttle between earth and orbiting space stations carrying relief crews, equipment, and supplies.

As at present envisaged, the heart of the space shuttle concept will be a delta-winged orbiter vehicle that will be launched, piggyback fashion, from the back of a huge, jettisonable liquid-propellant fuel tank, the latter being flanked by two recoverable solid-propellant booster rockets. The orbiter, in addition to its two-man crew, will have a large payload compartment that can accommodate complete satellites or flying laboratories with up to twelve passengers or scientists, the latter being able to live and work inside the orbiter in a "shirt-sleeve" environment just as though they were aboard a conventional modern airliner. Tasks foreseen for the shuttle include placing satellites into, servicing them in, and recovering them from, orbit; reconnaissance and space rescue; and working as space refueling tankers.

After centuries of dreams, disasters, and disappointments before he learned to fly, man has accomplished this much within the comparatively minute span of his own "three score years and ten". He has indeed traveled far, in all senses of the term, since that frail biplane lurched off the sands at Kitty Hawk.

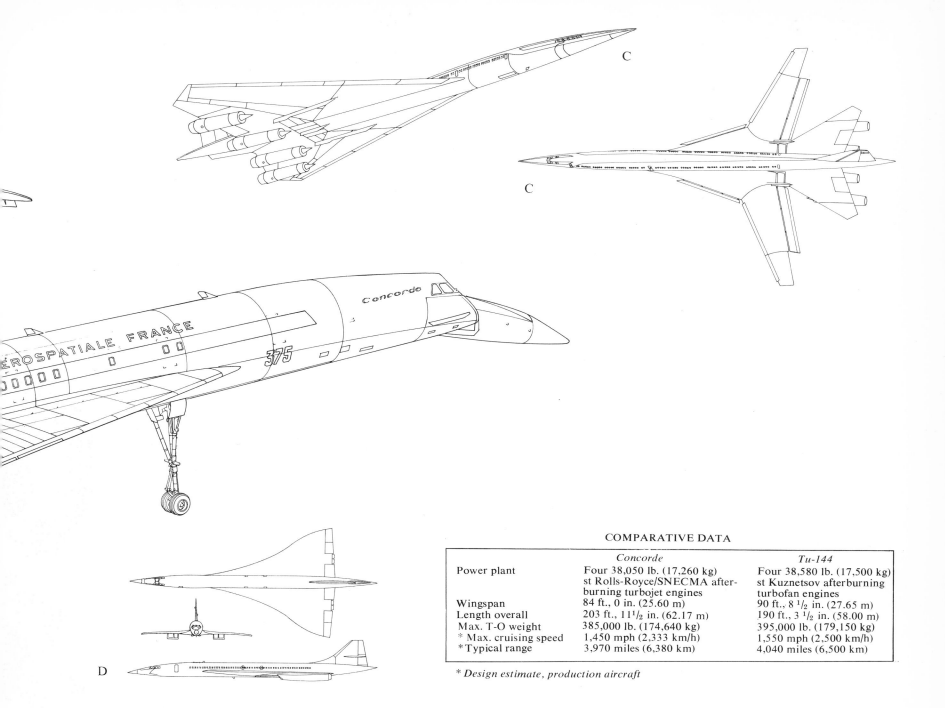

COMPARATIVE DATA

	Concorde	Tu-144
Power plant	Four 38,050 lb. (17,260 kg) st Rolls-Royce/SNECMA afterburning turbojet engines	Four 38,580 lb. (17,500 kg) st Kuznetsov afterburning turbofan engines
Wingspan	84 ft., 0 in. (25.60 m)	90 ft., 8 1/2 in. (27.65 m)
Length overall	203 ft., 11 1/2 in. (62.17 m)	190 ft., 3 1/2 in. (58.00 m)
Max. T-O weight	385,000 lb. (174,640 kg)	395,000 lb. (179,150 kg)
* Max. cruising speed	1,450 mph (2,333 km/h)	1,550 mph (2,500 km/h)
*Typical range	3,970 miles (6,380 km)	4,040 miles (6,500 km)

Design estimate, production aircraft

A BOEING 2707-300
  Boeing abandoned its rather too complex swing-wing SST design in October 1968, for the Model 2707-300, using a fixed wing of delta planform; but in March 1971, before any prototypes could be built, the United States Senate voted against providing funds for the project.

B TUPOLEV TU-144
  Mach 2.35 is the maximum cruising speed for the Tu-144, which became the world's first supersonic airliner to fly, on December 31, 1968. Its seating capacity is 120.

C BOEING 2707-200
  At the end of 1966 America selected a swing-wing design by Boeing as its entry in the supersonic airliner stakes. Known as the Model 2707-200, it was to have cruised at Mach 2.7 and would have been built largely of titanium alloy.

D CONCORDE
  The choice of Mach 2.2 as the maximum cruising speed for the Concorde was influenced by the fact that the resulting airframe skin temperature, averaging about 248°F (120°C), is within the tolerance of selected conventional aluminum alloys. The similarity between the Concorde and the Tu-144 demonstrates that two different design teams agree broadly upon the best aerodynamic compromise between the conflicting demands of minimum drag at supersonic speed and good handling and control at low speeds.

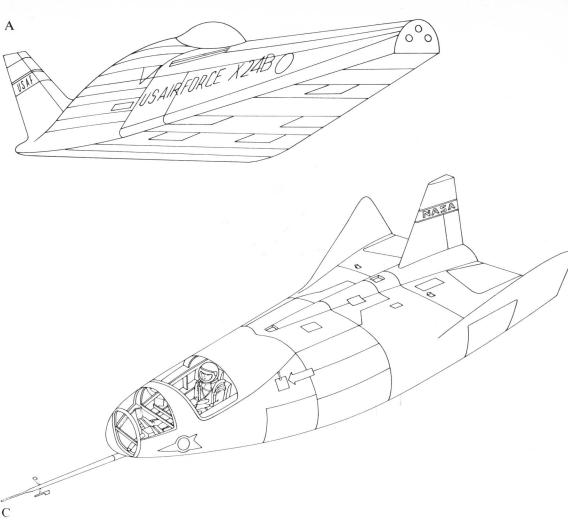

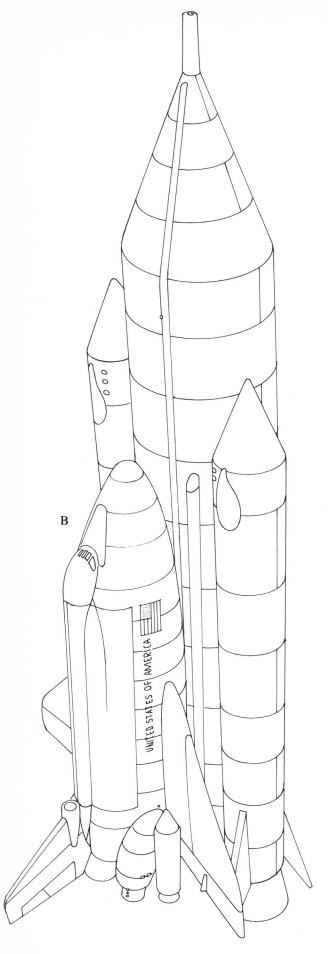

A MARTIN X-24A

This lifting-body vehicle, originally a snub-nosed craft like the HL-10, has been re-built as the X-24B with a completely new external appearance that combines a nee-dlelike nose with a double-delta planform of twice the original area.

B SPACE SHUTTLE

This will be the first "airliner" able to go out into space and return to make a con-ventional airplane-type landing. It will carry crews to orbiting workshops like that of America's Skylab. The complete shuttle vehicle will be launched vertically, with all engines firing. The booster rockets will be jettisoned at about 25 miles (40 km) altitude and recovered from the sea; the huge external fuel tank will be jet-

tisoned in space, once the orbiter vehicle is established in orbit. The payload com-partment will be up to 60 ft. (18.30 m) long and 15 ft. (4.60 m) in diameter. A new form of heat shielding will enable the orbiter to survive a hundred reentry missions.

C NORTHROP HL-10

This "flying stone" is one of the pioneer-ing designs for the space "taxis" that will carry crews to and from orbiting space stations. Their shape must be such that they will not overheat and burn up as they reenter the earth's atmosphere from space, yet they must also be controllable in at-mospheric flight and able to land con-ventionally at an airfield.

DE LANA

JOSEPH MONTGOLFIER

THE PARACHUTE

A *Francesco de Lana-Terzi was actually rather pleased when his airship proved to be impractical, as it could not then be used for such unpleasant things as dropping boiling oil on enemy ships in wartime.*

B *After watching scraps of burned paper drifting upward from a fire, Joseph Montgolfier is said to have held a paper bag over it, thus trapping hot air and causing the bag to rise when released.*

C *Garnerin was the first man to jump from a balloon with a parachute and survive. This illustration by a rather fanciful artist shows parasols being used for the same purpose.*

193

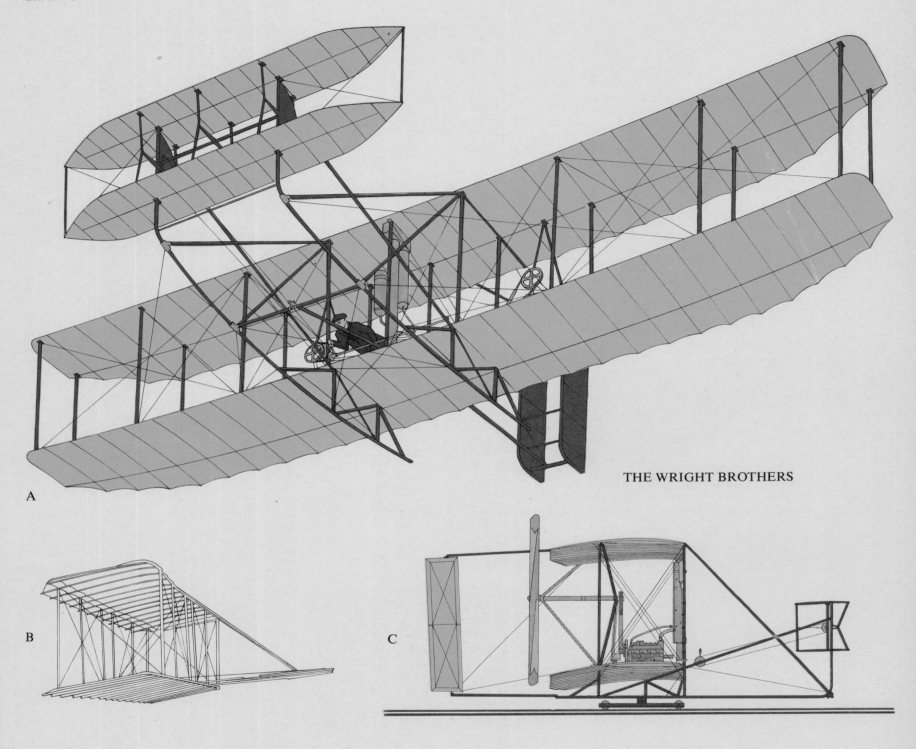

THE WRIGHT BROTHERS

A

B

C

A Satisfied with the warping-wing control system, the Wrights added a front elevator control surface on their second glider and then fitted a rear rudder on their third, which made hundreds of flights in 1902–1903. Then they were ready to progress to a powered airplane, the Flyer I which made four flights on December 17, totaling 97 seconds in the air, to become the most honored airplane in history.

B Realizing the shortcomings of Lilienthal's technique of controlling his gliders by body movement, Orville and Wilbur Wright devised the warping-wing control system which played a big part in enabling them to make the first sustained, powered, and controlled airplane flights. First, however, they tested the warping-wing system on a 5 ft. (1.52 m) biplane kite and on this 17 ft. (5.18 m) span No. 1 glider, which was flown mainly as an unpiloted kite.

C The Wright Flyer of 1903 took off on a small trolley fitted with two adapted bicycle wheel hubs, running on a wooden rail. To maneuver the aircraft on the ground, the brothers used two small wheeled trolleys placed under the lower wing.

LOUIS BLÉRIOT

D *With a little luck, the cross-Channel honors went to Blériot, who successfully made a crossing on July 25, 1909—a flight which for the first time focused worldwide attention on the future potential of the airplane for both peace and war. Blériot might have failed had not a providential shower of rain cooled his overheating 25 horsepower Anzani engine en route. The landing gear was carried in cycle forks which left the wheels free to castor, facilitating crosswind landings. Within two days*

after his achievement, Blériot received orders for more than 100 similar aircraft.

E *Plan and front elevation of the Blériot Type XI monoplane. The original aircraft is today preserved at the Conservatoire des Arts et Métiers in Paris; a replica was flown at the Paris air show in May and June 1969.*

F *During his cross-Channel flight, Blériot was not able to follow a straight course. Blown northward by the wind, he eventually found Dover by going in the same direction as ships bound for the port, after a 37-minute flight for 10 minutes of which he could see neither England nor France and had no means of knowing whether he was on course.*

A

B

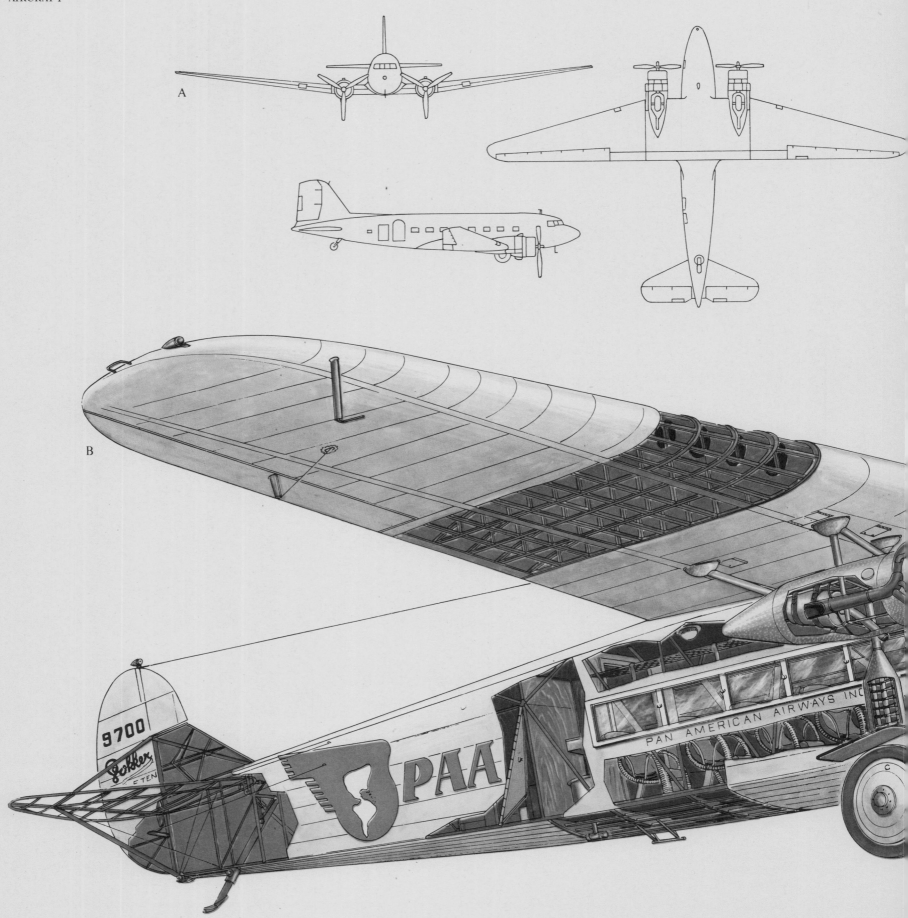

DOUGLAS DC-3

FOKKER F.X

A *Having evolved the 12-passenger DC-1 and 14-passenger DC-2 for TWA, Douglas was asked to develop a "sleeper" version of the latter for the same number of passengers. It was quickly realized that the larger fuselage necessary would thus seat 21 daytime passengers—and the DC-3 was born. From mid-1936, airlines ordered DC-3s as fast as Douglas could build them and by 1939 an incredible 90 percent of the world's total airline traffic was being flown in what has aptly been called "the plane that changed the world".*

B *In the late 1920s and early 1930s a prominent airliner type was the high-wing, trimotor monoplane, examples of which were built in substantial numbers by Fokker in Holland, Junkers in Germany, and Ford in the United States, among others. Typical of the breed was this American Fokker F.X of Pan American Airways. Powered by three 300 horsepower Wright engines, it could carry eight passengers at a speed of 103 mph (166 km/h).*

BOEING 747

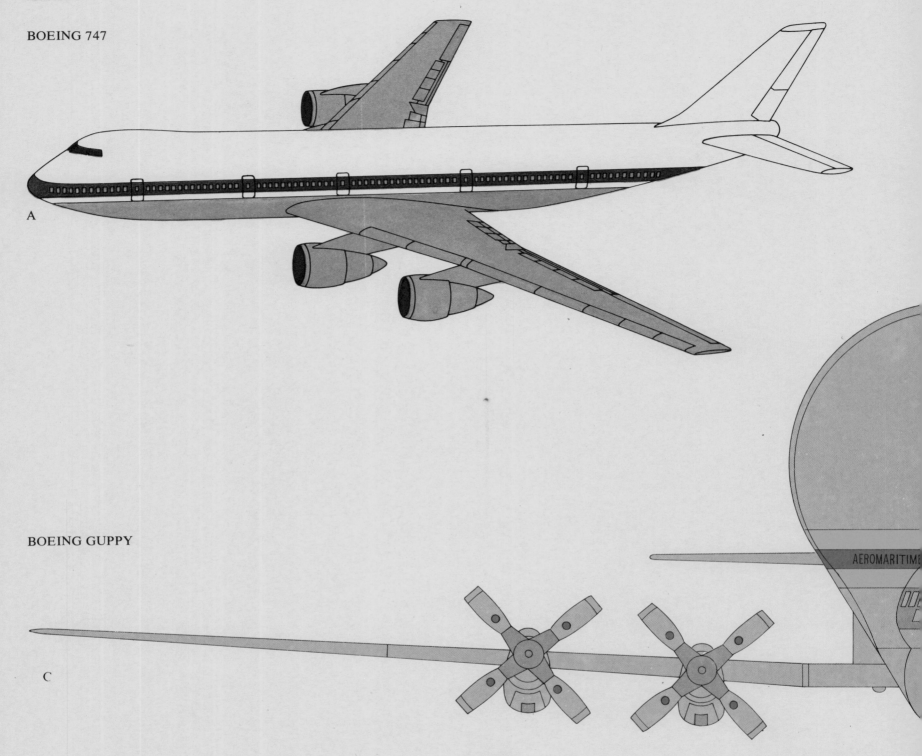

A

BOEING GUPPY

C

AEROMARITIME

A *Believing that passengers were fed up with traveling in close-fitting metal tubes, Boeing introduced in its Model 747 the first modern airliner with the new "wide-bodied" look. First put into service in January, 1970, it is capable of carrying up to 500 passengers, ten abreast, in a 20 ft. (6.1 m) wide cabin that is 185 ft. (56.39 m) long and 8 ft. 4 in. (2.54 m) high.*

B *First flown in 1949, Britain's de Havilland Comet 1 was the airplane that introduced the speed and comfort of jet travel to the airline industry on May 2, 1952. It carried up to 44 passengers at a cruising speed of 490 mph (789 km/h). This drawing shows the later Comet 4.*

DE HAVILLAND COMET 4

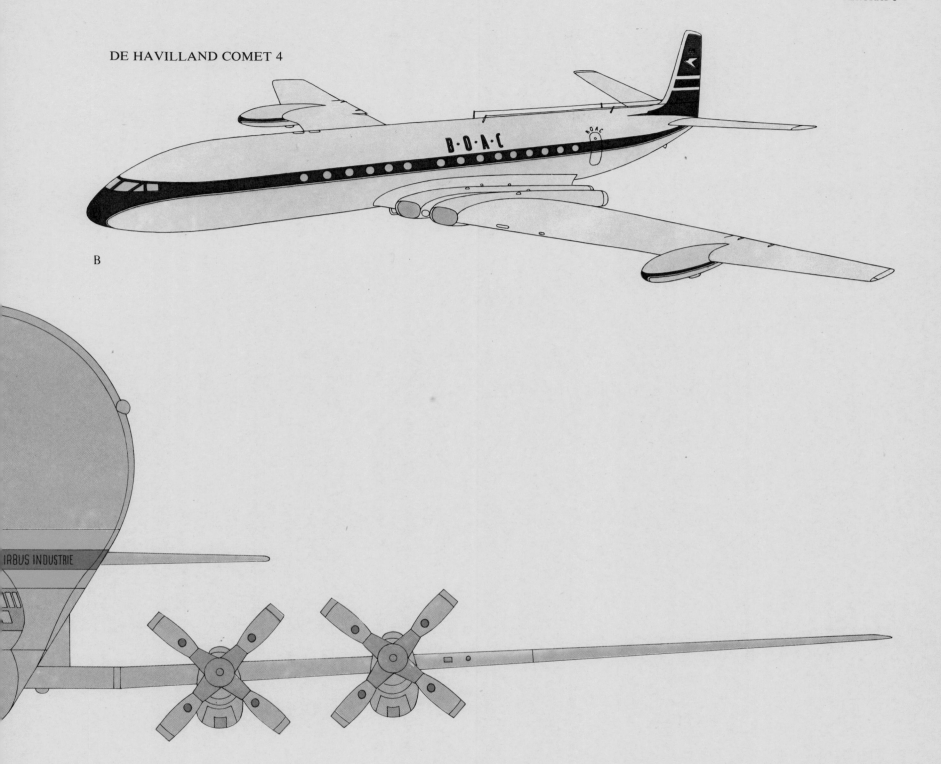

B

C *Among the most grotesque transport airplanes ever built are the "Guppies", converted from Boeing Stratocruiser airliners as specialized vehicles to carry outsize loads such as huge space program booster rockets or complete wings or other major components of large airliners like the Concorde or European Airbus. The entire nose or tail section swings open for straight-in loading of the cargo.*

LOCKHEED TRISTAR

EUROPEAN AIRBUS

DOUGLAS DC-10

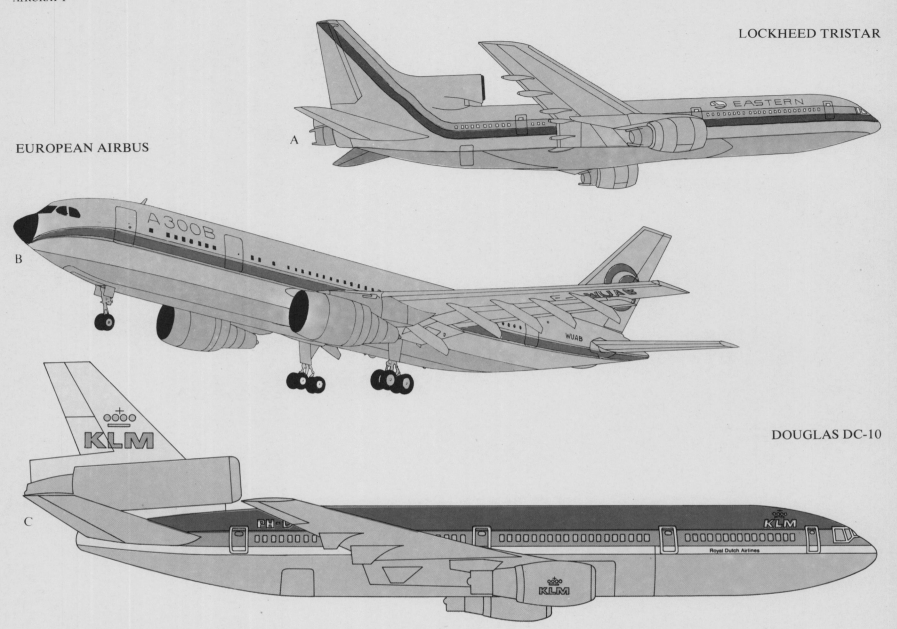

(TriStar data)
Three 42,000 lb. (19,050 kg) st Rolls-Royce
RB.211-22B turbofan engines
Wingspan 155 ft., 4 in. (47.34 m)
Length overall 178 ft., 8 in. (54.35 m)
Maximum payload 90,725 lb. (41,150 kg)
Maximum T-O weight 430,000 lb. (195,045 kg)
Maximum cruising speed 562 mph (905 km/h)
at 35,000 ft. (10,670 m)
Range with maximum payload 2,878 miles
(4,629 km)

(A 300B data)
Two 51,000 lb. (23,130 kg) st General Electric
CF6-50C turbofan engines
Wingspan 147 ft., 1 1/4 in. (44.84 m)
Length overall 175 ft., 9 in. (53.57 m)
Maximum payload 67,924 lb. (30,810 kg)
Maximum T-0 weight 302,000 lb. (137,000 kg)
Maximum cruising speed 582 mph (937 km/h)
at 25,000 ft. (7,620 m)
Range with maximum payload 1,000 miles
(1,610 km)

(DC-10 data)
Three 40,000 lb. (18,144 kg) st General Electric
CF6-6D turbofan engines
Wingspan 155 ft., 4 in. (47.34 m)
Length overall 181 ft., 4 3/4 in. (55.29 m)
Maximum payload 103,221 lb. (46,820 kg)
Maximum T-0 weight 430,000 lb. (195,045 kg)
Maximum cruising speed 579 mph (932 km/h)
at 31,000 ft. (9,450 m)
Range with maximum payload 2,429 miles
(3,909 km)

A *Slightly later than the DC-10, Lockheed's
Model 193 TriStar began regular passenger services on April 30, 1972. It too has
a single-deck layout; the internal cabin
dimensions are almost identical to those
of the DC-10, and a maximum of 400
economy-class passengers can be carried.*

B *Individual European companies can no
longer afford to finance projects like the
TriStar and C-10, but six of them plan to
fill a gap in the market with the A 300 B
European Airbus, a 200/300-seat "mini-
jumbo" which flew for the first time in
October 1972. They were supposed to
enter airline service in early 1974, but the
fuel shortage may alter these plans.*

C *The DC-10, which entered regular airline
service on August 5, 1971, can carry up
to 380 economy-class passengers in a
single-deck cabin with a maximum headroom of 8 ft. (2.44 m). A sharp contrast in
scale is shown by the company's earlier
piston-engined DC-3, whose 21-passenger
cabin was about the size of the DC-10's
rear engine pod.*

ILLUSTRATED INDEX

INDEX

This section of the book, comprising more than 2,500 entries and 100 illustrations, is a valuable complement to the main section. Here are both references to the first part of the book and new entries which provide additional information of especial interest to the reader. All figures in italics refer to page numbers of illustrations. Figures in roman are main text references.

Air brake, see also Flap
A device that can be raised or lowered into the airflow to create drag to reduce speed. Sometimes known as "speed brakes," air brakes are necessary on high-speed aircraft to enable them to reduce speed to that required by air traffic control and to increase descent rates. On some aircraft, wingmounted air brakes are used differentially to assist the ailerons for lateral control at low speeds, particularly during turbulent conditions when landing and taking off. In certain applications, air brakes may be known as "spoilers" as, in addition to creating drag, they "spoil" the lift of the wing.

Léon Bollée designed this 1899 Darracq, which has a horizontal air-cooled engine and 5-speed belt-and-pulley primary drive.

Air-cooled engine, 13 137 150 (see also Piston engine; Turbine)
All engines have to be cooled in order to remove the excessive heat caused by the exploding gases and the frictional heat from moving parts. The oil in the crankcase acts as a coolant, and in some engines the main cooling is done by means of drawing a volume of cool air over the cylinders with a fan driven by the engine. Cylinders are made with fins to take the heat quickly to the outside areas of the metal. The Volkswagen is one of the most popular cars using an air-cooled engine, the main advantage being that no water cooling is required which prevents troubles caused by radiator leaks and freezing.

The first recorded use of an airplane to deliver letters occurred in India on February 18, 1911, when a mail bag was flown some 6 miles (9½ km) from Allahabad to Nairi by the French pilot Pequet. The British operated a 3-day service between London and Windsor in September 1911, which carried more than 100,000 letters and postcards. In the United States, Earle Ovington ran aerial postal flights from Long Island, N.Y., in September/October 1911, and similar flights in several other countries took place before the 1914–18 war. In the 1920s the delivery of newspapers and mail by air became an important part of a pilot's activities, and several of today's leading airlines, particularly in the United States, started business with mail contracts.

Airspeed indicator, see also Pitot head
The airspeed indicator (ASI), one of the most vital instruments a pilot uses, relies on variation between the static and dynamic pressure of air to obtain a reading of the required value. Air is drawn from a pressure (pitot) head into the instrument. The pitot head contains a sealed static head of air that feeds one side of a diaphragm, while an open dynamic tube in the pitot head feeds the other side. The movement of the diaphragm in relation to the varying pressures is linked to a pointer in front of a dial in the cockpit.

Instrument by which a pilot calculates the height at which he is flying. The standard altimeter indication is given as a result of the difference between the outside air pressure and a standard capsule of air in the instrument. The altimeter does not necessarily give the height of the aircraft above the ground, but above a fixed datum pressure, and it is necessary to know the ground level pressure and set the instrument in relation to this before the height above ground level can be known.

Altimeter, radar or radio
Used as a supplementary height indicator, the radar altimeter gives an instantaneous presentation of the height of an aircraft over the land or sea directly beneath it. It does so by emitting radio waves to the ground and measuring the time taken to return to the aircraft.

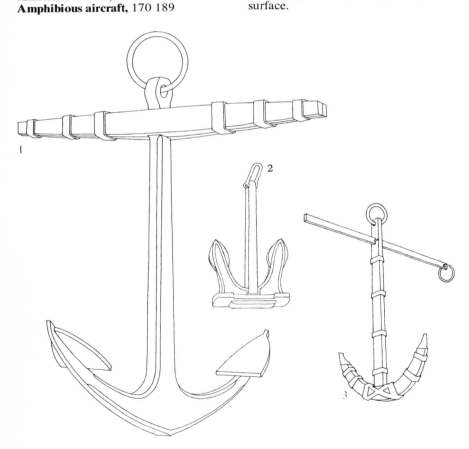

Anchors, see also Capstans; Windlasses
The common anchor (Fig. 1) was used from pre-Roman times until the late nineteenth century. It was difficult to handle and to stow. The stock that came to rest on the seabed in a vertical position was liable to foul the cable as the ship swung to wind or tide.

The modern stockless anchor (Fig.

2) has pivoted arms that will always turn and bite into the seabed however the anchor is dropped. When stowed, the shank is hauled taut into the hawsepipe and the arms fit snugly against the ship's side.

Fig. 3 shows an anchor discovered in Lake Nemi and bears a striking similarity to the later iron common anchor.

Angle of attack, see also Cierva, Juan de la; Flight, principles of
The angle formed between the chord line of an aerofoil surface and a line representing the undisturbed airflow relative to that surface. It is an aerodynamic term, and should not be confused (though it often is) with "angle of incidence."

Angle of incidence, 161
The angle formed between the chord line of an aerofoil surface and the datum line, or longitudinal axis, of the body (e.g. fuselage) supporting that surface.

Trade name of the engines and aeroplanes built by Leon Levavasseur, who named them after his partner's daughter.

Flight instrument, first introduced by the Sperry Gyroscope Company, which uses a gyroscope, aligned to the level of the earth and connected to the instrument, to give a pictorial representation of the aircraft in relation to the horizon. The aircraft picture rises above the horizon when the aircraft climbs and falls below the horizon when it dives.

It is difficult to determine when the term "Blue Riband of the Atlantic" was first used. Books written in the 1880s use this term, and it is possible that it had been used in connection with the fastest liners of the Atlantic for many years previously. Until 1934, the "Riband" was entirely a nominal award and some ships indicated their claim to the title by flying a long narrow blue pennant from the mainmast when entering or leaving harbor. In

highest rewards through full passenger lists and mail subsidies. It was just as important for people in Australia to receive their mail and passengers from Europe in the shortest possible time, but in general the travelers between Europe and the United States were more influential, the ships were larger and faster than those employed elsewhere and therefore they captured the popular imagination.

Sir Herbert Austin (1866–1941) began as a sheep-shearing machine engineer in Australia. He returned to England and built his first Wolseley car in 1895 which was followed by a succession of excellent small cars made for that company. Anxious to be his own master, he formed the Austin Motor Company in 1905, and the firm continued under that name until it was amalgamated with the Morris concern in 1952 to become the British Motor Corporation. Austin's greatest contribution to motoring was in the design and production of the Austin Seven in 1922, the first successful cheap British car.

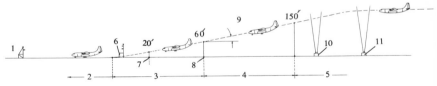

1934 Mr. H. K. Hales presented a magnificent trophy which was to be awarded to the owners of the fastest ship, and an international committee was formed to lay down the terms under which the trophy would be claimed. The award was not, however, an unqualified success, one of the reasons for this being that the Cunard Line refused to claim it, their policy having always been safety and comfort first, with no deliberate attempts to break the record for the prestige of owning the fastest ship.

It has to be remembered that on all the principal trade routes the owners of the fastest ships also received the

Autopilot, 171
Mechanical system of controlling an aircraft in flight without human assistance, developed primarily to minimize pilot fatigue on long flights. At first, simple gyro stabilization was accepted, but soon the magnetic compass was coupled in as a heading reference. During World War II, more complicated autopilots were produced in which the aircraft could be held on a steady heading at a constant altitude made to describe a steady rate of turn in either direction, or change altitude in a precise manner. From here it was a short step to the auto-approach coupler in which signals from an instrument

landing system (ILS, which see) were made to control an aircraft automatically during landing approach. Further refinement has led to modern autopilots that can bring an aircraft right onto the runway, keep it on the center-line, and turn off onto the taxiway, all in totally "blind" conditions. Within the past few years automatic landings of scheduled passenger flights have been introduced. These are still restricted to use in certain weather conditions, and can be used only at airports with ILS equipment.

Autorotation, see Cierva, Juan de la
Auto Union, DKW, *127*
Auxiliary motor, 36 38 59
Aviation Traders Carvair, 175
Avion III, Ader's, *161*
Avro, see Roe, Alliott Verdon
A. V. Roe triplane, *165* 166
A. V. Roe Type F monoplane, *164*
Axial-flow turbine, see Turbine
Axle, leading, 85 86
AZLK, Moscow, *133*
BA, see British Airways
BAC VC10, *184*
Backbone frame, 139
Backstay, 25
Bacon, Roger, 154
Balbo, General Italo, 169
Baldwin, Matthias, 75
Baldwin Locomotive Works, 80
Balloons, 15 161 (see also Flight, principles of)
Balloon, hot-air, 15 156 161
Balloon races, 122
Baltimore clipper, 25 *31* 36
Baltimore & Ohio Railroad, 66 72 81 88
Bamboo batten, 29
Bank of oars, 25
Banner, 29
Baras, speed record, 114

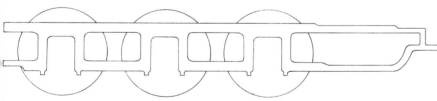

Bar frames

Bar frames, 69 70 71 74 75 76 81 82 84 85 91 104
The locomotive frame on which the boiler rests and which carries the wheels and axles is either of the plate or the bar form. Plate frames are of mild steel just over 1 inch thick and typical exemples of outside plate frames are shown in the illustrations. Bar frames on the other hand are much thicker and normally take the form of top and bottom bars running the length of the locomotive braced together by vertical members. The frames on either side of a locomotive are held together by stretchers across the locomotive; the buffer beams at either end often having a second duty as stretchers at those parts of the frames.
Barge, 30 36 46 54

Bark, 34 35
Bark, French, *33*
Bark, German five-masted, *34*
Barkentine, 27 35
Barsi Light locomotive, *93*

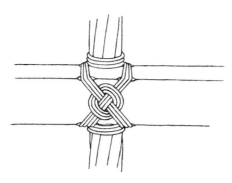

Wooden batten secured to shroud with seizing wire

Batten, 29 56
Battery, 114
Electrical energy necessary for the ignition starting and lighting systems in a car is stored in a lead-acid battery that is charged by a dynamo or alternator driven by the engine. The battery is made up of a number of cells to give the required capacity, the lead plates being kept out of contact with each other by porous wooden or plastic separators that do not conduct electricity. The whole block is immersed in an electrolyte of acid and distilled water in a strong casing with two terminals at the top onto which the wires for the various circuits are connected.
Battery-powered vehicles, early, 88
Battery vehicles, see Witkars

Bavarian State S 3/6 locomotive, *90*
BEA, 175 176 185 (see also British Airways)
Beaded edge pneumatic tires, 123
Beagle B.206, *187*
Beagle Pup, *180*
Beakhead, 23 25
Beam, 25 27 30 34 43 51
Beam, concrete, 96
Bearings, 70 82 143
Beaver Meadow Railroad, 71
Bedlington Ironworks, 66
Beech Aircraft Corporation, 179 187
Beechcraft Queen Air B80, *187*
Beetle, Volkswagen, 137 *150*
Belgian State Railways, 46 85 91
Belgian State Type 5 locomotive, *90*
Bell, Henry, 36 37
Bell Aerosystems X-22A, *178*
Bell Jet Ranger, 187
Bell XP-59A Airacomet, *173*
Bell XS-1 (X-1), 174 *177*

Bell XV-3, 188
Bellonte, Maurice, 169
"Bellows" bumpers, 152
Bellows, mechanical, 69
Bengal-Nagpur Railway, 93
Bennie monorail, 94
Benoist flying boat, *169*
Bentley, W. O., 131 149
Bentley, *148*
Bentley 3 liter, 149
Bentley 4½ liter, *121* 149
Benz, Carl, 111 112 118
Benz, "Blitzen," *114*
Benz, first car, *112*
Benz, gas-driven bicycle, 112
Berlin-Anhalt Railway, 103
Berlin Trades Exhibition, 88 95
Berths, 79
Bessemer process, 10
Best Friend of Charleston, locomotive, 66 71 *73*
Beyer, Peacock & Co., 78 (see also Garratt articulated locomotive)
Biplane:
    Antonov An-2, 179
    box-kite, Voisin brothers's, 166
    Curtiss's, 168
    Farman-Voisin, *162*
    Golden Flyer, 165
    Rumpler C.1, *164*
    "Russian Knight," *164*

Santos-Dumont's 14-bis, *163*
    tailfirst, 166
    Voisin, *162*
    Wright brothers's, 166 172
Biplane kite, *194*
Birds and birdmen, 154 162
Birkinshaw, John, 66
Bismarck, S.S., 42 43 45
Black Ball Line, 36
Black Diamond, locomotive, 69
Black Hawk, locomotive, *75*
Blanking plates, 175
Blast pipe, exhaust-steam, 69 100
Blenkinsop, John, 102
Blenkinsop's rack locomotive, *103*
Blériot, Louis, 165 166 195
Blériot 1909 (Type XI) monoplane, 166 *195*
Blind, 29
"Blitzen" Benz, *114*
Block sheave, 35
Blue Riband, see Atlantic, Blue Riband of
BMW 3.0-CSL, *134*
BOAC, 175 (see also British Airways)
Bodies, 113 116 117 119 120 122 125 128 129 130 143 146
The first car bodies were built by coach builders who were not necessarily associated with the people who built the chassis and mechanical parts of the

 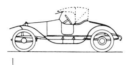 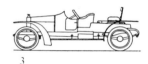

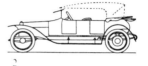 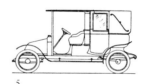 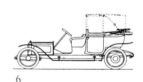

 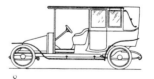 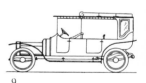

  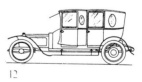

Car bodies
1 2-seater, or roadster, with dickey seat, *c.* 1914
2 Flush-sided "torpedo" tourer, *c.* 1913
3 Racing or sports car, re-bodied for road use, *c.* 1910
4 Coupé de Ville or Brougham, *c.* 1912
5 Landaulet, *c.* 1908
6 Landaulet fully opened; canopy and windshield removed, *c.* 1908
7 Limousine, *c.* 1912

8 Three-quarter landaulet with non-detachable roof opening at rear-quarter, *c.* 1910
9 Touring car with detachable 'hard-top', *c.* 1910
10 Fixed-head "doctor's coupé", *c.* 1914
11 Owner/driver's saloon: rear doors only, access to front by gangway between front seats, *c.* 1914
12 Enclosed-drive 7-seater Berline, *c.* 1911

205

car. These bodies were made from a wooden framework covered with metal sheets. During the 1930s, metal was substituted for wood, but the completed body was still separate from the chassis and fixed to it by nuts and bolts. Modern cars are built as complete box units, all the metal parts being welded together to form both body and chassis. This has the advantage of being both easier to produce and having much greater strength than the earlier forms.

The Adams bogie, introduced in 1865 by William Adams for the North London Railways.

Boilers

Boilers were originally rectangular iron tanks with a fire underneath. Later, the fire was placed inside the boiler to increase the heating area and flues were taken up from the firebox so that the

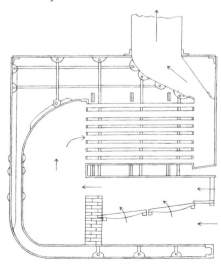

Return flue boiler (circa *1850–60). Combustion gases pass from the furnaces to a chamber and back through large diameter flues to the uptake. The flues are surrounded by the water in the boiler which at steaming level is above the highest flue.*

escaping gases were also made to heat the water. These early boilers could not withstand pressures of more than about 35 psi.

Fire tube boilers, in which the combustion gases passed through a series of tubes in the heart of the boiler, made it possible to increase pressures and increase thermal efficiency. Boilers were swiftly improved when steel became available for their construction. By the end of the century ships were equipped with boilers capable of producing pressures of up to 135 psi, although the Scotch boiler, as the fire tube variety came to be known, was widely used at lower pressures. Pressures of 300 psi were common between the two wars.

The water tube boiler, which is now vastly superiour in performance to the fire tube boiler, passes the water through a series of tubes that are surrounded by the boiler gases. In modern ships, superheated water tube boilers deliver steam to the turbine inlet valve at pressures in excess of 800 psi and at temperatures of over 1,800°F. A comparison can be made with these ships and the Cunard Liner *Aquitania*, built in 1914 and with a gross tonnage of 45,647. She was fitted with 21 double-ended Scotch boilers, each with a working pressure of 195 psi. The turbines of this ship, of which there were four, produced 60,000 horsepower. Apart from the engineers, 324 trimmers and firemen, divided into three watches, were required to look after these boilers. A single modern oil-fired boiler will produce steam to drive 30,000 horsepower turbines. There will probably be less than 20 engineers and boiler staff altogether and, if the engine room is automated, it is possible that there will be nobody in the engine or boiler rooms for several hours at a stretch

Boilers, multitubular, 66 69 81 100
Production of steam in the boiler is influenced by the extent of the areas in which hot gases lie on one side of a steel plate and water on the other. This heating surface is found not only round the firebox, it is extended by passing numerous tubes through the

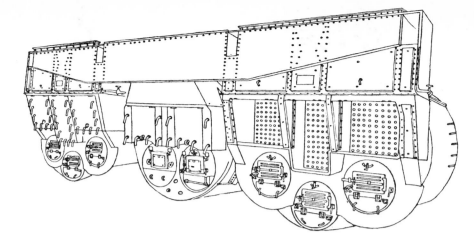

Scotch boiler. A boiler of the cylindrical-shell, internally-fired type, fitted with corrugated furnaces, wet-back combustion chamber, and return fire tubes. The main difference between it and the earlier flue boiler was in the size of the flue or tube, the arbitrary limit being 5 in (0.13 m). The normal working pressure of a Scotch boiler was around 175 psi.

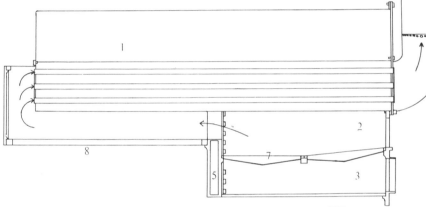

Marc Séguin's 1829 multitubular boiler
1 Boiler
2 Firebox
3 Ashpan
4 Chimney
5 Cast iron hollow box communicating with the boiler
6 Cast iron hollow boxes forming the sides of the firebox
7 Grate
8 Semi-cylindrical hollow casing, communicating at one side with the cold water tank, at the other with the feed pump

boiler barrel to carry the hot gases to the chimney. The tubes are $1^{1}/_{2}$ in. to $2^{1}/_{2}$ in. diameter. They must not be too large, in which case hot gas would pass through them without losing heat to the water, nor so small that they resist the free flow of gas.
Boiler fuel, 50
Boiler:
　horizontal, 72
　jointed, 81
　large-diameter, 85
　long, 81
　reversed on frames, 84
　vertical, 66 72 81
Bölkow Junior, MBB, *180*
Bollée tandem tricar, see Tricar

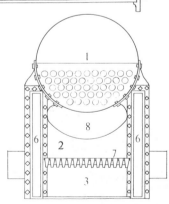

Brakes, 118 123 137 138 144 146
As the speed of cars has increased, it has been necessary to improve the braking systems. With maximum speeds in the region of 10 to 12 mph all that was needed was a spoon that could be pulled on to the outside of the solid tire. With pneumatic tires a band or drum brake had to be used, but only on the rear axles. Early designers found it difficult to combine both braking and steering on the front wheels, and four-wheel braking did not become general until the mid-1920s. The most recent development

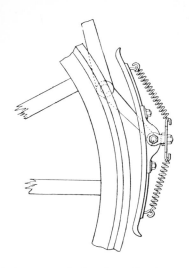

Price's patent brake shoe, fitted as an optional extra to some of the Benz cars in England. These patent shoes were less apt to damage the tires than the little 'spoon' brakes supplied by Benz.

is in the disk brake, and most modern cars use this type on the front wheels and the more conventional drum brakes on the rear.

British Airways
In 1973, BEA and BOAC amalgamated to form this new airline.

Bypass ratio
In a turbofan engine, the ratio of the airflow (A) handled by the fan alone (i.e., that which does not pass through the combustion chamber and turbine) to the airflow (B) that passes through the high-pressure compressor, combustion chamber, and turbine. Thus, in an engine with a 3:1 bypass ratio, the total airflow through the engine is divided in the ratio of three parts through the fan duct to one part through the turbine. The first turbofans had bypass ratios in the range 0.3 to 1.3, but more recent units have ratios ranging from 3 to 8.

Camshaft
To enable the valves of the engine to open and close to allow the inlet gases into the combustion chambers and the exhaust gases to the silencer, a camshaft is used to operate the valve mechanism. It is usually driven from the crankshaft (which see) through gears or by a chain running over

1 Drumhead
2 Capstan-bar
3 Barrel
4 Whelps
5 Whelp chocks
6 Pawls
7 Pawl rim
8 Capstan partners
9 Deck planking

stan. Bars were inserted into the holes (2) and the crew pushed on them to raise the anchor.

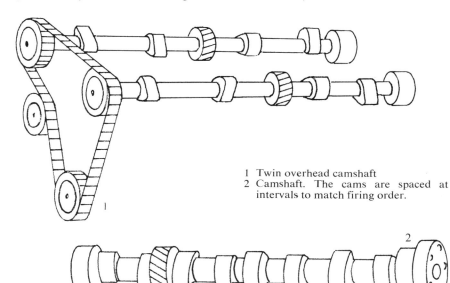

1 Twin overhead camshaft
2 Camshaft. The cams are spaced at intervals to match firing order.

sprockets. The valve rocker mechanism is above the valves and operated by push rods from each of the elliptical surfaces of the camshaft.

Camshaft, twin overhead, 119 139
So that the inlet and exhaust valves may be inclined at different angles, in the high performance cars there are two separate camshafts above the valves for each set of valves.

The capstan was a vital piece of equipment in a sailing ship, and also the source of many shanties. The diagram shows a typical nineteenth-century cap-

Carburetor, *12* 110 111
A device for mixing air and gasoline vapor to provide an explosive mixture. The first type to be used was called a surface vaporizer in which the fuel was heated by a tube containing hot water from the engine's cooling system. As the gasoline vaporized the gas was mixed with the correct volume of air to create an explosive mixture which entered the engine cylinder at the inlet valve. The next development, and still the basic principle used today, was the carburetor. A constant level of fuel is kept in a chamber by means of a float-operated needle valve. Suction caused by the movement of the piston down the cylinder draws air across a jet containing gasoline, the correct proportions give an explosive mixture to be fed to the cylinders. Engine speed is

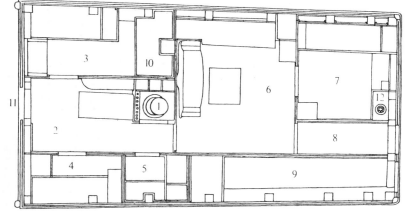

Cabin accommodation on board a barkentine, built in 1878.

1 Mizzenmast
2 Mess room
3 Mate's room
4 Second mate's and steward's room
5 Pantry
6 Cabin
7 Captain's bedroom
8 Alleyway
9 Sail locker and deck stores
10 Provisions
11 Entrance from deck
12 Steering compass

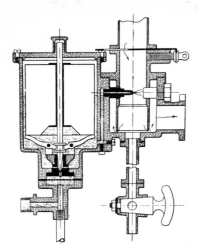

Peugeot carburetor, 1899. The spray from the horizontal jet impinged upon a conical plug which was supposed to help atomize the drops of fuel.

increased by causing a greater flow of air to be drawn across the jet.

Carburetor, Maybach's float-feed spray, 12
Car-carrying air service, 175
Car decks, portable, 54
Car ferries, 46 48 54
Cars, hand-built, 122 123
Carnarvon Castle, see Funnels
Carrack, 22 25
Carriages, passenger, 71 85

One of the carriages drawn by the Atlantic *locomotive in 1832 for the Baltimore & Ohio Railroad.*

Carrying wheels, 81 82 85 103 (see also Wheel arrangements)
Carvelbuilding, 21 25 (see also Materials, shipbuilding)
Cast-iron pistons, 141
Castle Line, 40
Castles, 20 21 23 25
Catch-Me-Who-Can, locomotive, 67
Cathead, 32
Cavendish, Henry, 161
Cavitation, see Engine, turbine
Cayley, Sir George, 157 158 159 161 166
Cayley's:
  glider, *158* 161
  triplane glider, 1849, *158* 161
  whirling arm, *158*
CC 70,000 and 72,000 class diesel-electric locomotives, 92

Centerboard, 59
Centrifugal force, 99 172
Cessna Aircraft Company, 179 187
Cessna Model 172, *181*
Cessna Model 337 Skymaster, *180*
Chain drive, 112 126
Many of the early cars used chains for the drive from the engine to the rear wheels. The system was much more reliable than the leather belt transmission, which was very likely to slip under load conditions and in the wet. Chains continued to be used for some years until the propeller shaft system was perfected. One particular manufacturer, Frazer-Nash, persisted with chains into the 1930s.

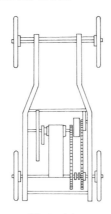

Chain drive

Champion, locomotive, 80
Champlain, S.S., 46 *47*
Charles, Professor J. A. C., 156 161
Charles's hydrogen balloon, *156*
Charleston & Hamburg Railroad, 66 71 72
Charlotte Dundas, P.S., 36 *37*
Charron, 122
Chasseloup-Laubat, Count de, 1899 speed record, 114
Chassis, 119 122 125 129 138 143
The term chassis is not strictly appropriate for modern car design. In its correct sense it refers to the frame onto which axles, engine, transmission, and other major components are fitted. It is separate from the body. Since the introduction of unitary construction there has been no separate chassis, but the understructure of a car is still sometimes referred to as the chassis.

Chevrolet Impala, *136*
Chevrolet Master sedan, *125*
Chicago & Alton Railroad, 85
Chicago Exhibition, 1893, 112
Chicago Milwaukee St. Paul & Pacific Railroad, 91
Chimney, 60 69 71 72 85 88
China clipper, American, *31*
Chinese junk, *28*
"Choppers," 187
Chronometers, see Navigational aids
Chrysler Imperial, 1963, *131*
Cie. des Bateaux-Omnibus de la Seine, 11
Cierva, Juan de la, 172 173 (see also Flapping hinge; VTOL)
Spanish engineer who produced or influenced the design of almost every successful Autogiro of the 1920s and 1930s. His first successful Autogiro, flown near Madrid on January 9, 1923, owed its success to the articulated hinges that allowed the rotor blades to "flap" up and down as they advanced

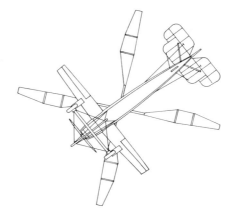

Cierva C.8L Autogiro

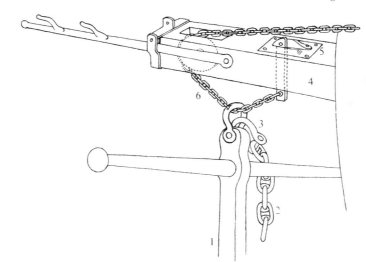

Cathead with anchor gear
1 Anchor
2 Cable
3 Shackle
4 Cathead
5 Releasing gear
6 Cathead stopper

and retreated, so balancing the lift forces and keeping the machine stable in flight. Cierva also discovered the basic principle of autorotation, showing that there is a small positive angle of attack (which see) at which the blades can be set to ensure that a rotor will continue to rotate automatically in an airstream, without an engine to drive it, and still develop enough lift to sustain flight. In 1933 Cierva evolved the first successful "jump-start" Autogiro.

Cisitalia, 1947, *128*
Citroën, André, 119
Citroën 2CV, 137
Citroën DS19, 1956, *131*
Citroën SM, 137
Citroën Traction Avant, 1934, *125*
Citroën Type A, 1919, *119*
City & South London Railway, 88 95
City & South London electric locomotive, *94*
City of Truro, locomotive, *82*
Civil aviation, see ICAO
Classification, locomotives, see Wheel arrangements
Clerestory, 60 85
Clermont, 36
Clinker-planking, 21 25 (see also Materials, shipbuilding)
Clippers, 25 31
Clipper, American, *31* 32
Clipper, Baltimore, 25 *31* 36
Clipper, British, *32*
Clipper bow, 31 41
Closed-circuit flight, Farman's, *163*
Clutch, 111 112 122 128 144 149
A mechanical device for connecting and disconnecting the engine from the transmission system. Because the gasoline engine, unlike a steam engine, is inflexible, it is necessary to take up the drive gradually when moving from a standstill. In the earliest cars this was done by a leather belt that was able to slip on a pulley. By 1908 leather-lined cone clutches were being used. These were fierce in operation and the latest development is a plate clutch.

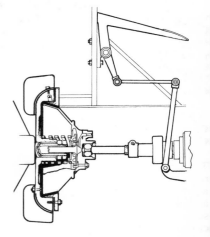

Cone clutch of a 1908 2-cylinder Renault.

Coal gas, 110
Coal trains, 66 80 81
Coastal trade, American, 59 60

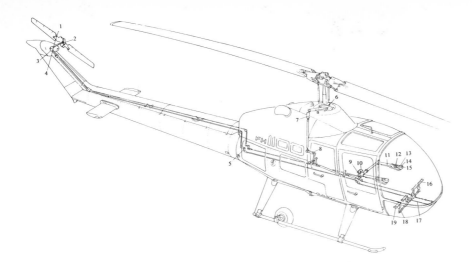

A small enclosed body, most often with two interior seats, much favored before 1914 by doctors and sometimes referred to as a "doctor's coupé."
The main component of a gasoline engine to which the connecting rods are fixed by bearings of low-friction metal. The shape of the crank is designed to convert the reciprocal motion of the pistons into the circular motion required to drive the car.

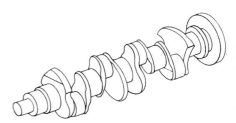

Crankshaft. Revolving in most cars at 6000 times to the minute, the crankshaft transmits engine power to the gearbox, and so onto the wheels.

Crash (unsynchronized) transmission
The early type of transmission in which the gear wheel teeth meshed without any assistance. In order to make a quiet change from one gear to another, great skill was necessary to ensure that the

Collective pitch
1 Acme thread and spline
2 Tail rotor gearbox pitch change rod
3 Bevel gear set
4 Tail rotor pitch sprocket
5 Cable disconnects for tail-boom removal

6 Swashplate
7 Hydraulic power cylinder
8 Isolation linkage
9 Throttle linkage
10 Collective friction control
11 Control stick
12 Engine throttle twist-grip

13 Engine start and motoring switch
14 rpm switch
15 Landing light switch
16 Left hand rudder pedals
17 Rudder balance cable assembly
18 Rudder pedal in-flight adjuster button
19 Right hand rudder pedals

Control in a helicopter that is used to vary the rate of vertical ascent or descent. It enables the angle of pitch of the blades of the main rotor(s) to be altered simultaneously, in conjunction with the power setting of the engine. Together with cyclic pitch (which see) it forms the main directional control system for a helicopter.
The ordinary magnetic compass required some modification to make it suitable for aircraft use since, mounted in a liquid such as alcohol, it was very sensitive to the movements of an aircraft. It remained the basic navigational instrument until relatively recently, although the gyrocompass was introduced between the wars. The gyrocompass is unaffected by some of the shortcomings of the magnetic compass

(i.e., variation according to position on the earth, deviation according to the amount of metal in the aircraft, lag due to swinging in response to aircraft movement, etc.). However, the ordinary gyroscope is prone to "precession," a gradual moving away from its original directional heading, and so the first gyrocompasses had to be reset periodically against a magnetic compass. Since World War II the gyrocompass has been considerably refined, and is now the normal navigational instrument.

A propeller in which the pitch of the blades is varied automatically by a governor, so that the engine may maintain a constant rotational speed as set by the pilot.

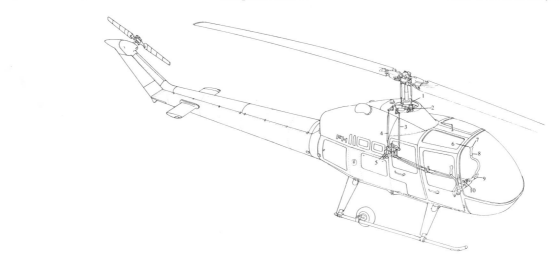

Cyclic pitch
1 Swashplate
2 Hydraulic power cylinder
3 Longitudinal push-rod

4 Lateral push-rod
5 SAS units
6 Radio and intercom switch
7 Trim switch

8 Control stick
9 Yoke
10 Trim motors

Deadeye, turned in a shroud
1 Deadeye
2 Shroud
3 Throat-seizing
4 End-seizing
5 Lanyard

wheels in the transmission were rotating at the correct relative speeds.
Crosshead, 11 13
Crossley, 15 hp, 1929, *121*
Crosstrees, see Masts
Crown, see Piston engine
Crow's nest, see Masts
Cruise liner, 56
Cruiser, 59
Cruises, 14 46 55
Cugnot, Joseph, 145
Cugnot, Nicholas, 67 110
Cugnot's machine, *145*
Cunard Adventurer, S.S., *56*
Cunard Line, 36 41 43 46 (see also Atlantic, Blue Riband of; Boilers; Funnels; Propellers)
Current, alternating and direct, 88 95
Current inverter, electronic, 92 94 97
Curtiss, Glenn Hammond, 165 168
Curtiss flying boats, *165 167* 168
Cyclic pitch, see also Collective pitch Control in a helicopter that regulates the forward or other directional movements other than those of vertical ascent or descent. It is achieved by altering the angle of attack (which see) of the main rotor blades and by tilting the rotational plane of the entire rotor in the direction desired. To provide a good forward speed, the angle of tilt is greatest in that direction.
Cyclone engines, double, 170
Cylinders, 11 13 68 73 81 84 85 86 88 110 111 142 166
Cylinder:
high pressure, 84 (see also Engine, steam)
horizontal inside, 68 70
inside, 68 70 81 83 85
low pressure, 84 85 (see also Engine, steam)
outside, 81 83 85
vertical, 11
DAF 33, *135*
Daimler, Gottlieb, 110 111 112 118 124
Daimler, first car, 110 *111*
Daimler, first high speed engine, *111* 118
Daimler, motorcycle in America, 112
Danish East Asiatic Company, 49 (see also Funnels)
Darracq, 112 114
Darracq, 1904, *115*

Darracq, 1905 V8, *115*
Darrin, 130
Dassault Mirage F-1, 14
Dassault Mystère 20/Falcon 20, *186 187*
Dassault Super-Mystère B2, 14
Datsun 240Z, *135*
Davits, 30 32
Deadeye, 25 35 (see also Shrouds)
Dean, William, 82
Decca System, see Navigational aids
Deck, 21 25 27
Deck beams, 25
Decorations, ships, 23 25 29 31 34
De Dion, Comte, 118
De Dion Bouton engine, 113
Defrosters, 141
de Glehn compound locomotive, *93*
de Havilland, Sir Geoffrey, 167
de Havilland, Geoffrey, 178
de Havilland D.H. 60 Moth, *166*
de Havilland D.H. 106 Comet, 175 179 198 (see also Fatigue in aircraft)
de Havilland D.H. 108, *178*
de Havilland D.H. Comet 4, *199*
de Havilland Canada DHC-6 Twin Otter, *185*
Deicing equipment, 171
Delag, 164
Delage 6-cylinder sedan, 1929, *126*
De Laval turbines, 51
Delaware & Hudson Canal Co., 66 71
Delta-winged aircraft, 190 191 192
Depth sounders, see Navigational aids
Der Adler, locomotive, *70*
Derricks, 49 (see also Masts)
Deutsche Lufthansa, 169
Deutschland II, 169
Deviation, see Compass; Navigational aids
Devon, Austin A40, 128
DFP 2-liter tourer, 149
Dhow, Arabian, *28*
Diagonal planking, see Materials, shipbuilding
Diesel, Dr. Rudolph, 45 92
Diesel locomotives, 12 92 94 97
Diesel-electric locomotive, 92 97
Diesel-electric "hood" locomotive, 96

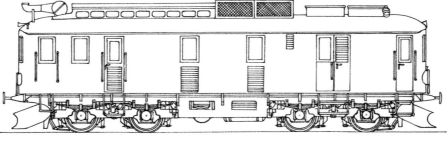

This 200 hp diesel-electric locomotive was built in 1928 for the Halmstad–Nässjö Railway in Sweden.

Diesel-electric railcar, 1912, *96*
Diesel engines, see Engine, motor
Diesel-hydraulic locomotives, 92 97
Diesel-hydraulic shunting locomotive, 92
Diesel railcars, 92
Differential action, 10
Dihedral, wing, 159
Diligence, locomotive, 69
Dion, Comte de, 118

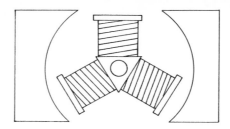

Electricity generator; principle

Direct current electrifications
An electricity generator possesses wire coils mounted round a shaft that revolve between magnets, usually electromagnets. The magnets induce an electric current in the coils revolving between them. When one coil is uppermost the induced current will appear to flow through it in a clockwise direction, but when it is downward the current will appear to flow in an anticlockwise direction from the same viewpoint. The shaft and coil assembly is known as an armature, and mounted on the end of the shaft is a device known as a commutator. Electric leads run from the coils to the commutator and the latter reverses the flow of current when necessary. A generator without a commutator produces alternating current, with a commutator it produces direct current and it is known as a dynamo.
Dirigibles, 16 *159*
Disk brakes, see Brakes
Dispatch vessel, *59*
Distilled water, 36
DKW, 1938, *127*
Doctor Lykes, S.S., 52
Doctor's coupé, see Coupé
Dolphin striker, 33
Door locks, non-burst, 152
Doors, sliding, 144
Doppler principle, see Navigational aids

Dornier Do X, *168*
Dornier Do 31, *188*
Dornier Skyservant, *185*
Double cyclone engines, 170
Double ender, 25 29 60
Douglas DC-1, 171 197
Douglas DC-2, 171 197
Douglas DC-3, 171 179 *197* 200
Douglas DC-4, 175
Douglas DC-8, McDonnell, 179 *184*
Douglas DC-9, McDonnell, 187
Douglas DC-10, McDonnell, 179 *200*
Douglas World Cruiser, *168*
Dowels, 25

Draft, 51
Drag, see Flight, principles of; Air brake
Dredger, 54
Dripps, Isaac, 73 81
Drive, 73
Driving axle, 70 71 78 86
Driving wheels, 68 76 81 82 86 88 98 142 (see also Wheel arrangements)
Drum brakes, see Brakes
Dry docks, 49
Dübs & Co., 76
Dunalastair, locomotive, *83* 85
Dundas, Lord, 36
Dundee & Perth Railway, 81
Dunlop, John Boyd, see Pneumatic tire
Dunottar Castle, S.S., 40
Duryea, wins America's first race, 112

Duster
In the days before tarmac surfaces, roads were covered in a fine white dust in summer. As all the cars were open many motorists and passengers wore protective dusters with head covers. The one illustrated dates from 1903.
Dutch flute, *22*
Dutch Statenjacht, *58*
Dutch State passenger locomotive, *78*
Dynamo, 92 95 97 (see also Battery; Direct current electrifications; Lighting, railway cars)
East African Garratt locomotive, *89*
East Indiaman, 9 27
East Indian Railway, 86
Eastwick & Harrison works, 71
Economy cars, 122 123 124 126 137 141 143 144
Edge, S. F., 122
Edison, Thomas Alva, 172
Egyptian bird "glider," *154*
Egyptian ship, *19*
Eiffel Tower, 161 163
Eight-coupled locomotives, 74 *80* 81 86
Eight-cylinder engine, 115 121 124 130 132 136 138
Eight-wheeled bogie coaches, 85
Ejector exhaust, 76

A gasoline engine working in the horizontal position in which the pistons travel parallel with the chassis.

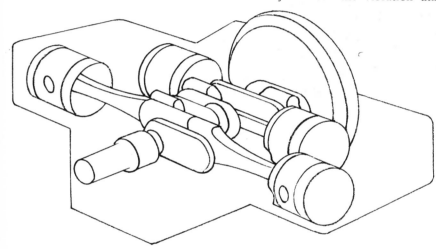

The horizontal engine has its cylinders arranged in two flat banks, with the crankshaft between them.

The diesel engine (or internal-combustion engine) is very similar in operation to the modern car engine, but with the difference that the oil, after being mixed with air, is exploded by the compression of the upward stroke of the piston.

Internal-combustion engines are built in a variety of types to meet the needs of practically any ship. Modern engines are supercharged and the development of the large bore engine has kept the internal-combustion engine competitive with the turbine for the propulsion of very large tankers. Many of the fastest cargo liners are also fitted with diesel engines, although several years ago it seemed that they had lost the race with turbines.

The compound engine used a given amount of steam in two cylinders, one high pressure, the other low pressure. In this way the steam was made to do twice as much work as it had done in earlier engines that had cylinders of equal size, each of which drew steam direct from the boiler.

In some compound engines the high pressure cylinder had a low pressure cylinder on either side. These engines were called tandem engines and considerably reduced the vibration that was a disadvantage of the ordinary compound engine.

The triple expansion engine was a logical step forward and used steam in three stages before it was passed to the condenser. Many large liners of the late nineteenth and early twentieth century were fitted with quadruple expansion engines.

The turbine is a complex rotary steam engine with no reciprocating parts. The rotor, or revolving part, is fitted with thousands of blades that revolve between other blades — or guides — fixed to the casing. Steam at high temperature and velocity is directed at the moving blades and in order to expand the steam the blades on the rotor are made successively longer.

The rotor revolves at extremely high speeds and in the early days the direct drive to the propeller caused cavitation.

The propellers revolved so fast that they created cavities in the water and thus became only partly effective. Various means were tried to overcome the problem and in the *Turbinia* three turbines were eventually fitted, each driving a shaft to which was fitted three propellers. Eventually gears were introduced between the turbine and the shaft and it is now possible for a 30,000 horsepower turbine to drive propellers revolving at under 100 revolutions per minute.

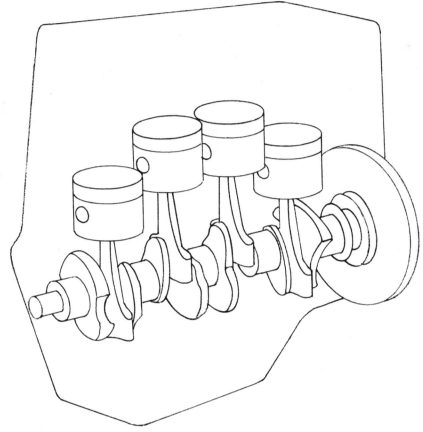

Vertical engine

A gasoline engine working in the vertical position in which the pistons travel perpendicular with the ground.

Engine fumes
The exhaust system sends out a mixture of burnt and unburnt gases. Some of these are lethal, particularly carbon monoxide. Faulty exhausts car allow these gases to enter the car with disastrous results. New legislation will lay down standards of emission to help prevent pollution.

A car body, popular in the late 1920s, in which an artificial leather fabric is stretched across a wooden framework of rigid or semiflexible construction.

Founded in 1905, the FAI is the internationally accepted body that formulates and enforces rules governing the conduct of sporting air meetings and international air records. Its headquarters is in Paris. The first speed record recognized officially by the FAI was the flight at Bagatelle, France, on November 12, 1906, in which Alberto Santos-Dumont reached 25.06 mph (40.33 km/h) in the 14-bis.

It is easy to design a structure to withstand a known steady load; but aircraft are subjected to widely varying loads in flight, and many components even experience load reversals. An obvious example of this "fatigue" process is that used to weaken and break off the lid of a tin can by bending it to and fro: eventually it breaks without the need to apply any large tensile load. Aircraft fatigue was dramatically highlighted in 1954 when fatigue of the pressure cabin, a hitherto unthought of menace, caused the breakup in flight of two Comet 1 jetliners. Since 1945 airliners have had to be designed for total flight "lives" of the order of 40,000 hours or more. New airframe designs are nowadays fatigue-tested by being subjected to thousands of load reversals; but the proof really comes in actual service, when fail-safe design (such as duplication of load paths) allows fatigue to be seen and rectified before structural failure can cause breakup of the aircraft in flight.

Feathering float, see Paddles
Fédération Aéronautique Internationale, see FAI
Feeder type miniairliner, 187
Fenders, 122 125 129 130 143
Ferrari 250 GT, 1959, *138*
Festiniog Railway, Wales, see Garratt articulated locomotive
Fiat, 112 135
Fiat, 1903, *112*
Fiat 9, 1930, *121*
Fiat 128 Giannini, *135*
Fiat 300 GP, *114*
Fiat 500 Topolino, 1938, *127*
Fidded mast, 29 30
Fighter planes, 16 171 172 174
Fighting top, 21 25 29
Figurehead, 25 27 31

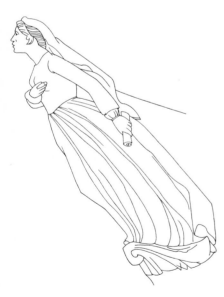

Figurehead of unknown vessel, from the middle of the 19th century.

Filter
A device for cleaning either the air before it enters the carburetor or the oil as it circulates around the engine. The filter elements are made of a paper compound and are removable so that

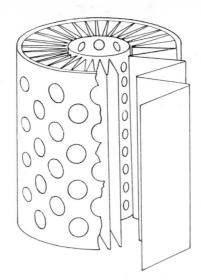

This type of filter in common use today is made of resin-impregnated paper.

they can be replaced at regular intervals as part of the servicing process when they become clogged with deposit.

Finland State No. 11, locomotive, *76*
Fins, antiroll, 53 (see also Stabilizers)
Fireboxes, 69 71 76 78 81 82 85 104 (see also Haystack fireboxes)
Firetube boiler, see Boilers
First:
   aerial voyage, 156
   air mail, see Air mail
   airline service (by airplane), 168
   airline service (by airship), 164 169
   airplane crossing of the English Channel, 16 166
   airplane crossing of the North Atlantic (in stages), 167 168
   airplane crossing of the North Atlantic (nonstop), 16 167 169
   airplane design, *158*
   airplane industry, 166
   airplane with totally enclosed accommodation, 164
   airship, *159*
   airship fitted with a gasoline engine, *163*
   airship that could be steered, *160*
   automobile dealer, 118
   balloon used to practical purpose, 15
   British railway, 10 66
   car-ferry service by airplane, 175
   commercial turbine ship, 43
   compound locomotive, 85
   deep-level underground railway, 88
   design for a lighter-than-air aircraft, 154 156
   diesel locomotive, commercial, 92 96
   electric locomotive, 88 *94*
   electrified city railway, 95
   fare-paying steam railway passengers, 67
   flight by a Briton to be officially recognized, 165
   flight of a heavier-than-air aircraft, 16
   flight under control by a powered airplane, 194
   flight with a powered heavier-than-air aircraft, 159

First:
   floatplane, 166
   flying boat, 168
   French steam railway, 66
   gas-turbine locomotive, 94 *98*
   glider (man-carrying), *158* 161
   helicopter (fully practical), 172 *173*
   helicopter (semipractical), 172
   hot-air balloon (man-carrying), *156*
   hot-air balloon (model), *156*
   hydrogen balloon, *156* 161
   jet aircraft, America's, *173*
   jet aircraft, Britain's, 172 *174*
   jet aircraft, Italy's, 172 *173*
   jet aircraft to make a cross-country flight, 173
   jet airline service across the North Atlantic, 179
   jet-lift VTOL aircraft, 178
   jet-powered aircraft to fly, 172 *175*
   jet-powered airliner to enter service, 16
   Jumbo jet airliner, 179
   locomotive built in Belgium, 81
   locomotive in the United States, 66 *68*
   locomotive with a multi-tubular boiler, 100 *101*
   main line electrification, 88
   man to leave the ground, 161
   mass-produced automobile, 15 123
   motorship in regular North Atlantic service, 45
   multiengined airplane to fly, 168
   pilot to flay faster than 1,000 mph, 176
   pilot to fly faster than sound, 174, 176
   powered airplane flight in Europe, 163
   railways, 10 11 66
   railway engines, 110
   regular mail and passenger service on the North Atlantic, 39
   restaurant car, 85
   rocket-powered aircraft to fly, 172
   roll-on roll-off service, 46
   round-the-world flight, 168
   sea plane, *162* 168
   sleeping car, 85
   solo airplane crossing of the North Atlantic, 165 169

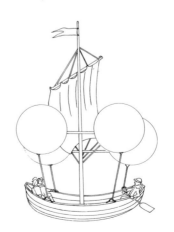

The first definite project for a lighter-than-air aircraft, proposed by Francesco de Lana-Terzi in 1670. It was intended to be lifted by four thin copper spheres from which all the air had been extracted.

First:
   solo airplane flight around the world, 168
   speed record recognized by the FAI, see FAI
   steam locomotives, 66 67 *68 103*
   steam propelled passenger vehicle, 110
   steam public railway, 66 71
   supersonic airliner to fly, 179 191
   supersonic airplane flight, 174 176
   supersonic world airspeed record, 174
   takeoff by a powered airplane, 161
   train disaster, 11
   turboprop-powered airliner to enter service, 176
   twin-engined airplane, 168
   United States railroad, 66 71
   vertical high speed engine, *111*
   vertical takeoff by an airplane, 173
   voyage, Columbus's, 20
   VTOL aircraft, *173*
Fitch, John, 36
Five-cylinder radial engine, Manly's, *12*
Fixed-float paddle wheel, see Paddles
Fixed-wing aircraft, 161 162 168 170 172 191

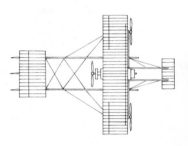

The Short S.39 Triple Twin was the first multi-engined airplane to fly safely after failure of an engine in the air.

Flanges, 66 (see also Plateways)
Flap
Hinged surface, usually at the trailing-edge of a wing, used to increase the lift of the wing at slow speeds; to steepen the glide path; or to act as an air brake (which see) during approach and landing. Flaps can take various forms, the simplest being to hinge the entire trailing-edge of the wing. A more sophisticated form involves the split flap, where only the lower surface of the trailing-edge is hinged, the upper surface being fixed and maintaining a normal airflow. Slotted flaps, when opened, allow an airflow over the upper surface of the flap, thus increasing lift.
Flapping hinge, 172
Hinge used on nonrigid helicopter rotors to allow the blades to move up and down and so relieve the severe bending loads. When initially introduced on the Cierva Autogiro (see Cierva), flapping hinges allowed the blades to rise and fall automatically under natural forces and so balance the unequal lift that otherwise would have been generated by the advancing and retreating blades, owing to their different speeds through the air.

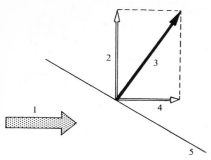

1 Airflow
2 Lift
3 Resultant force
4 Drag
5 Inclined plane

Flight, principles of, 161 172
Most aerodynes (heavier-than-air aircraft) are supported in flight by the reaction of air flowing past their wing(s). (Direct-lift VTOL aircraft are supported by the thrust of their engines exhausting downward.) A wing has a curved cross section known as an aerofoil; the degree of curvature on the upper and lower surfaces, and the ratio of wing thickness to wing chord, vary according to the role and performance required of the aircraft. Most wings generate lift because the air has to travel a greater distance in passing across the more curved top of the wing than in passing along the shallower curve beneath it. The air is therefore accelerated to a higher speed, relative to the aircraft, across the top of the wing, and thus is correspondingly reduced in pressure. Most of the lift results from this reduction in pressure across the top of the wing. The principle can easily be demonstrated by blowing across the top of a piece of paper shaped in an arched, curving form like the upper surface of a wing; the airflow tends to lift the paper into

a straight line behind the "leading edge." If the airflow suddenly breaks away from the upper surface of the wing, the wing leaves a massively turbulent wake and the aircraft drops almost like a stone until the pilot can restore the angle of attack (which see) to a low value, typically by pushing down the aircraft nose and increasing airspeed. This is known as the stall, and can be postponed by fitting slats to the wing leading-edge to keep the airflow "attached" as it crosses the upper surface. The onset of turbulence should warn the pilot of the impending stall (advanced aircraft measure angle of attack and provide a positive warning in the cockpit).

In steady cruising flight the lift of the wing equals the weight of the air-

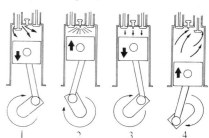

The jet-reaction control system on the Hawker Siddeley Harrier attack aircraft is used at low speeds when the aerodynamic flying controls are ineffective.
1 Pitch control jet
2 Roll control jet
3 Yaw and pitch control jets

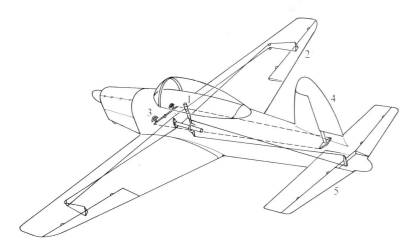

In a conventional flying control system, foot pedals operate the rudder, while a central control column operates the elevators and ailerons.
1 Control column
2 Aileron
3 Rudder pedals
4 Rudder
5 Elevator

craft and the thrust of the propulsion system equals the total aircraft drag. If these four forces do not all pass through the same point, then one pair must tend to tip the aircraft nose down by exactly the same amount as the other pair tend to tip it nose up. Flight of the aircraft is controlled by delibera-

tely spoiling this balance by applying disturbing forces far from the center of gravity. In nearly all aircraft these forces are imparted by movable aerodynamic surfaces – elevators to move the nose up and down to cause a climb or dive; rudder to yaw the aircraft left or right or cancel the asymmetric thrust caused by a "dead" engine on one side; and ailerons or spoilers near the wing tips to roll the aircraft. Jet-lift VTOL aircraft have to be able to fly at speeds too low for such surfaces to be effective, and their control forces are generally provided by compressed-air jets at the extremities of the body and wings.

Aerostats (lighter-than-air aircraft) are supported against the acceleration due to gravity by the fact that their overall density is initially less than that of the surrounding atmosphere, so that they rise. When they reach a height at which local air density is the same as their own, they stop rising. Further change in altitude is effected by releasing low-density gas (hydrogen or helium) to descend, and releasing ballast (such as sand) to rise.

Flywheel, 67 92 110
In an engine with a single cylinder the explosion stroke exerts a rotating force on the crankshaft (which see). It is followed by three idle strokes during which the shaft still has to turn without a reduction in speed. The flywheel is bolted to the crankshaft to maintain

uniform motion. During the explosion stroke it absorbs surplus energy and gives it up to the working parts during the other three strokes.

The reciprocating (piston) engine operating on the four stroke cycle was first described by Beau de Rocha in 1862 and then modified by Otto and others. Today it is known as the Otto cycle.
1 Induction stroke
2 Compression stroke
3 Power stroke
4 Exhaust stroke

Four stroke cycle, Otto's, 111
The principle of operation of the modern gasoline engine in which there are four successive strokes.

it is doubtful whether they were so. This is borne out by the fact that one famous line painted its ships black all over for many years, and brown or stone-colored upperworks were common for a long time.

From about 1860 until the early 1920s funnel shapes showed little change although many two and three funneled liners were built during this period. The fashion for four funneled ships that commenced at the turn of the century was over by the early 1920s. It is said that during this period many people estimated the power of a liner by the number of her funnels. How true this was is questionable, but one famous line did go so far as to produce a poster with an illustration of one of their ships – it had five funnels!

The first motor ships were given

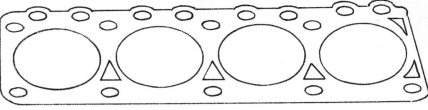

Gasket

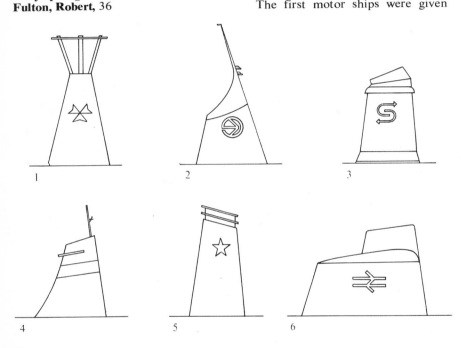

Funnels
1 Deutsche Atlantik Linie
2 British & Irish Steam Packet Co.
3 Seatrain
4 Cia Transmediterranea
5 Achille Lauro
6 British Rail (Sealink)

Funnels, 36 38
The earliest funnels were simple stove pipes, painted black, if they were painted at all, because the heat rising from the boiler would soon have scorched off any paint applied. Before very long an outer casing was built around the funnel and it became possible to use a wide variety of colors on the casing. From the outset Cunard liners had the red (actually a shade of orange) and black funnel with three black bands, which continued almost unaltered until the *Queen Elizabeth 2* was designed.

Early contemporary paintings of steamships suggest that they were spruce and clean, with gleaming funnel colors, but with the volume of smoke and smut that early boilers produced,

extremely small stove pipe funnels and the Danish East Asiatic Company introduced the practice of exhausting fumes from a narrow pipe secured to a mast. The last ship they built in this fashion was the *Selandia* of 1938. In

1927 Messrs. Harland and Wolff of Belfast built the *Carnarvon Castle*, the first of a long series of ships to have squat funnels. In 1930 the Cie. Messageries Maritimes put into service a group of liners with low rectangular funnels. A second group followed with pear-shaped funnels that were so low that from certain angles it was almost impossible to see them.

Since the late 1950s great attention has been given to the design of funnels so that the slipstream would carry fumes and smut clear of a ship's deck. It is now a regular practice to subject scale-model funnels to wind-tunnel tests in order to achieve an effective shape. There have been many solutions and more distinct variations than occurred in the preceding one hundred years.

Gaff, 27 33
Galleass, 25
Galleon, 25
Galleon, Elizabethan, *24*
Galley, 25 29
Galley, Phoenician War, *19*
Galliot, 25
Gantry crane, 46
Garnerin, 193
Garratt articulated locomotive, 86 *89*
H. W. Garratt evolved this type of articulated locomotive and the first one was built by Beyer, Peacock & Co. for a 2 foot gauge railway in Tasmania in 1909. At the end of its active life this locomotive was brought back to England by Beyer, Peacock & Co. (the firm had built a large number of

other much bigger Garratts in the meantime) and today it is preserved on the Festiniog Railway in Wales.
Gas engines, 15 118
Gas engine, Lenoir's, 110
Gasket
Means by which joints between metal surfaces in a car can be made water, gas, or oiltight. Paper and cork gaskets are most often used to prevent oil leaks between joints, and copper or copper and asbestos gaskets on exhaust systems and at cylinder heads where there is a high temperature.
Gasoline, bought from chemists, 118
Gasoline engines, 15 16 92 110 111 112 114 118 143 161 162 163 166 168
Gasoline railcars, 92
Gas-turbine chambers, *14*
Gas turbine-electric locomotive, 94 *99 108*
Gas-turbine engines, 14 56 172 189 (see also Turbine; Turbofan; Turbojet; etc.)
Basic means of propulsion for almost all but light aircraft since its introduction at the end of World War II. It works on the principle whereby air is drawn into a tube in which it is compressed and ignited, giving it increased energy, and exhausted through a tapering nozzle increasing its velocity. To this there is a resultant reaction that propels the tube in the opposite direction. A normal aircraft gas turbine consists of an intake, a compressor (mounted on the same shaft as the turbine that drives it), a combustion chamber or

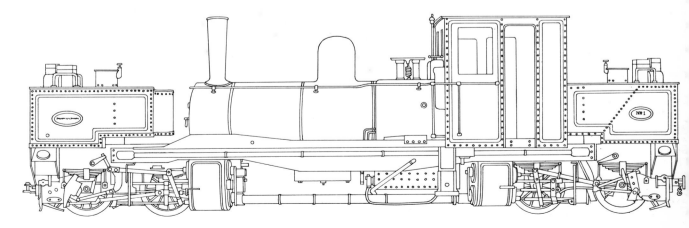

Garratt's first articulated locomotive

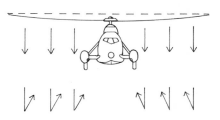

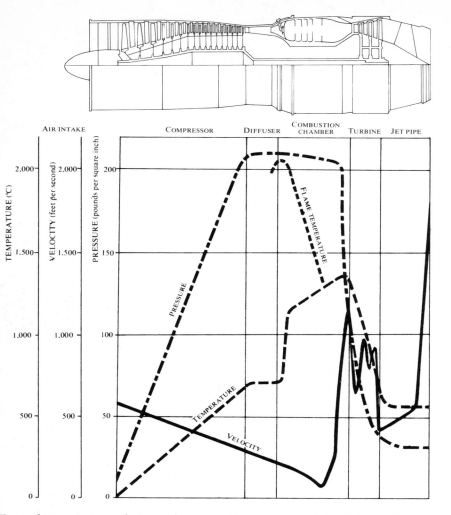

Gas turbine: pressure, velocity, and temperature variation chart

chambers, a turbine (through which the ignited gases pass and that drives the compressor), and a jet pipe through which the gases exhaust to atmosphere.

Great Eastern
Designed by I. K. Brunel (which see), the *Great Eastern* was the largest ship in the world when she was built in 1858. She was not surpassed in size until 1899 by the White Star liner *Oceanic*, by which time the *Great Eastern* had been broken up. Originally designed for the Indian service, she never entered that trade. Propelled by paddles, screw, and sail, she was underpowered and was virtually a failure, but achieved some success later in her career in laying the first reliable transatlantic cable. The *Great Eastern* was 692 feet long and was originally fitted to carry 4,000 passengers in three classes.

Ground effect
The effect of the "pushing" of air compressed against the ground by a landing airplane or helicopter. This effect can be turned to special advan-

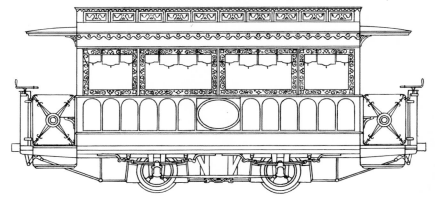

Ground effect or ground cushion; a supplementary source of lift, caused by the down-wash of air from the rotor being reflected back upward from the ground.

In 1883 Ireland saw the first use of electric traction with hydro-electric power on the little Giant's Causeway line from Portrush. This is a 20-seat car built for the line by the Midland Railway-Carriage and Wagon Co., Shrewsbury, England.

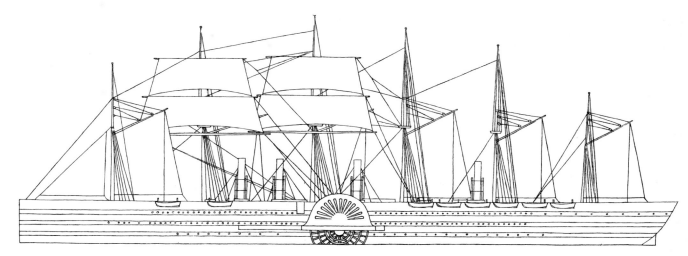

Great Eastern

tage by helicopters when required to land on high plateaus or mountainsides, their proximity to high terrain then enabling them to operate at heights greater than that of their normal hovering ceiling over low ground.

G. Sigl Works, 78
Gudgeon pin, see Piston engine
Guericke, Otto von, 156
Guides, see Engine, turbine
Guion Line, 41
Guns, 21 23 24 27 28 110
Guppy, Boeing, *198*
Gusmão, Bartolomeu Lourenço de, 156
Gustaph Adolph, *26*
Gypsies, see Windlasses
Gyrocompass, see Compass; Navigational aids
Gyroscope, see Artificial horizon
Gyro stabilization, see Autopilot
Hackworth, Timothy, 68 69 72 81
Hales, H. K., see Atlantic, Blue Riband of
Halyard, 25 35
Hancock, 110
Handley Page H.P.42, *167*
Handley Page Jetstream, *187*
Hang-glider, Lilienthal's, *160*
Hansa, MBB HFB 320, *187*
Hansina, *32*
Hargrave, Lawrence, 163
Harland and Wolff, Messrs., see Funnels; Materials, shipbuilding
Harrison, John, see Navigational aids
Hatches, 49
Hawker Siddeley 125, *186* 187
Hawker Siddeley 748, *183*
Hawker Siddeley Harrier, 188

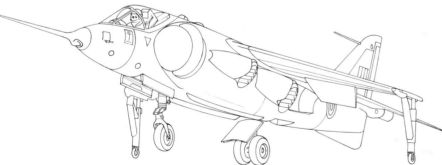

The Hawker Harrier VTOL strike aircraft embodies a tandem main gear, with small outrigger wheels at the wing-tips.

Hawker Siddeley P.1127, 188
Hawker Siddeley Trident, *184*
Hawsepipe, 32 (see also Anchors)
Haystack fireboxes, 69 71 74 (see also Fireboxes)
The haystack firebox roof had a characteristic domed shape flattened at the top. At first the dome covered a vertical cylinder inside which the grate was carried and into which the boiler barrel cylinder fitted. Later the normal rectangular firebox was also covered by a dome with a flattened top.
Head lamps, 126 130
Head lamps, retractable, 139
Headlight wipers, 152
Headsail, 26 27 30

Heaters, 125 141
Heating, train, 79 85
Steam heating of the train from the locomotive boiler became general in the 1890s and from a decade later it was joined by electrical heating on electrified railways. Electrical heating became general on European railways after 1945 and often air is warmed and blown into the railway cars, which helps ventilation. Air conditioning of railway coaches started in the United States in 1928 and rapidly spread in that country, as well as being used on luxury trains elsewhere. It became standard in new coaches in Europe from 1971.
Heavier-than-air research, 159 162
Hedley, William, 102
Heinkel He 176, 172 *174*
Heinkel He 178, 172 173 *174*
Heinkel He S1 engine, 172

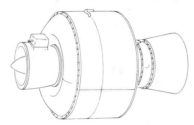

1939 Heinkel-Hirth HeS 3B 1,100 lb thrust.

Helicopters, 16 155 172 *173* 187 188 *189* (see also Ground effect; Turboshaft engine)

Helm, see Steering
Hemp, tarred, 33 35 (see also Shrouds)
Hengist, T.S., *55*
Henson, William Samuel, 159 161 166
Henson Aerial Steam Carriage, *158* 161
Hercules, locomotive, 71
Hernalser & Co., 79
Hernalser sleeper, *79*
He S1 jet engine, 172
Hiawatha, locomotive, *91*
High-speed railways, 91 100 108
High strength metal, 171
Hindenburg, 16 166 169
Hispano Suiza Type 12 Nbr, *13*
Hitachi-Alweg monorail, 94 *100*
Hofecker, Philip, 80
Holland America Line, 55
"Hood" locomotive, diesel-electric, *97*
Hoods, 116 122 125 141
Hope, locomotive, 69

Horizontal engine, see Engine, horizontal
Hornsby's diesel locomotive, *96*
Horse-traction railways, 66
Hot-air balloon, 15 156 161
Hot-air engine, 159 161
Hovercraft, 56 *64*
Hoverlloyd, 56
Hovertrains, 96 *100*
Hub mechanism, see Rotor head
Hukare, Swedish, 26
Hulk, *21* 25 38
Hull, 18 20 21 25 27 29 31 37
Hull, composite, see Materials, shipbuilding
Hull, double-ended, 25 29 60
Hull, iron, 18 35 43 (see also Materials, shipbuilding)
Hull, steel, 13 18 34 43 (see also Materials, shipbuilding)

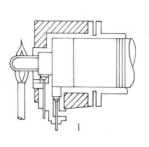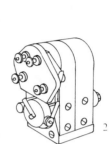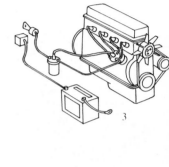

Humber, T.T., car, 149
Hungarian State Railways, Royal, 78 92 98
Hungarian State V40 class locomotive, *98*
Hydraulic transmission, 94
Hydrofoil, 56
Hydrogen balloon, Charles's, *156* 161
Hydrokinetic transmission, 92
Hydrostatic transmission, 92
IATA (International Air Transport Association)
IATA was founded in 1946 as an international trade association of the principal airlines. It maintains a worldwide pattern of rates, fares, and other matters relating to airline traffic, at the request of various governments. It has divided the world into nine areas, and a Traffic Conference for each area meets to establish fares and rates in that area together with related subjects such as relationships with travel agencies, cargo agencies, etc., together with more general development of such practical matters as cargo handling.
ICAO (International Civil Aviation Organization), see also Weather minima
In December 1944 the representatives of 54 nations met in Chicago to discuss matters of mutual interest and collaboration concerning postwar civil aviation. One outcome was the establishment, with effect from June 1945, of a Provisional International Civil Aviation Organization (PICAO): this became a permanent body as of April 1947, and by the end of that year 46

nations had become members. Today the membership is well over 100 countries and the declared objectives of ICAO are: "To promote the safe and orderly development of commercial and private international civil aviation with equal opportunity for all its member nations; the establishment of worldwide standards for safety, reliability, and regularity of air navigation; the economic development of aviation; the reduction of formalities of customs, immigration, health and currency control, and the continuous evolution of international air law."

The ICAO headquarters is in Montreal, Canada. In addition, it has regional offices in Mexico City, Lima, Paris, Cairo, Dakar, and Bangkok.

Icebreaker, *49* 50

1 Flame ignition
2 Magnetoignition
3 Coil ignition

Ignition, 111 112 116 123
Intense heat is required for a specific duration to ignite the compressed explosive gases in the cylinders on the power stroke. The earliest type of ignition was by means of a hot tube in which a probe of platinum was introduced into the combustion chamber, being heated from the outside by a spirit lamp. Apart from being highly dangerous, it was not possible to control the combustion, consequently these engines ran erratically. Electric ignition followed. An electric spark was created by a magnetoelectric machine geared up to the engine, the current was fed through a distributor to each cylinder, and could be timed to reach the gases at the precise moment required. A sparking plug acted as a spark gap to the electric current and ignited the mixture. Now a battery (which see) and coil provide the current that passes through a distributor to the sparking plugs.

ILS (Instrument Landing System), see also Autopilot
One of the most important radio aids developed since World War II, ILS is now in worldwide use by both military and civil aviation. It can be used either for pure navigational purposes or as an approach and landing aid at night or in bad weather. It comprises two radio transmitting units at the airfield

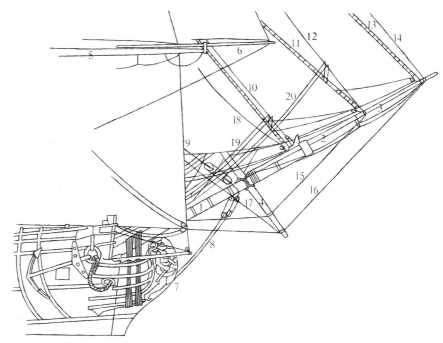

and a receiver in the aircraft linked to a display instrument in the pilot's cockpit. In the basic ILS, one airfield transmitter emits a radio beam along the axis of the runway, known as a localizer. The other transmitter alongside the runway emits a beam along the desired glide slope to land on that runway. This beam is interpreted in the aircraft by a vertical needle in the ILS instrument that must be aligned with a vertical line on the dial. Similarly, the glide slope beam is interpreted by a horizontal pointer that must be aligned with a further line on the dial to ensure a correct approach to the runway. In some cases ILS display is coordinated with a basic flight instrument such as an artificial horizon (which see), to inform the pilot not only how to get onto the runway but also what attitude his aircraft is taking while he is doing so.

ILS
1 Localizer clearance antenna
2 Localizer course antenna
3 Runway
4 "Fly down and left"
5 Localizer path width
6 "Course correct"
7 Outer marker
8 Glide path width
9 "Fly up and right"
10 Middle marker
11 Glide path

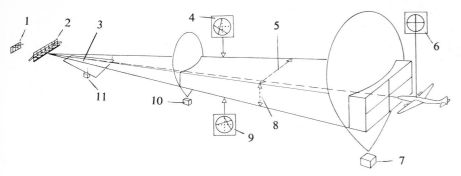

A familiar sight at Croydon in the early 1930s was the Armstrong Whitworth Argosy used on Imperial Airways's European routes.

Jet stream
Popular name of a meteorological phenomenon encountered chiefly off the eastern coasts of Asia and North America and over North Africa. It is a circumpolar airstream, usually traveling in a west-to-east direction, and is identified by a narrow stream of high velocity wind, particularly near the base of the stratosphere. Use has frequently been made of this phenomenon, acting as a very strong tail wind, to reduce the scheduled west-to-east flying time of transoceanic airliners.

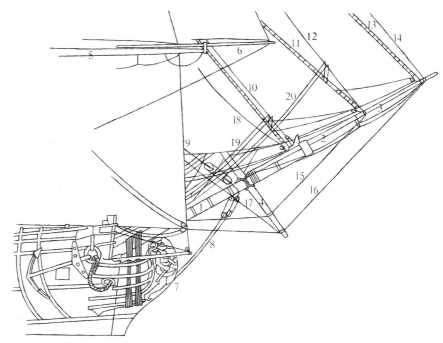

Bowsprit with jib boom and rigging, end of the 18th century.
1 Bowsprit
2 Jib boom
3 Flying jib boom
4 Spritsail yard
5 Foreyard
6 Studding sail boom
7 Fore tack bumpkin
8 Bobstay
9 Forestay
10 Fore topmast stay
11 Jibstay
12 Fore topgallant stay
13 Flying jibstay
14 Royal stay
15 Jib boom guy
16 Flying jib boom guy
17 Spritsail braces
18 Fore topmast staysail downhaul
19 Weather side jib sheet
20 Weather side flying jib sheet

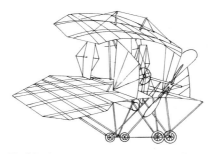

Karl Jatho covered up to 200 ft in his 9 hp kite-like airplane in November, 1903, but it is not accepted that his flights were controlled and sustained.

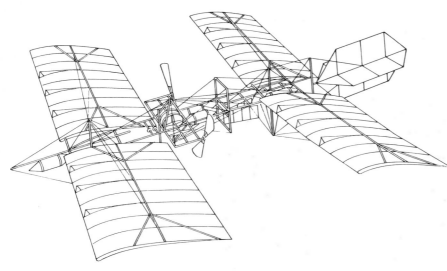

Dr. S. P. Langley flew this 14-ft span steam-powered model airplane well over three quarters of a mile, at 25 mph, in 1896.

This glider was built by Jean-Marie Le Bris in 1857. Inspired by the albatross, it made a short glide over a quarry after being launched from a horse-drawn cart.

A device extended to "spoil" the airflow over the wing and hence reduce or "dump" lift. Lift dumpers are used to reduce the total wing lift as soon as possible after touchdown, to increase the vertical load on the wheels, thus permitting a greater braking effort to be applied and so shorten the landing run.
A means of providing driving lights from burning the gas obtained from

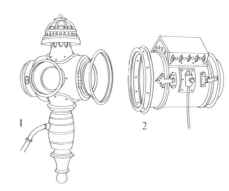

1 Acetylene lamp
2 Paraffin lamp

water dripping onto calcium carbide in a generator. The light obtained was powerful and free from glare.
A continuation of the lighting system used on horse-drawn vehicles that continued to be employed on car side and tail lamps until 1918.
Electricity is generated by a dynamo belt driven from a coach axle and used to charge a battery, which in turn supplies the railway car lamps. In recent years a generator is mechanically driven from the axle, the alternating output of which is rectified to direct current for charging the battery. Fluorescent tubes often replace the old lamps as well.
Load lines and the load line disk are prominently displayed on the sides of merchant ships. They indicate the amount of freeboard (reserve buoyancy) that a ship must have when loaded with cargo in a variety of conditions.

The illustrations show the markings, which are painted white, and action is taken against the master and owner of a ship that is found to be overloaded. The expression "down to her marks" derives from the load lines.

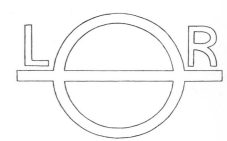

Load line disk or Plimsoll mark. The letters LR denote the classifying society, here Lloyd's Register.

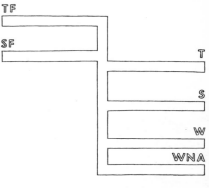

Load lines. The letters indicate:
TF = *fresh water tropical load line*
SF = *fresh water summer load line*
T = *salt water tropical load line*
S = *salt water summer load line*
W = *salt water winter load line*
WNA = *winter North Atlantic load line*

1 Digital Mach/airspeed indicator
2 & 3 Mach/airspeed indicators
4 Machmeter

Machmeter, 191
Instrument in high-speed aircraft indicating not only the airspeed but also the Mach number. Because the speed of sound in air is not constant, an ordinary airspeed indicator dial cannot show both figures simultaneously. Sonic speed falls with increased altitude (i.e., decreased pressure) and rises with air temperature, and so a Machmeter has to vary its reading according to air pressure and incorporate a thermometer to measure these added parameters not needed in an ordinary airspeed indicator. Most such instruments also indicate particular Mach numbers, which may be specially advantageous or dangerous, and particularly the limit that should not be exceeded in any particular aircraft configuration. A subsonic airliner, for example, may be cruised at Mach 0.785, or some similar figure, to obtain maximum fuel economy.

The method used to manufacture cars in quantity by producing numbers of identical components by accurate machine processes, and assembling them on a production line. Each worker on the line fits the part for which he is responsible and the vehicle travels onward to the next section. First used by Colt and later at Enfield for the production of weapons, the system was first adopted in the car industry by Henry Ford, whose Model T was the first car to sell in sufficient numbers to warrant mass production.

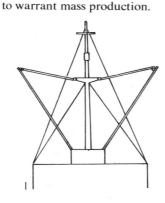
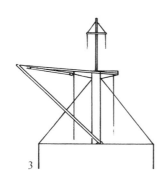
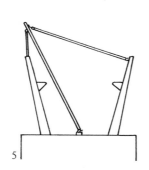

1 Conventional mast
2 Goalpost mast
3 Heavy lift mast (*c.* 1950)

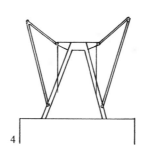
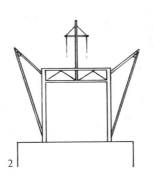
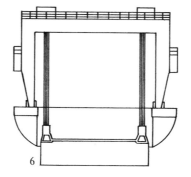

4 Bipod mast
5 Stulcken heavy derrick
6 *Lash* elevator

Mast:
   fore, 25 26 27 29 30
   main, 26 27 29 30 33 34
   mizzen, 29 30
   spritsail topmast, 33
   topmast, 26 29 30 33

Masts
The purpose of masts in sailing ships is obvious, but it is not so obvious why such lofty masts were fitted long after the need for auxiliary sail had vanished. For many years the masts were used to carry steaming lights, the crow's nest, and the crosstrees to which were secured the rigging for derricks. They were also used, of course, for displaying flags and, after the invention of wireless, for supporting the lengthy aerials that early sets required. Some ships were equipped with "goalpost" masts, but by the late 1930s a few ships had appeared with a single mast and additional derrick posts (also called king posts). Rapid development occurred after 1945 and many cargo liners were fitted with extremely strong masts to handle heavy derricks. Bipod masts are also now used as these require no supporting rigging, and the Stulcken derrick permits the use of one heavy derrick at two hatches. Now that the majority of big ships have all the superstructure at the after end of the ship the mast has at last become a purely functional piece of equipment. It is often faired into the foreside of the funnel and carries navigation lights, radar scanners and radio direction-finding aerials, plus a yard for the display of flags.

Materials, shipbuilding
   (see also p. 220) The main materials used for shipbuilding have been wood, iron, and steel.
   Wood planking was, and still is, used in three basic ways: clinker, carvel, and diagonal, in which two layers of planking are laid at right angles to each other.
   During the height of the clipper ship era composite hulls were built, iron keel and frames clad with carvel planking. The hulls of the first iron steamships were exactly the same as those of sailing ships, and little development occurred until the early sixties when Messrs. Harland and Wolff built a series of ships for the Bibby and White Star Lines that were designed specifically to get the best performance out of the engines. The hulls were about ten times as long as they were wide.
   Steel allowed stronger and lighter hulls to be built and by the turn of the century the combination of theoretical knowledge and improved quality of materials led to the evolution of the types of hulls that permitted ships such as the *Mauretania* to steam at high speed in seas that would have shaken earlier ships to pieces.
   The welding of parts of the hull had been carried out to a limited extent prior to 1939. This process was accelerated by the war, and by the sixties few ships were riveted. Light alloys and aluminum were also used to a limited extent to lighten the weight of the superstructure. Glass reinforced plastic (GRP) is a strong and light material that is being used extensively in the construction of yachts. Already a small minesweeper has been built of glass reinforced plastic and it is possible that it will be used in still larger ships as experience is gained, and if it lives up to expectations.

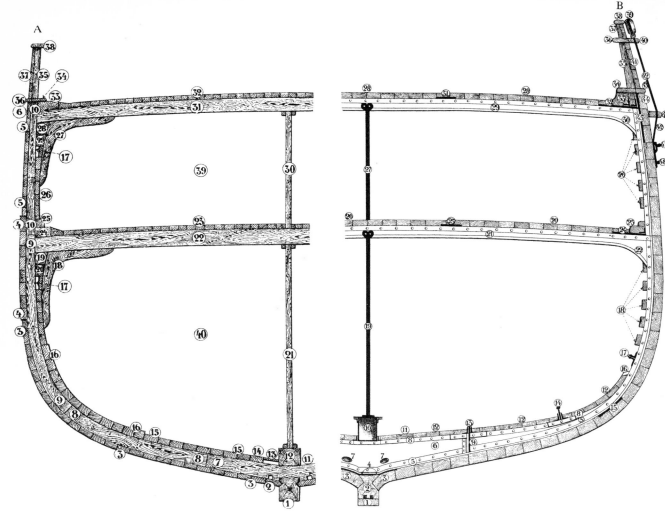

A *Midship section of wooden ship, second half of the nineteenth century*

1 Keel
2 Garboard strake
3 Bottom planking
4 Bends or wales
5 Topside planking
6 Sheer strake
7 Floor
8 2nd futtock
9 4th futtock
10 Long toptimber
11 Limbers, water course
12 Keelson
13 Limber board
14 Limber strake
15 Floor ceiling
16 Thick strakes of ceiling
17 Air courses
18 Lower deck hanging knee
19 Lower deck shelf
20 Lower deck clamp
21 Hold stanchion
22 Lower deck beam
23 Lower deck, lower deck planking
24 Lower deck waterway
25 Lower deck spirketing
26 Tween deck ceiling
27 Upper deck hanging knee
28 Upper deck shelf
29 Upper deck clamp
30 Tween deck stanchion
31 Upper deck beam
32 Upper deck, upper deck planking
33 Upper deck waterway
34 Covering board
35 Bulwark stanchions
36 Planksheer
37 Bulwark planking
38 Main rail
39 Tween decks
40 Hold

B *Composite ship (wooden vessel with iron frames), second half of the nineteenth century*

1 False keel or shoe
2 Keel
3 Garboard strake
4 Keel plate
5 Frame
6 Floor
7 Limbers
8 Reverse frame
9 Side intercostal keelson
10 Center line keelson
11 Limber boards
12 Ceiling
13 Side keelson
14 Bilge keelson
15 Bilge plate
16 Covering board
17 Bilge stringer
18 Cargo battens (in hold)
19 Hold pillar; hold stanchion
20 Lower deck
21 Lower deck beam
22 Bracket end (of lower deck beam)
23 Lower deck tie plate
24 Lower deck stringer
25 Lower deck waterway
26 Cargo battens (between decks)
27 Upper deck pillar, upper deck stanchion
28 Upper deck
29 Upper deck beam
30 Bracket end (of upper deck beam)
31 Upper deck tie plate
32 Upper deck stringer plate
33 Upper deck waterway
34 Covering board
35 Bulwark stanchion
36 Main rail
37 Topgallant bulwark stanchion
38 Topgallant rail
39 Deadeye
40 Upper channel
41 Bulwark planking
42 Chainplate
43 Planksheer
44 Sheer strake
45 Iron sheer strake
46 Lower channel
47 Chain bolt
48 Preventer bolt

More than 10,000 MiG-15 fighters were built, using a developed version of the Rolls-Royce Nene engine; they transformed the quality of Soviet first-line defence.

Monocoque
A structure in which all the loads are taken by the outer skin and not by any internal members; an example in nature is the shell of an egg. In addition to being strong structurally, the smooth streamlined shape of a monocoque fuselage provides an aerodynamic bonus in the form of reduced drag. Today most aircraft structures embody some internal stiffening members, even though most of the loads are carried by the skin. Initially the term "semi-monocoque" was used to describe such structures, but today the more generally accepted term used is "stressed-skin."

Monoplane:

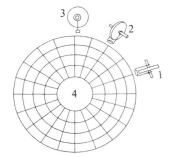

The gyrocompass principle
1, 2 & 3 A pendulous gyro always adjusts
    its axis towards the North Pole
3 A gyro axis pointing north
4 The North Pole

The magnetic compass works on the
principle that an unrestricted magnet
will always come to rest in a north-
south line, i.e., pointing toward the
magnetic pole. Magnetic compasses
are still fitted to all merchant ships

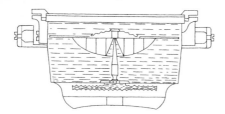

*Liquid compass, sectional drawing. In
most ship's compasses the compass card
is immersed in a liquid which moderates
its motion.*

because they are nonmechanical and
are therefore rarely subject to break-
down. They are compensated for:
(a) Deviation. This is the effect on the
    magnet by the steel of the ship. The
    effect is not constant and a ship has
    to be "swung." Bearings are taken
    on a known magnetic bearing and
    the differences between the known
    bearing and the ship's compass bea-
    ring are noted. In setting a magnetic
    course allowance is made according
    to the "deviation card."
(b) Variation. A correction that must
    be applied to the magnetic course
    in order to steer a true course since
    the magnetic pole and the true pole
    do not coincide. The variation
    changes constantly and all charts
    provide the necessary information
    for the correction to be applied.

The Gyrocompass
The theory of the gyrocompass is
complex, but depends upon the fact
that the axle of a wheel, which is allowed to spin freely in a horizontal plane,
but which has other external forces and
restrictions applied to it, will always
settle in a true north-south direction.
The gyrocompass is unaffected by mag-
netism and will give true bearings
within a degree or two each way. These
errors can easily be compensated for in
laying off a course.

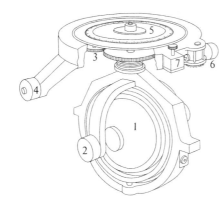

*Inside view of a gyrocompass. A gyro-
compass is not influenced by deviation,
but shows true north.*
1 Rotor case
2 Compensating weights
3 Motor
4 Bearings
5 Compass card
6 Repeater transmitter
7 Correcter for speed and latitude

Radio Direction Finders
Receiving apparatus records the bearing of a radio wave transmitted from
a shore station. This enables a ship to
fix its line of bearing on that shore
station, but unless two stations a suitable distance apart can be picked up
and a cross bearing plotted an exact
position cannot be obtained.

Decca System
A navigational system based upon the
reception at the same time of radio
waves transmitted by a master station
and two slave stations, which together
form three pairs of transmitters. The
three bearings are recorded on different colored dials, which, when inter-
polated onto special charts with a three-
colored grid superimposed, give an
amazingly accurate position. LORAN
is a similar system, but is as yet mainly
used for aircraft navigation.

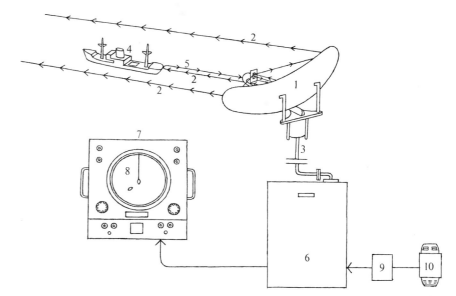

*Principles of radar. A scanner (1) sends
out high-frequency radio pulses in a beam
(2), which is very narrow in the horizontal
plane. The beam sweeps around the horizon through the rotation of the scanner.
The radio pulses are fed to the scanner
through a wave guide (3). The target (4),
which is hit by the beam, reflects part of
it (5) back to the scanner, and through the
wave guide the echo signal goes to the
T.R. unit (6). Here, the signal is transformed so that the P.P.I. (7), which is the
Plan Position Indicator, can give a picture*

Radar
Name derived from Radio Direction
and Range. British research from 1934
showed that radio waves of suitable
form and frequency are reflected by
metal objects, such as aircraft, and that
the reflected signal can be detected by
a suitable receiver near the transmitter
or elsewhere. Not only can the reflec-
ting "target" thus be detected, but the
time taken by the waves to reach it and
return enables the target distance to be
obtained. The first radars were large
ground stations, but by 1941 radars
had been made small enough to fit

inside aircraft. Modern radars fulfill
many functions connected with navigation, traffic control, collision avoid-
ance, missile and spacecraft guidance,
and such other diverse duties as providing detailed pictures of friendly or
enemy territory, indicating storm-cloud
or atmospheric turbulence ahead of
aircraft and, using the Doppler principle, measuring aircraft speed over
the ground.

The diagram explains in simple
terms the working of radar, which not
only indicates the position of ships for
great distances around, but will also
reproduce the shape of a coastline.
The exact position of the ship can
therefore be determined. For the purposes of avoiding collisions, skill is
needed in determining the speed and
actions of ships in the vicinity and the
master of each ship must still proceed
in accordance with the "rule of the

*signal. On the P.P.I. tube's screen (8) a
line appears at the center to the edge of
the tube and in the same direction as that
in which the scanner is pointing. The light
intensity on the line is strengthened by
the target's echo signal, and in this way
marks the target on the screen. The bearing is given by the direction of the line
from the center of the screen, and the
target's range by the distance of the echo
from the center of the screen.*
 9 Voltage regulator or stabilizer
10 Motor generator

road," particularly in fog. In early sets
the receiving ship was shown as a fixed
position in the middle of the radar
screen with other ships moving around
that point. The latest sets also record
the course and speed of the receiving
ship and this is called "true motion
radar."

Chronometers
Until the invention of a really reliable
clock it was impossible for sailors to
calculate longitude with any accuracy.
Longitude is calculated by comparing
the time of the zenith of the sun with

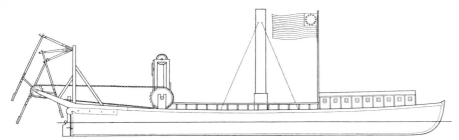

John Fitch's paddle steamboat Experiment *of 1788. She was propelled by three "duck leg" paddles at the stern operated by cranks and rods from a horizontal shaft fitted across the square stern of the hull. The engine was geared to a shaft*

having sprocket wheels and a chain or rope drive transmitted power to the stern shaft that operated the paddles. Steam was provided by a so-called pipe or tubular boiler in which the hot gases passed through tubes surrounded by water.

Paddles, 12 18 36 37 38 43 60
The idea of using paddle wheels crops up throughout history. Until the nineteenth century manpower, horse, or ox power was the motive power suggested and from time to time these ideas were put to the test, usually with little success. The practical use of steam intensified the need to produce an efficient propulsive agent and experiments were carried out with both paddles and paddle wheels. Quite complicated, but mechanically ineffi-

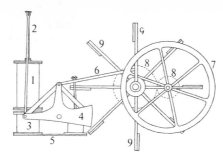

Geared steam engine of the Clermont *by Fulton, 1807.*
1 Cylinder
2 Piston rod
3 Condenser
4 Balance
5 Bearing
6 Connecting rod
7 Flywheel
8 Gear
9 Paddle wheel

cient systems were devised to transmit the power from the engine to the paddles, but it is often forgotten that until the invention of the crankshaft (which see) all efforts to harness steam power were bound to be limited in their effect.

For many years the fixed-float paddle wheel was used. Efficiency was impaired by the resistance set up by the angle at which the floats entered and left the water. The feathering float was eventually perfected and this continued

in use until the end of the paddle-propelled ship.

Paddle steamers (diesel engines were rarely used) continued to be used on rivers and in estuaries until well after 1939. They are, however, now rare specimens and several societies have been set up to preserve them. One of the last paddle steamers to be employed on the River Clyde is now moored on the River Thames in the center of London, and an old paddle tug is set up in working order at the National Maritime Museum in the same city. Paddle steamers are also preserved in America, where the Mississippi riverboats, so well described by Mark Twain, have become part and parcel of the history of that country.

Oil-based paints were applied to the body work of cars originally by hand brushing. To speed up the process of application during the 1920s, they were sprayed onto the coach work. This did not reduce the time necessary for drying and it was not until the invention of cellulose paint in the mid-1920s that cars could be sprayed and ready for the road in a matter of hours.

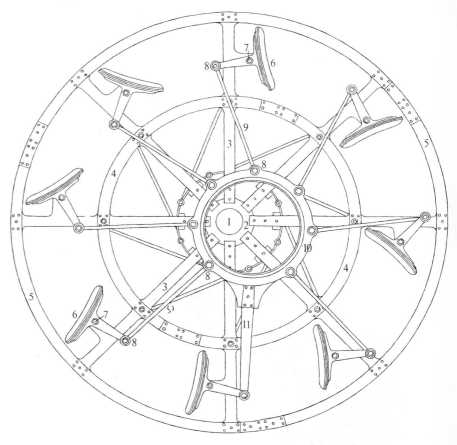

Paddle wheel
1 Paddle shaft
2 Hub
3 Spoke
4 Inner rim
5 Outer rim
6 Paddle
7 Wrist pin
8 Limbs
9 Drag link
10 Eccentric strap
11 King rod

(see also Four stroke cycle, Otto's)
Reciprocating engine in which a plug-like unit (the piston) oscillates to and fro in each cylinder to convert the high pressure of the burning fuel/air mixture into useful mechanical work, and also to draw in the fresh charge, compress it and expel it after combustion has been completed. The piston is usually a forging machined in a heat-resistant aluminum alloy, and has the form of an inverted cup, the head (known as the crown) being solid and the bottom terminating in an open "skirt" section. The diameter of the piston is less than the bore of the cylinder, but a gas-tight fit is achieved by a series of rings of springy, high tensile steel that fit corresponding grooves around the piston. Some of these rings serve to ensure that no gas leaks down from the combustion space, while the lowest is usually an oil scraper ring to prevent lubricating oil from leaking up past the piston and being wasted by being burned in the combustion chamber. Across the center of the piston are arranged strong bearings for the wrist pin (gudgeon

pin), which pivots the piston to the connecting rod and then to the crankshaft. Piston engines are of two basic types, air-cooled or liquid-cooled.

The pitot head has been installed on aircraft ever since instruments for giving flight information have been carried. The pitot head, or its later development, the pressure head, comprises two tubes facing forward into the airflow. One tube is closed and maintains a standard atmospheric pressure; the other is open-ended and records the pressure of the airflow on the aircraft. The tubes feed to opposite sides of a diaphragm, which moves according to the pressure differential, the diaphragm being linked to the pointers of the airspeed indicator.

Iron plates about two feet long, pegged down on cube or near cube blocks of stone, were easy to manufacture in the eighteenth century. Flangeless wheels ran upon the plates and the plates themselves had flanges to hold the wheels on the track. This track worked well enough provided the wagons were not too heavy.

John Boyd Dunlop invented the pneumatic tire for bicycles. The first tires were very unreliable and it was not until the speeds increased that the pneumatic tire was fully developed. Recent developments have been in tubeless covers and radial-ply tires using steel wire instead of fabrics in the carcass. The future could well bring a tire that will continue to give service for up to a hundred miles after it has been punctured. This could do away with the need for a spare wheel.

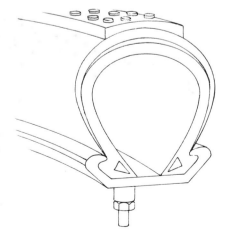

Pneumatic tire

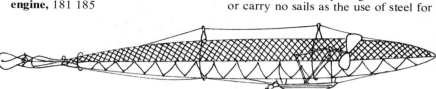

Pierre Jullien's clockwork-driven, gas-filled airship model of 1850, Le Précurseur.

Pressurization is used in most modern aircraft to enable them to operate at great heights. The cabin, or cockpit, is enclosed in a metal cell that is automatically sealed when all doors and hatches are closed. As the aircraft climbs, the pressure in the cell is maintained at that of a lower altitude than the one at which the aircraft is flying, by introducing more air into the cell by mechanical means. Thus, when flying at extremely high altitudes the cabin is maintained within a comfortable pressure band without the need to resort to oxygen or other assisted means of breathing.

was developed into a single wheel because of mechanical complications. The rudimentary form of the propeller as we know it today soon followed and in 1843 the *Great Britain* became the first screw-driven deep-sea ship. The propeller was, nevertheless, slow in being adopted and it was not until the 1860s that the Cunard Line abandoned the paddle in favor of the screw. By the 1880s steamships began to reduce or carry no sails as the use of steel for the construction of propeller shafts overcame the previously ever-present risk of a fractured shaft and loss of power. The development of twin screws also meant that ships rarely broke down completely at sea from this cause.

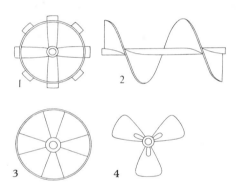

Propeller development
1 1800
2 1812
3 1840
4 1860

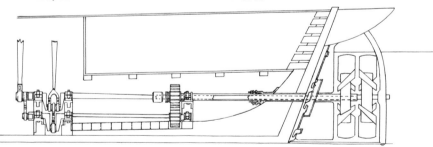

John Ericsson's screw propeller as originally mounted in the Robert F. Stockton *in 1838.*

The propeller is often called a "screw," and the propeller is in fact the helix of a screw. In 1836 Francis Pettit Smith constructed a vessel equipped with a propeller that was two complete turns of an Archimedean screw. During trials half of the screw fell off and the speed of the little vessel immediately increased. In the same year, Captain John Ericsson produced two counterrotating hoops, or wheels, each bearing eight fans, or blades. Later this invention

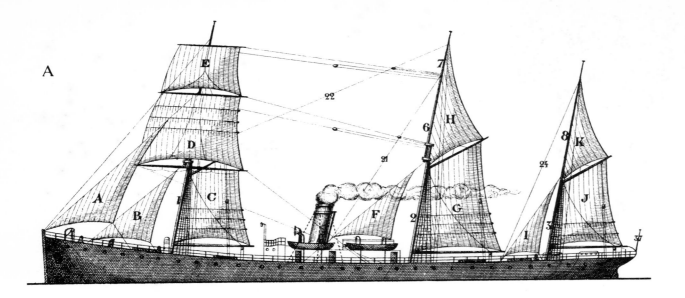

A

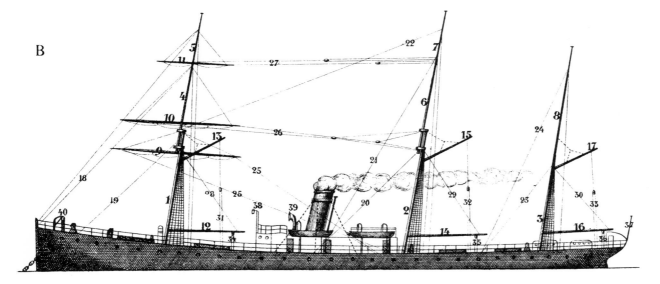

B

A device for cooling the water used to circulate around the engine in order to control the operating temperature. Water is pumped to the engine, removes the excess heat, and travels to the top

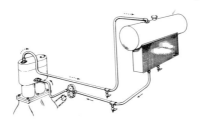

An early example of the "honeycomb" type of radiator forming part of the cooling system of the Canstatt-Daimler belt driven cars of c. *1897.*

of the radiator, which is made up of a number of tubes to cool the water as it travels around the system. A fan is driven by the engine to induce a draft of cool air across the radiator.

Rails, at first of rolled iron and then of steel, were originally carried on the sleepers in cast-iron chairs. Now, in contrast to the former bullhead rail, track is laid with flat-bottomed rails resting on a baseplate bolted to the sleeper. Modern practice inserts rubber pads between the rail and the baseplate and the latter and the sleeper for quiet running and the rail is secured to the baseplate by some type of steel spring clip.

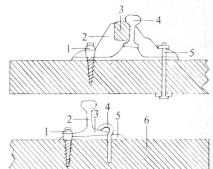

Rails, angle-iron, 100
Railway Act, 71
Railway companies, early, 66
Railway Foundry, E. B. Wilson & Co., 77
Rainhill trials, 68 69 100
Ram, 25
Ramjet, 177
An air-breathing propulsion system in which air is compressed in a ram intake, further compressed and slowed to a velocity suitable for combustion by passing along a suitably profiled diffuser duct, heated by the combustion of fuel in a combustion chamber and finally expelled as a supersonic jet of hot gas through a propulsive nozzle. The ramjet is best suited to highly supersonic propulsion: at Mach numbers greater than about 3 to 3.5, it is markedly superior to the turbojet, but it always suffers from the disadvantage that it cannot start from rest but must have air "rammed" into the intake.

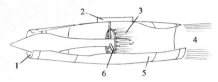

Ramjet
1 Intake
2 Diffuser
3 Flame
4 Supersonic jet
5 Nozzle
6 Fuel manifold

Ramp, 46
Rarefied air, 156
Reactor, pressurized water, 48
Rear-engine aircraft, 177 179 185
Rear-wheel drive, 143
Reciprocating engine, see Steam engine; Piston engine
Reconnaissance biplane, Rumpler C.1, 164
Rectifier, mercury arc, 92
Rectifier, solid state electronic, 92
Rederi A/S Panis, 34
Reduction gear, 13
Reef points, 27
Refreshment car, see Restaurant car
Registration of aircraft
In all countries where civil flying is undertaken, there exists a national authority responsible for registering, or authorizing, each specific airplane type that flies in that country. Many of these authorities have reciprocal agreements whereby the conditions required to be satisfied by one authority are accepted by its counterpart in another country. The principal national authorities include the SGAC in France, the LBA in Federal Germany, the RAI in Italy, the JCAB in Japan, the CAA in the United Kingdom, and the FAA in the United States.
Reheat, see Afterburner
Rheims air meeting, 163
Renard, 161
Renault, Louis, 113
Renault, 1898, *113*
Renault 1906, *116*

Renault 5, *134*
Renault 12/16 Doctor's Coupé, *116*
RENFE 3100 Class locomotive, *93*
Restaurant cars, 85 86
Restaurant cars travel under many names: dining car, refreshment car, buffet car, Gril-Express, Gril-Bar and so on. The one feature common to all is some sort of a kitchen to prepare food. Sometimes a whole coach is devoted to a kitchen to supply meals to the other coaches in the train. As train journeys become shorter in time because of speed, buffet cars become popular to serve simple meals and snacks. Buffets can be crowded into a compartment or small section of a coach so that little more than boiling water to make coffee can be carried out – there are all sorts of varieties.
Reverse pitch
A setting some 30° beyond the normal fine pitch stop of an aircraft propeller, by the use of which its net thrust can be changed from forward to rearward.
Reverse thrust
Mechanism fitted to a turbojet or turbofan engine to deflect the exhaust gases either vertically or sideways and thus impart reverse (braking) thrust to shorten the landing run. It is in use in many large jet aircraft and is particularly useful in wet conditions as it does not incur skidding or aquaplaning.
Rex, 46
Richard Hornsby & Co., 92 97
Rigging, 21 22 25 26 27 30 31 32 33 35
Rigging screws, see Shrouds
Right hand drive cars, 116
Rigolly, 100 mph record, 114
Riley 2½ liter, 1946, *130*
Riley 9, 1927, *118*
Riverboats, 25 (see also Paddles)
Riveted ships, 25 (see also Materials, shipbuilding)
Road coaches (on rails), 66
Road tolls, 15
Roads:
concrete, 118
early, 15
Macadam, 15 118
Roman, 15 66
Robert, Marie-Noël, 156
Robert Stephenson & Co., 66 70 81 100
Rocket, locomotive, 66 *101*
Rocket:
engine, four-chamber, 174
engine, liquid-propellant, 179
engine, Walther, 174
-powered aircraft, 172 174 176
Rockets, 156 188 190 192
Roe, Sir Alliott Verdon, 164 165 (see also Avro)
Roger, Emile, 118
Rogers Locomotive Works, 104
Roller bearings, 35
Roll-on roll-off, 14 46 48 55 56
Rolls-Royce, 116 120 124 185
Rolls-Royce:
Avon engine, 176
Continental engine, 181
Corniche, *132*
Eagle engine, 168 169
"Marine Proteus" gas turbine, 64
Nene engine, 174 178

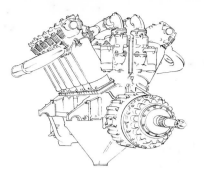

1918 Rolls-Royce Eagle 360 hp.

Pegasus vectored-thrust engine, 188 189
Phantom III, 1939, *127*
RB. 162 lift jet engine, 189
RB. 211-22 B turbofan engine, 200
"Silver Ghost," 1908, *117*
SNECMA engine, 182 191
Thrust Measuring Rig ("Flying Bedstead"), *178* 187 188
turbojet engine, 186
turboprop engine, 183

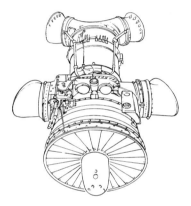

1968 Rolls-Royce Bristol Pegasus 20,000 1b thrust.

Roman Empire, 15 23 25 66
Roman merchant ship, 20
Rope, 19 33 35
Rope fittings, 33
Rope ladder, 25
Rope trusses, 25 35
Rošňava Cathedral, 66
Rotary engine, see Engine, rotary; Engine, turbine
Rotor, 143 172 188
Rotor, coaxial, 172

Rotor head employing flexible laminate mountings on a Hughes LOH.

Rotor head
General name given to the complex hub mechanism of the rotor of a helicopter or Autogiro.
Rotterdam, S.S., 54
Rotterdam Lloyd, 45
Round ship, 18 21 25

Royal Aircraft Establishment, 179
Royal Air Force, 172
Royal George, locomotive, 72 81
Royal Hungarian State Railways, see Hungarian State Railways, Royal
Royal Navy, 179
Royal William, P.S., 36
Royal yard, 33
Rozier, François Pilatre de, 156 161
Rudder, 21 (see also Steering)
Rudder:
bar, see Trim tab
rear (Wright brothers'), 194
surfaces, movable, 163

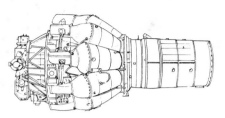

1945 Rolls-Royce Nene 5,000 1b thrust.

Rumpier C.I., *164*
Running boards, 129
Running gear, 25 33 35
Running rigging, 35
Russia, P.S., 43
Russian:
freight locomotive, *88*
Imperial car, *79*
Knight biplane, *164*
skimmer, *64*
Ruts, artificial, 66
Ryan NYP (New York-Paris) monoplane, *165* 169
SA 330 Puma, *189*
Sachsen, 165
Safety cars, 142 152
Safety glass, 129
Sails, see p. 226–227
Saloon coaches, *79* 85
Salvage tug, 54
Sans Pareil, locomotive, 68
Santa Maria, 20
Santos-Dumont, Alberto, 161 163 166 (see also FAI)
Santos-Dumont airship, *163*
Santos-Dumont 14-bis, *163* 166 (see also FAI)
"Saracen of Constantinople," 154
Satellites, 190
Savannah, P.S., 36 *38*
Savannah, nuclear-powered ship, 50
Savoia-Marchetti flying boats, 169
Saw, 25
Scarf joints, 25
Scavenging, 12
Schneider Trophy, 16 164
Schooner, 31 32 34 59 60
Science Museum, London, 102
Scotch boiler, see Boilers
Scottish Aviation/Handley Page Jetstream, *187*
Screws, see Propellers
Screw, Leonardo da Vinci's helical, *155*
Screw staircase, 55
Seabee ship, 52
Sea King antisubmarine helicopter, 189

Sails

The square sail has been in use throughout recorded history and has changed little in shape or design. Problems were encountered in the early days as sufficiently strong materials were not always available. It is known, for instance, that early Nordic sails were made of homespun wool and lacked the durability of cotton or canvas. The cloth would stretch under the force of the wind and the large sail would sag more and more until it burst. To strengthen the sail and hold it more

evenly, a supporting net was fastened to the forward side.

    The earliest sailing ships could only sail with the wind astern or on the quarter, but as hull design improved and more sails were carried it became possible to sail with the wind at an angle of 90 degrees, or slightly less, to the line of advance. The jib was the greatest advance made in thousands of years as it enabled ships to sail still closer to the wind. Eventually, the better designed ships could, by beating, reaching, or running, follow a mean course through about 270 degrees of a circle.

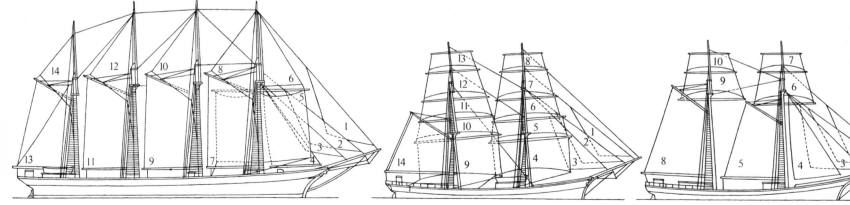

A   *Four-masted fore-and-aft schooner*
1   Flying jib
2   Outer jib
3   Inner jib
4   Fore staysail
5   Square foresail
6   Raffee
7   Foresail
8   Fore gaff topsail
9   Mainsail
10   Main gaff topsail

11   Mizzen
12   Mizzen gaff topsail
13   Jigger or spanker
14   Jigger gaff topsail

B   *Brig*
1   Flying jib
2   Jib
3   Fore topmast staysail
4   Foresail
5   Fore lower topsail

6   Fore upper topsail
7   Fore topgallant sail
8   Fore royal
9   Mainsail
10   Main lower topsail
11   Main upper topsail
12   Main topgallant sail
13   Main royal
14   Trysail

C   *Two-topsail schooner*

1   Flying jib
2   Outer jib
3   Inner jib
4   Fore staysail
5   Foresail
6   Fore topsail
7   Fore topgallant sail
8   Mainsail
9   Main topsail
10   Main topgallant sail

226

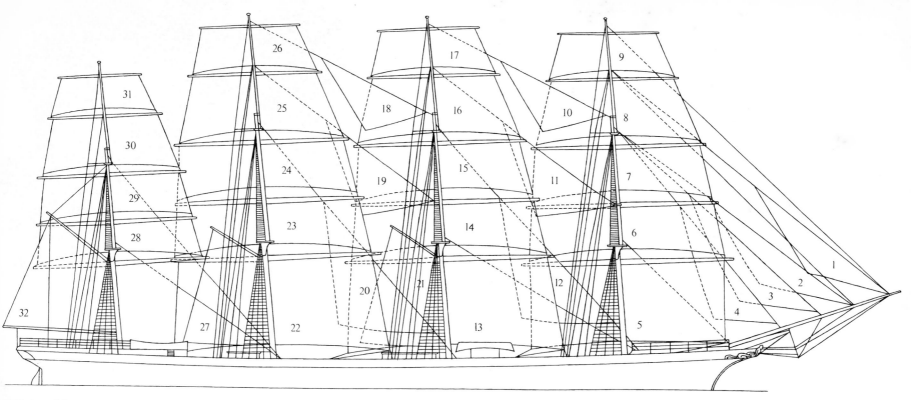

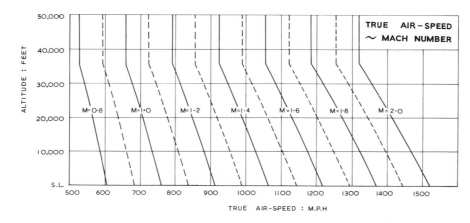

Live sparks shot into the air through
locomotive chimneys and falling on
dry grass, trees, or crops have started

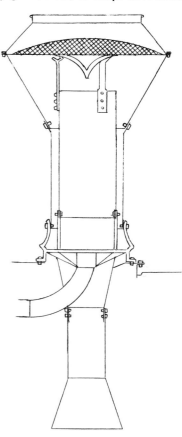

*Section of the American "diamondstack."
This arrangement was supposed to prevent cinders flying up from the wood-
burning engines.*

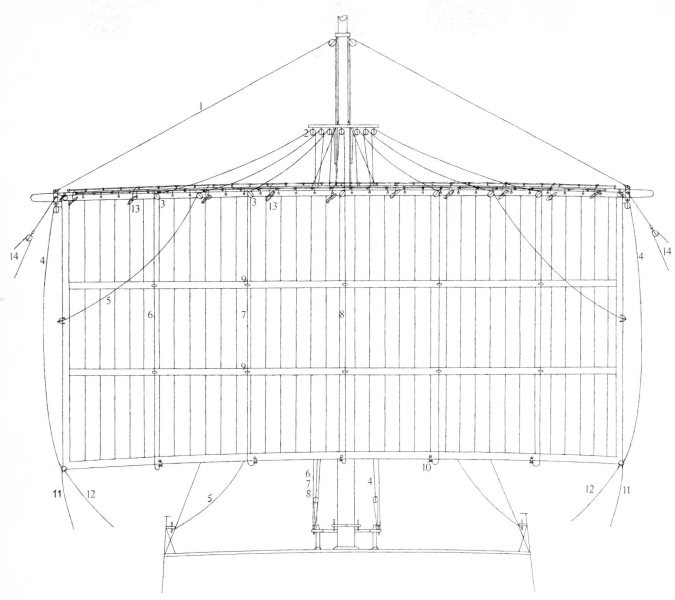

many fires and it is a special danger when wood is used as fuel. A multitude of grills and baffles have been devised to prevent sparks leaving the locomotives, many of the systems being mounted inside the chimney to give it a characteristically bulbous appearance.

Stabilizers

The fin stabilizer is a recent invention and is extremely effective in reducing rolling. The fins act as hydroplanes and can be turned through an arc of 50 degrees. They work hydraulically on impulse from a gyroscope. When not in use they are retracted into the ship's hull.

Antirolling tanks are now being increasingly used in container ships and vehicle ferries.

Stabilizer

Steam engine: (see also Engine, steam)
  compound two-cylinder, 36 43
  reciprocating, *10* 18 42 43 45 46 144
  triple expansion, *11* 12 41 43
  twin-screw, *11*
Steam-powered airships, 16 *159* 161
Steel, 10 18 38 43
Steerage accommodation, 46 62
Steering, 21 25
Early ships were steered by heavy oars. When the rudder was first hung from the stern a tiller was used to operate it. Later on the whipstaff was developed. This was in fact a lever attached to an elongated tiller. Steering wheels (the helm) came into use in the eighteenth century. With the coming of steam the rudder was operated by a series of chains and rods powered by a simple steam engine in or near the wheelhouse. Hydraulic steering gear was developed in the twentieth century, but many small ships such as coasters and trawlers continued to use the steam steering engine until relatively recently.

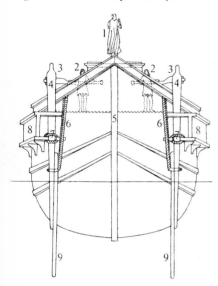

Rudder arrangement in a Roman merchant ship about A. D. 200
1 Stern ornament
2 Helmsmen
3 Tillers
4 Rudder stock
5 Sternpost
6 Carrying ropes
7 Lashing
8 Balcony
9 Rudder blade

Steering:
  hydraulic, 130
  rudder, 21
Stem, 27 30
Stephenson, George, 66 *101*
Stephenson, Robert, 66 70 72 81 *101*
Stephenson's Locomotion, 69
Stephenson's Patentee locomotives, 70 *71* 81
Stephenson's Planet, *70* 81
Stephenson's Rocket, locomotive, *101*
Stepped mast, 26 29
Stern, 25 29 30 31 33 46 60
Stern:
  castle, 20
  counter, 32
  post, 21 60

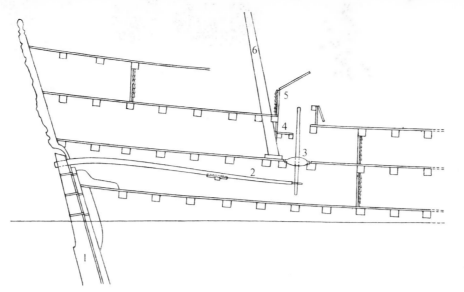

Steering arrangement in a big ship of the seventeenth century, when the rudder was controlled by a vertical lever called the whipstaff.
1 Rudder
2 Tiller
3 Whipstaff
4 Platform for the quartermaster
5 Hood for the quartermaster
6 Mizzenmast

  rudder, 21 25 (see also Steering)
  square, 25
  windows, 25 27
Stevens, Colonel John, 11 66 68
Stevens's locomotive, 68
Stevens's twin-screw steam engine, *11*
Stirling, Patrick, 77
Stockholmshäxan, *60*
Stockton & Darlington Railway, 66 69 72 81 100
STOL, 181
Abbreviation, formed from the initials of Short Take-Off and Landing, for aircraft in a class specially designed to take off and land in a very short space.

The Breguet Br 941 is a practical STOL transport, resulting from Breguet's many years of developing the deflected-slip-stream technique. This involves blowing the slipstream from four propellers over the entire wing span and utilizing an extensive slotted-flap system on the wing trailing edge. An engine synchronization system ensures a constant airflow over the entire wing, with the result that low landing speeds and short take-offs and landing distances are achieved. The Br 941 is a four-engined high-wing mono-plane, with accommodation for 57 passengers, 40 troops, or 24 stretchers. The prototype flew in 1964 and has been followed by four pre-production Model 941S aircraft. The design is sponsored in the USA by McDonnell Douglas as the McDonnell Douglas 188.

Such aircraft are usually fitted with wings incorporating high-lift devices; with auxiliary lift-jets; with tilt-wings; or combinations of these devices.
Stone paving, 66
Stourbridge Lion, locomotive, 66 *71*
Stove (for heating coaches), 79 85
  (see also Heating, train)
Streamlined cars, *114 124* 126
Streamlined locomotives, 91
"Stressed-skin," see Monocoque
Stringfellow, John, 161

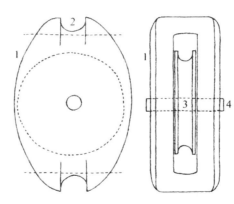

Block for hemp strop
1 Shell
2 Score for strop
3 Sheave
4 Pin

Strop, 35
Studding sail, *27*
Stulcken derrick, see Masts
Sud-Aviation Caravelle, *176* 179 185
Sunbeam, 149
Super 8 engine, 130
Supercharged engine, see Engine, motor
Superheater, 84
Supersonic flight, see Sound, speed of
SuperSonic Transport (SST), 179 191
Superstructure, 25 41
Surface vaporizer, 110 (see also Carburetor)
Suspension, 98 99 118 130
A term derived from the ancient method of hanging or suspending the body of a carriage from a chassis by leather straps. Steel springs of the same type used on carriages were adopted for the early cars and are still used today on the rear suspensions of the majority of cars. All cars now have independent front suspension using coil springing.
Suspension, independent, 119 124 128 131
Wheel springing on each of the wheels on an axle that allows either to operate independently of the other to improve road-holding and stability. Used on the front suspension of all modern cars and at the rear of many of the more sophisticated and expensive models.
Suspension, self-balancing, 130
Suspension, transverse, 146
Swearingen Metro, *183*
Swedish America Line, 45
Swedish hukare, *26*
Swedish kravel, *23*
Swedish krejare, *26*

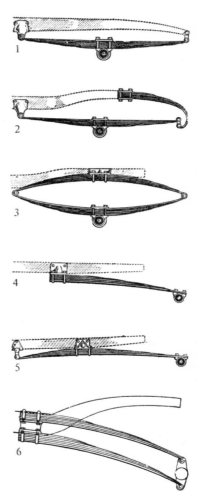

Suspension springs
1 Semi- or half-elliptic spring: the most usual type
2 Three-quarter-elliptic spring, popular for rear suspension
3 Full-elliptic spring. Not much used after 1900
4 Quarter-elliptic spring
5 Cantilever spring, originally used by Lanchester
6 Double-quarter-elliptic spring. This type was not often seen, but provided 'parallel motion' without the expense of radius links

Léon Bollée's tandem tricar; a noisy and temperamental machine, but capable of more than 30 mph (48 km/h).

Tricar, 112 118

A three-wheeled car much favored in the early days. The best known example was the 1895 Bollée tandem, which carried its passenger in the front. Some three-wheelers had one wheel in the front, but the Bollée seems to have been the most stable.

Trim tab, 171

A small hinged flap, usually set in the trailing-edge of an aircraft control surface. Its purpose is to offset the control surface in order to trim out any out-of-balance force on the control column or rudder bar and make the flying of the aircraft easier for the pilot.

A device for converting the energy of a fluid flow into mechanical power available from a rotating shaft. Various types of turbine have been built, but almost all gas turbines used to propel aircraft incorporate an axial-flow turbine consisting of one or more disks, around the edge of each of which are arranged a large number of curved blades, projecting radially, between which the flow of hot gas from the combustion chamber passes. In doing so the pressure and temperature of the gas fall violently and the energy thus lost appears as a tangential force on the blades, which results in a large torque being imparted to the disk. Disks and blades are both made of special high strength heat-resistant metals, and in the hottest engines the blades are cooled by an internal air-flow. The number of stages of disks and blades depends upon the work which the turbine must do. In a pure turbojet a single-stage turbine often suffices to drive the compressor, but to drive a compressor of high pressure ratio a two-stage turbine will be more efficient and possibly lighter. Three-stage turbines are often used in turbofan and turboprop engines (which see) in which much more energy is extracted from the gas flow.

Turbine, steam, see Engine, turbine
Turbinia, T.S., 10 43 (see also Engine, turbine)
Turboelectric engine, 46
Turbofan engine, 182 184 185 186 188 191 200 (see also Bypass ratio; Reverse thrust)

A gas-turbine engine used for propulsive purposes in which the air delivered by the compressor is divided into two streams, one of which passes to the combustion chamber and turbine while

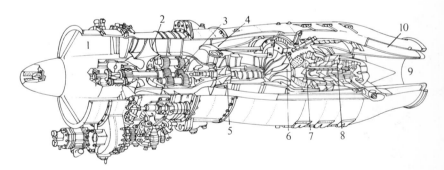

The French Turboméca Aubisque turbofan engine. An unusual feature of the Aubisque is that its single-stage fan is driven through a reduction gearbox. If it were driven directly by the shaft on which the small-diameter turbines and centrifugal compressors are mounted, it would reach supersonic speed at the tips of its blades and achieve poor efficiency. As it is, it enables a specific fuel consumption of the order of 0.6 to be achieved for the first time in the 1,000-lb thrust class.

1 Intake section
2 Single-stage low-pressure compressor
3 Step-down gearing
4 Flow divider
5 Axial compressor
6 Centrifugal compressor
7 Vaporizing combustion chamber of annular type
8 Two-stage turbine
9 Jet nozzle
10 Discharge nozzle from fan duct (bypass duct)

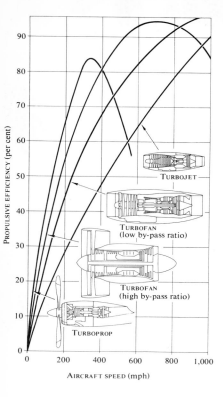

Aeroengine propulsive efficiency chart

the other is discharged directly to atmosphere through a propulsive nozzle. It has greater propulsive efficiency at subsonic speeds, but the turbojet becomes superior at supersonic speeds.

Turbojet engine, 172 173 174 175 176 178 186 187 191 (see also Reverse thrust)

The simplest type of gas-turbine engine. Air is drawn into it from the atmosphere, compressed and fed to a combustion chamber in which fuel is burned. From the combustion chamber a steady stream of very hot gas passes to the turbine, which extracts just enough energy to drive the compressor and such accessories as the fuel pump and electric generator. The gas, still with high temperature and high pressure, then escapes to atmosphere through a nozzle in which as much as possible of the flow's energy is converted to kinetic energy in a high-velocity jet.

Turboméca turboprop engine, 183 187

Turboprop engine, 175 176 181 184 185 187

A gas-turbine engine driving an air propeller. The propeller can be basically similar to those used with piston engines of comparable power, but a speed-reducing transmission is necessary. The turboprop handles a larger airflow than any other aircraft propulsion engine and thus, at low flight speeds, generates the largest thrust for a given fuel consumption. On the other hand, the thrust falls off rapidly with increasing forward speeds, and at about 450 mph (725 km/h) the propeller efficiency has begun to fall drastically as a result of the blade tips nearing or exceeding sonic velocity.

Turboshaft engine, 187 189

A gas-turbine engine used to provide a mechanical power output in the form of a rotating shaft. Such an engine can be regarded either as a turbojet with an extra stage or two on the turbine; or with an added free turbine driving a mechanically independent output shaft; or as a turboprop without its propeller and reduction transmission. In aircraft propulsion a turboshaft engine is used to drive mechanical transmission systems of helicopters and some classes of V/STOL machines.

Turn and slip indicator

A gyro instrument, introduced between the two world wars, which gives to the pilot indications of the rate of turn which the aircraft is making, and whether the aircraft is slipping inward or skidding outward. This information is presented either by a pointer connected to a pendulum or by a ball in a curved glass tube. By means of these two indications in the one instrument the pilot can ensure that he is making accurate turns at the desired rate.

Variable geometry

Term used, specifically in the aerodynamic field, to describe structures that can change their configuration during flight. Variable geometry is prominent in two particular fields, one being that of aircraft such as the General Dynamics F-111, whose wings are fully spread forward for slow-speed flying but can be fully swept back in flight for supersonic efficiency. The principle on which this system is based was developed by Dr. Barnes Wallis in the United Kingdom. The term is also applied to intake ducts of certain turbojet or turbofan engines that have variable geometry intakes to cater for the vastly differing airflow problems at the upper and lower ends of the speed range.

Vectored-thrust engine, see also Rolls-Royce Pegasus

Strictly speaking, any aero-engine having a thrust line which can be vectored in different directions falls into this category, and this definition would include all jet engines fitted with reversers. In practice the description is reserved for powerplants for V/STOL aircraft, and especially for turbojets and turbofans provided with deflectors so that their thrust vector may be rotated from rearward to downward, to provide lift to support the aircraft at times when forward speed is too low for wing lift to be adequate. Frequently the thrust vector may also be directed forward to brake the aircraft. Such power plants are also known as lift/cruise engines, since they serve the dual function of providing lift for the VTOL regime and forward propulsion in cruising flight. The first such engines were modified Rolls-Royce Derwent turbojets, but the first vectored-thrust unit designed as such was the Rolls-Royce (Bristol) Pegasus, in which the front fan and rear hot jet each discharge through left and right pairs of nozzles fitted with deflectors which turn the flow through approximately 90°. All four nozzles are mechanically linked

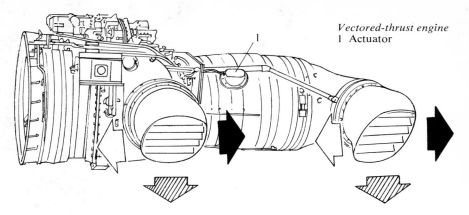

Vectored-thrust engine
1 Actuator

General Dynamics/Grumman F-111 A demonstrating its ability to sweep its wings from 16° to a maximum supersonic angle

of 72° while maintaining station with a KC-135 tanker.

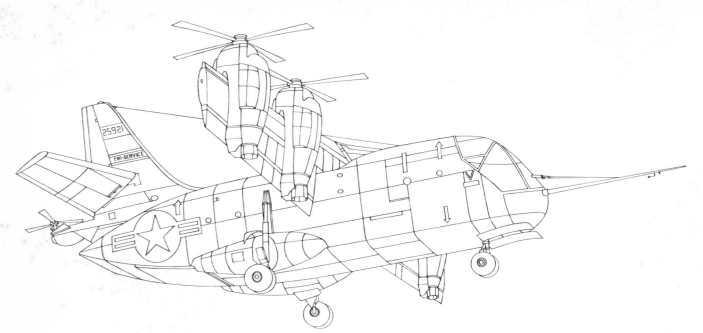

Weather minima

For the purpose of air travel the ICAO (which see) has laid down categories of weather minima for aircraft landings. These relate to the height at which a pilot must decide whether he can see enough of the runway to attempt a safe landing. In practice, commercial aircraft not equipped for automatic landing can operate only down to Category 2 weather minima. The five categories in current use are:
Category 1. Operation down to decision height of 200 ft. (60 m) with a visibility of more than 2,600 ft. (800 m).
Category 2. Decision heights between 200 and 100 ft. (60 and 30 m) with visibility between 2,600 and 1,200 ft. (800 and 400 m).
Category 3A. Operation to and along the surface of the runway, with external visibility during the final phase of the landing down to 700 ft. (200 m).

The LTV-Hiller-Ryan XC-142 is the biggest VTOL aircraft utilizing the tilt-wing principle. Weighing 44,500 1b, the XC-142 is designed to carry a payload of 8,000 1b over a combat radius of 200 miles. Power is provided by four General Electric T64 turboprop engines driving conventional propellers and a horizontally mounted tail rotor through a system of cross-shafting which enables flight to be maintained on any two engines in an emergency. The wing is able to rotate through an angle of 100°, giving the XC-142 ability to hover in a tail wind.

During VTOL flight, roll control is achieved by means of differential collective propeller pitch, yaw control by means of the ailerons working in the propeller slipstream, and pitch control by means of the variable-pitch tail rotor. During transition, a mechanical mixing linkage integrates the VTOL control system with the conventional ailerons and tail control surfaces in the correct proportions required at various wing tilt angles. In normal cruising flight, control is by the conventional control surfaces, with the tail rotor locked.

and actuated by a motor and drive shafts to point in the desired direction. Arrangements in which the whole engine is pivoted, or in which an engine is fixed but drives a tilting propeller, do not properly qualify for this description.

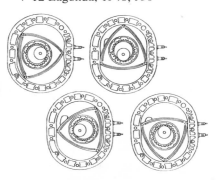

Wankel engine: principle

Abbreviation for Vertical Take-Off and Landing, used to cover classes of aircraft that, beginning with the helicopter and Autogiro, are now developing apace in many fields and many shapes.

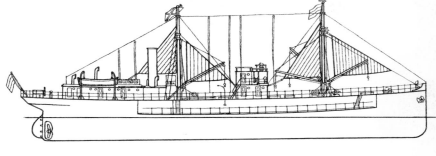

The first sea-going vessel to be propelled by a diesel engine was the Vulcanus, *a tanker constructed by the Nederlandsche Scheepsbouw Maatschappij, Amsterdam, in 1910.*

Category 3B. Operation to and along the surface of the runway and taxiways down to a visibility of 150 ft. (50 m), which is sufficient only for visual taxying.
Category 3C. Operation to and along the surface of the runway without

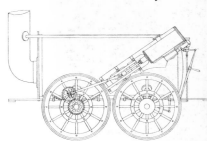

Watt's "sun-and-planet" drive as proposed for a Stephenson Rocket *locomotive, c. 1828. The construction was never made use of.*

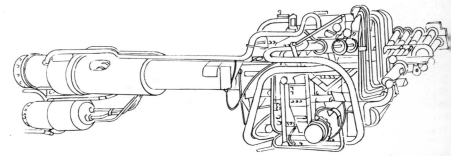

1943 Walther 109–509 3,300 1b thrust

Wheel arrangement: steam power. The wheel arrangement of steam motive power by the Whyte system.

OO	0-4-0	Four-wheel shunter
OOo	0-4-2	
OOO	0-6-0	Six coupled
OOOO	0-8-0	Eight coupled
OOOOO	0-10-0	Decapod (English)
oOO	2-4-0	
oOOo	2-4-2	Columbia
oOOO	2-6-0	Mogul
oOOOo	2-6-2	Prairie
oOOOoo	2-6-4	
oOOOO	2-8-0	Consolidation
oOOOOo	2-8-2	Mikado
oOOOOoo	2-8-4	Berkshire
oOOOOO	2-10-0	Decapod (American)
oOOOOOo	2-10-2	Santa Fé
oOOOOOoo	2-10-4	Texas
ooOO	4-4-0	American
ooOOo	4-4-2	Atlantic
ooOOoo	4-4-4	Double-ender
ooOOO	4-6-0	Ten-wheeler
ooOOOo	4-6-2	Pacific
ooOOOoo	4-6-4	Baltic (European) Hudson (American)
ooOOOO	4-8-0	Twelve-wheeler
ooOOOOo	4-8-2	Mountain. Mohawk (New York Central)
ooOOOOoo	4-8-4	Northern. Niagara (New York Central)
ooOOOOO	4-10-0	Mastodon

ooOOOOOo	4-10-2	Southern Pacific
ooOOOOOOo	4-12-2	Union Pacific

While many of the above types are seen in both tender and tank engine form, those below are almost entirely tank engine wheel formations. A tank engine is indicated by a "T" after the wheel formation thus: 4-4-2 T.

OOOoo	0-4-4
OOOo	0-6-2
OOOoo	0-6-4
OOOOo	0-8-2
OOOOoo	0-8-4
oOOOooo	2-6-6

Articulated types fall into two main groups: those in which both engines are placed under the boiler, as in the Mallet – these are nearly always tender engines – and those in which the boiler is slung between the two engine units as in the Garratt. In the first group it is customary to show the wheel arrangement as having four groups only thus: 2-6-6-2.

In the second group there may be six groups of wheels and the notation is shown thus: 4-8-2 + 2-8-4. These engines are always tank engines in that they do not have a separate tender, but the suffix "T" is never used in the case of Garratt type engines.

Mallet type:

oOOO oooo
2-6-6-2
oOOOOOooo
2-6-6-6
oOOOOOOOo
2-8-8-2
ooOOOOOOOooo
4-8-8-4

Garratt type:

ooOOO OOOoo
4-6-0 + 0-6-4
ooOOOo oOOOoo
4-6-2 + 2-6-4
oOOOOo oOOOOo
2-8-2 + 2-8-2
ooOOOOoo ooOOOOOoo
4-8-4 + 4-8-4

Wheel arrangement: diesel and electric wheel notation. As the original system of Whyte notation evolved for steam locomotives is not suitable to indicate the wheel arrangement of diesel and electric locomotives, a different form has been

INDIVIDUALLY DRIVEN AXLES	COUPLED WHEELS	CARRYING WHEELS	
			B
			Bo
			Bo–Bo
			Bo+Bo
			B–B
			C
			Co
			C–C
			Co–Co
			Co+Co
			AIA–AIA
			ICo–Col
			I-Co-Co-I
			2-Co-Co-2
			I-Do-I
			2-Do-2
			IA-Do-AI

devised in which letters are used for driving axles, and numbers for carrying axles. In this system, "A" stands for one driving axle, "B" for two, "C" for three, and "D" for four. When, however, the axles are in groups, each axle being individually driven, a suffix "o" is added after the letter (except for "A" which can of course only be individually driven). A hyphen is used to break up separate wheel groups, such as bogies, although a + sign replaces this when an articulated joint links the wheel groups together.

In the case of shunting locomotives having two or three driving axles only, the Whyte notation is often used, and these may be indicated as 0-4-0 or 0-6-0 locomotives instead of type "B" or type "C".

The table to the left sets out some of the wheel notations for diesel-electric and gas turbine locomotives at present in existence.

This C–C description applies to a locomotive whose axles are mechanically coupled together; should each axle have its own electric motor the wheel arrangement becomes Co-Co to show this. As so many diesel and electric locomotives have no carrying axles the o is omitted in their wheel arrangements, but where carrying axles exist these go in. Thus, British Rail has many diesel locomotives with two six-wheel bogies and a carrying axle at each end. These are 1–Co–Co–1, or as is often written 1Co–Co1.

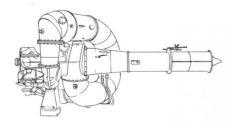

1937 Whittle 480 1b thrust

external visibility (not in use up to 1973, although a small number of modern airliners are cleared for operation down to these conditions).

Steam locomotives are normally classified by wheel arrangement, usually of three numerals. First a figure gives the number of leading carrying wheels, the next figure the number of driving wheels, and finally the number of trailing carrying wheels. Should there be no carrying wheels, either at the front or at the rear, an 0 is put in the wheel arrangement. Thus a single-driver locomotive with a pair of carrying wheels both front and rear is described as a 2–2–2. A ten-coupled freight locomotive with a single axle leading truck is a 2–10–0. The Pacific type with a four-wheel bogie leading, six driving wheels, and a trailing pair of wheels is a 4–6–2, and so on.

In several European countries it is the convention to count axles instead of wheels, that is the 4–6–2 becomes a 2–3–1. In Germany in particular a letter was substituted for the driving wheel figure, so that a 4–6–2 became a 2–C–1. This latter method has become generally accepted to describe electric and diesel locomotives. An electric locomotive mounted on two six-wheel bogies is known as a C–C.

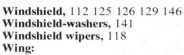

Windlasses

Windlasses performed the same function as capstans (which see). The earliest types were actually horizontal capstans. They were crude, provided no mechanical advantage, and were terribly slow in operation since the windlass bars could only function over less than half the arc of a circle.

Steam windlasses were designed to handle chain cable. Modern windlasses are electric-powered. The gypsies are shaped so as to grip each link of the cable in turn. The chain is stowed in the chain locker by way of the navel pipe. The inboard link is secured to

the deck of the cable locker by a stopper. Modern anchors are "let go." When this happens the gypsies are declutched and the cables run free; the weight of the anchor pulls the cable from the locker. Once the anchor is on the bottom the stern way on the ship lays the cable in a straight line on the seabed and the ship is "brought to" when the anchor has gripped the seabed and is holding firmly. At anchor in normal circumstances cable is laid on the bottom for two or three times the depth of water. Anchor bearings are checked regularly and in bad weather a regular anchor watch is kept.

Wing-warping

Early method of lateral control of an aircraft, first used in practical form by the Wright brothers. It remained standard for some time even after the aileron had become generally accepted.

Witkars

Electric battery vehicles being used experimentally as commuter cars in Amsterdam. Users are given stiff cards to insert into machines in the vehicles, the destination is dialed into a computer, which checks that space is available. A key is then given and the

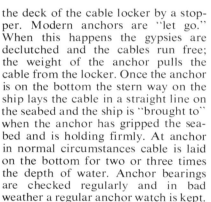

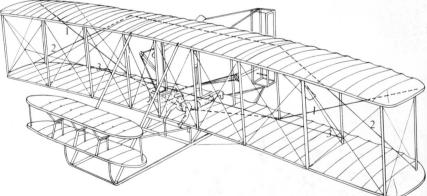

In the wing-warping system of the 1903 Wright Flyer, two cables ran from the pilot cradle, over pulleys, one cable leading to the top of the outer rear starboard wing strut and one to the top of the port strut. The lower ends of these outer struts were interconnected by a separate auxiliary cable which ran upward and passed over pulleys attached to the top of the two center struts. This auxiliary cable was not attached to the control and cradle. To bank to port, the pilot-cradle was twisted to port; this pulled on the starboard cable which, acting on the top of the starboard strut, pulled down the outer part of the trailing-edge of the top starboard wing, the struts pushing down the lower wing in sympathy. Simultaneously, this downward warping of the starboard wing pulled on the auxiliary cable (connecting the lower ends of the outer struts) and automatically pulled up the outer port strut, to give negative warp on the port side and lower the port wing. On later aircraft the cradle was replaced by hand-operated control levers.

1 Pulley
2 Auxiliary warping cable
3 Main wing warping control cables connected to pilot cradle

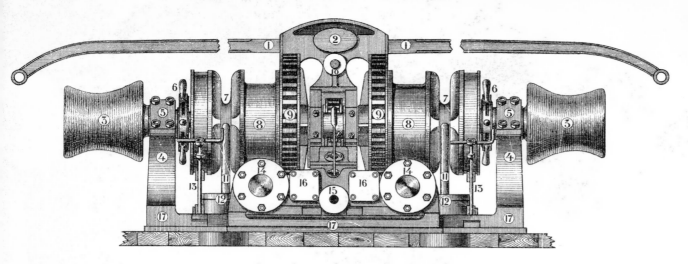

Patent steam windlass
1 Levers, handpower levers
2 Crosshead
3 Warping heads
4 Side bitts
5 Bearing caps

6 Screwbrake nuts
7 Wildcats (Gypsies)
8 Windlass barrel or drum
9 Main cone driving wheels
10 Crosshead bracket
11 Cable relievers

12 Chain pipes
13 Bandbrakes
14 Cylinders
15 Steampipe flange
16 Valve casings
17 Bedplate

vehicle may be driven to the desired destination. While parked, automatic battery charging takes place.

Wolseley, 122 (see also Austin, Sir Herbert)
Wood, see Materials, shipbuilding
Wooden mining tramway, *67*
Woolwich Arsenal, London, 92 97
World Cruiser, Douglas, *168*
World map, early, *20*
World War I, 13 15 16 35 45 120 122 123 138 149 164 168

Acworth, W. M. *Railways of England* (Ian Allan Ltd., Shepperton; originally published by John Murray, London, 1900)

Adams, Charles Francis. *Railroads: Their Origin and Problems* (G. P. Putnam & Co., New York, 1878)

Ahrons, E. L. *British Steam Railway Locomotive 1825–1925* (Ian Allan Ltd., Shepperton, 1927)

Albion, Robert Greenhalgh. *Square-Riggers on Schedule* (Princeton University Press, Princeton, 1938; *The Rise of New York Port 1815–1860* (Charles Scribner's Sons, New York, 1939)

Angas, W. Mack. *Rivalry on the Atlantic* (Lee Furman, Inc., New York, 1939)

Ansdale, R. F. *The Wankel RC Engine* (A. S. Barnes & Co., South Brunswick & New York, 1968)

Baird, Anthony. *Roads and Vehicles* (Longman's, Green and Co. Ltd., 1969)

Ballantyne, A. M., and Pritchard, J. L. *The Lives and Work of William Samuel Henson and John Stringfellow*. (J. Royal Aeronautical Society, London, June 1956)

Barker, Ronald, and Tubbs, Douglas B. *Automobiles and Automobiling* (Patrick Stephens Ltd., Cambridge, 1973)

Barrow, Clayton R., Jr. *America Spreads Her Sails* (Patrick Stephens Ltd., Cambridge, 1973)

Barsley, Michael. *The Orient Express* (Stein and Day, New York, 1967)

Basset-Lowke, W. J., and Holland, G. *Ships and Men* (Harrap, 1946)

Bennett, A. E., and Borley, H. V. *London Transport Railways* (David and Charles Ltd., 1963)

Bird, Anthony. *The Motor Car, 1765–1914* (B. T. Batsford Ltd., London, 1960); *Veteran Cars in Colour* (1962)

Birmingham, A. T. *Riley; The Production and Competition History of the pre-1939 Riley Motor Cars* (G. T. Foulis & Co. Ltd., 2nd ed., 1974)

Bowen, Frank C. *A Century of Atlantic Travel, 1830–1930* (Little, Brown and Co., Boston, 1930)

Boyd, James I. C. *The Festiniog Railway 1800–89* (Vol. 1. Oakwood Press, 1956); *1890–1959* (Vol. 2, 1959); *Isle of Man Railway* (1963)

Brabazon of Tara, Lord. *The Brabazon Story* (Heinemann, London, 1956)

Brewer, G., and Alexander, P. Y. *Aeronautics: an Abridgement of Aeronatuical Specifications filed in the Patent Office. 1815–91* (London, 1893)

Bruce, J. M. *British Aeroplanes, 1914–18* (Putnam, London, 1957)

Burgess, George H., and Kennedy, Miles C. *Centennial History of the Pennsylvania Railroad Company, 1846–1946* (The Pennsylvania Railroad Co., Philadelphia, 1949)

Carpenter, M. Scott., et al. *We Seven, by the Astronauts Themselves* (Simon & Schuster, New York, 1962)

Chanute, O. *Progress, in Flying Machines* (American Engineer, New York, 1894)

A Century of Progress, History of the Delaware and Hudson Company, 1823–1923 (The Delaware and Hudson Company, Albany, 1935)

Chapelle, Howard I. *The Baltimore Clipper, Its Origin and Development* (Salem, Massachusetts, 1930); *The History of American Sailing Ships* (Bonanza Books, Heffer, 1935); *The National Watercraft Collection* (Washington, 1960); *The Pioneer Steamship Savannah: A Study for a Scale Model* (Washington, 1961)

Chayne, Charles A. *Engineering Safety Into Today's Cars* (Milford/Michigan, 1956)

Chittenden, Hiram Martin. *History of Early Steamboat Navigation on the Missouri River* (2 vols., Francis P. Harper, New York, 1903) *The Chevrolet Story 1911–1960* (Published by Chevrolet)

Clark, Arthur H. *The Clipper Ship Era* (G. P. Putnam & Co., New York, 1910)

Clarke, Basil. *Supersonic Flight* (Frederick Muller Ltd., London, 1965)

Cleveland, Frederick A., and Powell, Fred Wilbur. *Railroad Promotion and Capitalization in the United States* (Longman's, Green and Co., New York, 1909)

Cleveland, R. N., and Williamson, S. T. *The Road is Yours; The Story of the Automobile and the Men Behind It* (New York, 1951)

Clymer, Floyd. *Treasury of Early American Automobiles* (New York, 1950); *Those Wonderful Old Automobiles* (1953)

Cobham, Sir A. J. *Skyways* (Nisbet, London, 1925)

Cohn, David L. *Combustion on Wheels* (Boston, 1944)

Conway, H. G. *Bugatti "Le pur-sang des automobiles"* (G. T. Foulis & Co. Ltd., 3rd ed., 1974)

Cooper, B. K. *Electric Trains and Locomotives* (Leonard Hill Ltd., London, 1953)

Cox, E. S. *British Standard Steam Locomotives* (Ian Allan Ltd., Shepperton, 1966)

Cutler, Carl C. *Greyhounds of the Sea. The Story of the American Clipper Ship* (United States Naval Institute, Annapolis, Maryland, 1930); *Queens of the Western Ocean. The Story of America's Mail and Passenger Sailing Lines* (1961)

Davy, M. J. B. *Henson and Stringfellow, Their Work in Aeronautics* (His Majesty's Stationery Office, London, 1931)

Dendy Marshall, C. F. *Centenary History of the Liverpool and Manchester Railway* (Locomotive Publishing Co. Ltd., 1930)

Dendy Marshall, C. F. (ed.) *A History of the Southern Railway* (Southern Railway Publications Department, 1963–64; revised by Kidner, R. W.)

Derrick, Samuel Melanchton. *Centennial History of the South Carolina Railroad* (The State Company, Columbia, 1930)

Diesel Locomotive Handbook (British Railways, 1962)

Dodman, Frank E. *The Observer's Book of*

Ships (Frederick Warne & Co. Ltd., London, 1961)

Dorman, G. *Fifty Years Fly-past: from Wright Brothers to Comet* (Forbes-Robertson, 1951)

Dow, George. *Great Central, 1813–63* (Vol. 1, Locomotive Publishing Co. Ltd., 1960); *1864–99* (Vol. 2, 1962) *1900–22* (Vol. 3, 1965)

Dunn, Laurence. *Passenger Liners* (Adlard Coles Ltd., Southampton, 1961)

Ellis, C. Hamilton. *The Midland Railway* (Ian Allan Ltd., Shepperton, 1953); *The North British Railway* (1955); *The South-Western Railway* (George Allen & Unwin Ltd., 1956); *The London, Brighton and South Coast Railway* (Ian Allan Ltd., Shepperton, 1960); *The Lore of the Train* (Crescent Books, New York, 1973)

Emde, Heiner. *Conquerors of the Air; The Evolution of Aircraft 1903–1945* (Patrick Stephens Ltd., Cambridge, 1973)

Epstein, Ralph Cecil. *The Automobile Industry; Its Economic and Commercial Development* (Chicago, 1928)

Ferguson, T. *Electric Railway Engineering* (Macdonald & Evans Ltd., 1955)

"Fiat" A Fifty Years' Record (Fiat, Turin, 1951)

Flint, Henry M. *The Railroads of the United States: Their History and Statistics* (John E. Potter and Company, Philadelphia, 1868)

Fox, W. J., and Birnie, S. C. *Marine Steam Engines and Turbines* (George Newnes Ltd., London, 1952)

Freeston, Ewart C. *Prisoner of War Ship Models 1775–1825* (Nautical Publishing Co. /Harrap Books, 1973)

Fry, Henry. *The History of North Atlantic Steam Navigation* (New York, 1896)

Gallico, Paul. *The Hurricane Story* (Michael Joseph Ltd., London, 1959)

General Motors. *Adventures of the Inquiring Mind* (Detroit, 1957); *Story of General Motors* (1957)

Gentle, Ernest J., and Chapel, Charles E. *Aviation & Space Dictionary* (Aero Publishers, Inc., Los Angeles, 1961)

Gibbs, C. R. Vernon. *Passenger Liners of the Western Ocean* (London, 1952); *British Passenger Liners of the Five Oceans* (London, 1963)

Gibbs-Smith, C. H. *A Short History of the Aeroplane* (Her Majesty's Stationery Office, London, 1957); *Sir George Cayley's Aeronautics 1796–1855* (1962); *Flight Through the Ages* (Thomas Y. Crowell Co., New York, 1974)

Gibbs-Smith, C. H., and Bradford, L. E. *World Aircraft Recognition Manual* (Putnam, London, 1956)

Gilfillan, S. C. *Inventing the Ship* (Follett, Chicago, 1935)

Gill, Crispin, Booker, Frank, and Soper, Tony. *The Wreck of the Torrey Canyon* (David and Charles Ltd., Newton Abbott, 1967)

The Glasgow and South-Western Railway, 1850 to 1923 (Stephenson Locomotive Society, 1950)

Gould, E. W. *Fifty Years on the Mississippi; or Gould's History of River Navigation* (Nixon-Jones Printing Co., St. Louis, 1899)

Gracie, Colonel Archibald. *The Truth About the Titanic* (Patrick Stephens Ltd., Cambridge, 1973)

Green, W., and Cross, R. *The Jet Aircraft of the World* (MacDonald, London, 1955)

Gregory, H. F. *The Helicopter* (George Allen & Unwin Ltd., London, 1948)

Grinling, W. J. *History of Great Northern Railway* (George Allen & Unwin Ltd., London, 1962; reprinted from 1898)

Hansen, Hans Jürgen, and Wundshammer, Benno. *Windjammer Parade* (Ian Allan Ltd., Shepperton, 1973)

Harding, Anthony (ed.) *Car Facts and Feats, a Record of Everyday Motoring and Automotive Achievement* (Guinness Superlatives Ltd., Enfield, 1971)

Hartsough, Mildred L. *From Canoe to Steel Barge on the Upper Mississippi* (The University of Minnesota Press, Minneapolis, 1934)

Heinkel, E. *He. 1000* (Hutchinson, London, 1966)

Hendry, P. G. *Vintage and Veteran Cars* (Bartholomew Books, Edinburgh, 1974)

The Highland Railway Company and its Constituents and Successors (Stephenson Locomotive Society, 1955)

The Highway Transportation Story (Highways Users Conference, New York, 1958)

Hinde, D. W., and Hinde, M. *Electric and Diesel-electric Locomotives* (Macmillan & Co. Ltd., 1948)

A History of Travel in America (4 vols., The Bobbs-Merrill Company, Indianapolis, 1915)

Hopfinger, K. B. *Beyond Expectation; The Volkswagen Story* (London, 1954)

Howe, Octavius T., and Matthews, Frederick C. *American Clipper Ships, 1833–1858* (2 vols., Marine Research Society, Salem, Massachusetts, 1926–27)

Hughes, Tom. *The Blue Riband of the Atlantic* (Patrick Stephens Ltd., Cambridge, 1973)

Hungerford, Edward. *The Story of the Baltimore & Ohio Railroad, 1827–1927* (2 vols., G. P. Putnam's Sons, New York, 1928)

Hunter, Louis C. *Steamboats on the Western Rivers* (Harvard University Press, Cambridge, 1949)

Inman Hunter, Marcus C. *Rotary Valve Engines* (Hutchinson's Scientific & Technical Publications, 1951)

Jackson, G. Gibbard. *The Ship Under Steam* (Charles Scribner's Sons, New York, 1928)

Jane's All the World's Aircraft (Jane's All the World's Aircraft Publishing Co. Ltd., Yearbooks)

Jellinek-Mercédès, Guy *My Father Mr Mercédès* (G. T. Foulis & Co. Ltd., London, 1966)

Kalla-Bishop, P. M. *Italian Railways* (David and Charles, Newton Abbott); *Tandem Compound Locomotives; Hungarian Railways* (1973)

Kaye, David. *Buses and Trolleybuses before 1919* (Blandford Press, London, 1972)

Kennedy, Ludovic. *Pursuit; The Sinking of the Bismarck* (Collins, 1974)

Kidner, R. W. *London, Chatham and Dover Railway* (Oakwood Press, 1951); *The Cambrian Railways* (1955); *South-Eastern Railway and the S.E.C.R.* (2nd ed., 1963)

King, G. A. B. *Tanker Practice; The Construction, Operation and Maintenance of Tankers* (Wokingham, 1956)

Kirkaldy, Adam W. *British Shipping: Its History, Organization and Importance* (E. P. Dutton & Co., New York, 1914)

Kirkland, Edward Chase. *Men, Cities and Transportation, A Study in New England History, 1820–1900* (2 vols., Harvard University Press, 1948)

Krause, Ian. *Great Western Branch Line Album* (Ian Allan Ltd., Shepperton, 1969)

Labatut, Jean, and Lane, Wheaton. *Highways in Our International Life* (Princeton University Press, Princeton, 1950)

Lane, Carl D. *American Paddle Steamboats* (Coward-McCann, Inc., New York, 1943)

Lane, Wheaton J. *From Indian Trail to Iron Horse: Travel and Transportation in New Jersey, 1620–1860* (Princeton University Press, Princeton, 1939)

Langley, S. M., and Manly, C. M. *Langley Memoir of Mechanical Flight* (2 vols., Smithsonian Institution, Washington, D. C., 1911)

Lascelles, T. S. *The City and South London Railway* (Oakwood Press, 1956)

Lee, Charles E. *The Metropolitan District Railway* (Oakwood Press, 1956); *The Welsh Highland Railway* (David and Charles Ltd., 1961); *Sixty Years of the Bakerloo* (London Transport, 1966)

Leech, K. H., and Body, M. G. *Stirling Singles of the G.N.R.* (David and Charles Ltd., Newton Abbott, 1965)

Legget, Robert F. *Railways of Canada* (David and Charles Ltd., Newton Abbott, 1973)

Lehmann, E. A., and Adelt, L. *Zeppelin* (Longman's, Green and Co., 1937)

Lent, Henry B. *The Helicopter Book* (The Macmillan Company, New York, 1956)

Lewis, Edward V., O'Brien, Robert, et al. *Ships* (Time-Life Books, 1965)

Lewis, Eugene W. *Motor Memories, A Saga of Whirling Wheels* (New York, 1947)

Lilienthal, O. *Bird Flight as a Basis of Aviation* (Longman's, Green and Company, London, 1911)

Lindbergh, Charles A. *The Spirit of St. Louis* (Murray, London, 1953)

Lindsay, W. S. *History of Merchant Shipping and Ancient Commerce* (London, 1876)

Lubbock, Basil. *The Opium Clippers* (Brown, Son & Ferguson Ltd., Glasgow, 1933); *The China Clippers; The Colonial Clippers; The Blackwell Frigates; The Western Ocean Packets; The Last of the Windjammers* (2 vols.); *The Log of the "Cutty Sark"; The Down Easters; The Nitrate Clippers; Coolie Ships and Oil Sailers; The Arctic Whalers*

MacDermot, E. T. *History of the Great Western Railway, 1833–63* (Vol. I, Ian Allan Ltd., Shepperton, 1964; revised by Clinker, C. R.); *1864–1921* (Vol. II, 1931); *1922–47* (Vol. III, Nock, O. S., 1967)

MacGregor, David. *Fast Sailing Ships 1775–1875* (Nautical Publishing Co./Harrap Books, 1973)

Macintyre, Donald, and Bathe, Basil B. *Man-of-War* (McGraw–Hill Book Company, New York, 1968)

Maclean, John S. *Newcastle and Carlisle Railway, 1825–62* (R. Robinson & Co. Ltd., 1948)

Maginnis, Arthur J. *The Atlantic Ferry, Its Ships, Men, and Working* (The Macmillan Co., New York, 1893)

Marshall, J. *The Guinness Book of Air Facts and Feats* (Guinness Superlatives, London)

Marvin, Winthrop L. *The American Merchant Marine: Its History and Romance from 1620 to 1902* (Charles Scribner's Sons, New York, 1910)

Mason, Francis K., and Windrow, Martin C. *Air Facts and Feats, a Guinness Record of Aerospace Achievement* (Guinness Superlatives Ltd., Enfield)

Meyer, Balthasar Henry (ed.) *History of Transportation in the United States before 1860* (Carnegie Institution of Washington, 1917)

Meyer, J. R., Kain, J. F., and Wohl, M. *The Urban Transportation Problem* (Harvard University Press, Cambridge, 1965)

Miller, Sidney L. *Inland Transportation: Principles and Policies* (McGraw-Hill Book Company, New York, 1933)

Mills, John. *Ford; the Construction of Specials* (London, 1960)

Mondey, David. *Aircraft. An All Colour Story of Modern Flight* (Octopus Books, London, 1973)

Moody, G. T. *Southern Electric* (Ian Allan Ltd., Shepperton, 1960)

Morison, Samuel Eliot. *The Maritime History of Massachusetts, 1783–1860* (Houghton Mifflin Company, Boston, 1921)

Morrison, John H. *History of American Steam Navigation* (Stephen Ungar, New York, 1958; first published by W. F. Sametz and Company, New York, 1903)

Morriss, Lloyd, and Smith, Kendall. *Ceiling Unlimited. The Story of American Aviation from Kitty Hawk to Supersonics* (The Macmillan Company, New York, 1953)

Mott, Edward Harold. *Between the Ocean and the Lakes: The Story of the Erie* (J. S. Collins, New York, 1902)

Munro-Smith, R. *Applied Naval Architecture* (Longman's, Green and Co., London, 1967)

Munson, Kenneth. *Civil Aircraft of Yesteryear* (Ian Allan Ltd., London, 1967); *Private Aircraft; Business and General Purpose since 1946* (Blandford Press, London, 1967); *Helicopters and Other Rotorcraft since 1907* (1968); *Pioneer Aircraft 1903–1914* (1969)

Murray, Andrew. *The Theory and Practice of Ship-Building* (Edinburgh, 1861); *Ship-Building in Iron and Wood* (1863)

Nader, Ralph. *Unsafe at Any Speed* (Grossman Publishers, New York, 1965)

Nevins, Allan, and Hill, Frank Ernest. *Ford: The Times, the Man, the Company* (New York, 1953); *Ford: Expansion and Challenge 1915–1933* (1957)

Nielsen, T. *The Zeppelin Story* (Wingate, 1955)

Nixon, St. John C. *The Invention of the Automobile* (London, 1936); *Daimler, 1896–1946* (1946); *Wolseley* (1949); *The Story of the S.M.M.T.* (1952)

Nock, O. S. *British Locomotives from the Footplate* (Ian Allan Ltd., Shepperton, 1950); *Fifty Years of Western Express Running* (Edward Everard Ltd., 1954); *The Locomotives of R. E. L. Mansell* (1954); *The Railway Engineers* (B. T. Batsford Ltd., 1955); *British Railways in Action* (Thomas Nelson & Sons Ltd., 1956); *Father of Railways* (Thomas Nelson & Sons Ltd., 1958); *Historical Steam Locomotives* (A. & C. Black Ltd., 1959); *Fifty Years of Railway Signalling* (The Institution of Railway Signal Engineers, 1962); *Great Western Railway in the 19th Century* (Ian Allan Ltd., Shepperton, 1963); *Great Western Railway in the 20th Century* (1964); *British Steam Railway Locomotive 1925–65* (1966); *L.N.W.R. Precursor Family* (David and Charles Ltd., 1966); *The Railway Enthusiast's Encyclopedia* (Hutchinson & Co. Ltd., London, 1968)

Nock, O. S., and Treacy, Eric. *Main Lines Across the Border* (Thomas Nelson & Sons Ltd., 1959)

Nockolds, Harold. *The Magic of a Name (Rolls-Royce)* (London, 1949)

Noel, John V., Jr. *Naval Terms Dictionary* (2nd revised ed., United States Naval Institute, Annapolis, Maryland, 1966)

Norbye, Jan P. *The Wankel Engine* (Chilton Book Company, Philadelphia, 1971)

Olyslager Organisation. *The Observer's Book of Automobiles* (Frederick Warne & Co. Ltd., London, 1972)

Partridge, Bellamy. *Fill'er Up! The Story of Fifty Years of Motoring* (New York, 1953)

Petersen, William J. *Steamboating on the Upper Mississippi* (Iowa City: State Historical Society, 1937)

Poor, Henry V. *History of the Railroads and Canals of the United States of America* (New York, 1860); *Manual of the Railroads of the United States for 1868–69* (H. V. and H. W. Poor, New York, 1868)

Pound, Arthur. *The Turning Wheel* (New York, 1934)

Preble, G. H. *Origin and Development of Steam Navigation* (Philadelphia, 1895)

Purser, P. E., Faget, M. A., and Smith, N. F. *Manned Spacecraft: Engineering Design and Operation* (Fairchild, Stamford, Conn., 1964)

Rolfe, D., and Dawydoff, A. *Airplanes of the World, from Pusher to Jet, 1490–1954* (Simon & Schuster, New York, 1954)

Rolt, L. T. C. *Isambard Kingdom Brunel* (Longman's, Green and Co., London, 1957); *Stephensons, George and Robert* (1960); *The Aeronauts. A History of Ballooning 1783–1903* (1966)

Saint-Exupéry, A. de. *Night Flight* (Appleton, 1935); *Wind, Sand and Stars* (Heinemann, London, 1939)

Setright, L. J. K. *The Grand Prix* (Nelson, 1973)

Shapiro, Jacob. *The Helicopter* (Muller, London, 1957)

Sinclair, J. A. *Airships in Peace and War* (Rich & Cowan, 1934)

Skeat, W. O. *George Stephenson; The Engineer & His Letters* (The Institution of Mechanical Engineers, London, 1973)

S.M.M.T. *The British Commercial Vehicle Industry* (London, 1950)

Snell, J. B. *Classics of Transportation: Trains* (MacDonald, London, 1968); *Trains Seventy* (Ian Allan Ltd., Shepperton)

Spears, John R. *The Story of the American Merchant Marine* (The Macmillan Company, New York, 1910)

Stanton, Samuel W. *American Steam Vessels* (New York, 1895)

Starr, John W., Jr. *One Hundred Years of American Railroading* (Dodd, Mead & Co., New York, 1928)

Steel, W. L. *History of London and North-*

Western Railway (Railway Publishing Company Ltd., 1914)

Stevens, Frank Walker. *The Beginnings of the New York Central Railroad: A History* (G. P. Putnam's Sons, New York, 1926)

Stevens, J. H. *The Shape of the Aeroplane* (Hutchinson, London, 1953)

Stever, H. Guyford, Haggerty, James J., et al. *Flight* (Time Inc., New York, 1965)

Tanner, Hans. *Ferrari* (4th ed., G. T. Foulis & Co. Ltd., 1974)

Tanner, Henry S. *A Description of the Railroads and Canals of the United States Comprehending Notices of All the Works of International Improvement Throughout the Several States* (T. R. Tanner & J. Disturnell, New York, 1840)

Taylor, George Rogers. *The Transportation Revolution. 1815–1860* Volume IV, *The Economic History of the United States* (Holt, Rinehart and Winston, Inc., New York, Chicago, and San Francisco, 1951)

Taylor, John W. R. *A Picture History of Flight* (Hulton, London, 1955); *The Lore of Flight* (ed.) (Tre Tryckare AB, Gothenburg, 1970); *Rockets and Missiles* (The Hamlyn Publishing Group, London, 1970); *Aircraft* (1971); *Jane's Pocket Book of Commercial Transport Aircraft* (Jane's Pocket Books, 1973)

Thompson, Slason. *A Short History of American Railways, Covering Ten Decades* (D. Appleton and Company, New York, 1925)

Thurston, Robert H. *A History of the Growth of the Steam-Engine* (D. Appleton and Company, New York, 1907)

Troyer, Howard William. *The Four Wheel Drive Story* (London, 1954)

Turnbull, Archibald Douglas. *John Stevens, an American Record* (The Century Company, New York, 1928)

Turner, Stuart, and Organ, John. *MGB* (G. T. Foulis & Co. Ltd., London, 1968)

Tyler, David Budlong. *Steam Conquers the Atlantic* (D. Appleton-Century Company, New York, 1939)

Verdon-Roe, Sir Alliott. *The World of Wings and Things* (Hurst & Blackett, London, 1939)

Wallace, G. *The Flight of Alcock and Brown* (Putnam, London, 1919)

Whittle, Sir Frank. *Jet* (Muller, 1954)

Wiech, Raymond E., and Strauss, Robert F. *Fundamentals of Rocket Propulsion* (Reinhold, New York, 1960)

Williams, F. S. *History of the Midland Railway* (Bemrose & Company, 1877)

Wilson, William Bender. *History of the Pennsylvania Railroad Company* (2 vols., H. T. Coates and Company, Philadelphia, 1899)

Wonder Book of Aircraft (Ward Lock, London, 1956)

Woods, Clinton Edgar. *The Electric Automobile, Its Construction, Care and Operation* (Detroit, 1904)

Wragg, David W. *World's Air Fleets* (2nd revised ed., Ian Allan Ltd., London, 1969)